THE HOTELMAN'S BASIC LAW

by

Ronald A. Anderson

THE HOTELMAN'S BASIC LAW
(1974 SUPPLEMENT)
by
Ronald A. Anderson

Member of the Philadelphia Bar

Author of Couch Cyclopedia of Insurance Law (2d ed)
  The Insurer's Tort Law
  Anderson on the Uniform Commercial Code
  Anderson's Pennsylvania Civil Practice
  Purdon's Pennsylvania Forms
  Government and Business (4th ed)

Co-author of Business Law (12th ed)
  Business Law, Principles, Cases, Legal Environment (9th ed)

Consulting Editor of Pennsylvania Law Encyclopedia

Professor of Law and Government
  Drexel University

The Littoral Development Company
Philadelphia, Pennsylvania

Copyright © 1974
by
Decima M. Anderson
Philadelphia, Pennsylvania
All rights reserved

The text of this publication, or any part thereof, may not be reproduced in any manner whatsoever without permission in writing from the publisher.

INTERNATIONAL
STANDARD BOOK NUMBER
0-914770-00-4

The Littoral Development Company
252 South Van Pelt Street,
Philadelphia, Pennsylvania 19103

PREFACE

The problem

Once upon a time a hotelman ran a hotel and that was all he did! Today the hotelman is many men. He runs a hotel — yet he may be a tenant, who rents his building from a corporation; he is a buyer and a seller, both buying food, drink, drugs, and various goods and reselling to his patrons; he is a supplier, with or without charge, to his patrons, of automobiles, sports equipment, and other goods; he is an employer and probably subject to the Federal Labor Management Relations Act and the Civil Rights Act of 1964; he handles checks and signs commercial paper in receiving and making payment in transactions with patrons, suppliers, and others; he is an automobile owner whose car is driven by an employee; he is a parking lot, a restaurant, a swimming pool, a ski run, and many other things. And in all these, the hotelman is subject to general bodies of law not limited to hotels — all this in addition to the law relating directly to hotels.

And to complicate matters, the law in many of these areas is new or changing. Today the hotelman finds himself in the field of labor law and civil rights legislation; administrative law affecting hotel management; the Uniform Commercial Code, **adopted in 49 states and for the District of Columbia and the** Virgin Isles, with respect to checks and commercial paper and the hotel's position as a buyer and seller of food and goods; increased liability for the wrongful acts of third persons and employees, even when the latter are not within the course of their employment — as science makes possible more harm-creating situations by way of the fast-moving automobile, the sealed container of food or drugs, and even the lowly paper bag converted into a water bomb by the hands of the prankster conventioneer; and laws governing the hotelman's liability for the property of his patrons and defining his duty toward the public.

The purpose

The object of this book is to bring to the hotelman in plain, non-legal language a simple but accurate statement of the important principles of the various areas of today's law which concern him. The emphasis is upon the reason for the rules of law and the values or interests involved. The object is to give the reader an understanding and a sense of balance rather than merely a handful of specific rules to be memorized.

The book is designed for the student of hotel management and for everyone who runs any phase of the hotel. In some cases, particular chapters should be read by persons not ordinarily regarded as "running" the hotel. For example, the registration clerk should in particular read Chapter 3 on accommodations and discrimination; the cashier and any fiscal employee, Chapter 17 on checks; the driver of the hotel automobile, Chapter 13 on liability for the hotel automobile; the person in charge of the hotel restaurant, drugstore, or sports goods shop, Chapter 14 on liability for sold products; the persons who hire and supervise employees, Chapters 5, 6, and 20 on vicarious and supervisory liability and labor law; and the persons in charge of building maintenance and activities, Chapter 11 on liability for condition of the premises.

In the planning of this book, I have had the benefit of the answers to a questionnaire and the suggestions of various members of the staff and the Board of Directors of the American Hotel & Motel Association. I hereby express but do not thereby discharge my debt to them for their kindness.

Ronald A. Anderson

THE HOTELMAN'S BASIC LAW

I. General principles

1. Introduction	3
2. Definitions	13
3. Accommodations and discrimination	31
4. Liability-imposing conduct	43
5. The hotel's supervisory liability	50
6. The hotel's vicarious liability	71
7. Causal relationship	84
8. Intentional torts and death claims	94
9. Negligence	119
10. Contributory negligence and assumption of risk	137

II. Particular situations

11. Liability for condition of premises	153
12. Liability for condition of leased premises	198
13. Liability for the hotel automobile	209
14. Liability as to sold products	218
15. Liability as to supplied products	239
16. Liability as to guest's property	244
17. Checks and credit cards	288
18. Liens and eviction	320
19. Management and government regulation	328
20. Labor law	354
21. Crimes	394
22. The anatomy of a lawsuit	412
23. How to be a good client	444
1974 Supplement	473
Index	475

I. General principles

Chapter 1. INTRODUCTION

§ 1:1. Why bother?
    (a) Why should a hotelman understand hotel law?
    (b) Public relations and good will.
    (c) Litigation is a nuisance.
    (d) Uncertainty of litigation.
    (e) Co-operation with your attorney and insurer.

§ 1:2. Understanding the law.

§ 1:3. The absolutes and the arbitraries.
    (a) The absolutes.
    (b) The arbitraries.
    (c) What does a straight line mean?
    (d) What does "one" mean?

§ 1:4. The quest for justice.
    (a) Generally.
    (b) Conflicting aims.

§ 1:5. Specific objectives of the law.

§ 1:1. Why bother?

(*a*) *Why should a hotelman understand hotel law?* There is a natural tendency to feel that you can push your problems off onto your lawyer or your insurance company and they will take care of everything. Therefore why should you bother about the law? There are a number of sound reasons.

(*b*) *Public relations and good will.* The most important reason for understanding the law is that it may enable you to avoid certain situations which might give rise to liability. While in most cases you can pass the headache of litigation on to your lawyer or to your insurer, the fact remains that to some degree, if only with respect to one person and his friends, your image as a hotel has been harmed. If for any reason the matter is given newspaper publicity the harm to you may be greater. But be the harm large or small, one who lives by dealing with the public will want to preserve his public image at the best possible level.

(*c*) *Litigation is a nuisance.* When you pass the matter over to your lawyer or your insurer you are still involved for you must co-operate with your attorney and your insurer. You must provide information. You must attend meetings and trials, and you and your employees are subject to discovery proceedings. None of this is so burdensome that it will impair your operations over the years but these events are an annoyance and a nuisance. Is it not good management to avoid subjecting yourself to such nuisances by running your hotel in a litigation-proof manner? In order to do so, you must have some understanding of what the law requires of you.

(*d*) *Uncertainty of litigation.* The only certain way of not losing a law suit against you is by never being sued. There is great uncertainty in the law because much of your case will hang upon what the jury believes to have happened. If they do not believe you and your witnesses, there is the danger that you will lose the case. Moreover, there is the possibility that because of a change in the law the insurance policy which you have does not cover the liability which tomorrow's court decides exists.

(*e*) *Co-operation with your attorney and insurer.* When you turn the case over to your attorney or to your insurer you are under a duty to co-operate and be as helpful in the defense of the case as possible. Actually the need for co-operation begins before then. As discussed in Chapter 23, from the very beginning of the occurrence or transaction from which the claim arises there should be a careful recording of what was done and a preservation of any evidence that is involved. This enables you, when you see your attorney or your insurer, to turn over the best case possible rather than one which is difficult, if not impossible, to defend. Moreover, an appreciation of the law will make you more sensitive as to when you are involved in a matter which calls for consultation with your lawyer or your insurer.

The more you know about the law, the more you will be able to act like a good client and be of help to your lawyer and your insurer. Remember that the lawyer is not a magician and cannot save you when you have let a hopeless case build itself around you. While the insurer would still be bound by its contract, remember that the insurer may cancel most of its contracts with you or increase the rates, so that there may be harmful side-effects of your not having acted in such a way as to assist your attorney and insurer. Moreover, the liability might be so great that it is in excess of the insurance coverage.

§ 1:2. Understanding the law.

Much of the difficulty in seeking to understand the law is the result of regarding it as an absolute and exact science. The ideal of a definite body of law is not only attractive to the student but is dear to the heart of everyone. Long-revered is the maxim that "in the known certainty of the law lies the safety of all." The purpose of establishing our Constitution is to the end that we may have a government of laws and not of men.

The truth of the matter is that the certainty, the precision, and the logic of the law are very relative matters. In truth the law is an arbitrary set of rules that we have agreed upon to govern ourselves. And our reason for so doing is the quest for justice and the advancement of the various social objectives that we hold dear.

§ 1:3. The absolutes and the arbitraries.

(*a*) *The absolutes.* Law is not absolute, for anything which is absolute is the same at all times and all places. For example, the gravitational pull of the earth, that is, the law of gravity, is the same in every state of the United States. It is also the same in every other country. Thus, it is geographically constant. The law of gravity is also the same at all times. Go back to the remote day when the prehistoric cave man threw a spear. It fell to the ground because of the same force that centuries later would make an apple fall on Newton's head, that today makes an airplane crash to the earth, and that centuries hence will continue to bring you down.

The law of gravity is also inevitable. It operates at the same point with the same power regardless of what you do. It is true that you can fly, but that does not mean that you have repealed or destroyed the law of gravity. It only means that you have overcome it with a superior force — and remember that the moment you stop working with the superior force, down you come. The law of gravity is therefore an absolute; for it is universal, timeless, and inevitable.

(*b*) *The arbitraries.* In contrast with those things which are absolute, as the law of gravity, are those things which are the way they are merely because we want them that way. For example, we outlawed the flying wedge in football, just because we decided that it should be outlawed. Similarly, we have changed the rules for basketball. We change women's hair styles. We change the size and length of automobiles. And so on, whenever it suits us, meaning society, to so do, we change.

Our action in making such decisions is arbitrary. This word often has a bad sound because we generally think of a person who is arbitrary as being capricious, corrupt, or tyrannical. Let us use arbitrary in the simple sense of a standard which is the opposite of an absolute; which is dependent upon will or discretion. That is to say, it is just what it is because someone in charge wants it that way; not because it must inevitably and at all times and at all places be that way.

(c) **What does a straight line mean?** Look at this and state what it means:

—

Depending upon your experience and training, you may say it is a dash, a hyphen, an underscore, a minus sign, the indication of a negative charge, or even the letter "n" in Gregg shorthand. Now rotate or turn this line 45 degrees, thus:

/

Now you may think of a fraction, divided by, or you may associate it with the address form of "c/o," or if you are familiar with the Fortran language of computers, you will recognize that the slant line may be used to indicate the beginning of a new record. Let us rotate the line 45 more degrees, and we have:

|

Now of course we see that it is a "one." Is it not peculiar that this little line changes its meaning in terms of its position? It is still the same line. It has just as much lead or ink in it regardless of its position, but you and I choose to give it a particular meaning in terms of its position. Of course, it is a little discouraging to think that if you stand up, or sit down, or lie down, or even stand on your head, you are always the same old you. This little line has us stopped.

But to return to the main theme, suppose that we place two little straight lines parallel to each other. If horizontal, as:

=

we will probably all agree that it means "equals." But let us rotate it 90 degrees, as:

||

Now we say that it is eleven, but if we were ancient Romans, we would recognize it as meaning two. But to a binary computer it means three.

The practical explanation for the foregoing is that there are only so many kinds of lines that can be drawn on paper and that if we all agree, that with reference to a particular subject, a particular line shall have a particular meaning, no one is harmed. Just the opposite, we are able to have effective and exact communication between us. But note that we are "arbitrary" in agreeing upon any meaning, for there is no "absolute" which makes any particular meaning universal, timeless, and inevitable.

*(d) **What does "one" mean?*** Suppose we agree that

|

stands for "one." Do you know what "one" means? Does it have an absolute value? Or an arbitrary value which can mean anything you want it to mean? Let us turn to the law for our answers of what "one" means and consider various situations which raise the question of what is "one."

Assume that a thief steals your suitcase. We say that he has committed larceny. How many larcenies? Why, one, of course. Suppose, however, that your suitcase contains a pair of your shoes. How many larcenies now? Is it one larceny for the aggregate of everything taken, or are there three larcenies: one for the suitcase, one for the left, and one for the right shoe? And if the shoes have laces, are there two additional larcenies for the two laces? I am sure that most of us would regard the one act of taking your property from you as merely one larceny, and also regard my question as somewhat silly.

Suppose, however, that the suitcase belongs to one person and the shoes to another person. Now we have two persons wronged by the one act of taking the suitcase. Is it still one larceny because there was one "taking," or are there two larcenies because there are two victims?

Assume that the suitcase was owned by one person and various objects contained in the suitcase were owned by three different persons. If we say that four persons are wronged by the defendant, which is the fact, and that therefore there are four larcenies, we have the possibility that the defendant by one stroke has committed four crimes and made himself a habitual criminal upon whom a life sentence could be imposed.

Let us take a variation of this theme. This time, in the night our hero drives up to a warehouse with a truck. He enters and steals a bag of flour. He takes only one bag because that is all he can carry at one time. He puts the bag into the truck and then goes back for another bag. Bag after bag he steals. Forty-eight bags in all. Is he now guilty of forty-eight larcenies and subject to the punishment of one larceny times forty-eight? We might even have him steal forty-eight bags of coffee and then have the interesting question of whether the taking of each bag of coffee constitutes one larceny for the bag, one larceny for the binding twine, and one larceny for each coffee bean.

Take the offense of maliciously destroying property. Now our defendant enters a hothouse and one by one breaks 517 potted geraniums, he himself being in a similar condition. The penalty for maliciously destroying property is a $50 fine. Is he liable for $50 or 517 times $50?

And again, our hero, whether sober or not, speeds cross country driving at an illegal rate of speed. During the course of his wild drive he passes through five boroughs, two townships, and four cities — always at the continuously illegal rate of speed. Is he guilty of one offense of illegally speeding or of 11 offenses?

I suspect you have the feeling that in all these cases there is merely one act by the defendant, even though it may be an act which continues over time, or through a geographic distance, or which affects a number of items, or a number of items owned by different persons; and that since the defendant did one act, he should only be punished for one crime. In general, the law agrees with you, and most courts will say in the cases above given that there is only one offense because there is only one act.

What's hard about all this? After all, it's just plain common sense that if a person does only one act he commits only one crime. Well, let's just apply this common sense principle logically. "Logic" means that from now on we will say that it is the number of acts rather than the number of things or persons affected which determines the number of crimes which are committed: one act, one crime.

Let's see how logical we really want to be. Let's apply the rule of "one act" to the case of a bus which runs off the road into a ditch with a driver and forty-eight passengers. The bus is damaged and each person in the bus is injured. How many accidents are there? The newspaper headline says: "Bus Accident." But if there is only one accident, what happened to each of the persons in the bus? Does each of the persons go home and say, "I just had one-fiftieth of an accident" — or does he say that he had "an" accident? Actually there was only one act, that of the bus going off the road, or the negligence or fault of some person which caused it to do so. The fact that the bus was damaged and each of the forty-nine persons in the bus was injured does not alter the fact that there was only one "act." If, however, we say that each person who is injured in the bus has had his own private "accident," then we find ourselves engaged in the curious doubletalk that for one purpose there is one accident and for another purpose there are fifty accidents. Now you see that logic has created a real dilemma. If we say that the act determines the number, we must say one act means one accident. This, of course, becomes of practical importance where the automobile liability policy sets a maximum limitation on liability "per accident." In contrast, if we look not at the number of acts but at the number of interests or persons harmed, we would say that there were fifty accidents and the liability of the insurer would accordingly be enhanced.

Don't feel bad if you are troubled, because the courts are divided as to whether the situation described above is one accident or multiple accidents.

If we are still sure, however, that one act means one legal consequence, assume that the defendant recklessly runs over and kills two pedestrians at the same moment. Is it one manslaughter or two manslaughters by automobile? Suppose he kills a person with a high-powered rifle bullet which passes through the first person, killing both that victim and another person. Again, the problem, is it one or two homicides? Suppose the defendant throws a bomb into a crowded hall and kills 100 people. Has he committed one murder or 100 murders?

Let us carry the matter a step further and put the question in its possible procedural setting. The defendant who has killed 100 people with one bomb is prosecuted for the murder of one of the victims. For some reason, he is acquitted on that charge. He is then prosecuted for the murder of the second victim. He then raises the defense that as he did only one act he committed only one murder, for which he has already been put in jeopardy and he cannot be tried again for the same act. If we sustain this defense, we say that the defendant cannot be held liable for the remaining 99 killings, but has them free on the house.

Obviously, when it comes to taking a human life, we are just not going to say that one act is only one crime. Instead, "common sense" tells us that every person killed represents a separate crime, and that is what most courts do say. But what about logic? If I take the lives of four different people by one act, I am guilty of four homicides, but if I steal the property of four persons by one act, I commit only one larceny. Why should the test for the number of crimes be the number of the acts done when it is larceny but the number of the victims when it is a question of human lives?

The only answer is the obvious one that society just doesn't want to be too tough when merely property is concerned, but when life is involved it will be as tough as possible. This distinction, you recognize, is arbitrary in that it is not inevitable, it is not universal, it is not timeless, and it is not even consistent. But you and I like the distinction. It sits well with us emotionally, because it fits in with our feelings deeply rooted in our socio-theological mores and our democratic concepts of the dignity of the human life. We, and the law with us, therefore reject the cold and logical consistency and make the rule of law vary to suit our feelings of what is "just." We make "one" mean one thing in some cases and something else in others.

§ 1:4. The quest for justice.

(*a*) *Generally.* In the last section we have come face to face with the heart of the problem. Law seeks justice, which is exactly what we want it to do, but in seeking justice it must often sacrifice logic and precision. This is where the difficulty comes in, for if we do not understand the law's concept of justice, we cannot understand why it makes its variations and the departures from the rules. Moreover, unless we recognize law as a quest for justice, we cannot understand why it is that law grows and changes as man's concept of justice changes and as the socio-economic world in which he lives changes.

Of course we add to our difficulties when we speak of "justice" as changing, but it would be a mistake to assume that justice is a universal value which means the same to all people in all ages. Many factors and institutions have made their contribution in the molding and change of the concepts of justice. Home and school training, religion, enlightened self-interest, social and business groups, and the various media of modern communication and entertainment all have played and continue to play a part. Furthermore, each individual's concept of justice varies in terms of his personality, his training, and his social and economic position. Obviously, justice has different meanings to the employer and to the employee, to the millionaire and the pauper, to the industrial worker and the farmer, and above all, to the plaintiff and the defendant.

(*b*) *Conflicting aims.* The problem is made further complicated by the fact that you cannot devise rules of law to keep everyone happy. Somebody wins, and somebody must lose. You cannot have both sides win. This means that quite frequently you will have conflicting social objectives and then society, through the law, must make a choice as to which objective is to prevail.

For example, we all believe in preserving the United States and we all believe in preserving freedom of speech and freedom of action. Yet if the defendant makes treasonable statements and seeks to protect them under the garb of free speech, we do not hesitate to suppress free speech in the interest of the greater social objective of preserving the government. Likewise, although we exalt freedom of the individual, we recognize that a military draft is necessary for the protection of the state.

If you examine any rule of law or statute, you will find that it has one or more underlying objectives, and that frequently in advancing certain objectives it defeats other equally praiseworthy objectives. But remember all this conflict is for the sake of justice.

§ 1:5. Specific objectives of the law.

If we know the specific objectives that society, through the medium of the law, is trying to advance in its quest for justice, we will obviously have a better understanding of the law itself and of the pattern of growth of the law. We will also realize the better why the law is often so vague and uncertain and why litigation is frequently very hazardous.

The objectives most commonly involved are:
(1) Protection of the state
(2) Protection of public health, safety, and morals
(3) Personal protection
(4) Property protection
(5) Title protection

(6) Freedom of personal action
(7) Freedom of use of property
(8) Enforcement of intent
(9) Protection from exploitation
(10) Protection from oppression
(11) Protection from fraud
(12) Furtherance of trade
(13) Creditor protection
(14) Debtor rehabilitation
(15) Stability
(16) Practical expediency[1]

---

[1] For a more extensive examination of these objectives of the law, see Anderson, Fox, and Twomey, Business Law (12th ed 1987), South-Western Publishing Co.) chapter 2; Anderson, Fox, and Twomey, Business Law, Principles, Cases, Legal Environment (9th ed 1988), South-Western Publishing Co.) chapters 1,2.

Chapter 2. DEFINITIONS AND RELATIONSHIPS

§ 2:1. The significance of definitions.
    (a) Generally.
    (b) Obliteration of distinctions.

§ 2:2. Definitions.
    (a) Hotel.
        (1) Services rendered as the test.
        (2) Guest defined.
            (i) Boarders and lodgers distinguished.
            (ii) Tenants distinguished.
    (b) Motel.
    (c) Boarding house.
    (d) Apartment house.
        (1) The hotel as a landlord.
        (2) Exclusive character of tenant's possession.
            (i) Other patrons distinguished.
        (3) Test of landlord-tenant relationship.
            (i) Duration of relationship.
            (ii) Absence of specific test.

§ 2:3. Creation of guest-hotel relationship.
    (a) Generally.
    (b) Registration.
        (1) Registration not essential.
        (2) Specific accommodations not essential.
        (3) Other relationships.
    (c) Unknown additional guests.
    (d) Known additional guests.

§ 2:4. Duties of guests and patrons.
    (a) Generally.
    (b) Conduct.

§ 2:5. Emergency medical care of patron.
    (a) Generally.
    (b) The unconscious guest.
    (c) The objecting guest.
    (d) Non-guests.
    (e) Inventory and control of patron's property.

§ 2:6. Transfer of right of occupancy or possession.
    (a) Guests and boarders.
    (b) Tenants.
        (1) Contract terms and regulations.

§ 2:7. Termination of relationship between hotel and guest.
    (a) Agreement for indefinite accommodations.
    (b) Accommodations for specified duration.
    (c) Eviction on termination of relationship.
        (1) Available remedies.
        (2) Changing locks and removing property.

§ 2:8. Termination of relationship between hotel and tenant.
    (a) Termination of lease.
        (1) Nonpayment of rent.
        (2) Breach of regulations.
        (3) Collateral matters.
    (b) Effect of termination of lease.

§ 2:9. Burden of proof.
    (a) Existence of relationship.
    (b) Termination of relationship.
        (1) Justification for terminations.

§ 2:1. The significance of definitions.

(*a*) ***Generally.*** As this book is written on hotel law it becomes important to know what is a hotel. In everyday life, this is not true because except in the very unusual case you know whether you are running a hotel or not. Moreover, if your hotel has been in business any length of time, these matters have been ironed out long ago and you are no longer concerned with this problem. Furthermore, the most simple things are often very difficult to define, even when we know exactly what we are talking about. For example, define "man," "walking," or "sunlight," in such a way that a person born without sight would be able to perceive in his mind's eye just what you meant. That is why the Chinese say that one picture is worth a thousand words.

(*b*) ***Obliteration of distinctions.*** The work of definition is also a thankless task because practical reasons make the definitions and distinctions worthless or purely theoretical in many cases. For example, the law tells us that we must make a distinction between the relationship of hotel and guest, on the one hand, and hotel and permanent resident, on the other.

While this is true, it is obvious that for the purpose of administrative simplicity and giving instructions to your ordinary employees, it is necessary to treat all patrons alike. The law tells us that it is to the transient guests only that the hotel owes the duty of courtesy; but because of the force of competition, it is obvious that the hotel will be courteous to all its patrons regardless of their guest or non-guest status. And to further obliterate the distinctions, the lawmaker will probably make various statutes apply to all "housing" enterprises without regard to their technical differences. For example, the fire safety statute will generally treat the transient guest and the permanent guest the same because the raging fire is not concerned with how long the patron would be residing in the place if it had not been burned to the ground. Differences likewise become increasingly less significant as we find the hotel and the non-hotel reaching out into each other's activities, such as those of the restaurant, nightclub, swimming pool, drugstore, merchandise store, and so on; where either the force of competition or geographic location of the enterprises makes it desirable or necessary to furnish patrons with all the services and conveniences that they desire.

§ 2:2. Definitions.

(*a*) *Hotel.* The hotel, or inn, as it was formerly called, offers lodging accommodations for a temporary sojourn to transient persons called guests. The hotel furnishes cleaning services but is not required to furnish any other service.

The modern hotel has expanded beyond these limited functions to embrace restaurants, and bars, dance floors, swimming pools, stores, and so forth. It is the lodging accommodations aspect, however, which creates the hotel-guest relationship. Contrarily, other services which do not relate to lodging accommodations do not give rise to such a relationship. Accordingly, a person who is merely a customer at a bar, restaurant, barber shop or newsstand operated by a hotel is not a guest of the hotel.

(1) Services rendered as the test. When it is necessary to determine what relationship is involved, the law looks to the substance of the transaction and not to the name or labels which the parties choose to attach to it. Therefore an enterprise which describes itself as a "motel" will be treated as a "hotel" when in fact it offers "hotel" services. There is authority, how-

ever, that the name of the enterprise is an element which may be considered in determining its character, so that the fact that the enterprise uses the word "hotel" in its name may be considered in deciding whether it is actually a hotel.

(2) Guest defined. A guest is a transient person who obtains accommodations at a hotel. He is distinguished from a boarder or lodger who regards the "hotel" as his home or residence, rather than a place of temporary, passing, or transient accommodation.

(i) Boarders and lodgers distinguished. The distinction between the boarder and lodger is merely that the latter is provided with rooming accommodations but no meals.

(ii) Tenants distinguished. The guest is distinguished from a tenant on the basis that the guest has merely the right to use the quarters assigned to him. This is a right of occupancy, whereas a true tenant has the right to possession of his room, apartment, or quarters.

The clarity of definition becomes confused, however, by the fact that for certain purposes a guest of a hotel is treated as having more than an interest of occupancy. For example, it has been held that the hotel does not have the authority to consent to an unlawful search and seizure of a guest's room; for whatever right a hotel has with respect to control and access to a room does not include the authority to admit strangers without legal process or give the hotel authority to waive the constitutional rights of a guest. If the guest had merely a right of occupancy and nothing more, the ordinary rule would be that the hotel, as being in possession, would be entitled to give permission for a search of and seizure upon the premises.

(b) Motel. A motel is a group of separate housing units rented on a short term basis to persons who are ordinarily traveling by automobile. This definition views the motel as a small cluster of cottages or a row of joined units which offers to the traveler no more than the right of occupancy of a unit, together with periodic cleaning services. As in the case of the hotel, the patron of the motel has the right to occupy the accommodations assigned to him.

With the expansion of motel services into non-lodging areas, such as a restaurant, skating rink, swimming pool, and so on, the motel gradually finds itself only physically different from a hotel and soon becomes the hotel-motel enterprise, and is frequently held to be a "hotel" within a regulatory statute.

(*c*) **Boarding house.** The distinction is generally made between a hotel and other enterprises, such as a boarding house, lodging house, or a rooming house, on the basis that the former is open to serve all persons without any express agreement as to the duration of their stay; in contrast with the latter in which there is an express contract for a specified period of time at a specified rate and the management has the right to deal with whom it sees fit.[1]

There is nothing, however, which prevents a hotel from acting as a boarding house as to certain persons. That is, as to some it is a "hotel" providing them with lodging on an indefinite transient basis, while as to others it is a "boarding house" furnishing them with lodging for a specified period.

(*d*) **Apartment house.** The apartment house is a building in which there are two or more residential units which are leased by the apartment house owner to the individual tenants. The relationship between the apartment house owner and the tenants is technically that of landlord and tenant. This means that the tenants are more or less permanent residents, having the right to the possession of part of the premises until the termination of the lease.

(1) The hotel as a landlord. A landlord-tenant relationship is not confined to buildings organized exclusively as apartment houses. Accordingly, the hotel may stand in the position of hotel to its transient patrons who are guests and also stand in the position of landlord to some permanent residents who are tenants.

Whether a given patron is a guest or a tenant is of course a question of the intention of the parties. In this respect, the distinction between the various permanent residents must be remembered: namely the tenants, who have a right to possession, and boarders, lodgers, and roomers, who have merely a right to occupy or use the assigned rooms.

(2) Exclusive character of tenant's possession. In a landlord-tenant relation as to an apartment, the possession of the tenant is exclusive except as the contrary is specified in the lease from the landlord. In the absence of such a provision in favor of the landlord, he would have no right to enter the leased premises without the tenant's permission. However, the right is generally reserved to the landlord to examine the premises

---

[1] Note however that by statute the freedom of choice of management may be restricted to prevent discrimination. See § 3:6.

from time to time to see that they are properly used and that other covenants of the lease are obeyed by the tenant, and for the purpose of showing the premises to prospective purchasers or to other tenants. The rights of entry reserved by the landlord may be so extensive that for practical purposes it is not important that the tenant technically has possession.

If the apartment house provides cleaning services, the right of such cleaning people to enter the apartment and perform their services will generally be a limitation upon the exclusive possession of the tenant and will be expressly stated in the lease.

(i) Other patrons distinguished. The right of occupancy or use enjoyed by a guest and by a boarder or lodger, is to be distinguished from the right of a tenant. The latter acquires an interest in the building itself, to the extent of the area leased to him, while the others do not.

In consequence of the nature of the tenant's interest in the premises, he has exclusive possession thereof, and may even bring actions at law to protect his right of possession. There is also significance in the status of a tenant as opposed to that of a guest, boarder, or lodger in that the hotel does not owe to the tenant the same duties as to the latter and in some cases statutes applicable to hotels and their liability do not apply when a tenant is concerned.

(3) Test of landlord-tenant relationship. If the hotel and its patron expressly stipulate that their relationship shall be of a particular character, the law will ordinarily give effect to such agreement. Thus if they specify that the relationship shall be as landlord and tenant it will be given that effect. Such an agreement may often be implied from the fact that the method of operating the building shows that the hotel is merely a landlord as to all of its patrons.

In many cases, the question turns on whether the occupant has exclusive possession of the premises occupied by him, in which case he is ordinarily deemed a tenant. In many instances the tenant's right to possession is not expressly stated but is to be deduced from the terms of the relationship. As a general rule, the relationship will be deemed a tenancy if the occupant is to maintain and clean the premises. The fact that the occupant is also to bring his own furniture and furnishings likewise indicates a landlord and tenant relationship. Conversely, the fact that the hotel has retained all keys for all apartments and

Definitions and Relationships 19

particularly that the hotel furnishes cleaning services and so forth are strong indications that the relationship is not that of landlord and tenant.

The presence or absence of cleaning services is not controlling, however, for if they are furnished as an additional service and charged for separately the relationship may still be that of landlord and tenant. For example, a landlord-tenant and not a hotel-guest relationship existed where a patron occupied a furnished apartment, paid a rent monthly in advance, did all cooking, and paid for maid service at an hourly rate; and it was specified that a thirty-day notice was required to terminate the relationship.

The size of the quarters do not establish whether the relationship is that of a roomer or a tenant for there may be a lease of one room. However, the occupant of one room in a house for whom the owner provided furniture, linens, towels, and daily maid service was a roomer and not a tenant. And as the acquisition or retention of possession is significant in determining the relationship of the parties, it is held that a person hiring a room is a lodger where the owner, who lives on the premises, retains the keys to the room.

(i) Duration of relationship. Speaking in generalities, a landlord-tenant relationship will ordinarily run for a longer period of time than a hotel-guest relationship; but duration is not the controlling distinction. This is particularly true in the case of trailer camps where a person renting trailer camp space by the week is not a guest in the sense of a person accepting transient accommodations, but is merely making a short-term rental of a piece of land, together with the purchase of such incidental "services" as water, electricity, and so on.

(ii) Absence of specific test. In determining whether the patron is a tenant or a guest, no one factor is controlling and a general appraisal of the entire situation is required. If there is a written agreement between the parties, the status of the patron can be determined by the court as a matter of law from an examination and interpretation of the written agreement. If there is no written agreement, the question is regarded as a mixed question of law and fact to be determined by the jury and on appeal the higher court will not reverse the conclusion of the lower court unless it is clear that it was manifestly wrong.

§ 2:3. Creation of guest-hotel relationship.

(*a*) *Generally.* The creation of the guest-hotel relationship is a matter of the intent of the parties that, on the one hand, the person offers himself as a guest, and on the other, that the hotel accepts or recognizes him as such. With respect to the first part of the statement it is of course obvious that a person cannot be made a guest and subjected to the obligations of a guest if he does not wish to become such. With respect to the second part, the hotel, although it is under the duty to serve the public without discrimination, does not become a hotel as to a particular individual until it manifests the intent that the person should be so received.

(*b*) *Registration.* Ordinarily no question arises as to whether the hotel-guest relationship has been established because the hotel's act in asking or permitting the applicant to sign a registry book or card is clearly an acceptance by the hotel of the applicant and the latter's act of registering is clearly his acceptance of the guest-hotel relationship. If the accommodations with respect to which this registration and acceptance takes place are transient accommodations, the relationship is that of hotel and guest.

(1) Registration not essential. While registration is ordinarily the transaction or the moment which definitely establishes that there is a hotel-guest relationship, the act of registration is not essential to the creation of the relationship. Accordingly when it can be established that by correspondence, telephone, or direct conversation, the applicant and the hotel had accepted each other with reference to particular transient accommodations, the guest-hotel relationship arises.

(2) Specific accommodations not essential. It is not essential that the parties agree to the exact rooms to be used by the guest in order for the hotel-guest relationship to arise. For example, the hotel-guest relationship will ordinarily arise at the time of registration, even though it might be some minutes later before the hotel has decided on just which rooms to provide the new guest. Furthermore, the relationship may arise where the incoming applicant applies for accommodations but none are available for him at that time, where it was the intention of the parties that he should be regarded as a guest. This aspect of the matter arises most frequently where the intended guest leaves his baggage with the hotel, hoping that

Definitions and Relationships 21

accommodations will become available to him later in the day or night.[2]

(3) Other relationships. Care must be taken to determine that the relationship which arises at the time of registration be one relating to transient accommodations as a guest and not the establishment of any other relationship such as that of a boarder or lodger on the one extreme, or a tenant, on the other.

(c) Unknown additional guests. As the guest-hotel relationship does not arise in the absence of an intent on the part of the hotel to receive the person as a guest, the unknown "guest" of the registered guest who shares the latter's room is not a guest of the hotel, as it was never intended by the latter that the unknown person should be so received.

(d) Known additional guests. It is not necessary that there be a direct contractual relationship between the hotel and a given person in order for the latter to be a guest. It is necessary, however, that it was within the comtemplation of the hotel that it was extending accommodations to such person. For example, members of the registering guest's family are guests of the hotel where the latter knew or was informed that such members would be using the accommodations.

§ 2:4. Duties of guests and patrons.

(a) Generally. The law imposes upon guests and patrons of the hotel, both with respect to the hotel and non-hotel enterprises, that such guests and patrons pay for services according to the terms of their contract or relationship with the hotel; obey all laws of the community and all lawful regulations of the hotel; and leave the premises when their right to stay has expired, as in the case of the expiration of the period of occupancy of rooms, or the closing of the bar at night.

(b) Conduct. The law imposes upon a guest the duty of so conducting himself that he does not annoy or harm other persons lawfully in the hotel nor harm the reputation of the hotel or subject it to criminal punishment. When a guest knows that he is carrying a contagious disease in a communicable stage he will be liable to the hotel when he causes harm through

---

[2] As to the status of the applicant as a guest and the obligation of the hotel with respect to his property, see § 16:1.

the spread of such disease to the hotel, its employees, and other guests.

§ 2:5. Emergency medical care of patron.

(*a*) *Generally.* As a phase of the hotel's duty to protect guests from harm, the hotel is under the duty to assist a guest in obtaining medical care in case of an emergency. No legal problem arises when the guest seeks the aid of the hotel and the hotel either gives the guest the information of where to find medical aid or takes him there. As long as the hotel has acted in a reasonable manner and has used reasonable care in dealing with the guest it is not liable for any subsequent negligence or fault of the doctor or hospital to whom it has directed or taken the guest.

(*b*) *The unconscious guest.* What should the hotel do if it finds that a guest is unconscious? If the guest is outside of his rooms and is unconscious, the hotel is under a duty to see that medical care and attention is provided for the guest. And again the hotel is not liable for any harm as long as it exercises reasonable care in selecting the physician or hospital for the guest. Moreover, as the hotel is acting in an emergency it is not negligent when it makes the best of the circumstances as it finds them, although when viewed in the light of the event after it has occurred, the hotel did not make the most judicious decision.

If the unconscious guest is in his rooms, a technical question arises as to how the hotel can reach the guest without violating the guest's right of privacy. The matter becomes very difficult for the hotelman when he is not certain that the guest is unconscious and in need of medical help; the hotelman being faced with the alternatives that (1) the guest is not in need of help and accordingly an entry into his rooms may be an invasion of privacy for which the hotel would be liable, or (2) the guest is in fact in need of medical help and if the hotel does not enter the guest's room to take care of him the hotel may be liable for the harm which follows from the neglect of the guest, including the possible death that may result from such failure. The answer is to be made in favor of entering to rescue the guest. Society places a higher value on giving the guest necessary medical care and perhaps saving his life than it gives to protecting his injured feelings from an invasion of his privacy.

Definitions and Relationships

In terms of dollars of liability, it is reasonably certain that the same jury would return a greater verdict against a hotel for failure to provide necessary aid than it would for making an unnecessary invasion of privacy. Moreover, since the potential of harm to the guest is so great, it is more than likely that the jury will be eager to find that you had reasonable cause to enter to rescue the guest although in fact there was no need for your rescue.

The manner in which the entry is made has of course much to do with the reaction of the jury. As discussed in § 22:3, the entry should be made if possible by a high ranking employee and a physician, if they are available and time permits their being summoned. If not, and reasonable ground exists for believing that there is an emergency, the hotel should take the chance of making a mistake, and enter to save the guest.

The condition of the guest when last seen or heard of is important in determining whether the hotel has acted with reasonable care. For example, if the guest comes into the hotel nearly dead drunk, the hotel is entitled to assume that the reason it does not hear from him the next morning is that he is sleeping off his indulgences. The hotel is not required to play the role of the mother hen and assume that the worst has happened to one of her brood. In such circumstances, the hotel is justified in believing that everything is normal and that there is no emergency.

(*c*) *The objecting guest.* A difficult situation may arise where the guest appears to be in need of medical treatment but insists that he is all right and refuses to go for or receive medical treatment. If in fact he appears fully possessed of his faculties and to know what he is doing, the hotel will not be liable because it leaves him alone, even though in fact he required medical care. If it appears to a reasonable man both that the guest needs medical attention and that the guest is too far gone to be making an intelligent choice, the case should be treated the same as that of the unconscious guest. The best solution of course is to get a doctor as soon as possible and let him decide what action he should take. Once the hotel, in the exercise of reasonable care, has procured a doctor for the guest, it need go no further unless requested or advised to do so by the doctor, in which case it is protected from liability for its conduct to the same extent as though the act directed or requested of it had been performed personally by the doctor.

(*d*) *Non-guests.* What should be done if the person considered in the previous situations is not a guest but a patron at the restaurant; or a lodger, or boarder; or a tenant? As the starting point, the distinction can be made that it is only to the guest that the peculiar duty of taking care exists. The hotel should, however, ignore this element and should treat anyone on its premises in the same way as the guest. This should be done for two reasons. First, there may not be any time to check on the identity and classification of the afflicted person, so that the logical necessity of the moment dictates that anyone on the premises should be cared for by the hotel which holds its place out as a place of safety for the members of the public. Second, the question of whether a person is a guest or a different kind of patron may present a difficult legal problem and it would be both absurd as well as brutal to require the hotel to analyze its legal status before it could determine whether it should act as a good Samaritan.

In any case, the easy solution is to get a physician to take charge of the patron, for from then on it is the problem of the doctor: the hotel being no longer responsible for the patron if it had exercised reasonable care in finding a physician for the patron.

(*e*) *Inventory and control of patron's property.* If the patron is a guest, tenant, lodger, or boarder in the hotel and is removed for emergency medical care, the hotel must take reasonable steps to protect the property of the patron while he is away. In the case of one who is a guest, this liability may rise to the point of being nearly an insurer, although statutes, contract clauses, and regulations generally limit such liability.[3]

If the hotel does not lock up the patron's property in the patron's room, the hotel should remove the property for safekeeping. Before it does this, an inventory should be prepared carefully; listing all items of property which have been removed. This phase of activity should be supervised by a high ranking employee of the hotel as discussed in § 22:3.

§ 2:6. Transfer of right of occupancy or possession.

(*a*) *Guests and boarders.* The right of a hotel guest is not transferrable or assignable. Hence, the permission which a hotel guest gives to a friend to live in the guest's room in place

---

[3] See Chapter 15.

of the guest does not bind the hotel which may therefore exclude the friend by changing the locks on the doors. The same is true of a boarder, roomer, or lodger, as his right is even less than that of a guest.

(*b*) *Tenants.* For practical reasons, the right of a patron under a lease is the same as in the case of a guest: if the hotel has taken the precautions to so declare in the lease. It is true that the right of a tenant under a lease is a property right which he can transfer or assign to another person without the permission and even over the objection of the landlord. But the law has long been established that the landlord can provide in the lease that no assignment, subletting, or transfer of any nature may be made by his tenant without the landlord's permission. When this is done, the tenant has no more right than a guest and the landlord may oust the transferee.

(1) Contract terms and regulations. In order to preserve control of the premises, the hotel should always specify on a card or an agreement which the patron signs when the landlord-tenant relationship is created that no assignment, subletting, or transfer of any nature may be made without the prior written approval of the hotel and that for breach of such provision the rights of the patron in the premises may be terminated.

If as a practical business matter, it is not expedient to require the execution of such an agreement because it is too difficult to separate the guests from the tenants, two alternatives could be followed: (1) have such a declaration on the reverse of the registration card signed by all patrons, the provision then applying to all patrons whether guests or tenants, with the registration card bearing appropriate indication of the presence of such conditions; (2) adopt a general regulation to the same effect which would be applicable to all patrons whether guests or tenants, provided proper notice was given of the existence of the regulation.

§ 2:7. Termination of relationship between hotel and guest.

(*a*) *Agreement for indefinite accommodations.* When the relation of the hotel is that of guest and hotel, the stay of the guest is initially indefinite in duration. Consequently the hotel may at any time give the guest reasonable advance notice that it is terminating the relationship and thereby compel him to leave, without giving the guest any reason for such termination and without having any grounds for ejecting the guest. Likewise the guest may terminate the relationship at any time and without giving any advance notice.

(*b*) *Accommodations for specified duration.* Contrary to the general rule above stated, it would appear that when the guest has been granted rooms on the basis of a reservation extending to a specified date that the stay of the guest cannot be terminated except for a cause which initially would have justified refusing the grant of accommodations to him.

The case is not free from doubt for the reason that there is in fact no contract between the parties as to the termination date but merely a statement of expectation. For example, when I stop at your hotel and inform you that I will be leaving next Friday afternoon, it is understood by both of us that I may leave on Thursday afternoon without being liable to you for the room rent up to Friday afternoon. That is, there is no binding contract between us that I should take and pay for the room down to Friday afternoon. In contrast, note that if I rent a house or an apartment for one year I must pay the rent for that year even though I choose to leave earlier and leave the place empty for the balance of the year.

While it is true that my statement of my intended checkout date is not really a term of our contract, it is likely that the changing pattern of the relation between hotel and guest will incline the courts to conclude that when the guest relies upon the hotel's statement that accommodations are being furnished to a specified date, the hotel cannot thereafter revoke such accommodations to the detriment of the guest. If it does so, as by locking the guest out of his room, it is not only liable for damages, but if it makes no good faith attempt to show an excuse or justification for its action, it is also liable for exemplary as well as compensatory damages.[4] Likewise, when a guest's rent is paid up, the hotel cannot lock her out without just cause and if it does, the hotel is liable for exemplary damages in so doing where the hotel manager stated publicly that the hotel did not want her and would not accept money for future rent. Likewise damages for mental anguish and suffering may be recovered by the tenant who has been unlawfully dispossessed.

---

[4]As to the classification of kinds of damages, see Chapter 22.

(c) *Eviction on termination of relationship.* When the relationship between the hotel and the patron is that of hotel and guest, the right of the guest terminates with the expiration of the period for which the guest had reserved the accommodations. This conclusion necessarily follows from the fact that the interest of a guest in his accommodations is less than that of a tenant and even a tenant who stays in possession after the expiration of his lease may be treated by the landlord as a trespasser and evicted. The guest with merely a right of occupancy can clearly have no greater right of hanging over in possession than a tenant. Consequently when a patron of the hotel, regardless of his classification as a tenant, guest, boarder, or lodger overstays the expiration of his accommodations, he may be evicted, the hotel using such force to do so as is reasonably necessary.

The use of excessive force will impose liability upon the hotel for the harm thereby caused the patron but does not extend his right to stay in the hotel.[5]

(1) Available remedies. Statutes may provide a special procedure for evicting the guest who remains in possession after the termination of the relationship. In some instances, statutory remedies for dispossessing occupants are limited to cases of true landlord-tenant relationships, with the result that a hotel cannot use such a remedy against a person who in fact was a transient guest and not a tenant.

(2) Changing locks and removing property. Since the hotel has the right to evict a guest who remains in possession after he should leave, it necessarily follows that the hotel can block the guest's returning to the accommodations, as by changing the locks on the door during a temporary absence of the guest.

Likewise, as the right to evict the person necessarily includes the right to eject property belonging to the guest, the hotel upon locking out the guest may also remove his property from the accommodations. When this is done the hotel should have a superior employee keep watch over the hotel employee doing the actual removal of the guest's property, both for the purpose of avoiding any harm or theft and also in order to have an additional witness as to what had been done. Moreover a careful written inventory should be made of all property so removed.

---

[5]See Chapter 18.

When the circumstances are such that the hotel has the right to a lien, the lien may of course be asserted against the property removed from the guest's room. In any case, whether or not there is a lien, the hotel should exercise reasonable care to protect the property from harm; although the liability of the hotel may be the insurer-like liability of the common law.[6]

§ 2:8. Termination of relationship between hotel and tenant.

(a) *Termination of lease.* When the relationship between the hotel and its patron is that of landlord and tenant, the hotel can only terminate the lease for such cause as under general landlord and tenant law or as the terms of the lease warrant a revocation of the lease. In the absence of facts justifying such revocation, the hotel must allow the lease to run to its expiration date.

If the lease is not for a fixed period but is continuing on a week to week, month to month, or year to year basis, the hotel will frequently find that there is a statute which provides that the lease shall run again for another unit of time unless the landlord-hotel gives notice to the tenant, or the guest, of the landlord's desire to terminate the lease. In the absence of statute, a similar notice requirement will commonly be in the lease; notice being given a rental period in advance. If a statute does not specify the exact form of the notice to be given, any notice is sufficient; but it must be clear and positive.

(1) Nonpayment of rent. If the relationship is that of guest and hotel, the hotel may exclude the guest immediately upon nonpayment of rent[6a] and may use such force as is necessary to evict the guest. The same is true of a boarder or lodger. For practical purposes, the same is also true of a tenant of the hotel for by the terms of the rental agreement the hotel will have undoubtedly, and should have, provided that in the event of nonpayment the hotel may terminate the lease and use a landlord's remedies to evict the tenant and so forth.

"If, however, no such provision is made in the lease, the tenant cannot be summarily removed for nonpayment of rent . . ."

---

[6] As to the common-law liability of the hotel for property of the guest, see § 16:2 et seq.; as to modification of this liability, see § 16:17 et seq.

[6a] This right is probably limited by the due process concept discussed on page 475 under §18:3.

Definitions and Relationships 29

and the hotel is liable if it attempts to do so. And in some states the hotel is limited to using a special statutory procedure available against tenants generally.

(2) Breach of regulations. Patrons who are guests, boarders, and lodgers, may of course be evicted for a violation of any valid regulation of the hotel and their right of occupancy terminated. Again, for practical purposes, the relationship to the tenant is the same, for the well-drawn lease will declare the right of the landlord from time to time to adopt such regulations as shall be proper or as the landlord shall deem necessary, and such lease further provides that the violation of such regulations shall be a ground for forfeiture of the lease.

(3) Collateral matters. Ordinarily a lease cannot be terminated at the will of the landlord because of conduct that is unrelated to the lease or the guest's duties as a tenant. So it has been held that where the patron had paid rent in an apartment building for one week in advance, the hotel had no right to oust her from possession because a check which she had indorsed and the hotel had cashed to accommodate the guest's escort had been dishonored.

(b) Effect of termination of lease. When the lease terminates according to its provisions, or because an authorized notice was given, or because the hotel has declared the lease forfeited for proper cause, the tenant no longer has any right to remain in his accommodation. From the moment of the expiration on, the former tenant is deemed to hold by sufferance of the hotel and is said to be a tenant by sufferance. This classification gives the hotel the right to elect (1) to accept the holdover tenant as a tenant for a new period or term of the lease or (2) to treat the holdover tenant as a trespasser and resort to any procedure available to a landlord for the eviction of a person improperly claiming to be a tenant.

§ 2:9. Burden of proof.

(a) Existence of relationship. A person claiming that at a particular time he stood in a certain relationship to a hotel has the burden of proving that fact. Thus the person claiming that he was a guest at a particular time in question has the burden of so proving, and it is not sufficient that he show that he was some kind of patron of the hotel. It must be remem-

bered, however, that for some purposes, the plaintiff will sufficiently prove his case if he proves that he was merely a patron, without regard to whether he was a guest. For example, a person injured by the condition of the lobby floor need only show that he was an invitee of the hotel, which could be established, among other things by showing that he was a patron of some service of the hotel, as a person going to the hotel restaurant or a purchaser in the hotel store in the lobby, and so on, whether or not he was a guest.

(*b*) *Termination of relationship.* The burden of proof is upon the hotel to show that a given relationship has terminated. That is, the general rule of law holds that once it is established that a relationship existed at a particular date, it is presumed to have continued thereafter until it is shown that it has terminated. Hence if the hotel wishes to show that the plaintiff was no longer a guest at the significant time in question, the hotel has the burden of proving that fact, as against the presumption that the guest was still a guest.

When the patron has ceased to be any kind of a patron at the hotel there is no difficulty in establishing that he was not thereafter a patron. More difficulty arises when the guest remains at the hotel but the latter claims that the guest became a boarder or a lodger, which if true, would reduce the liability of the hotel in certain respects.

(1) Justification for termination. When it is claimed that the relationship between the hotel and the tenant has been terminated by the voluntary act or revocation of the hotel, the hotel has the burden of proving that its action was justified when the patron claims that the hotel is liable for damages for improper termination.

Chapter 3. ACCOMMODATIONS AND DISCRIMINATION

§ 3:1. Right to enter hotel.
    (a) Generally.
    (b) Restriction of right to customers and related persons.
        (1) Right of eviction.
        (2) Loss of right of entrance.
    (c) Visitors of guests.
    (d) Business solicitors.
        (1) Equality of treatment.
        (2) Prohibited solicitation by person properly on premises.

§ 3:2. Nature and price of accomodations.
    (a) Generally.
    (b) Change of accommodations.
    (c) Accessory accommodations.
    (d) Hotel rates.

§ 3:3. Proper refusal of accommodations.
    (a) Generally.
    (b) Absence of available accommodations.
    (c) Bad character of applicant.
    (d) Bad conduct.
        (1) Basis for decision.
    (e) Disease.
    (f) Financial irresponsibility.
    (g) Salesmen and competitors.

§ 3:4. Improper refusal of accommodations.
    (a) Generally.
    (b) False statement of lack of accommodations.
    (c) Unreasonable regulations or conditions.
    (d) Age.
    (e) Time.
    (f) Racial discrimination.

§ 3:5. Civil rights protection against discrimination.
    (a) Generally.
    (b) Limitation to specified discrimination.
    (c) Remedy for violation of federal statute.
    (d) Relation to state law.

§ 3:6. — Hotels under Federal Civil Rights Act.
    (a) Definition.
        (1) Exceptions.
    (b) Conditions to applicability of statute.

§ 3:7. — Non-hotel functions and services.
    (a) Generally.
    (b) Restaurant and food service.
    (c) Gasoline stations.
    (d) Amusement and entertainment places.
    (e) Concessions.
        (1) Nature of concession business.
        (2) Legal relationship between hotel and concession.
    (f) Private clubs.

§ 3:1. Right to enter hotel.

(*a*) *Generally.* As the hotel by definition holds itself out to the general public to furnish accommodations, anyone has the right, without any prior invitation or permission, to enter the hotel seeking accommodations. With the broadening of hotel functions, as by operating a public bar, restaurant, beauty parlor, and so forth, the right of the public to enter naturally expands. Consequently any person may enter to patronize any facility or accommodation which the hotel holds open to the public.

(*b*) *Restriction of right to customers and related persons.* In ordinary speech, the hotel is only open to customers, and to those seeking to be customers, or who are present at the invitation of one who is already a customer, with respect to some accommodation or activity of the hotel. In contrast, one who has no such interest or relationship, for example, a newsboy or a peddler, has no right to enter the premises.

    (1) Right of eviction. With respect to persons who have no right to enter the hotel, the building is the hotel's own private home and the hotel may therefore employ such force as is reasonably necessary to exclude and physically eject, if necessary, all persons having no right to be there. Eviction upon the expiration of the patron's tenancy or reservation is discussed in Chapter 18.

    (2) Loss of right of entrance. A person otherwise qualified and entitled to enter may be evicted when his subsequent con-

Accommodations and Discrimination 33

duct is such that it threatens to or causes harm to other persons or their property, or to the hotel property. For example, a person who enters and acquires the status of a guest may be evicted where he thereafter becomes so drunk that he is a danger to persons around him or to the hotel building.

(*c*) **Visitors of guests.** Since it is not contemplated that guests will live in isolation, it is an implied term of the guest's relationship that business and social callers may visit him.

The hotel may restrict such right of visitation, even over the guest's objection, to exclude those visitors who for one cause or another would be a source of annoyance, disturbance, or harm to other persons' property in the hotel, or to the employees or property of the hotel. The hotel may also exclude visitors whose purpose is gambling or prostitution, even though there is no harm to person or property nor any disturbance or public annoyance. This right of exclusion in such cases may be reinforced in a given state where a law exists which would make it a criminal offense for a hotel, or any other owner of property, to permit it to be used as a gambling house or a house of prostitution.

(*d*) **Business solicitors.** A hotel may validly make and enforce a regulation prohibiting anyone from entering the premises for the purpose of promoting some other business, whether that of a competitor of the hotel or not. Thus the hotel may prohibit any automobile salesman; promoters of other businesses, such as transportation companies, theaters; and so forth, from coming on the premises at all.

(*1*) *Equality of treatment.* The hotel must treat all business solicitors equally without discrimination. Accordingly if it permits any solicitors for a particular kind of business, it must permit all to enter. For example, if it allows the representative of one railroad to enter the premises for solicitation of business, it must allow the representative of any other railroad to do so. Conversely, if the hotel wants to exclude any, it must exclude all, and a regulation of the hotel which excludes all is valid.

The foregoing is of course subject to the qualification that the hotel, or its concessionaire, is not engaged in a particular business; in which case it is proper to discriminate to the extent of prohibiting admission to the salesman of any business which competes with the business of the hotel or its concessionaire.

Equality of treatment does not require that everyone be evicted who violates the regulation of the hotel. The hotel has the discretion to determine that its past experience with a given sales agent has been such that the only reasonable thing is to be rid of him completely. On the other hand the hotel may reasonably believe that if it warns the salesman there will be no further violations of the no-solicitation regulation; in which case it is proper to permit the salesman in question to remain.

(2) Prohibited solicitation by person properly on premises. A person may enter the premises to be a guest, a patron, or a proper visitor of a guest or patron. Assume that after such person is on the premises he seeks to solicit customers for the business of his employer. If there is a regulation against such solicitation and he knows or is informed of such regulation, he may be evicted from the hotel because of its breach. That is to say, he loses, because of his improper conduct, the benefit of the status which permitted him to enter the hotel.

§ 3:2. Nature and price of accommodations.

(*a*) **Generally.** A hotel is required to furnish lodging to transient guests.

The only obligation upon the hotel is to furnish a room or rooms of the nature, class, or price level requested by the applicant. When there is a choice between two or more rooms, the hotel has the right to say which shall be provided the applicant, although as a practical business matter the hotel ordinarily does not insist on exercising this right if the applicant requests or demands if there are other like rooms.

(*b*) **Change of accommodations.** The hotel may change the room assignment and move its guest to another room or apartment. As long as the new quarters are reasonably fit and the guest is not charged any additional amount the guest cannot complain of the transfer. The guest cannot prevent the transfer by refusing to agree to it, nor can he sue the hotel as a trespasser for moving his belongings to the new accommodations.

Goodwill considerations prevent the frequent exercise of this power by the hotel over the objection of the guest.

(*c*) *Accessory accommodations.* It is no longer required that a hotel provide food and drink or stable facilities. Practical competitive reasons, however, cause the modern hotel to offer restaurant and garage facilities.

A hotel is not required to furnish rooms for the display of goods by its guests. Again the circumstances are frequently such that the hotel expressly offers showroom facilities in order to attract individual guests and conference groups.

There is no requirement on the hotel to provide entertainment for its guests. No real question arises in this connection because it is common for the larger hotels to go out of their way to provide entertainment. With respect to the hotels which do not provide entertainment, the law can imply from the surrounding circumstances that the guest as a reasonable man must recognize that he was not paying for any entertainment and therefore was not entitled to any.

(*d*) *Hotel rates.* The hotel rates must be reasonable in amount and equal to all persons. Whether or not rates are excessive or reasonable is ordinarily a question for determination by a jury.

Prepayment of the charges of the hotel is ordinarily not required; the hotel has the right to require such prepayment.

§ 3:3. Proper refusal of accommodations.

(*a*) *Generally.* Although the hotel is open to serve all and is required to act without discrimination, it may properly refuse accommodations for a number of reasons which in general terms relate to (1) physical inability to provide accommodations, or (2) the reasonable belief of the hotel that the applicant is objectionable.

(*b*) *Absence of available accommodations.* When the rooms of the hotel are filled, it is not required to permit an applicant to use a room not furnished for lodging. Moreover, the hotel is deemed filled even though each room is not filled to its maximum capacity.

(*c*) *Bad character of applicant.* The hotel may refuse accommodations to improper persons who are of a suspicious or immoral character or have a bad reputation.

(*d*) *Bad conduct.* The hotel may refuse accommodations to a person who at the time is disorderly, drunk, or whose conduct in any other way would be offensive or objectionable to other guests of the hotel. The hotel may also exclude under this ground persons who refuse to obey the hotel's proper regulations.

When the exclusion is based on the bad conduct of the applicant, such bad conduct may be actually occurring at the time of the application. That is, the applicant is offensively intoxicated at the time he comes up to the registration desk. In addition, it is sufficient if there is reasonable ground for believing that the guest will be guilty of future bad conduct, as in the case of the known drunk who applies for accommodations and although sober at the time is carrying a large paper bag from which comes a clanking sound suggestive of bottles.

(1) Basis for decision. In the bad conduct exclusion situation it is logical to permit, and the law does permit, the hotel to act upon expectations and fears to exclude the persons whose expectable conduct will cause harm before they have actually caused harm. The essential element is merely that the hotel acted reasonably in reaching the conclusion that bad conduct may occur.

The hotel, however, cannot exclude on the theory of class guilt or guilt by association. For example, it cannot exclude a member of a convention merely because the hotel has had trouble with other members of the convention. Similarly, a hotel cannot refuse accommodations to a soldier in uniform because the hotel has had trouble with other uniformed soldiers. That is to say, whether an applicant is a bad conduct case depends solely upon what the applicant has done, is doing, or is likely to do in the future while in the hotel; what other persons of his class have done is immaterial.

(e) Disease. Accommodations may and must be refused to any person carrying a contagious or infectious disease. Here the exclusion is more than a privilege and becomes a duty, for other guests could hold the hotel liable if with knowledge of the applicant's condition it furnished accommodations to him and the other guests became infected thereby.

The foregoing statement of course assumes that the infection of the other guests was the result of involuntary exposure to the applicant. If the complaining guest had voluntarily increased the probability of becoming infected, as in the case of a venereal disease, the guest's conduct would constitute an assumption of the risk involved and would bar liability of the hotel.

Accommodations and Discrimination 37

(*f*) *Financial irresponsibility.* As a hotel is not a charitable institution it may refuse accommodations to anyone who cannot pay for them. Moreover, the hotel may demand a payment of all or any part of the hotel bill in advance.

(*g*) *Salesmen and competitors.* The hotel may exclude any applicant whose purpose in coming to the hotel is to persuade the guests to leave and go to another hotel. Accommodations may also be refused to a salesman whose purpose in coming to the hotel is to enable him to contact the guests in the hotel in order to sell them his product.

§ 3:4. Improper refusal of accommodations.

(*a*) *Generally.* As the hotel is by definition an enterprise holding itself out to serve the public, it necessarily follows that the hotel must accept all members of the public, otherwise fit, who offer themselves as guests. Thus the hotel cannot pick and choose its guests, but must make facilities available to them on a "first come — first serve" basis. If the hotel refuses accommodations for an improper ground it is liable for damages, including exemplary damages. In addition, it may be liable under a civil rights or similar statutory provision, and may also be guilty of a crime.

(*b*) *False statement of lack of accommodations.* If the hotel falsely tells the applicant that no accommodations are available, the hotel is liable to the applicant for damages, unless the applicant could be excluded otherwise. That is to say, the hotel can tell the offensively drunk person that there are no rooms even though this is not true, because the hotel could exclude such a person because of his physical condition.

(*c*) *Unreasonable regulations or conditions.* The hotel cannot refuse accommodations because the applicant will not comply with terms and conditions imposed by the hotel when such terms and conditions are unreasonable, and therefore not binding.

(*d*) *Age.* A hotel cannot refuse accommodations to a person merely because the applicant is a minor, nor because he is an aged person, in the absence of other factors which indicate that because of such age the applicant will or may probably create some problem for the hotel, whether in terms of disobeying regulations of the hotel or imposing additional duties on it in taking care of the person, and so forth.

(*e*) **Time.** A hotel must be kept open at all times. Accommodations therefore cannot be refused on the ground that the applicant has arrived too late at night or that the day is a holiday or Sunday.

(*f*) **Racial discrimination.** This subject is now regulated by federal statute.[1]

§ 3:5. Civil rights protection against discrimination.

(*a*) **Generally.** In its original sense, a civil right was any right of the individual which was recognized or enforced by the law. In modern usage, however, it is identified with provisions against discrimination because of race, color, or any other cause based upon a person's membership in a class rather than his individual characteristics or behavior. Such civil rights provisions are now found in both the federal and the state constitutions and statutes.

By virtue of the Federal Civil Rights Act of 1964, neither a hotel nor its concessionaire can discriminate against a guest or patron, nor segregate them on the basis of race, color, religion, or national origin.[2]

(*b*) **Limitation to specified discrimination.** The Federal Civil Rights Act is limited to discrimination for the stated reasons and does not in any way interfere with the right of the hotel to exclude those who because they are drunk or criminally violent are unfit persons to admit, nor persons who are not dressed in the manner required by the hotel regulations which are applied to all persons.

(*c*) **Remedy for violation of federal statute.** When there has been improper discrimination or segregation or it is reasonably believed that such acts may occur, the statute authorizes the institution or proceedings in the federal courts for an order to stop such prohibited practices.

---

[1] See § 3:5.

[2] § 201(a). By federal regulation a similar limitation had earlier been imposed upon hotels operating within national parks and certain national recreational areas.

Accomodations and Discrimination   39

If the prohibited practice is also unlawful under state statutes or local ordinance, or any other federal statute, the complaining party may also proceed under such other statutes in the manner authorized by them. If the prohibited acts also constitute a crime under any other statute or ordinance, the hotel may also be prosecuted thereunder in addition to being ordered under the Civil Rights Act to stop the prohibited practices.

(*d*) *Relation to state law.* State law is displaced by the federal statute only to the extent that it is inconsistent with the federal statute. With the exception of such conflicting provisions, the state statutes or city ordinances remain in effect.

> *The facts:* A negro and his white wife were refused accommodations by the hotel because of his race. They sued for statutory penalties imposed by the Public Accommodations Law stating that no hotel "shall directly or indirectly refuse . . . to any person any of the accommodations . . . on account of race, creed, color, or racial origin." The hotel claimed that it was not liable for the penalty with respect to the wife.
>
> *Decision:* Judgment for both plaintiffs. It was obvious that accommodations had been denied the wife only because she was married to her negro husband. She was thus directly or indirectly discriminated against on account of race. [Hobson v. York Studios, 208 Misc 888, 145 NYS2d 162 (1955)].

§ 3:6. — Hotels under Federal Civil Rights Act.

(*a*) *Definition.* For the purpose of the above provision of the Civil Rights Act, any inn, hotel, motel, or other establishment which provides lodging to transient guests is subject to the provisions applicable to hotels.

(1) Exceptions. The Civil Rights Act does not apply to a small hotel which (a) does not contain more than five rooms for rent or hire and which in addition (b) is actually occupied by the proprietor as his residence. As a matter of statutory construction it should also be held that the act does not apply to an establishment which does not serve "transients."[3]

---

[3]Note, however, that to the extent that state-owned facilities are used by a lessee all racial discrimination is prohibited by Burton v. Wilmington Parking Authority, 365 US 715, 81 SCt 856, 6 L ed2d 45 (1961) (lessee of restaurant in building owned by state governmental authority). This principle is probably restated by §301 of the Civil Rights Act. See Supplement, p. 473.

(*b*) *Conditions to applicability of statute.* Assuming that the status of "hotel" is satisfied, the federal statute is still not applicable unless (a) the operations of the hotel or other enterprise affect interstate commerce, or (b) the discrimination which is practiced is state supported.

The limitation as to interstate commerce creates no problem as to hotels for, in effect, it is declared that every hotel is in interstate commerce. Likewise the interstate commerce element is satisfied as to non-hotel activities because the test established is such that it will ordinarily be satisfied in every case.[4]

Discrimination or segregation is state supported, and consequently the Civil Rights Act applies, without regard to the commerce aspect, whenever such conduct is permitted, authorized, or required by law, custom, ordinance, or statute.

§ 3:7 — **Non-hotel functions and services.**

(*a*) *Generally.* The Federal Civil Rights Act of 1964 embraces a number of functions and services which are not essential to being a hotel, although commonly engaged in by hotels.

(*b*) *Restaurant and food service.* To the extent that the hotel engages in these activities it is subject to the Civil Rights Act prohibition against discrimination or segregation. The Act applies to any restaurant, cafeteria, lunchroom, lunchcounter, soda fountain, or other facility principally engaged in selling food for consumption on the premises. When a hotel engages in such activities, it will undoubtedly be held subject to the same provisions as though the enterprise were only a hotel. That is, the provisions of the Act will be held applicable whether or not the enterprise is solely a restaurant or the restaurant function is merely a subsidiary or secondary function.

(*c*) *Gasoline stations.* If the hotel operates any gas station, the station is subject to the terms of the Act.

(*d*) *Amusement and entertainment places.* Any motion picture house, theater, concert hall, sports arena, stadium, or other place of exhibition or entertainment is subject to the Act.

---

[4] If a substantial part of the customers of an establishment are interstate travelers, or the goods sold or materials or persons participating customarily move from state to state, as in the case of hotels, the commerce aspect of the statute is satisfied.

Accommodations and Discrimination

Again the fact that such enterprise is merely a secondary activity of the hotel, or is merely a "free" service rendered the guests as part of the overall package of services, would not take the activity out of the statutory control to which it would be subject if operated as an independent enterprise.

(e) **Concessions.** Any concession of the hotel is bound by the Civil Rights Act to the same extent as the hotel itself. As long as (1) the concession is on the hotel premises or the same premises as the hotel, and (2) the concession holds itself out as serving patrons of the hotel, the concession is bound by the Civil Rights Act to the same extent as the hotel.

(1) Nature of concession business. Under the Act, the concessionaire is bound regardless of the nature of the business operated by him. This follows from the fact that the Civil Rights Act speaks broadly as applying to "any establishment" which meets the two requirements above noted. Hence a bookstore concession, a drug store concession, and any other concession will be subject to the Act.

(2) Legal relationship between hotel and concession. The nature of the legal relationship between the concessionaire and the hotel is immaterial. The fact that the hotel has no control over the operations of the concessionaire does not make the statute inapplicable to the concessionaire. Hence even the fact that the concessionaire holds possession of his store under a long-term lease does not affect the operation of the statute.

In most cases, the hotel may protect itself against possible violations of the Civil Rights Act by a concessionaire by providing in its lease or other agreement with the concessionaire that (a) the hotel reserves the right to terminate the relationship upon the breach by the concessionaire of the Civil Rights Act or any other law, and (b) requiring the concessionaire to pay to the hotel any money which the hotel has lost as the result of paying fines, legal expenses, and so on, which the hotel incurred because of the misconduct of the concessionaire. In most instances, the well-drawn modern concession agreement will contain such provisions, and possibly all that might be done to improve the position of the hotel is to state expressly that such clauses cover liability under the Civil Rights Act and other federal legislation, as well as under other laws.

(f) **Private clubs.** The private club device cannot be employed to evade the requirements of the Civil Rights Act. If a private club or other establishment is in fact not open to the public, the statute permits it to set up such restrictions as it chooses. If, however, the club is open to all or made available to the guests of the hotel, the club is to that extent subject to the Act. To illustrate, a truly private swimming club is not affected by the Act. Assume, however, that the club agrees to allow hotel guests to use the club's facilities, such as a swimming pool. In receiving guests from the hotel, the private club cannot make any discrimination or segregation which the hotel would have been prohibited from making.

Chapter 4. LIABILITY-IMPOSING CONDUCT

§ 4:1. Fields of Liability.
    (a) Generally.
    (b) Positive duty imposed by law.
    (c) Negative duty imposed by law.
    (d) Duty imposed by contract of the parties.

§ 4:2. Liability for tort.
    (a) Generally.
    (b) Fault of hotel.
    (c) Effect of liability insurance coverage.
        (1) Trend of the law.

§ 4:3. Theories of tort liability.
    (a) Generally.
    (b) Absolute liability.
    (c) Intentional harm.
    (d) Negligent harm.
    (e) Tort liability from breach of duty.

§ 4:4. Liability for breach of contract.
    (a) Generally.
    (b) Terms of contract with guest.
    (c) Authority of hotel employee to contract.
        (1) Contrary instructions.
    (d) Authority of apparent employees.

§ 4:1. Fields of liability.

(*a*) *Generally.* When does the hotel owe an obligation to its patron? When must it pay damages to the patron for the violation of such duty? The liability of the hotel may be based upon any of several theories. In many instances, the theory is one of general application not confined merely to hotels but instead, is applicable to anyone who does the act done by the hotel. In some instances, no liability is imposed upon the hotel for the harm sustained by the plaintiff.

(*b*) *Positive duty imposed by law.* A hotel is under certain duties because the law says that it is. For example, the duty to serve the general public without discrimination exists because the law has adopted that standard and requires all seeking to run a hotel to follow it. The law having imposed a duty, there then arises the question of what the law provides when there is breach of the duty.

Other positive duties imposed by law may be stated in general terms so as to be applicable to businesses and persons who are not hotels. For example, if a building code specifies the insulation which is to be required on electric wiring, this applies to all electric wiring, without regard to whether the building is used as a hotel.

(*c*) **Negative duty imposed by law.** The law may prohibit the hotel from doing certain acts. Ordinarily this is associated with the field of criminal law which declares it to be a crime when the hotel does certain acts. Again the law or statute may be aimed at hotels alone or it may apply to anyone in the position of the hotel, as a law prohibiting the sale of intoxicating liquor to minors. The negative duties may also be found in the field of general regulatory law, as a zoning ordinance which prohibits anyone from building a certain type of structure in specified areas.

(*d*) **Duty imposed by contract of the parties.** The hotel may enter into contracts which in general terms are the same in scope and effect as though the contracts were executed by any person or other business.

§ 4:2. Liability for tort.

(*a*) **Generally.** The law classifies as torts the various harms to person and property such as physical injury to the person, damage to or loss of property, and harm to personality, such as defamation and invasion of privacy.

A hotel is liable for its torts to the same extent as any individual or ordinary business corporation. The law which governs the hotel's tort liability is consequently the general tort law applicable to everyone.

(*b*) **Fault of hotel.** In general, it may be said that liability of a defendant for tort is based upon his fault. Consequently, the fact that harm occurs does not in itself establish fault. Moreover, the problem of determining when liability exists cannot be answered merely in terms of "fault" for two reasons. First the concept of "fault" recognized by the law is not necessarily the same as fault recognized by moral or ethical standards. Secondly, it is necessary to distinguish between fault which consists of the defendant's willful act and that which is his negligence, or which consists of the breach of a supervisory duty. Furthermore, the fault of others may in some instances be imputed to the defendant, as in the case of an employer, and he may accordingly be held vicariously liable. And in addition, there are instances where, contrary to the general rule stated above, absolute liability, or liability without fault, is imposed upon the defendant.

(c) *Effect of liability insurance coverage.* No principle is more firmly established than that a defendant is not made liable for the consequences of his actions by the mere fact that he is covered by liability insurance. Accordingly, a hotel which would otherwise not be liable for harm, does not become liable merely because it has liability insurance which could pay for the harm. Thus a question of tort liability is to determined as though there were no insurance coverage in the case.

(1) Trend of the law. While this is the correct statement of the law with respect to a given case, it is apparent that the course of the growth of the law has been affected greatly by the fact that insurance is available which can lighten the burden on defendants. Thus, those courts which have abolished the immunity of charities for liability have often stressed the fact that they could protect themselves by insurance; in some instances the courts making the decisions take effect as to future cases in order to give the charities the time in which to go out and procure insurance. Similarly the expansion of the product liability of manufacturers has been influenced by the fact that the manufacturer could cover his loss by insurance and transfer the economic incidence of liability to the insurer and the consuming public. And the validity of a statute imposing absolute liability upon aircraft for ground damage has been sustained on the dual grounds of the difficulty of proof and the fact that the air carrier, through its ability to procure insurance, was the better risk bearer. In addition, statutes sometimes declare liability coverage to be a waiver of the immunity of a charity or governmental unit or give such an insured the option to waive its immunity.

§ 4:3. Theories of tort liability.

(*a*) **Generally.** Liability is not imposed upon the hotel or anyone else merely because someone has been injured. In order to impose liability upon the hotel it is necessary for the plaintiff to show that there is some recognized legal principle which covers the facts and holds the defendant hotel liable.

(*b*) **Absolute liability.** In some areas of the law liability for harm exists without regard to whether there has been any fault. The hotel is not subject to this principle, although its common-law liability for goods of guests comes close to this. Under the common law, now greatly changed by statutes, the hotel was liable for the loss of or harm to the goods of the guests although it was actually free from fault; but this liability, which is absolute to this point, was not imposed if any one of the explanations discussed in § 16:3 could be established by the hotel to account for the loss or harm.

(*c*) **Intentional harm.** When the hotel intentionally causes harm to a person, it is ordinarily liable therefor, although there are certain exceptions which excuse or justify the conduct of the hotel. This area of liability is discussed in Chapter 5.

(*d*) **Negligent harm.** The basis on which a hotel is held liable to a guest or other person for any type of harm sustained by that person or his property is ordinarily that of negligence. Namely, the failure of the hotel to exercise such care as would be exercised by a reasonable man under the circumstances in order to avoid reasonably foreseeable harm. This subject is discussed in Chapter 9 with respect to the standard of due care, and in Chapter 7 with respect to the necessity of a cause and effect relationship between the negligence and the harm.

When the hotel is a corporation or similarly organized enterprise, the hotel of necessity acts through agents and employees and in any event most law suits arise from the conduct of an employee. It is therefore important to know to what extent a hotel has either supervisory or vicarious liability, that is, to what extent it is liable for the conduct of its agent or employee or other person over whom it exercises or may exercise control.

(*e*) **Tort liability from breach of duty.** The hotel has no immunity from ordinary tort liability by virtue of the fact that it is a hotel. Hence if the hotel causes willful or negligent harm to another person it is liable to the same extent as though the hotel were an ordinary individual.

§ 4:4. Liability for breach of contract.

(*a*) *Generally.* The hotel is liable for the breach of its contracts to the same extent as any person or business corporation. This is true both with respect to contracts made by the hotel as the buyer or customer, as in buying food and linen supplies from manufacturers and distributors; and contracts which the hotel makes with its guests and patrons.

In many cases, the questions which arise relate to the terms of the hotel's contract with its guests and the authority of its employees to make or modify such contracts.

(*b*) *Terms of contract with guest.* When a guest or other patron registers at a hotel or makes a reservation in advance, very little is ordinarily discussed. The availability of a specified type of space, its cost, the duration of the guest's stay — and the guest registers or agrees to the reservation. Nothing is said as to the various rights and duties which are imposed upon the respective parties to the contract. Nor is it necessary that anything be said about them because the law "reads" into every hotel-guest agreement various "terms" stating the respective rights and liabilities of the parties. This is not anything peculiar to hotel law, for if I make a contract to sell you my watch for $50 the law reads into that contract the obligation to pay $50 (a) in cash, (b) in money which is legal tender today, (c) and to make payment concurrently with delivery of the watch.

It is often said that the "silent" terms which the law reads into the contract are implied by law. But in a sense, this is not so since the parties have indicated or expressed by their conduct that they meant the particular relationship to exist between them and hence may be deemed by their conduct to have agreed to the rights and duties that go along with the relationship in question.

In a sense we have but two sides of the same coin. Actually, what occurs is merely that the parties have agreed to a certain relationship and the characteristics of this relationship are various rights and duties which go along and form part of the package. By what theory of law this is to be explained is not as important as is the fact that by virtue of the agreement to create the hotel-guest or similar relationship there do arise the various rights and duties discussed in this book.

(*c*) *Authority of hotel employee to contract.* The problem which most frequently arises in the administration of a hotel within this area of law is the authority of a given employee to make an agreement on behalf of the hotel, such as to take care of a guest's automobile; or his authority to modify any rights of the hotel, as by surrendering or waiving a right which the hotel would otherwise have.

An employee of a hotel has, to begin with, such authority to act on behalf of the hotel as the hotel has actually given him. In addition, he has such authority as the nature of his position apparently would give him. Thus the employee in charge of room reservations has in the eyes of the law authority to waive requirements as to room reservations and to make a modification to the hotel's plan of doing business. For example, the reservation man has authority to waive the checkout time requirements by agreeing that the guest may overstay that time and leave several hours later without any additional charge.

(1) Contrary instructions. The hotel may of course give its employees instructions which limit or reduce their authority. But when the employee's position is such that in the ordinary hotel life within the community a reasonable man would regard him as having a particular power, it is immaterial that the hotel has given the employee contrary instructions if they are unknown to outsiders. Suppose for example, that in the case of waiving the checkout time, the hotel had expressly prohibited its employees from allowing any running over. If this instruction to the employees was not known or made known to a guest, he would not be bound by such instruction and could hold the hotel to the checkout time agreed to by the reservation clerk in violation of these instructions.

(d) Authority of apparent employees. The hotel is bound not only by the contracts of its authorized employees but also by acts of third persons who, in the eyes of the world, reasonably appear because of the hotel's conduct to be its employees. To illustrate, a hotel allows an employee of a next door parking lot to stand about in the hotel lobby, wearing what appears to be a uniform of some nature, and receiving instructions with respect to the parking of cars; such instructions being given by guests or by the hotel itself. Under such circumstances, in the absence of something to indicate the contrary, such as the name of the true employer on the employee's uniform, the world is held to be justified in relying on the appearance which the hotel had created, or had allowed to continue, that the employee was a hotel employee and not the employee of another business, that is, the parking lot.

The consequence of this conclusion is that the hotel is bound by the contracts of its apparent employees, acting within what reasonably appears to be the scope of their authority.

Chapter 5. THE HOTEL'S SUPERVISORY LIABILITY

§ 5:1. Nature of supervisory liability.
    (a) Generally.
    (b) Theory of liability.

§ 5:2. Vicarious liability compared.
    (a) Generally.
    (b) Fault of hotel.
    (c) The actor.
    (d) The plaintiff.
    (e) Alternative applicability of theories.

§ 5:3. Standard of reasonable care.
    (a) Generally.
    (b) High degree of care.
        (1) Keys to room.
    (c) Persons involved.

§ 5:4. Standard of absolute liability.
    (a) Generally.
    (b) Rationale of absolute liability.
    (c) Persons involved.
    (d) Appraisal of absolute supervisory liability concept.

§ 5:5. — Liability for improper language and discourtesy.
    (a) Guests.
        (1) Nature of liability.
    (b) Non-guests.

§ 5:6. Apprehension of harm.
    (a) Generally.
    (b) Extent of observation.
    (c) Opportunity to act.

§ 5:7. Warning as a sufficient precaution.
    (a) Generally.
    (b) Reason to believe warning sufficient.
    (c) Relation to offender.

§ 5:8. Protection from acts of third persons.
    (a) Generally.
    (b) Reasonable care.

(c) Foreseeability or knowledge of harm.
(1) Degree of precautions.
(2) Athletic and amusement activities.
(d) Exclusion of strangers where harm not foreseeable.
(e) Contributory negligence and assumption of risk.
(f) False arrest.

§ 5:9. Protection of persons on street.
(a) Generally.
(b) Nature of duty.
(c) Foreseeability.
(1) Activities of hotel.
(2) Incidental acts of guests.

§ 5:10. Act of employee.
(a) Generally.
(b) Employee as wrongdoer.

§ 5:11. Acts of concessionaire.
(a) Generally.
(b) Independent character of concessionaire apparent.
(c) Independent character of concessionaire not apparent.
(1) Separate identity signs.
(d) Indemnity agreement.

§ 5:12. Acts of unrelated business tenants in hotel building.
(a) Generally.
(b) Particular applications.

§ 5:1. Nature of supervisory liability.

(*a*) *Generally.* The hotel, as is true of the proprietor of any public place, holds itself out to the public as a place which is safe and free from evildoers. The hotel must accordingly keep its premises clear of persons likely to cause harm whether they be criminal, intoxicated, or mentally defective; and must prevent otherwise proper persons from engaging in misconduct, horseplay, or other rowdy conduct which would cause harm to other persons.

(*b*) *Theory of liability.* Ordinarily the theory of supervisory liability of the hotel is stated in terms of negligence. That is, the question is whether the hotel did or did not exercise reasonable care under the circumstances to avoid the harm from third persons which would have been foreseen or anticipated by the reasonable man. In some instances, the theory is stated in terms of absolute liability; making the hotel liable if the act of a third person caused harm, without regard to whether the hotel had exercised due care or was negligent.[1]

§ 5:2. Vicarious liability compared.

(*a*) *Generally.* In order to place supervisory liability in its proper perspective, it is necessary to look ahead to the subject of vicarious liability discussed in the next chapter and compare the two theories.

Vicarious liability is the principle or rule of law by which an employer may be held liable for the harm caused by his employee while the latter is acting within the course of his employment.

(*b*) *Fault of hotel.* In the case of vicarious liability, the hotel is held liable for the act of its employee because that act constitutes a tort. The employer is not at fault, and it is the fault of the employee with which it is blamed. In contrast, supervisory liability is ordinarily predicated upon the fault of the hotel in failing to exercise the due care which a reasonable man would exercise to so supervise the premises as to prevent the occurrence of the harm which the reasonable man foresees as probable.

(*c*) *The actor.* In the case of supervisory liability, the identity of the actor causing harm is immaterial. Namely, the person actually causing the harm to the plaintiff may be a guest, a third person, a total stranger, and so on. In the case of vicarious liability, the wrongdoer must by definition be the employee of the employer for he must be a person acting within the course of his employment.

(*d*) *The plaintiff.* Under supervisory liability, any person may be the plaintiff if he is on the hotel premises as an invitee, as defined in § 11:2, or if he is on the adjoining pavements and land. Under vicarious liability, the plaintiff class is broader for the person injured may be anyone anywhere.

(*e*) *Alternative applicability of theories.* Ordinarily the concepts of supervisory and vicarious liability are alternative in that only one or the other applies in any given situation. The

---

[1] See § 5:3 et seq.

exception to this is the case in which the hotel employee negligently causes harm to the plaintiff while acting in the course of his employment and reasonable examination by the hotel would have shown that the employee was not fit for the position.

In this situation, the hotel could be both liable for the negligence of the hotel employee, imputed to it under the theory of vicarious liability, and could also have supervisory liability, under the theory that the hotel had failed to maintain reasonable supervision over its employees.

§ 5:3. Standard of reasonable care.

(*a*) *Generally.* As the rule is ordinarily stated, the hotel is only required to exercise reasonable care to see that its premises are free from such third persons or such conduct of others as would cause harm. Ordinarily the hotel is not regarded as an insurer that the hotel will be free of all danger from others. Consequently, the hotel is not liable where the presence of the evildoer was unknown or there was no reason to believe that a person on the premises would cause harm to others.

(*b*) *High degree of care.* In some circumstances it is said the degree of care is a high degree rather than the ordinary degree as above stated. Analytically it could be said that the standard is still that of reasonable care under the circumstances but the foreseeability of harm is so great that the circumstances require that greater precautions be taken.

(1) Keys to room. The hotel must exercise a high degree of care to prevent strangers from obtaining access to a guest's room by obtaining his keys from the desk or from an employee. It is to be noted that the hotel is not absolutely liable for a breach of this duty, on the one hand, but on the other, the standard of care is greater than that of ordinary care.

As the duty is one of care under the circumstances, even though it is a high degree of care, the case must ordinarily go to the jury when the guest is assaulted in his room by a stranger who apparently obtained the door key from the hotel desk, the purpose being for the jury to determine whether the required high degree of care had been exercised.

(*c*) *Persons involved.* For the purpose of applying the concept of supervisory liability based on negligence, it is immaterial what relationship exists between the person harmed and the hotel or between the offender and the hotel. Thus the victim may be a guest, a lodger, a tenant, a customer, an employee, or a stranger. The same is true of the offender. The only important factor is that the wrongdoer is within the area over which the hotel has the right and the duty to exercise control. As a practical matter the victim will also be within that area or closely nearby, as the pedestrian on the street outside of the hotel.

In reading this chapter it is necessary to bear in mind that "third person" or "other person" has this broad meaning and that an illustration's referring to certain persons as "guests" or "strangers" does not mean that the principle involved is limited to "guests" or "strangers."

§ 5:4. Standard of absolute liability.

(*a*) **Generally.** Contrary to the view stated in the preceding section that the supervisory liability of the hotel is stated in terms of negligence, there is some authority that the hotel has what is in effect absolute liability for harm sustained because of the conduct of employees.

For the purpose of simplicity, when the phrases "supervisory duty" or "supervisory liability" are used hereafter in this book, reference is made to the liability or duty stated in terms of due care and negligence. If the absolute liability concept is intended, it will be specifically so stated.

(*b*) **Rationale of absolute liability.** The absolute liability concept of supervisory liability proceeds on the theory that the hotel makes an implied contract with its guests to protect them from harm; hence if a guest sustains harm there is a breach of this term of the contract and the hotel is liable for the damages sustained regardless of the reason why there was a breach and in spite of the fact that the hotel was not negligent in any respect.

> *The facts:* The hotel detective told an unidentified person claiming to be a guest to wait in the lobby while the detective checked his registration. The detective checked and found that the person was a registered guest. Meanwhile the guest had not waited for the detective but had taken the elevator up to his floor. The detective followed him to his floor, demanded why the guest had not waited as directed, and then hit him. The guest sued the hotel. The hotel defended on the ground that the act of the detective was outside of the scope of his employment.

Decision: Judgment for guest. The tort of the detective was outside the scope of his employment, as the guest was in fact a guest and the detective had already verified that fact. The detective's act was therefore inspired by his own ill will or personal feeling and was not part of doing his job. Nevertheless, the hotel was liable to the guest because the hotel-guest contract carried with it the obligation of protecting the guest from harm. [Crawford v. Hotel Essex Boston Corp. (DC), 143 FSupp 172 (1956)].

To appraise this reasoning, consider the analogy of the case of my agreeing to paint your hotel by a specified date. If I fail to paint your hotel by that date I have broken my contract regardless of how careful I had been in trying to perform it. That is, with respect to performance under a contract I am under an absolute duty to perform and, while certain things will excuse delay or non-performance, or there may be escape clauses in the contract itself, the mere fact that I show that I had exercised due care will not excuse my failure to perform.

There is, however, an obvious difference between holding me responsible for my failure to perform and holding you as a hotel responsible for the conduct of third persons. The two situations are radically different. Furthermore, the mere fact that the hotel has undertaken to protect the guest really begs the question, namely, the question of whether the hotel has undertaken to protect the guest absolutely — that is, be liable regardless of what is the cause of the harm; or merely to exercise due care — that is, be liable only if the hotel were negligent in the performance of its duty to protect the guest.

The view of a supervisory liability in the nature of an absolute liability is supported, however, by the analogy of the long-recognized rule that a hotel is liable for improper language or discourteous treatment of a guest by an employee, without regard to whether he was acting within the course of his employment.[2] If the guest-hotel relationship imposes the duty of protecting from emotional harm caused by employees it could with equal logic be required to protect from physical harm at the hands of its employees.

(*c*) **Persons involved.** When the supervisory liability of the hotel is based on the absolute liability or breach of contract theory, it is necessary that the victim of the wrong be a guest of the hotel. While a duty is owed to patrons who are not guests, that duty is not an absolute duty but only a duty to use due

[2]See § 5:5.

care to keep the premises safe; and is not the absolute duty here considered.

As in the case of supervisory liability based upon negligence, it would appear theoretically immaterial whether the wrongdoer is an employee or not, although generally the cases imposing absolute supervisory liability have involved persons who were employees. The fact that the hotel has the opportunity of screening the employee when he applies for a position and has the continuing ability to supervise his actions may cause a limiting of the absolute supervisory liability rule to the cases of guests harmed by employees.

(*d*) *Appraisal of absolute supervisory liability concept.* If this were written fifty years ago, it would be safe to ignore the cases which follow the absolute liability view on the ground that they represented an illogical minority view that was contrary to the "true" rule. The fact that the last half century, and particularly the last two decades, has witnessed such a great expansion of liability concepts, including the imposing of liability without fault, opens the possibility that courts may in the future adopt the concept that the hotel is liable for harm caused its guests by third persons although the hotel was not negligent and although such acts were not by persons acting within the scope of their employment. In the light of this possibility, the liability insurance coverage of the hotel should be carefully reexamined.

§ 5:5. — Liability for improper language and discourtesy.

(*a*) *Guests.* A hotel is liable to a guest for insulting, profane, or abusive language directed to the guest by a hotel employee. This is part of the duty of a hotel to assure its guests respectable and courteous treatment. Ordinarily, as this liability is predicated upon the hotel-guest relationship, it does not exist when the insured person is a patron in a restaurant, whether run by a hotel or not; or is a patron in the cocktail lounge of a hotel; or is a visitor of a guest in the hotel. As indicated below under subsection (b), this limitation as to guests may disappear.

> *The facts:* A woman was a guest in the hotel. She was visited in her room by her husband. They were both insulted by false ac-

cusations made by employees of the hotel. They both sued the hotel for such insults.

Decision: The hotel was liable only to the wife since she was the only guest and the duty to refrain from insulting language was only owed to a person who was a guest. [Kirstein v. Hotel Taft Corp. 183 Misc 713, 51 NYS2d 162 (1944), affirmed without opinion 269 AppDiv 683, 54 NYS2d 376 (1945)].

(1) Nature of liability. The liability described above can be explained in several ways: (a) the hotel is absolutely liable because the guest has been offended, (b) the hotel is liable for the breach of its contract that the guest should not be offended, and (c) the hotel is liable because it failed to supervise its employees sufficiently to prevent the offending of the guest. It is not important what label is attached — the net result is that the hotel is liable when the event occurs without regard to whether the hotel had exercised due care or the employee was acting within the course of his employment.

(b) Non-guests. While the fact that a person is not a guest precludes him from recovering under the rule above stated, there may still be recovery if the victim of the employee is able to show that the offense of the employee was committed within the scope of the employee's employment, provided that the state in which this occurs recognizes vicarious liability for a willful act.[3]

Moreover it is very likely that the limitation that the duty of courtesy is owed only to guests will undoubtedly be expanded to apply to all patrons of the hotel, for the reason that this concept of a duty of courteous conduct is being increasingly recognized in the case of stores and other public places. Liability in such cases is being imposed upon the theory that the business invitor owes a public duty to protect its business invitee from language which is slanderous, opprobrious, insulting, or abusive, without regard to the identity of the speaker. Liability is not based on the theory that the invitor is the wrongdoer nor that such act is imputable to it under the rule of respondeat superior. Instead liability is based merely upon the breach of the supervisory duty owed to the public, without regard to whether the offending actor is a third person or an employee of the business.[4]

---

[3] See § 6:4.
[4] Zayre of Atlanta v. Sharpton, 110 GaApp 587, 139 SE2d 339 (1964).

§ 5:6. Apprehension of harm.

(*a*) ***Generally.*** Under the general supervisory liability rule, a hotel is not liable for conduct of others unless it had knowledge or reason to know that there was foreseeable harm if it did not take reasonable steps to prevent it.

> *The facts:* The plaintiff was eating at the defendant restaurant. Suddenly a fight broke out between two other customers. In the course of this fight, the plaintiff, who was a bystander, was injured. He sued the defendant restaurant.
>
> *Decision:* The restaurant was not liable. The mere fact that the fight took place between the other two customers did not establish that the restaurant was negligent; on the theory that it had either (1) negligently admitted persons it should have recognized might cause physical harm to other patrons, or (2) negligently permitted the fight to continue without making any efforts to stop it or to eject the wrongdoers. In the absence of such negligence the restaurant was not liable. [Hughes v. Coniglio, 147 Neb 829, 25 NW2d 405 (1946)].

(*b*) ***Extent of observation.*** The hotel may be charged with knowledge of the violent disposition of a patron although there has not been a long and continued course of conduct observed by the hotel. It is a matter of balancing variables and it is sufficient that there be such conduct as would indicate to a reasonable man that the other person had dangerous tendencies, even though the duration of the observation period was not long.

(*c*) ***Opportunity to act.*** The concept of apprehension of danger also involves the idea of knowing of or viewing danger within sufficient advance time to do something about it. Accordingly where there was no reason to anticipate harm until the very moment the wrongdoer began to commit it, the hotel is not liable where it had no opportunity to act in time to prevent harm to the guest. Thus where the third person's actions are over before anyone really knows what happened, it is clear that the hotel is not liable for it had no opportunity to act; remembering of course that there would be liability under the absolute supervisory concept.

§ 5:7. Warning as a sufficient precaution.

(*a*) ***Generally.*** The hotel may become aware that someone is likely to cause trouble. Assume that it then warns that per-

The Hotel's Supervisory Liability

son to behave or quiet down. Can the hotel then forget about the matter or will the hotel be liable if the troublemaker later resumes his conduct and harms someone?

There is no clear answer to this question and in a lawsuit the question will go to the jury to decide if under all the surrounding circumstances the hotel acted in the way in which a reasonable man would act to avoid reasonably foreseeable harm.

(*b*) *Reason to believe warning sufficient.* The hotel is not liable for the subsequent harm if the jury believes that a reasonable man would have believed that the warning to the offender was sufficient to put an end to the matter. So it has been held that the fact that the plaintiff on the street below was hit when a guest threw a bottle out of the window did not impose liability upon the hotel where the hotel clerk had stated to the guest that others had complained of the noise but when he visited his room he was assured that there would be no further noise; and no disturbance arose until two hours later when the defendant threw a bottle out of the window and injured the plaintiff.

If on the other hand, a reasonable man would recognize that the offender was either just pretending to comply with the warning and would resume his offensive conduct as soon as he could, or was in such a mental or physical condition that a warning would not stick in his mind very long, the hotel must recognize that the mere warning has not been sufficient and must take further steps to protect others from harm.

(*c*) *Relation to offender.* One of the facts which will influence the decision, whether consciously or unconsciously, is the length of prior dealings with the offender and his prior history. To illustrate, if the offender is someone who has been a regular patron of or guest in your hotel for the last five years and there has not been any trouble before, you would be entitled to rely upon this person's apology and his statement that he would behave. The shorter the period you have dealt with him, and the less you know about him, the less you are entitled to rely on what he says; until you reach the point where the offender is a total stranger and you might not be entitled to rely at all on his promise to behave.

> *The facts:* A stranger came into a restaurant. He did not order anything to eat or drink, and for twenty minutes used vile language and then drop kicked a glass of water into a wall. The manager stated that he was going to phone the police. The

stranger then apologized and paid for the glass. In a few minutes the stranger resumed this conduct and without any provocation suddenly assaulted a patron in the restaurant, causing him serious brain injury. The patron sued the restaurant which defended on the ground that it had taken reasonable steps to prevent harm and had no reason to foresee any harm after obtaining the apology.

Decision: The restaurant was negligent; the negligence consisting of the manager's accepting the apology and desisting from calling the police. The conduct of the total stranger was so offensive and violent in character that the manager was taking an obvious risk in accepting the stranger's word that he would behave. [Shank v. Riker Restaurants Associates, Inc., 216 NYS2d 118 (1961)].

§ 5:8. Protection from acts of third persons.

(*a*) *Generally.* The hotel is under a duty to protect its guests and patrons and to prevent their being harmed physically by the hotel itself and its employees; third persons, including other guests and patrons and animals. The hotel remains under this duty, and is liable for the damages for a violation, even though the hotel is not actually running the business which in fact is run by an independent contractor.

(*b*) *Reasonable care.* The duty stated in the preceding subsection is not a duty to protect in all cases, at all costs. It is only a duty to use reasonable care to see that harm does not befall or that wrong is not done to the guest or other person. Thus the mere fact that one is harmed does not in itself require the hotel to pay damages. It must be established that in addition to the harm which was caused, the hotel failed to take such steps as would be taken by a reasonable man under the circumstances to prevent the occurrence or realization of the kind of harm sustained by the plaintiff. Otherwise stated, the hotel does not insure that nothing will cause harm, but only that the hotel will take reasonable steps to see that nothing does. Hence the hotel is liable only if the plaintiff can prove that it was negligent.[5]

Ordinarily the question whether reasonable care was exercised under the circumstances raises a question of fact which is determined by the jury. When the supervisory liability of the

---

[5] As to the qualification of this statement by the concept of absolute supervisory liability, see § 5:4.

The Hotel's Supervisory Liability

hotel is involved, the questions submitted to the jury become more complex for there is then both the question of what caused the plaintiff's harm and the question whether the hotel was negligent in failing to so supervise the area as to avoid the realization of such harm. The result is that there is not a simple "yes" or "no" question submitted to the jury but instead a number of successive questions. For example, where the twelve-year old plaintiff was injured in the defendant's roller skating rink, the conflicting evidence made it necessary to submit to the jury whether in the first place the plaintiff fell down by herself or was knocked down by someone else; whether such other person, if any, was at the time skating in a reckless or negligent manner; and if so, whether the defendant was negligent in failing to supervise the patrons properly so as to prevent skating in such manner.

The facts: The taproom proprietor allowed a dog to roam at large through the taproom. The dog had just had a litter of pups and was irritable. For no apparent reason, the dog bit a guest of the taproom. He sued the taproom proprietor. The latter denied liability.

Decision: The taproom proprietor owed the guest a duty to keep the premises free of dangerous animals. It was a question for the jury to determine, however, whether the dog by its general nature and by its particular irritability should have been kept off of the premises on the theory that the taproom proprietor as a reasonable man should have foreseen that harm could arise from the animal's presence. [Poulos v. Brady, 167 PaSuper 150, 74 A2d 694 (1950)].

(c) **Foreseeability or knowledge of harm.** As the standard of conduct prescribed for the hotel is that of being not negligent, it follows that there is liability when there is either a foreseeability that harm will occur or actual knowledge that it will occur or is occurring. For example, the hotel is liable when it admits as a guest a visibly intoxicated person who appears likely to get into a fight with anyone he meets. The hotel is also liable when it receives as a guest a person with a known criminal nature involving violence. If in such instances the guest harms another person, the victim may hold the hotel liable.

The hotel is of course liable when it actually knows that its guest is being harmed but takes no steps to stop the wrongdoer.

(1) *Degree of precautions.* If the hotel knows or has reason to know that persons of criminal character may be

coming to the hotel as patrons or that some of its patrons belong to the criminal class, the hotel must exercise greater care than usual. This is still merely reasonable care under the circumstances, namely, embracing the circumstance that there is a higher probability of harm because of the known criminal characteristic of the guest, which would lead a reasonable man to take greater precautions to avoid the harm which could foreseeably arise.

The hotel must also take greater precautions in order to constitute reasonable care with respect to a restaurant or lounge in which liquor is sold. For the reason that harm may be more reasonably expectable from an intoxicated than a sober patron.

(2) Athletic and amusement activities. The hotel must exercise reasonable care to supervise athletic and amusement activities so that its patrons are not injured by the reckless or willful conduct of others. Thus the hotel is liable when its employees fail to stop a boisterous game of ball in the swimming pool, which resulted in a guest's being hit; or fail to stop horseplay on a high diving platform, which resulted in a girl being shoved off of the platform. Likewise where the hotel permitted boys to throw each other into the pool in unchecked horseplay and this was a daily occurrence, the hotel was liable to a guest in the pool who was injured when struck by a falling boy.

> *The facts:* The plaintiff was injured by a patron in the swimming pool operated by the insured. The injury occurred when the plaintiff aged 15 dove from the side of the pool directly into the path of three approaching teenage swimmers who had decided on the spur of the moment to race to the other side of the pool. The plaintiff was injured when he struck one of the racers. He sued the insurer of the proprietor on the ground that the latter had failed to supervise the pool so as to prevent unruly conduct.
>
> *Decision:* Judgment for defendant. There was nothing which created an unreasonable risk of harm in three boys swimming to see who would reach the other side first. To prohibit this would be to prevent any two or more patrons from swimming in the same direction. Moreover as there was no reason to foresee harm from such conduct, there was no liability. [Benoit v. Hartford Acc. & Ind. Co. ... La ..., 169 So 925 (1964)].

(d) *Exclusion of strangers where harm not foreseeable.* As an incident of its duty to supervise its premises, the hotel has the right to exclude strangers as distinguished from new guests and

The Hotel's Supervisory Liability

so forth, from its premises; however innocent their conduct appears to be and though no reason exists to foresee harmful or wrongful conduct. This is particularly so when the strangers are in the hallways of the upper floors of the hotel.

> *The facts:* The defendants were Jehovah's Witnesses who had been distributing religious pamphlets in the hallways of the upper floors of the hotel. They were told by the hotel proprietor and by a policeman that they had to leave and must not return. They were put out of the hotel but returned and resumed the distribution of the leaflets. They were then arrested for "disorderly conduct." They defended on the ground that (1) they had not been guilty of any disturbance, and (2) the constitutional right of religious freedom gave them the right to distribute their leaflets.
>
> *Decision:* The fact that a hotel is under a duty to serve the public does not destroy its basic character as private property. Accordingly, an unwelcome person cannot invade such private property because he wants to exercise a constitutional right thereon. Furthermore, the hotel as part of its supervisory duty to protect its guests had the authority to exclude from the hotel all persons who were not there as guests or in some way related to the hotel enterprise or to the guests of the hotel.
>
> The fact that there was no disturbance or open breach of the peace did not mean that the defendants were not guilty of disorderly conduct. Their act of returning to the hotel in defiance of the warning of the proprietor and the policeman was a defiance to law and order which could have led to a breach of the peace in the effort to expel them again from the premises. They were therefore guilty of disorderly conduct. [People on Complaint of DuBois v. Thorpe, 198 Misc 462, 101 NYS2d 986 (1950)].

(e) Contributory negligence and assumption of risk. Assuming that the guest is harmed by the misconduct of other guests and that the hotel would be liable to the victim on the theory that the hotel had failed to exercise reasonable care to protect the injured guest from such harm, it may still be concluded that the hotel is not liable on the theory that the injured guest had been contributorily negligent or has assumed the risk involved in the conduct of the wrongdoing guests.

> *The facts:* A guest went onto the dance floor of the hotel. The floor was not particularly crowded and a number of the dancers were jitterbugging. The guest was later injured when one of the jitterbugs backed into her. She sued the hotel.

Decision: There was no evidence that the hotel had been negligent either in permitting the dance floor to be overcrowded or in allowing the other guests to act in a disorderly or rowdy fashion. Moreover the guest, by going onto the dance floor while other persons were jitterbugging, had assumed the risk of being bumped into in the course of dancing. [Hibbs v. Brown Hotel (Ky) 302 SW2d 127 (1957)].

There is of course no liability where the plaintiff-guest is injured by a third person if the plaintiff-guest has provoked the difficulty or in effect "asked for trouble." So it has been held that the hotel is not liable for the harm caused the plaintiff by being struck by another guest who in several years of steady patronage had never been known to fight with anyone, particularly where the other guest, on being warned by the hotel to "break it up" when the fight began, obeyed such instruction, and was leaving the premises, when the plaintiff grabbed him and the guest then struck him back. And of course when the plaintiff guest or patron voluntarily enters into unneccessary physical combat with another guest or patron he assumes the risk of harm and cannot hold the hotel liable therefore. And this is true even where the plaintiff-guest engaged in combat because of wild statements made at the time by the other guest; for the reason that the use of mere words is not deemed to justify engaging in combat or the commission of an assault.

(*f*) *False arrest.* A hotel is not under any duty to protect its guests from arrest where the hotel has no reason to know that the arrest is in any respect improper. Accordingly the hotel was not liable when because of mistaken identity, police officers arrested the guest, as the hotel did not have any knowledge or reason to know that the guest was not the right person to be arrested.

§ 5:9. Protection of persons on street.

(*a*) *Generally.* A person on the street, whether a stranger or a hotel guest or patron, may be injured by objects falling from a hotel window as the result of the conduct of a guest or employee. This may be the result of negligence, as the careless placing of flower pots on the windowsill, or it may be the result of the intentional conduct of a guest as by throwing various objects, such as light bulbs, bags filled with water, and so forth, down onto the street.

The Hotel's Supervisory Liability 65

The hotel is under a duty to use reasonable means to see that no one within the hotel causes harm to any person outside of the hotel, whether such other person is a guest or merely a member of the general public passing by the hotel. If the hotel fails to exercise reasonable care to prevent reasonably foreseeable harm to persons on the street it is liable when the hotel's guests or patrons or their guests, cause harm to such third persons.

(*b*) *Nature of duty.* This obligation rests not so much upon the status of the hotel's being a hotel but upon the broader principle that one who assembles a large number of persons upon his premises for the purpose of his own financial gain must assume the responsibility of using reasonable care to protect others from injury from causes reasonably to be anticipated from such assemblage. In the exercise of this duty it is necessary for the assembler to furnish a sufficient number of guards or attendants and to take other precautions to control the actions of the crowd. Whether the guards furnished or the precautions taken are sufficient is ordinarily a question for the jury to determine under all circumstances.

(*c*) *Foreseeability.* The hotel is not an insurer against harm from conduct as above described. It is only liable to the injured third person if the hotel had reason to know that the actor in question would engage in such conduct or was in fact so doing. And to the contrary, if the hotel had no reason to foresee or anticipate conduct of such nature from the actor in question, the hotel is not liable for the harm so caused.

(1) Activities of hotel. The activities of the hotel are circumstances to be considered, for while the standard of care remains constant, the precautions to be taken vary with the facts and circumstances of each case. Hence, the fact that the hotel operates a bar or sells liquor is a factor to be considered in determining whether the hotel should foresee that its guests might become unruly or cause harm to others.

> *The facts:* A convention was held in the hotel. About four hundred young men were registered guests in connection with this convention and approximately four thousand more attended. In the course of several days there was much drinking at the hotel bar and in private rooms. In the course of the several days of the convention, the drinking increased and conduct became increasingly disorderly. Hotel property was damaged, and the premises both inside and out were daily littered with broken glasses and

bottles. A policeman and a pedestrian complained that water bags were being thrown out of the windows.

The hotel, prior to the convention, had taken the precaution of cutting off the corners of laundry bags to prevent their use as water bombs. The plaintiff was a stranger who was walking on the pavement outside the hotel and was struck by a gob of mud which came from an unidentified upper part of the hotel. The plaintiff sued the hotel.

Decision: The hotel was liable because it permitted its premises to be used in such a way that harm to persons outside the building was foreseeable. The hotel was negligent in failing to take reasonable steps to avoid the danger from falling objects, which in the light of the hotel's own act of cutting the laundry bags and the course of the immediate events was a reasonably foreseeable harm. The hotel should have required the persons in charge of the convention to exercise greater control over their members and should have obtained additional policemen to make the premises safe. [Connolly v. Nicollet Hotel, 254 Minn 373, 95 NW2d 657 (1959). (But note that four judges dissented on ground that the majority imposed so strict a standard as to require practically individual guards for each person on the premises)].

(2) Incidental acts of guests. The hotel is not liable for the incidental act of a guest where there is no prior course of events or known character of the guest which should make the hotel anticipate that the particular incidental act would be committed. For example, the fact that a guest threw an armchair out of the hotel window in his jubilation over V-J Day did not impose liability on the hotel where this was a single, isolated event and there was no reason to foresee that there would be any such conduct. Likewise there is no liability of the hotel where the third person was injured when a flower pot fell from a windowsill where it had been placed by a transient guest.

§ 5:10. Act of employee.

(a) Generally. As noted in § 5:2, the hotel may be liable for the act of its employee either on the theory of vicarious liability or of supervisory liability; the former being based on the concept of harm caused by the employee while acting within the scope of his employment; the latter upon the concept of harm caused to a guest by any person on the premises.

(b) Employee as wrongdoer. When the wrongdoer is an employee, the availability of these two principles means that the

hotel may be liable for the act of its employee because it was committed within the course of his employment, or liable for the harm caused by the act of an employee on the theory that the hotel had failed to supervise the employee properly.

While these two theories are alternative, it has been noted already that if the harm is caused by the employee acting in the course of his employment and the hotel had failed to supervise him properly, liability may be based upon both theories. Conversely, the facts may be such that neither theory is available to impose liability. This occurs when the employee is acting outside the scope of his employment and the hotel had exercised reasonable care in supervising the employee's actions.

To illustrate the latter point, the fact that the houseman used the house key given to him by the hotel to enter the plaintiff's room and commit an assault, did not make the hotel vicariously liable for his act as it was outside of the scope of his employment and the hotel was not subject to supervisory liability as it had not been negligent in employing the houseman as it had had no reason to foresee that there would be any harm arising therefrom. If the absolute supervisory liability concept is followed,[6] the fact that harm was caused to a guest by an employee on the premises would impose liability. This would have the practical effect of allowing a guest to recover in any case of an act committed by an employee; on either the theory of liability for an act committed within the scope of employment or on the theory of absolute liability for his misconduct as a person on the premises who should have been supervised so as to prevent such harm.

§ 5:11. Acts of concessionaire.

(*a*) *Generally.* It is common for various enterprises, stores, and so on, to be housed in the same building as the hotel. When the patron of the concessionaire is injured in his shop, the liability of the concessionaire depends upon the general principles applicable to determine liability for condition of the premises, product liability, and so on. The question which is here considered is whether the hotel is also liable for harm to the concessionaire's customer.

The legalistic problem is complicated by the fact that the concessionaire may occupy a space under a lease directly from the hotel, or there may be a holding corporation which has leased part of the building to various concessionaires. The

---

[6]See § 5:4.

matter is also complicated by whether the concession is run in such a way as to appear to be the hotel itself or a separate enterprise.

(*b*) ***Independent character of concessionaire apparent.*** When a reasonable person dealing with the concessionaire would recognize that the latter was an independent operator and was not the hotel, the latter is not liable for the misconduct of the concessionaire unless the case can be brought within the principle that the hotel has been negligent in failing to exercise control over the concessionaire so as to prevent reasonably foreseeable harm from the conduct of such a third person.

This latter concept of supervisory liability requires both that (1) the concessionaire engage in such acts that the hotel knows or has reason to know of the danger potential, and (2) the hotel have the legal right under the terms of its lease with the concessionaire to exercise control. The first qualification is the same as that considered above in § 5:6. The second qualification necessarily limits liability to the case where the concessionaire is the tenant of the hotel. If, however, the concessionaire is the tenant of a real estate holding corporation, the hotel would have no power to control the concessionaire's conduct and should not be liable for the concessionaire's act. In view of the fact that the hotel is on the premises and is the one more likely to know what is going on, it is possible that the hotel, although not the landlord of the concessionaire, might be held liable for failing to notify the real estate holding company, the common landlord, and demanding that the latter take steps to remedy the situation.

It is suggested as a matter of caution that in the common landlord situation, there be an immediate phone call to a responsible person in the real estate holding corporation, and a follow-up letter to such person confirming the conversation, with the making of proper records of such phone call and letter as are described in Chapter 22; the purpose being to go on record as exercising reasonable care.

(*c*) ***Independent character of concessionaire not apparent.*** When a reasonable person dealing with the concessionaire would think that it is part of the hotel, both the concessionaire and the hotel may be held liable for the misconduct of the latter. This liability is based on the theory of estoppel, or, in simple terms, deception. It is obvious that a person will be more likely to patronize a shop or restaurant in the big hotel building if he thinks that this is part of the operation of the big hotel. Conversely, if he knows that the concession is some small outfit of unknown reputation he is more likely to go to some place better. Accordingly, if the hotel has allowed the concessionaire to give the public the impression that it is part of the big hotel operation, the big hotel cannot run away from the liability when a member of the poor trusting public has relied to his sorrow on the appearance so created.

(1) Separate identity signs. In order to protect the hotel from liability in the above situation, the hotel should insist, whenever it is able to do so, that there be appropriate signs on the concessionaire's windows or an added statement to his regular sign that the concession is independently owned and operated by the named concessionaire. If these signs are of sufficient size that a person with normal vision would perceive them, the apparent identity of the concessionaire and the hotel is destroyed and members of the public are not deceived into believing that they are dealing with the hotel.

(d) Indemnity agreement. Whenever the hotel is able to obtain such an agreement, it should require the concessionaire to agree to indemnify the hotel against liability or loss caused the hotel by any act of the concessionaire. If possible, the hotel should also require that the concessionaire give the hotel a surety bond to indemnify it as above stated or to deposit in escrow a fund to be held for such purpose.

Whether the hotel can procure such an agreement, bond, or deposit, is a matter of relative bargaining positions. If the premises are in high demand by concessionaires, the hotel is in a position to pick and choose and can set its own terms. If the premises are not in demand, either because of the general economic conditions of the community or the hotel's size and location, the hotel may not be able to obtain such favorable terms.

§ 5:12. Acts of unrelated business tenants in hotel building.

(a) Generally. The hotel building may be rented in part to outside businesses which by their nature are unrelated to hotels and the reasonable man would therefore not think that they were part of the hotel operation. When such is the case, the hotel is not liable on any of the theories considered earlier for

any harm caused by the conduct of such other tenants. Here the relation of the hotel can rise no higher than that of an ordinary landlord, in which case there is ordinarily no liability for harm caused by a tenant. Moreover, the hotel might not even be the landlord of such other tenants in the building, as in the case where the building is owned by a holding real estate corporation which leases the hotel part to the hotel and the other parts to the other tenants.

(*b*) ***Particular applications.*** The situation here considered is illustrated by the renting of office space to a brokerage house or to a manufacturing company. Here it is clear from the nature of the enterprises that they are not part of the hotel nor functions of the hotel but merely outside businesses that have come seeking as customers persons who are in the hotel. The hotel, having no control over or supervisory duty with respect to such tenants, is not liable for their misconduct.

As a further illustration, when a doctor has offices in the hotel building but is not in any other way associated with the hotel, the latter is not liable for the misconduct of the doctor. This is so, even though the doctor had been recommended to the injured guest when he had inquired of the location of a doctor.

Chapter 6. THE HOTEL'S VICARIOUS LIABILITY

§ 6:1. Nature of vicarious liability.
    (a) Generally.
    (b) Direct and vicarious liability compared.

§ 6:2. Scope of vicarious liability.
    (a) Generally.
    (b) Immunity from suit.
    (c) Damages.

§ 6:3. Acts of employees.
    (a) Generally.
    (b) Scope of employment.
        (1) Determination of scope.
    (c) Optional employees.

§ 6:4. — Particular kinds of conduct.
    (a) Negligence.
        (1) Existence of negligence.
        (2) Use of excessive force.
    (b) Willful and malicious conduct.
        (1) Particular applications.
        (2) Supervisory liability for willful act of employee.
    (c) Fraud.

§ 6:5. Acts of independent contractors.
    (a) Generally.
    (b) Direct liability of hotel.
        (1) Faulty specifications.
        (2) Faulty materials.
        (3) Performance of duty.

§ 6:6. Hotel automobile loaned or rented to patron.
    (a) Generally.
    (b) Statutory liability.
    (c) Unfit driver.

§ 6:7. Acts of concessionaire.
    (a) Generally.
    (b) Joint venture.
    (c) Supervisory liability distinguished.

§ 6:1. Nature of vicarious liability.

(*a*) ***Generally.*** When the wrongdoer commits a tort he is ordinarily liable to the victim. In some instances, another person, such as the employer of the wrongdoer, is also liable to the victim for the wrongdoer's tort. This liability of one person based upon the tort of another is called vicarious liability. It is also said that the liability of the wrongdoer is imputed to the other person. When applied to employment relationships, the rule of law involved is also named the rule of respondeat superior, namely, that by which the superior person, the employer, is made to respond or pay out money for damages.

The principles considered in this chapter are part of the general law of torts and are not peculiar to or limited to hotels.

(*b*) ***Direct and vicarious liability compared.*** The vicarious liability of a person is to be distinguished from a direct liability for his own conduct, which liability may co-exist with his vicarious liability. To illustrate the differences, assume that an employee of the hotel, while driving the latter's truck in the course of his employment, runs into and injures the plaintiff. Three types of situations may be involved:

(1) The driver negligently drove a mechanically-sound truck. He, as the driver, is liable for his own tort and the hotel is likewise liable under the rule of respondeat superior, although it was not personally at fault.

(2) The driver was not negligent and the plaintiff was harmed because the hotel had negligently supplied its driver with a mechanically-defective truck. Here the driver is not liable if he did not have reason to know that he was driving a defective truck, for in such case he has neither been negligent nor willfully inflicted harm upon the plaintiff. On the other hand, the hotel is liable for its own tort in launching a dangerous vehicle on the highway when a reasonable man would foresee that harm could be caused thereby to persons and property lawfully on the highway.

(3) The driver negligently drove the truck and the hotel was negligent in supplying a truck with defective brakes, and the negligence of both the employee and the hotel contributed to the accident. For example, the employee did not look at the road ahead and did not see the plaintiff in the intersection nor see the red stop light, and when he did perceive that he had

negligently endangered the plaintiff, he was unable to stop the truck in time to avoid harm because the brakes on the truck were defective. In this case, the employee is liable for the plaintiff's harm because his negligence has caused the plaintiff's harm. The hotel has a double-barreled liability to the plaintiff, for it is liable to the plaintiff as the consequence of its own negligence and is also vicariously liable with respect to the negligence of the employee.

Direct liability of the hotel may arise not only through negligently supplying defective equipment, but also from negligently employing incompetent employees; or assigning work to employees unqualified for that kind of work; or negligently giving improper instructions or negligently failing to warn of dangers; when as the consequence of such negligence the employee causes harm to the plaintiff which the hotel should have reasonably foreseen.

The mere fact that a hotel employee has a mental age less than his actual age does not mean that it was negligent for the hotel to employ him.

§ 6:2. Scope of vicarious liability.

(*a*) *Generally.* Ordinarily the liability which is vicarious and the liability of the actual wrongdoer are the same in all respects. Hence, when the victim brings suit against either the wrongdoer or the person vicariously liable, he must prove the wrongful conduct of the actual wrongdoer and is correspondingly subject to the defense of contributory negligence regardless of which one he sues.

(*b*) *Immunity from suit.* When the theory of vicarious liability is literally applied, the person who is so liable stands in the shoes of the actual wrongdoer and may assert any defense which may be asserted by the wrongdoer. It may be that the wrongdoer has a personal immunity against suit by the victim of his tort. For example, the wife or child of the employee may be injured by the latter in the course of his employment. In most jurisdictions, the wife or child cannot sue the employee because of the immunity based on the domestic relationship existing between them. In many states, however, the fact that the wrongdoer has such an immunity from suit would not protect the hotel when sued for vicarious liability. That is, although the employee cannot be held liable, his employer is not protected by that immunity and is liable to the injured wife or child.

(c) **Damages.** There is a conflict of authority whether the person vicariously liable may be held for punitive or exemplary damages. By the one view, the person vicariously liable is held not subject to punitive damages on the ground that he has not acted with the evil mental state which is to be punished by the imposition of such damages.

In other jurisdictions, the liability of such person is made the same as that of the wrongdoer. That is, if the employee is subject to punitive damages. the employer is also subject to them. The adoption of this view is influenced to a large degree by the fact that in the average vicarious liability case, such as the employer-employee situation, the plaintiff will not be able to collect his judgment for punitive damages against the employee. Accordingly, if he is to obtain the actual money for punitive damages, it will necessarily be from the employer. The ability of the employer to obtain employers' liability insurance has also influenced courts to favor this view, although standard policies do not cover liability for punitive damages.

§ 6:3. Acts of employees.

(a) **Generally.** A hotel is vicariously liable for the tort of its employee when committed within the course of the latter's employment. This liability is in substance based upon the consideration that as the hotel stands to benefit by the activities involved in the employment it should also pay for the harm done in the course of such activities. Thus the liability of the hotel to the third person injured by the employee is in effect an operational cost. Furthermore, the hotel may generally shift the actual burden of this vicarious liability to the public in the form of increased rates or may obtain public liability insurance to cover such hazards.

This is merely the application of a basic rule of law: an employer is liable under certain circumstances for the harm which is caused by his employees, agents, or servants. Otherwise stated, the rule of liability for harm is not reduced by the fact that the employer is running a hotel, instead of a factory, a department store, or any other kind of business.

(b) **Scope of employment.** The hotel is liable for the harm

The Hotel's Vicarious Liability 75

caused others by the tortious negligent acts or omissions of a hotel employee while acting within the scope of his employment. Conversely, only the employee is liable if at the time he is not acting within the scope of his employment.[1]

To illustrate, assume that the hotel employee runs a private hotel taxi to pick up guests at the train. If he drives negligently, in consequence of which there is a collision which causes harm to guest passengers, the hotel is liable because the negligent harm was caused by the employee while acting within the scope of employment. In contrast, assume that the employee after working hours takes the hotel taxi out, without permission, and uses it to drive his own friends around. A friend who is injured under such circumstances because of the employee's negligence can only sue the employee. The hotel is not liable because at the time the employee was not acting within the scope of his employment.

(1) Determination of scope. The determination of the scope or course of the employment, which in turn may mean whether the hotel is liable or not, may be relatively simple, as when the employee is doing the very thing he is employed to do, such as driving the hotel taxi from the railroad station to the hotel with guest passengers; or it may be reasonably defined or deduced from the nature of the work assigned to the employee.

To illustrate the latter point, consider the case of the night clerk who has authority to receive guests, assign rooms, and in general run the hotel through the night. Although nothing is said by the hotel as to his authority to evict a guest to preserve order, it is obvious that he has such authority as an incidental aspect of the authority which is expressly given to him. Accordingly, he acts within the scope of his employment when he evicts a guest by force, summons the police to arrest her, and uses violent language. That is to say, the hotel cannot be allowed to escape liability on the theory that it never told the night clerk to evict guests who became noisy or that when he used force, or strong language, or called the police he was doing acts which were not called for by his official duties. Since the hotel was under the duty to preserve order, its employee placed in charge of the operation necessarily had authority to take steps to preserve order.

---

[1] Note that the hotel may have supervisory liability in some cases of employees acting outside the scope of employment. See Chapter 5.

Whether the act was done within the scope of employment, so as to impose vicarious liability, or whether it was such a departure from the employment so as to avoid such liability, is a question of fact which depends upon the extent of departure — whether or not the act, as performed in its setting of time and place is so different in kind from that authorized, or has so little relation to the employment, that it is not within the scope. An act does not cease to be within the course of employment merely because it was not expressly authorized nor even because it was committed in violation of instructions. For example, the hotel does not avoid liability for the harm caused by its driver by telling him, "Do not be negligent. Do not hit anyone."

(*c*) *Optional employees.* The fact that a hotel is not under any duty to provide a particular service or have a given employee does not alter its liability for his negligence. For example, the fact that a hotel is not required to employ a doorman does not relieve it from liability if the latter's negligence in directing traffic is the cause of the plaintiff's injury.

§ 6:4. — Particular kinds of conduct.

(*a*) *Negligence.* It is everywhere recognized that the hotel is vicariously liable for the negligence of its employee while acting within the course of his employment without regard to the identity of the person injured or the victim's relationship, if any, to the hotel. That is to say, when liability is predicated upon the theory of vicarious liability it is immaterial whether the victim is a total stranger injured off the premises, or is a patron, tenant, and so forth, of the hotel.

(1) Existence of negligence. When it is claimed that the hotel is liable because of the negligence of an employee, it is of course necessary to show that the employee was negligent. This means that it must be shown by the guest that the employee did not exercise such care as would be exercised by a reasonable man under the circumstances to avoid the occurrence of reasonably foreseeable harm.

The fact that the employee has acted in an emergency may excuse both him and the hotel from liability. For example, where an employee was carrying out a burning gasoline lamp, and his clothing caught on fire, the hotel was not liable to a guest who was injured when the employee, acting in the emergency to save himself, threw the lamp away from him which resulted in its exploding and injuring the guest.

The Hotel's Vicarious Liability

(2) Use of excessive force. The hotel employee may use excessive force in doing that which it is his job to do. The force may be excessive in that he uses more force than is required, or force where none is required. If no force or a lesser force is required the employee may be negligent in reaching the conclusion that the force he used was necessary. In such case the ordinary vicarious-liability rule is applied, as distinguished from any special willful tort rule as described in the next section.

Illustrative of the foregoing, when an employee who has the authority and responsibility of maintaining order uses excessive force in so doing, both he and the hotel are liable to the injured person, the employee for his own direct tort, and the hotel on the basis of vicarious liability.

> *The facts:* The plaintiff went as a guest to a private club of which he was not a member. He got into an argument with employee no. 1 running a gambling table. Someone went to bring employee no. 2 whose job was to maintain order. By the time that employee no. 2 arrived, the plaintiff was already walking away from employee no. 1. In spite of this, employee no. 2 struck the plaintiff a severe blow on the jaw and injured him. The plaintiff sued employee no. 1, employee no. 2, and the employer club.
>
> *Decision:* Employee no. 1 was not liable to the plaintiff, as he had not done anything beyond having the exchange of words, which does not impose liability. Employee no. 2 was liable for his use of force when in fact none was required, since in such case the force used was "excessive."
>
> The employer club was liable on the basis of respondeat superior. Employee no. 2 had authority to use force in order to keep order and the employer was consequently liable when he used force when not required or used excessive force. The employer was thus liable although it was not known whether employee no. 2 had struck the plaintiff without realizing that the argument was over, and did so to maintain order; or whether he realized it was over but feared that it might reopen and took steps to prevent a renewal. [Beggerly v. Walker, 194 Kan 61, 397 P2d 395 (1964)].

(b) *Willful and malicious conduct.* Wanton and malicious injury is within the scope of employment when the employee inflicts such harm for the purpose of furthering the hotel's interest; although some courts follow the older rule that the employer is never liable for a willful or malicious act of his employee regardless of its purpose.

Looking at the law generally, there is a tendency toward widening the employer's liability for the tort of his employee, but there is great conflict among the decisions. There is a conflict of authority as to the liability of an employer for the use of force by an employee employed to guard property or in the protection of the employer's interest; with the weight of authority probably in favor of imposing liability. When the employee is employed to recapture or retake property of the principal, as the employee of a finance company employed to repossess automobiles on which installments have not been paid, the courts will generally impose liability on the employer for the unlawful force of the employee used in retaking the property or in committing an assault upon the buyer, but there is some authority to the contrary. In contrast, the majority of decisions do not impose liability on an employer for an assault committed by his bill collector upon the debtor. There is a conflict of authority as to whether the employer is liable for the assault of his employee committed during a dispute over a traffic accident in which the employee has been involved while driving the employer's truck or vehicle.

(1) Particular applications. Applying the foregoing principles to the hotel, assume that the guest seeks to leave the hotel without paying his bill. The desk clerk runs after him and a fight ensues in which the guest is injured. By the older rule of employer law, the hotel would not be liable for the injuries so caused; on the theory that when the employee committed a willful assault and battery he stepped outside the scope of his employment, because he had not been hired to commit assault and battery. The modern view takes the sounder position that the employee in this case was not beating up the guest for his own private benefit but was doing so merely because he was trying to carry out his duties of collecting room rent from the guest. The fact that he acted "not wisely, but too well" does not mean that he was any the less acting as employee and therefore the employer, who would benefit by the collection of the room rent, should pay for harm done by the employee in the first place.

> *The facts:* A registered guest went to the hotel clerk at 5:00 in the morning and requested him to arrange for credit for his wife in another hotel. The clerk stated that this could not be done because the two hotels were not connected in any way and suggested that the guest take the money to the other hotel himself. The guest began counting out the money on the counter. The

The Hotel's Vicarious Liability 79

clerk went into the back room and returned with a blackjack with which he began to beat the guest severely. The hotel when sued claimed that it was not liable because the clerk was not acting within the scope of his employment in committing such assault.

Decision: Judgment for guest. The jury could have found on the facts that the employee was in fact acting within the scope of his employment, as contrasted with committing an assault for his own personal reason. [Manchester v. Selectmen of Nantucket, 335 Mass 156, 138 NE2d 766 (1956)].

In some cases the significant element is not the particular rule of law but the time sequence. For example, an assault may be committed by an employee in the course of evicting a guest, enforcing the regulations of the hotel, or collecting room rent: here the assault is part of the line of conduct by which the employee seeks to bring about the result desired by the hotel. In contrast, the illwill generated during the course of an otherwise proper transaction may cause the employee to assault the guest afterwards. For example, if the clerk has a dispute with the guest as to the hotel bill due and after the bill is paid by the guest, the clerk then hits the guest, it is clear that such assault is merely inspired by the clerk's own personal feelings and has nothing to do with the performance of his duties which were already accomplished when the bill was collected.

(2) Supervisory liability for willful act of employee. In the preceding discussion, liability of the hotel employer was considered on the basis of secondary or vicarious liability for the acts of an employee. Apart from this question, the hotel may in a given case be held liable on the theory that it had failed to exercise reasonable care in screening and selecting employees, and that it was liable for the willful act of an employee because it had exposed the guest to harm at the hands of a person whom the hotel should never have hired. That is to say, the hotel may be liable for the willful, wrongful acts of a hotel employee, either because the hotel had been guilty of a wrongful act in exposing the guests to the peril of an unqualified employee, or the hotel, although innocent of fault, is held secondarily or vicariously liable for the fault of its employee acting within the scope of his authority. For example, when an employee enters a hotel room for the purpose of committing larceny or a felonious assault upon a guest, the employee had departed from the scope of his employment, but the employer may still be

liable if he was negligent in hiring or retaining in his employ a person having a tendency to commit such improper conduct.[2]

In some instances this concept of liability based on the direct fault of the hotel has not been extended to restaurants although the distinction does not seem valid because of the duty which the restaurant would owe a patron as a business invitee, a duty which is very similar, if not the same, as the duty of a hotel to its guest.

There is also authority that the normal rule of liability for a willful tort committed by an employee of the hotel outside of the scope of employment is not applied to apartment houses.

(c) *Fraud.* A hotel is liable for the fraudulent acts or the misrepresentation of its employee made within the scope of his authority. In some states the principal is not liable when he did not authorize or know of the fraud of the agent at the time of the agent's fraudulent statement or misrepresentation.

§ 6:5. Acts of independent contractors.

(a) **Generally.** The hotel, entering into a contract with an independent contractor, is ordinarily not liable for any tort committed by the latter; the theory being that the hotel is not liable because it does not have any control over the action of the independent contractor. There is a trend, however, to make exceptions to this rule on the theory that the hotel is still the one which benefits by the performance of the work and that it has the power to select the contractor whom it desires and to contract on such terms as it chooses.

(b) **Direct liability of hotel.** The fact that the hotel contracts with an independent contractor does not protect it from liability for harm which may be traced directly to the hotel's negligence or misconduct. For example, the hotel is liable if it has not exercised reasonable care in the selection of a qualified and competent contractor.

(1) Faulty specifications. The use of an independent contractor to perform work in connection with the premises does not shield the hotel from liability where the independent contractor did exactly what the hotel's contract specifications required. For example, where the glass installed as a street panel

---

[2] Note that there is also authority imposing supervisory liability even when there was no negligence of any kind on the part of the hotel. See § 5:4.

of the lobby was inadequate because it was too thin to withstand the expectable leaning of people against it, the hotel could not claim that it was not liable because the installation had been made by an independent contractor where the latter had installed in the proper manner the exact glass which had been ordered by the hotel.

(2) Faulty materials. If the hotel supplies materials or equipment to the contractor which are defective and the hotel has been negligent in this respect, the hotel is liable to a third person injured as the consequence of such negligence. To illustrate, the existence of the independent contractor relationship does not insulate the hotel from liability for its own negligence in supplying the contractor with ropes for scaffolding which the hotel, using a reasonable man's judgment, would have perceived were defective and the scaffolding thereafter fell and injured a passerby in the street because the defective rope broke.

(3) Performance of duty. The employment of an independent contractor does not insulate from liability when the performance to be rendered by the contractor is the performance of a duty which the hotel is required by law to perform for another or for the general public. This parallels the concept of the assignment of a contract, which, in the absence of a provision to the contrary, does not release the assignor from his obligation to perform, although the assignee has undertaken to render the performance required.

Accordingly, the fact that an independent contractor is employed by the hotel to repair its building or maintain its elevators does not protect a hotel from liability for failing to maintain its property in a safe condition. Thus the hotel which is under the duty to provide a safe store or working place for its patrons and employees, remains liable for a breach of that duty even though it has retained an independent contractor to perform such duty.

§ 6:6. Hotel automobile loaned or rented to patron.

(*a*) *Generally.* The hotel may loan or rent a car to a guest or patron. The mere fact that the hotel owns the hotel automobile does not make it vicariously liable for the negligence of the person who is driving the automobile. The same conclusion is reached even though a hotel employee is physically present in the automobile driven by such other person. That is to say, the hotel is not vicariously liable for the negligent acts of the driver guest or patron when the hotel gives over the control of the automobile to the driver and a hotel employee is merely going along for the ride as a passenger, rather than engaging in "operating" the automobile.

(*b*) **Statutory liability.** An increasing number of states have adopted statutes by which a person granting permission to another to use his automobile thereby automatically becomes liable for any negligent harm caused by the person to whom he has entrusted the automobile. That is, permissive use imposes liability for the permittee's negligence. In some states, the operation of such a statute is limited to cases where the permittee is under a specified age, such as 16 years. Under some statutes, the owner is only liable with respect to harm sustained while the permittee is using the automobile for the purpose for which permission was granted; the problem here being similar to that of the question whether an employee is acting within the course of his employment.

Such statutes are ordinarily so worded as to be as applicable to hotels as to any other owner. Whether such a statute is applicable is determined by the law of the state where the injury is sustained and not by the law of the state where suit is brought.

(*c*) **Unfit driver.** It is generally held, apart from statute, that the owner or bailor is liable, as well as the bailee, for harm caused by the latter's negligence when the bailee is a known incompetent or a reckless driver. Accordingly, a hotel which permits an incompetent driver, whether patron or employee, to drive a hotel car is liable for the latter's negligence in driving regardless of the purpose for which the car is being used, when the hotel knows or has reason to know of such incompetence.

§ 6:7. Acts of concessionaire.

(*a*) **Generally.** Whether or not the hotel has any liability for the acts of a concessionaire depends upon whether the hotel has any control over the concessionaire's operations in the sense of saying how things should be managed or run.

In the absence of such voice in the operation of the concession, the hotel is ordinarily merely the landlord of the concessionaire. The hotel in such case has no right of management other than the negative and limited right to terminate for breach of the lease terms. When the hotel is in this position, it is not liable for the acts of the concessionaire. Otherwise stated, the concessionaire is a total stranger to the hotel, as far as the latter's vicarious liability is concerned; and hence the concessionaire's misdeeds do not impose liability upon the hotel.

When both the concessionaire and the hotel hold separate leases from the real estate corporation it is all the more clear that the hotel is not liable for the concessionaire's acts.

(*b*) *Joint venture.* In lieu of an ordinary landlord-tenant, or no relationship whatever when the hotel is not the landlord, there may exist a more or less formal joint venture between the hotel and the concession. That is to say, it may be found that the hotel and the concessionaire were working the concession together in some common plan, apart from the existence of the lease from the hotel or from the common landlord. The working arrangement in question looks very much like an informal or short-term partnership, but will probably be deemed a joint venture.[3]

If the relationship is held a joint venture, then the hotel is liable for the acts of the concessionaire in the same way that one partner is liable for the tortious harm caused by the other partners.

When the evidence is conflicting as to whether it should be concluded that there was a joint venture control of the concession enterprise, the question must go to the jury.

(*c*) *Supervisory liability distinguished.* Although the hotel has no liability for the concessionaire who is merely a tenant, the hotel may be liable to any patron who is harmed by the conduct of the concessionaire where the hotel has reason to foresee that the nature of the concession or the manner in which the concessionaire is acting or running the concession may cause harm to patrons, and the hotel then had the power and the legal right to do something about it. If the hotel and the concessionaire each hold a lease from a common landlord there is ordinarily no power or right the tenant-hotel may exercise over the tenant-concessionaire, and the hotel consequently cannot be held liable for the acts of such a stranger. Note that possible expansion of the absolute supervisory concept might make it necessary for the hotel to complain to the common landlord, as discussed in § 5:11(b).

---

[3] A joint venture arises when two or more persons combine labor or property for a single undertaking and share profits and losses equally, unless otherwise agreed.

Chapter 7. CAUSAL RELATIONSHIP

§ 7:1. Necessity of causal relationship.
    (a) Generally.
    (b) Particular applications.

§ 7:2. Proximate cause.
    (a) Generally.
    (b) Proximate relationship.
        (1) Determining existence of proximate relationship.
        (2) Substantial factor test.

§ 7:3. Intervening force.
    (a) Generally.
    (b) What constitutes an intervening force?
    (c) Foreseeable reaction or conduct distinguished.
        (1) Medical treatment and rescue harm.
        (2) Harm to rescuer.
        (3) Subsequent accident induced by harm.

§ 7:1. Necessity of causal relationship.

(**a**) ***Generally.*** As a matter of elementary justice, liability should not exist for the harm of the plaintiff unless the hotel's conduct was a cause or the cause of that harm or the hotel is responsible for the conduct of another which was such a cause. The burden is therefore on the plaintiff to show that such a causal relationship existed between the harm he has sustained and the act or omission of the hotel or its employee.

The principles here applied in this chapter are part of the general body of tort law and are not peculiar to or limited to hotels.

(**b**) ***Particular applications.*** Illustrative of the necessity for a causal relationship, the mere fact that an area is dimly lit, so as to amount to negligence, does not establish liability where the guest fell over a box on the floor which was clearly visible, and the dim lighting had nothing to do with the fall.

Similarly the hotel is not liable for the construction of the hall and steps when the reason for the plaintiff's fall and injury is that when he reached for a door knob the door was unexpectedly opened from the other side and threw him off balance.

Causal Relationship

Likewise where one room of the lobby was lower than the other with one intervening step, and the plaintiff guest fell when her heel caught on the floor of the upper level, the fact that the hotel did not maintain a handrail on the step was not material as there was no evidence that the plaintiff had attempted to keep herself from falling by the use of a handrail or that the steps were so hazardous that a rail was required. Hence, as the harm occurred without the absence of a handrail being significant there was no liability, and even if there were negligence in failing to have a handrail, that failure was not the proximate cause of the plaintiff's harm.

Similarly where the guest's assailant did not enter her room by going through the door, it is immaterial whether the lock on the door was of adequate strength.

The failure of the hotel to take precautions of a nature designed to protect the plaintiff from the harm which the plaintiff sustains does not establish that the hotel is liable, nor that its negligent failure was a proximate cause of the harm sustained by the plaintiff. Otherwise stated, when the harm would have been sustained by the plaintiff even had the precautions been taken, the fact that the hotel failed to take the precautions does not establish liability.

The facts: The defendant owned and operated an amusement park and swimming resort. Two teenage boys went swimming and the first two hours passed without any significant event. By 5:00 P. M., one of the boys realized that he had not seen his companion for a half hour and began looking for him. The companion was finally found dead by drowning, in 9' of water in a roped-off area of the lake near one of the diving towers. There was a conflict of testimony as to whether life guards had been on duty during this time. It was estimated that some 300 to 500 persons had used the swimming area during the afternoon. The dead boy was a good swimmer and no one had seen him in distress.

Decision: The fact that the boy had drowned and the defendent may have negligently supervised the lake did not establish liability of the defendant for it must be shown that its negligence had borne a causal relationship to the drowning. As there was no cry for distress by the drowned boy nor anything seen or heard which indicated that he was in danger, it could not be said that if guards had been present they could have detected the beginning of the boy's difficulty and have rescued him. The mere fact that it might be conjectured that if there had been guards, or more guards, they might have seen the boy, and might have rescued him, is not sufficient on which to base liability. Since it cannot be said definitely that the boy was drowned because of the absence of guards, there was no liability on the part of the defendant. [Blacka v. James, 205 Va 646, 139 SE2d 47 (1964)].

§ 7:2. Proximate cause.

(*a*) ***Generally.*** Assuming that there is a sufficient causal relationship between the defendant's act and the plaintiff's harm, how far is the defendant liable for what he does? Is he liable for every consequence that flows from his acts? To illustrate the problem, we will concede that the defendant who negligently runs over and kills a person is liable for the harm he has caused. But whose harm are we talking about? Where does the harm end?

We can readily say that there should be recovery sustained by the man's wife and children. Suppose, however, that the man is the key man of a large industrial enterprise which, because of his death, very quickly goes out of business. In that event, there are innumerable employees, stockholders, and creditors who have lost money in consequence of the unfortunate death of the key man. Does this mean that the negligent driver must pay for the economic loss which he has caused to all of these other persons? And to take the question of causation a step further, consider any one of the stockholders, creditors, or employees, and assume that because of the crash of the enterprise such person is not in a financial position to send his child to college. Can the child then sue the negligent driver for the economic loss and the loss of future opportunities which the child sustains thereby? To assume an even larger-scale pattern of actual harm, consider the case of the negligent driver who runs over and kills a great political leader, as the result of whose death the country is plunged into a depression or a war. It is perfectly obvious that although it can be said that the subsequent events and subsequent losses would not have occurred or probably would not have occurred if the defendant had not run over and killed the key man or the political leader, the law will just not go to the extreme of imposing liability for the infinity of consequences which flows from the act of the defendant, even though it was a wrongful act.

(*b*) ***Proximate relationship.*** In order to indicate when a causal relationship will impose liability, the law uses the phrase "proximate cause." This merely means that the cause is sufficiently close to the harm that society regards it proper to impose liability. A phrase often used for the same purpose is "legal cause," which again merely means that in the eyes of the law a given cause is regarded as imposing liability for the result.

(1) Determining existence of proximate relationship. Thus far, two things are clear: (a) society does not want to impose endless liability upon the actor, and (b) when harm is such that society wants to impose liability it uses the label of "proximate" or "legal" cause. But how does society determine how far liability should reach: how does it determine when it has reached the cut-off point for liability?

In some cases the court flatly declares that an act is or is not the proximate or legal cause of the harm without specifying how that conclusion was reached. In many cases, the court declares that the act was not the proximate cause because the harm could not have been foreseen and that it would be unreasonable to impose liability when harm could not be foreseen; or because no duty was owed to the plaintiff. Some hold that proximate cause is not a question of foreseeability or the existence of a duty but merely a question of fixing a cut-off point, as though there were a clause in a contract stating the maximum liability of the party bound thereby. By this view, the conclusion may be reached that there is no liability, even though the harm was foreseeable, because "socio-economic and moral factors dictate that there must be a stopping point to the liability of the negligent defendant."[1]

While the foregoing enables you to understand what is going on in the law, it does not furnish you, nor can anyone furnish you, with an easy guide for actually deciding a case. The significant thing to remember is that while the conduct of the hotel or of any other defendant must have "caused" the plaintiff's harm, all conduct of the defendant "causing" harm will not necessarily impose liability even though the more remote harm can trace its occurrence to the earlier act. In short, "proximate" and "legal" as applied to "cause" are merely ways of indicating whether the cut-off point has been reached.

(2) Substantial factor test. In general, there is a causal relationship when the defendant's conduct played a substantial

---

[1] Maya v. Home Ice, Fuel & Supply Co., 59 Cal2d 295, 379 P2d 513 (1963). See Supplement p. 473.

part in bringing about the plaintiff's harm. Notice that this does not require that the defendant's conduct be the only cause. Hence, when harm is caused by two actors, as when the plaintiff is harmed by being run over by two different automobiles, neither defendant can escape liability, if otherwise at fault, by asserting that his act did not cause the harm because the plaintiff would have been harmed anyway by the act of the other defendant. To the contrary, each defendant is liable for the harm which he causes to the plaintiff even though others cause similar harm. Likewise, a defendant's act is a liability-imposing cause although by itself it might not have caused harm had not some other person acted, so that the combined conduct "causes" the plaintiff's harm.

§ 7:3. Intervening force.

(*a*) *Generally.* If the hotel negligently acts or omits to act, another force or factor may enter into the picture. For example the hotel may negligently leave rubbish in the hallways and a careless guest later drops a cigarette, causing the rubbish to catch on fire, thus causing a hotel fire which harms other guests. The intervention or occurrence of such outside force may excuse the hotel from liability on the basis that it was not its conduct which caused the harm but the operation of the other force. In other instances, the intervention of other forces does not effect liability.

In general, the determination is made in terms of foreseeability. That is, if the hotel should have reasonably foreseen the intervention of the other forces, it remains liable although there may also be liability on the part of the third person creating such other force. If the element of foreseeability is lacking, there is generally no liability; although even in some non-foreseeable situations there has been liability on the theory that the intervening harm was "normal" to the situation created by the hotel.

> *The facts:* The walls of the garage adjoining the motel unit were not solidly constructed and had cracked. A guest drove into one of these unit garages and allowed the motor to run. Exhaust fumes seeped through the cracks in the garage wall into the adjoining motel unit and made the guest therein sick. He sued the motel.
>
> *Decision:* Judgment for motel. Even if the garage walls were regarded as defective, the motel was not liable for there was no reason to foresee that a driver would bring his automobile into

the garage unit and then let the motor run to the extent that fumes would fill the garage and seep out into the adjoining living unit. [Cunningham v. Marable, 48 OhioLAbs 614, 76 NE2d 254 (1947) appeal dismissed 148 Ohio 276 (1947)].

(*b*) *What constitutes an intervening force?* An intervening force is a new element or agency which arises after the hotel has acted. A force does not "intervene" when it is merely a natural step or link in the chain of consequences initiated or set off by the hotel's act. To illustrate, assume that the hotel car negligently runs into the plaintiff's automobile and causes physical damage but no fire. If a few seconds after the collision the plaintiff's car would be struck by lightning and set on fire, the fire loss would be caused by an intervening force. If, however, a few seconds after the collision, the plaintiff's car caught on fire when the gas line in the plaintiff's car exploded from overheated short-circuited wires in the plaintiff's car there would not be an intervening force because the factual elements involved were all present at the time when the hotel acted. That is to say, the wires which overheated were there, the battery which furnished the electricity which overheated the wires was there, and the gas line which exploded was there. The only new element was the combination of these factors by the hotel's act, so as to produce an overheating, an explosion, and a fire. The fire was therefore a natural consequence of the hotel's negligent conduct and not the intervention of a new force.

(*c*) *Foreseeable reaction or conduct distinguished.* When it is reasonably foreseeable that the hotel's conduct may be followed by the particular voluntary acts of other persons, such voluntary acts do not constitute intervening forces which exonerate the hotel from liability. Accordingly, when a hotel rents or loans an automobile to one who is obviously intoxicated, the careless driving of the latter is not an interrupting or intervening force but is a natural consequence of the hotel's act. Likewise, if the hotel creates a situation of hazard it remains liable if the plaintiff is injured when he does some act which exposes him to the peril. That is, if electrical wires are left uninsulated, an elevator shaft is left open, or an obstruction of ice and snow is left on the pavement, the hotel which we will assume was initially negligent in permitting such condition to arise or continue, remains liable when the plaintiff touches or comes in contact with the dangerous situation; as opposed to the argument that the plaintiff's action in touching the wire, and so on, was an independent act which was the actual cause of the plaintiff's harm and for which the hotel is therefore not liable. Similarly when a glass panel faces directly on the street, the hotel must anticipate that persons on the pavement may lean against the glass and it is therefore liable when one of its own guests standing outside of the hotel leans slightly against the glass and it then shattered causing him harm. And a motel which leaves swimming pool cleaning equipment on the ground should anticipate that the water floats may be removed by children and thrown into the pool, and it is consequently liable when this occurs and another child is injured thereby.

In short, it is immaterial that the hotel's negligence does not directly cause the plaintiff's harm when it is caused by a foreseeable factor which a reasonable man would recognize as likely to grow out of the situation created by the hotel. Accordingly, the hotel remains liable although the additional facts which are essential to the realization of harm consist of (1) the plaintiff's voluntarily touching or coming into contact with the dangerous condition created by the defendant; (2) the plaintiff's voluntarily or automatically seeking to save himself, as by jumping out of an automobile before the crash; (3) the occurrence of ordinary forces of nature, such as rain; (4) the natural reaction of animals under the circumstances, or (5) the conduct of third persons, whether negligent or criminal.

> *The facts:* The plaintiffs were patrons at the restaurant of the defendant. While dining in the restaurant, an automobile which was being parked by another restaurant patron crashed through the restaurant wall and injured them. They sued the defendant on the ground that he had been negligent in failing to put barriers on the parking lot which would have prevented cars from overriding the lot and running into the restaurant building. It was further contended that the general custom of the community was to provide such barriers. The court dismissed the action on the theory that the facts as above recited did not constitute a cause of action against the restaurant.
>
> *Decision:* The case should have gone to the jury rather than be determined by the court. The test was whether the defendant should have foreseen that his failure to have parking lot barriers would probably and from usual experience result in patrons' overdriving the parking lot and running into the restaurant building. Conversely, if such an occurrence was unusual or unlikely to happen or was a slight probability or remote event, then the harm sustained was not foreseeable. The case must be considered by the jury on the basis of this test and could not be decided by the court itself.

Causal Relationship

The fact that the harm was actually caused by the act of another guest overriding the lot did not act as an independent agency which broke the causative chain between the defendant's negligence, if any, and the harm sustained by the plaintiff. And here again the test is whether such conduct or actions of third persons were reasonably foreseeable. In view of the fact that the very purpose of barriers at the side or the end of a parking lot is to prevent overriding the lot and colliding with persons and property, it could not be said as a matter of law by the trial judge that such harm was not foreseeable, but should have been determined by a jury. [Denisewich v. Pappas, 97 RI 432, 198 A2d 144 (1964)].

(1) Medical treatment and rescue harm. As the result of negligence, the plaintiff may be injured. Assume that the medical treatment he thereafter receives increases the harm, as when the negligence of the doctor makes it possible for the minor cut caused by the negligence of the hotel to become infected and the plaintiff thereafter must undergo an amputation or even dies because of such infection. Or assume that the negligent conduct of the hotel exposes the plaintiff's property to fire damage and volunteer rescuers in removing the plaintiff's property to safety cause substantial damage to the property. In both of these cases it is clear that the direct cause of the harm or the additional harm was not the act of the hotel but the act of other persons. In fact, in the case of the medical treatment it could be said that there are three additional forces present: (1) the plaintiff's voluntarily going to any doctor and this particular doctor; (2) the doctor acting in a negligent manner; and (3) the entry and spread of infection in the system of the plaintiff.

In spite of this aspect of the case, it is clear that a reasonable man in the position of the hotel should foresee the possibility that its conduct may open the door to the conduct of third persons and the harm produced by them is not so abnormal or strange that the hotel should not be held liable for such consequences. It is therefore ordinarily held liable for such harm.

(2) Harm to rescuer. In general, the hotel is held accountable for harm which is caused third persons when they attempt to remedy the situation created by the hotel. Hence, a hotel is liable to a rescuer who is injured in attempting to rescue the person improperly exposed to peril by the hotel. To illustrate, if the hotel swimming pool is not properly guarded

and a child starts to drown, whereupon another guest tries to save the child but is injured in so doing, the hotel is liable for the harm sustained by the rescuer. It is true that the act of rescuing is a voluntary act of the rescuer but the law recognizes that the generous effort of the third person to rescue is such a normal incident that it is foreseeable and the hotel is therefore liable for the harm caused the rescuer. Another practical aspect of the situation is that the hotel which is negligent and would have been liable had its conduct continued to operate with respect to the apparent original victim should not be given a windfall by the fact that someone else happens to throw himself into the scene and receive the effect of the hotel's unlawful act.

The liability to the rescuer is not, however, without limit. Thus, while an attempt to rescue is a reasonably foreseeable occurrence, there is no reason to foresee that a hopeless rescue will be attempted and therefore there is no liability to the injured rescuer in such a case. Hence, when a reasonable man in the position of the rescuer would recognize that it was not possible to save the victim and that an attempt to do so would merely cause harm to the rescuer, the hotel is not liable for the harm sustained by the hopeless rescuer.

There is likewise no liability when the rescuer is himself careless in making the rescue in an unreasonably dangerous way, although here the "emergency" rule comes into play so that the hotel is not exonerated merely because there was a safer way in which the rescue could have been made.

(3) Subsequent accident induced by harm. The plaintiff after being injured by the hotel's negligence may be more likely to contract diesase than before or may be more accident prone. If the plaintiff sustains later harm because of his weakened condition or a disability resulting from the hotel's negligent conduct, the latter is generally liable for such additional harm, as opposed to the contention that the latter harm was sustained because of an intervening force.

This rule of liability is even extended to cases where the injury caused by the hotel's negligence causes the victim to become insane and the latter commits suicide during an insane period. Again the argument is rejected that it was the voluntary act of the victim which caused his harm; for the hotel had set the stage for such harm by causing the plaintiff's insanity.

The facts: The defendant druggist sold barbiturate capsules to a customer without any prescription and without informing him of the fact that they were habit forming nor of the possible effect of continued use. He continued to sell them to the customer for a year, during which time the customer deteriorated mentally and physically. While under the influence of the capsules or while suffering from moroseness caused by such continued use, the customer committed suicide. An action for wrongful death was brought against the druggist. Was he liable?

Decision: No. The druggist could foresee that drug addiction could follow from his conduct but not that the drug addiction would in turn lead to suicide, for the reason that so many factors may enter into a suicide's decision to take his life and the fact that many drug addicts do not commit suicide. [Scott v. Greenville Pharmacy, 212 SC 485, 48 SE2d 324 (1948)].

Chapter 8. INTENTIONAL TORTS AND DEATH CLAIMS

A. Intentional torts directed at the person.

§ 8:1. General tort principles.
    (a) Generally.
    (b) Classification of intentional torts.

§ 8:2. Battery.
    (a) Definition.
        (1) Absence of consent.
        (2) Absence of privilege.
    (b) Damages.

§ 8:3. Assault.
    (a) Definition.
    (b) Present contact.

§ 8:4. False imprisonment, arrest, and malicious prosecution.
    (a) False imprisonment.
        (1) Detention.
        (2) Privilege and consent.
    (b) False arrest.
        (1) Liability of complainant.
    (c) Malicious prosecution.
    (d) Authority of hotel employee.
    (e) Damages.

§ 8:5. Intentional causing of mental distress.
    (a) Generally.
    (b) The law in transition.
        (1) Physical harm.

§ 8:6. Intentional torts directed at property.
    (a) Generally.
    (b) Damages.

B. Defamation.

§ 8:7. Injury to reputation.
    (a) Generally.
    (b) Libel and slander.

Intentional Torts and Death Claims

§ 8:8. Proof of damage.
    (a) Libel.
    (b) Slander.

§ 8:9. Privileged statements.

C.   Violation of privacy.

§ 8:10. Nature of the right.

§ 8:11. Hotel privilege of surveillance.
    (a) Generally.
    (b) Surveillance of visitors.
        (1) Entry into room.

§ 8:12. Hotel privilege of entry into rooms.
    (a) Generally.
    (b) Protection of patron.
    (c) Protection of other patrons.
    (d) Protection of hotel.
        (1) Cleaning and maintenance.
        (2) Enforcement of regulations.
    (e) Prevention of crime.
    (f) Overlapping aspects.
    (g) Manner of exercising privilege to enter rooms.
    (h) Protection of hotel from liability.
        (1) Regulations.
        (2) Lease term.

§ 8:13. Public privilege.
    (a) Generally.
    (b) Lapse of time.
    (c) Liability of hotel.

§ 8:14. Private privilege of investigation.

D.   Death claims.

§ 8:15. Effect of death.

§ 8:16. Wrongful death action.
    (a) Generally.
    (b) Nature of action.
    (c) Defenses.

§ 8:17. Surviving action.

§ 8:18. Survival action.

A. Intentional torts directed at the person.

§ 8:1. General tort principles.

(*a*) ***Generally.*** The principles of law discussed in this chapter are general rules of tort law applicable to any person involved in the same set of facts and are not limited or peculiar to hotels.

The inclusion of death claims within this chapter should not be deemed to indicate that death claims arise only from intentional torts; they may arise from any tortious killing of another, whether the wrong involved be deemed willful or negligent.

(*b*) ***Classification of intentional torts.*** The intentional torts may be directed at causing harm to any interest. Thus they may be directed to (1) causing harm, or fear of harm to, or interfering with, the plaintiff physically, in which case we have such torts as assault, battery, and false imprisonment; or (2) causing harm to or interfering with the plaintiff's relationships with others, in which case we have defamation, interference with privacy, interference with contract and economic relationships and so on; or (3) causing harm to physical things such as going or trespassing on the plaintiff's land. The hotel is ordinarily only concerned with the first class and part of the second class of these torts.

§ 8:2. Battery.

(*a*) ***Definition.*** A battery is an intentional, unprivileged touching of another person without his consent. For example, if I throw a stone at you with the intention of hitting you, the touching is a battery unless you have consented to being hit. If I intentionally throw you out of my hotel when I do not have the right to evict you I have also committed a battery.

(1) Absence of consent. There is no battery when there is consent to the touching. Thus two persons voluntarily wrestling give consent to each other to be touched and such touching does not constitute a battery. It is necessary, however, that the touching stay within the range of consent. Accordingly consent to engage in wrestling contacts is not consent to the use of a knife in the course of the contest.

(2) Absence of privilege. The circumstances may be such that although there is no consent to the touching, the law gives

a privilege or permission to make the touching without incurring liability therefor. To illustrate, if you are attacked by a robber or put in peril of your life, you have the right to use force in your own defense. Likewise, if the hotel has the right to evict the plaintiff, it has a privilege to use such force as is reasonably necessary for that purpose, and the touching involved does not constitute a battery.

(*b*) **Damages.** In harmony with general principles, an award may be made to the plaintiff of both compensatory and punitive or exemplary damages. The compensatory damages pay or compensate the plaintiff for the loss he has actually sustained, such as medical expenses, loss of wages, and the less definite elements of pain and suffering and loss of future earning power. The punitive or exemplary damages are additional damages which the defendant is required to pay the plaintiff because the law thinks that what he has willfully done is so serious that he should pay additional damages to punish him or make an example of him to the community so that there will not be a repetition of such conduct. Such damages are awarded only when the defendant is an intentional wrongdoer.

§ 8:3. Assault.

(*a*) **Definition.** An assault is the unprivileged act of intentionally making another person apprehend that he will be touched without his consent. In brief, it is the action which looks to the victim as though there will be a battery but which never reaches that point.

With respect to elements for which damages are allowed, the basic element is the disturbing of the plaintiff's mind through the apprehension of the physical contact. Recovery is also allowed for humiliation when present, and for any physical illness or harm which follows from the shock sustained by the plaintiff.

(*b*) **Present contact.** There is no assault if a present contact is not apprehended. Thus there is no assault when the actor, that is, the one who acts, merely uses insulting language but does not give any reason to believe that he will strike the plaintiff. Nor is there an assault when the actor merely makes threats as to what he will do in the future or what he would do in the future depending upon the conduct of the plaintiff. Likewise there is no assault when the actor makes his offer of violence at such a distance that a reasonable man would recognize there could not be any contact.

§ 8:4. False imprisonment, arrest, and malicious prosecution.

(*a*) *False imprisonment.* This tort is the intentional, unprivileged detaining of a person without his consent. False imprisonment may take the extreme form of kidnapping. At the other extreme a person who is detained in the hotel manager's office and questioned as to certain thefts is the victim of false imprisonment where there was no reasonable ground for believing that he was the thief. False imprisonment also includes the detention under an official arrest when in fact there is no legal justification for the arrest so that it is a false arrest.

(1) Detention. Any detention at any place by any means for any duration of time is sufficient. Stone walls are not required to make a false imprisonment. If a bank robber holds a bank teller at gun point with the purpose of preventing him from attacking the other robbers or in order to escape there is a detention. Also there is a detention when the patron is stopped by the house detectives and not allowed to leave.

> *The facts:* An employer believed that an employee was embezzling money. The employer retained a private detective agency to make an investigation. The plaintiff was an employee who was suspected. With the employer's approval, he was taken into the employer's office and kept there for some time. Several times, when he went to leave, he was prevented from so doing by the private investigator who told him he was not finished. He was personally afraid of the investigator, who sat in a chair against the door and prevented the plaintiff's leaving. The employee sued the employer for false imprisonment. The employer defended on the ground that (1) the plaintiff was an employee and was still getting paid for the time that he was detained, and (2) the detention had been committed by the detective who was working for the detective agency which was an independent contractor.
>
> *Decision:* The defenses raised by the employer were not valid. The fact that the employee had to be at the place of business and was getting paid for the detention time did not make it any the less an unlawful detention. The fact that the employer retained an independent contractor did not insulate him from liability because the examination of the plaintiff was approved by the employer who had made his office and the employee available

Intentional Torts and Death Claims

for the purpose. [Greenbaum v. Brooks, 110 GaApp 661, 139 SE2d 432 (1964)].

The duration of the detention is immaterial, as in the case of the falsely and unreasonably accused guest who was detained for ten minutes, or the kidnapped victim who is detained for ten days. The duration of course bears importantly upon the question of damages.

(2) Privilege and consent. A privilege to detain or imprison arises when a person reasonably suspected of crime is detained in a reasonable manner. The privilege may also arise in non-criminal situations as in the case of the quarantine officer who lawfully confines you to your home because of the presence of a contagious disease.

There is no false imprisonment if there is consent to the detention. For example, a doctor entering a dangerous mental patient ward with knowledge that he cannot get out of the ward unless the guard outside of the door opens it for him, consents that he be confined or detained in such manner and to such extent.

The facts: A customer was shopping at the handbag counter of the defendant's store. She did not make any purchase and left the store. When she was a few feet away from the store, an employee of the store tapped her lightly on the shoulder to attract her attention and asked her if she had made any purchase. When she inquired why, he asked, "What about that bag in your hand?" The cusomer said that it belonged to her and she opened it to show by its contents that it was not a new bag. The employee gave the customer a "real dirty look" and went back into the store without saying a word. The customer then sued the store for false imprisonment.

Decision: Judgment for store. There was no false imprisonment because there was no actual detaining of the customer. The circumstances did not show the use of force or the threat of force which stopped the customer from proceeding. Her action of stopping and showing the contents of her handbag was her voluntary act. [Abner v. W. T. Grant Co., 110 GaApp 592, 139 SE2d 408 (1964)].

In some instances, the distinction is made either expressly or impliedly between restraint under color of authority and restraint by force or fear of force. That is to say, there are decisions which find no false imprisonment when a person stops and answers questions or submits to a search "voluntarily" when requested to do so by a police officer or other person apparently possessing an officer's authority.

> *The facts:* The customer was leaving the store and was about to leave the parking lot in the car driven by her friend. Two men appeared, one showed a badge, and asked to see the customer's pocketbook. She showed it to him. He examined it, returned it to the customer, and asked her to take a bracelet out of the pocketbook and hand it to him. The customer did so, the man examined it, asked her where she had purchased it, the customer explained, and the man returned the bracelet, and walked away. The customer then sued the store for false imprisonment.
>
> *Decision:* Judgment for store. To constitute false imprisonment there must be a detention through force or fear of force. But here no force was used, and the customer was not in fear of any force but had acted voluntarily with all requests of the man with the badge. Accordingly, there was no false imprisonment. [Black v. Clark's Greensboro, Inc., 263 NC 226, 139 SE2d199 (1964)].

(c) False arrest. A false arrest is committed when an arrest is for any reason deemed void. In essence it is a false imprisonment made under the color of authority. The situation may arise because the court from which the warrant of arrest was issued lacked the jurisdiction to issue the warrant; the warrant under which the arrest was made is fatally defective; or the officer or private person making the arrest had no authority to do so, either generally or under the particular warrant.

(1) Liability of complainant. When the arrest is made because someone complains about someone else and swears out a warrant for his arrest, the question arises whether this complainant who sets the wheels of the law in motion is liable for damages for false arrest when the arrest thereafter made is void for any reason.

If the circumstances are such that the complainant knows or should know that what is being done lacks validity, he is liable for the unauthorized interference with the liberty of the person arrested. A difficult question arises when the proceedings are in every respect proper but the arrest is a false arrest because the warrant is void. Here some courts take the position that as long as the complaining party acted in good faith, he cannot be held liable for a false arrest when so far as he is concerned he has done nothing illegal. In contrast, other courts charge him with liability for the chain of events which he initiated although he could not know that the arrest was illegal because he was not learned in the law. It is obviously very important for the hotel to learn from its attorney whether it is located in a liability-imposing state, and if it is, to have its attorney keep an eye on all arrest proceedings begun by the hotel.

> *The facts:* The owners of stores in the community sought to obtain the enforcement of the law which prohibited the making of sales on Sunday except where required by necessity or charity. The manager of one of the stores went to the local constable and signed a complaint on the basis of which a warrant was issued for the arrest of the personnel operating a store which was open on Sundays. As the identity of the person who would be arrested was then unknown, the warrant authorized the arrest of "Mary Doe, correct name unknown," and described her as working at a store, the name and address of which were given.
>
> The plaintiff was a salaried employee in the offending store and was arrested on the basis of this warrant. She was detained for approximately two hours by the arresting officer and the justice of the peace, and then released on the ground that the warrant was void. She sued the manager for false arrest and a verdict was returned in her favor. The manager appealed on the ground that the warrant was valid, and that he was not liable even if it were invalid.
>
> *Decision:* A warrant for arrest must identify the person by name or by a description which is sufficiently specific to distinguish the person from other persons. A warrant which uses merely a fictitious name is void and the arrest made thereunder is a void arrest, unless the circumstances are such as would authorize the making of an arrest without any warrant. Such other circumstances were not present and hence the plaintiff had been falsely arrested.
>
> The fact that the warrant contained the description of the place of employment did not identify the plaintiff sufficiently since the description applied equally to any other female working at the store in question. The warrant was therefore void.
>
> The defendant was liable for damages for the false arrest under the void warrant, because West Virginia follows the rule that when a person is arrested under a void warrant the person who causes the warrant to be issued is liable for the false imprisonment of the person arrested. [Winters v. Campbell, 148 WVa 710, 137 SE2d 188 (1964)].

(d) Malicious prosecution. This action is brought by a person who has been unjustly prosecuted against the person who has instigated or caused the prosecution. In order to establish such claim, it is necessary to show that there was a criminal prosecution begun against the plaintiff by the defendant without probable cause and acting with malice, and that such criminal prosecution terminated in favor of the plaintiff in the present malicious prosecution action.

The malice essential to give rise to this liability is difficult to define. It requires an actual malice, but it would appear that the requirement of malice is satisfied whenever it is shown that the person instigating the former criminal prosecution, that is, the present defendant, was not guided solely by the aim of bringing an evildoer to justice; but to the contrary, had the purpose of bringing pressure to bear so that he could collect a debt, or compel the performance of a contract, and, of course, where the purpose was to extort money from the present plaintiff.

(e) *Authority of hotel employee.* When it is claimed that the hotel is liable for malicious prosecution because of the act of its employee in instigating the prosecution against the present plaintiff, it is necessary for the present plaintiff to establish that the employee or agent in question had authority to act for the hotel, so as to provide the basis for the application of the rule of vicarious liability.[1]

When the hotel denies liability for conduct of an employee or agent on the theory that such person was not its employee or agent or had exceeded the scope of his authority, the question is to be determined by the jury where there is conflicting evidence, or the fact of agency is disputed.

> *The facts:* The manager of the motel and a guest had a dispute over the bill due by the guest. When the guest refused to pay the greater amount claimed by the manager, the latter swore out a warrant for the guest's arrest for the crime of failing to pay the hotel bill. The guest was acquitted and then sued the motel and the manager for malicious prosecution. The motel denied liability on the ground that the manager did not have authority to swear out a warrant for the arrest of the guest. The evidence showed that an agent of the motel corporation had entrusted the manager with the running of the motel in all respects, and that the manager was in charge of hiring and firing of employees, setting the hours of employment, and had charge of the maintenance of the motel.

---

[1] See Chapter 6.

Decision: The facts were sufficient to support a conclusion that the manager had complete charge of the motel's operation and that as incidental to such authority, he had the authority to commence a criminal prosecution for the nonpayment of a guest's bill. Consequently he had acted within the scope of his authority and the motel was liable. [Ross v. Dellinger, 262 NC 589, 138 SE2d 226 (1964)].

(*f*) **Damages.** Damages may be recovered for false imprisonment without proof of actual physical harm, for compensation is allowed for the mere interference with the plaintiff's freedom of motion. The damages recoverable will increase in terms of the duration and severity of the detention. As the false imprisonment is by definition intentional, punitive damages are properly allowed. The defendant is also liable for various other elements of harm that the plaintiff may sustain such as loss of time, harm to reputation and credit standing, expense of litigation in obtaining his release, humiliation, and physical and mental illness brought about by the shock of the false imprisonment.

In general, the recovery of damages in the actions for false arrest and malicious prosecution follow the same pattern as false imprisonment. In the case of false arrest, this is natural since the wrongs of false imprisonment and false arrest overlap: the detention of the plaintiff by means of a false arrest being itself a false imprisonment. In the case of malicious prosecution, the process and procedure are valid, so that the detention, if any is involved, is not a false imprisonment; but at the same time, much the same injuries caused a person falsely imprisoned are sustained by a person who has been subjected to criminal prosecution without cause. In addition, both false arrest and an improper prosecution are in a sense slanderous of the plaintiff, and add to his damages in this respect.

§ 8:5. Intentional causing of mental distress.

(*a*) **Generally.** When the defendant commits an act which by itself is a tort there is ordinarily recovery for the mental distress which he causes thereby. That is, mental suffering is merely an element of the damages sustained by the plaintiff for an assault, and so forth.

The question arises whether there is liability when the actor merely says things to the plaintiff or does acts for the purpose of causing him emotional disturbance or distress and the plaintiff does suffer such emotional distress, perhaps, even to the point of becoming physically ill from the experience.

(b) *The law in transition.* By the common law down to this century, words by themselves have been held not to give rise to any liability, unless slanderous or libelous. Likewise, conduct designed to distress was not actionable. With the turn of the century, and particularly in the last quarter century, recovery has been allowed in a number of cases in which no ordinary or traditional form of tort was committed and the common element was that the defendant had willfully subjected the plaintiff to unnecessary emotional disturbance. This result has been reached when the common carrier or the hotel insulted a patron, a collection agency used unreasonable means of collection designed to harass the debtor, an outrageous practical joke was played upon the plaintiff or his personal or physical condition purposely exploited by such joke, or the corpse of a close relative of the plaintiff's was mistreated or interference made with the burial.

Generally the theory on which recovery is allowed is beclouded by efforts to bring the case within the standard patterns of liability. Occasionally a court frankly recognizes that it is imposing liability merely because mental distress was intentionally caused.

(1) Physical harm. Assume that the defendant falsely and for the purpose of causing mental distress tells the plaintiff that he is going to lose his job or that a close relative has been killed. The emotional disturbance caused by such statements may be the full extent of the harm. However, the shock to the plaintiff may be so great that he becomes physically or mentally ill.

Is any distinction to be made between the situation in which there is no resultant physical or mental harm and the case in which there is such harm? Theoretically no, assuming that the jury believes the facts to be as just stated. There is a definite tendency or pattern, however, for some courts to deny recovery where there is merely mental distress and to allow recovery when there is some physical or mental illness which the jury finds to have been caused by the mental distress. This is easy to understand, for the ordinary person is likely to reason that if there was resulting physical or mental harm, there must of course have been serious mental distress and suffering.

The facts: A widow brought suit against the defendants for the death of her husband claiming that their acts had led him to commit suicide. She claimed that they had intentionally made threats, statements, and accusations against her husband for the purpose of harassing, embarrassing, and humiliating him in the presence of friends, relatives, and business associates, and that this caused the husband to become physically and mentally disturbed, as the direct result of which he committed suicide. Were the defendants liable?

Decision: The court declared that if the jury found that the defendants had intentionally caused the mental distress of the husband they were liable if such distress was really a substantial factor in causing him to commit suicide. [Tate v. Canonica, 180 CalApp2d 898, 5 CalRptr 28 (1960)].

§ 8:6. Intentional torts directed at property.

(a) Generally. Intentional torts may be committed with respect to property, as in the case of the unpermitted entry or trespass upon land. Thus someone walking across your front lawn without your permission commits a trespass, as does your neighbor when he builds a shed which extends over the boundary between your lots. The intentional tort may also involve the taking and keeping of the property as when the wrongdoer unlawfully mines and carries away coal from your land or steals your lawnmower. The intentional tort may also be merely an act of vandalism or destruction, as when the windows of your house are intentionally broken or holes are made in your automobile tires.

(b) Damages. In general, the plaintiff recovers damages representing the extent of the injuries which he has sustained through the harm to or taking of his property. In addition to compensatory damages, the jury may generally assess punitive damages against the wrongdoer. In many jurisdictions, the willful wrongdoer harming property is subjected to a special statutory penalty.

B. Defamation

§ 8:7. Injury to reputation.

(a) Generally. Defamation consists of any communication to one person which has the tendency of harming another person's reputation or the esteem or regard in which he is held. The

standard is easy to state but difficult to apply, for statements which might be regarded as undesirable or even offensive by the person described may not be regarded as defamatory by the courts. In addition, time and place are very important factors. For example, a statement made in London in 1776 that a person was seeking to obtain the independence of the American colonies would clearly be differently regarded than the same statement made in Philadelphia on July 4, 1776.

In general, defamatory statements will either (1) reflect upon the individual, as by stating that he is a drunkard, a coward, an anarchist, or refuses to pay his just debts; or (2) reflect upon the individual's status or condition, as by stating that he is a bastard, is a pauper, or is insane, or the child of a murderer.

(*b*) *Libel and slander.* Libel and slander are distinct in that (1) slander is spoken while libel is written, and (2) damages can be recovered for any libel without proof of actual injury whereas actual damage must be shown to recover for slander, except in certain cases. In many states this distinction has been eroded so that there is no distinction made as to the form of the defamation and the plaintiff must show actual harm, unless the statements are on their face of a defamatory character.

§ 8:8. Proof of damage.

(*a*) *Libel.* Proof of actual damage to the plaintiff is not required in the case of libel, the theory being that any defamatory libel is of course harmful and therefore not only is the plaintiff entitled to sue therefor but he is also entitled to recover damages. There is a tendency by decision or statute, however, to modify the view above stated so as to require proof of damage to the same extent as in slander.

(*b*) *Slander.* With respect to slander, the plaintiff has no right of action in the absence of proof that he has sustained damages, and conversely, recovery is necessarily limited to the damages which he has sustained.

As an exception to the foregoing statement, there are several instances in which slander follows the same rule as libel, so that the mere proof of the slander, without proof of any damages actually sustained, is sufficient to give rise to a right of action against the defendant and to warrant the recovery of substantial damages by the plaintiff. These statements which come within this special group are said to be statements which

Intentional Torts and Death Claims 107

are slanderous per se, or slanderous in themselves, and include statements charging the victim with a serious crime; stating that he has leprosy or a venereal disease; reflecting upon his business, professional, or official standing; or accusing a female of unchastity.

The facts: The plaintiff was a dentist and married. He sued the defendant for saying (1) that the plaintiff was a "Hitler," (2) that the plaintiff's father was a criminal, (3) that the plaintiff cheated the tax people, and (4) that he slept with his secretary. The plaintiff did not prove that he was in any way damaged by these statements. Is the plaintiff entitled to recover damages from the defendant?

Decision: Yes. As no damages were shown, the plaintiff is only entitled to recover as to those statements which were slanderous per se. The statement that he was a Hitler was not slanderous per se. Although it was a term of disapprobation, it did not accuse the plaintiff of any particular crime. The statement that the plaintiff's father was a "criminal" was not slanderous because it did not accuse of any specific crime and did not accuse the plaintiff. The statement that he cheated tax people was slanderous, as it accused the plaintiff of a specific crime. The statement as to the plaintiff's relations with his secretary was slanderous, as it accused the plaintiff of the specific crime of adultery. [Jordan v. Lewis, 20 AppDiv2d 773, 247 NYS2d 650 (1964)].

§ 8:9. Privileged statements.

In some cases the position of the speaker or the nature of the transaction is such that the law makes him immune from liability for defamation. This immunity, which is called a privilege, may be (1) a perfect or absolute immunity, as in the case of statements made in legislative or judicial proceedings; or it may be (2) a qualified or conditional immunity, as in the case of statements made in good faith to protect the interests of the speaker or the auditor. The difference is that absolute immunity exists regardless of the circumstances under which the defamatory statement is made. In the case of the conditional or qualified privilege, the immunity exists only if the necessary conditions or qualifications exist.

The hotel has a qualified or conditional privilege. Accordingly when it reports to the police that a guest is a thief there is no liability if the hotel has reasonable ground for making such statement, but it is unprivileged if it makes the statement without reasonable ground for its belief.

C. Violation of privacy

§ 8:10. Nature of the right.

An individual has a right "to be let alone" and an unreasonable invasion of this right of privacy constitutes a tort. Invasion of the right most commonly occurs in one of four ways: (1) invasion of physical privacy, as by entering a person's home or his hotel rooms without his permission or a privilege to do so; (2) giving unnecessary publicity to personal matters of the plaintiff's life, such as his financial status or his past career; (3) false public association of the plaintiff with some product or principle, such as indicating that he endorses a product or is in favor of a particular law, when such fact is false; or (4) commercially exploiting the plaintiff's name or picture, as using them in advertising without his permission.

> *The facts:* The landlord leased the premises to a husband and wife. Without their knowledge, he placed a microphone in their bedroom and ran the lead wire to the receiving device in his residence. While cleaning, the tenants found the hidden microphone. Both husband and wife sustained mental shock, distress, and humiliation, to the point of being made physically sick and unable to work. They sued the landlord for damages. He defended on the ground that there was no statute or decision which declared improper what he had done, and that he had not committed any invasion of privacy because there was no proof that he or anyone had every heard anything over the microphone, or that he had told anyone anything heard thereon, or that anything had been written or published as to what had been heard.
>
> *Decision:* Judgment for both tenants. There is a basic right of privacy which courts will recognize without any statute or prior decision. An essential part of this right of privacy is that of being let alone. When the privacy of the bedroom was invaded by the placing of the microphone the landlord had breached his duty to let the tenants alone and was accordingly liable for damages for the injuries sustained as the result of such conduct. The defenses raised by the landlord were not valid, since it was the fact of the invasion which was the wrong and what followed or did not follow would merely affect the damages recoverable but not the existence of the cause of action. [Hamberger v. Eastman, 106 NH 107, 206 A2d 239 (1965)].

Similarly a separated husband and anyone participating with him in putting a wiretap on the telephone line of the separated wife, so that the husband could get information on which to

Intentional Torts and Death Claims

base a divorce action, are likewise liable to the wife for the tortious invasion of her privacy.

§ 8:11. Hotel privilege of surveillance.

(*a*) *Generally.* A hotel has the right and, in most cases, the duty to employ detectives and night watchmen both for the protection of the hotel's own interest, as by preventing it from being subject to criminal punishment because of illegal acts committed on the premises, as well as to protect guests and other persons to whom it owes a special duty of care.

(*b*) *Surveillance of visitors.* The hotel has a right to supervise the visitors of its guests to insure that no illegal or criminal acts will be committed either as between the visitor and the guest or as against other persons.

(1) Entry into room. The right to supervise the conduct of visitors and of guests gives the hotel the right to enter the room of the guest to determine whether any immoral or illegal acts are being committed. And where a wife has registered in her name only, the hotel on entering her room and finding that the man with her was her husband, may require the husband to register as a guest. Conversely the hotel is not liable in such case for any invasion of privacy nor for any embarassment or humiliation.

§ 8:12. Hotel privilege of entry into rooms.

(*a*) *Generally.* As a starting point, the guest has an absolute right to privacy, as though he were in his own home, and it is unlawful for the hotel or other guests to enter his room without his permission. The hotel, however, is privileged under certain circumstances to enter the patron's room. The hotel privilege arises in terms of (1) protection of the patron whose right of privacy is involved; (2) protection of other patrons; (3) protection of the hotel; and (4) prevention of crime and arrest of criminals.

Factually, the basic problem is the same in each of these situations. Namely, the hotel representative senses or suspects that something improper is going on inside the rooms of the patron of the hotel; the word "patron" being used in the broad sense to denote any person in the hotel as a "customer," whether he is technically a "guest" or not. Acting on this belief, the hotel representative uses a passkey or breaks down the door to gain entrance to the patron's rooms. Is the hotel then liable for the invasion of privacy in the event that no crime or other misconduct was in fact being perpetrated, or that the patron condones any offense and refuses to testify against a wrongdoer?

(*b*) **Protection of patron.** The hotel on the basis of cries or other sounds emanating from the rooms of the patron may fear that the patron is the victim of a crime being committed within his rooms. If the hotel reasonably believes that the guest needs protection, the hotel is protected for such entrance because it is under the duty to use reasonable care to keep the premises clear of persons likely to cause harm to its patrons. That is, the supervisory duty of the hotel to keep the premises safe from wrongdoers must be deemed to extend to the protection of patrons in their rooms. This logically follows from the fact that a wrongdoer should not gain immunity from the supervisory action of the hotel merely because he had fled or sneaked through the lobby or other public area into the private room of a patron.

The case turns on the reasonableness of the action of the hotel. If it would appear reasonable to phone the patron, or knock on the door first, such steps should be taken. It is obvious that under some circumstances it may be a futile gesture and prove a dangerous waste of time to inquire in such manner; as when gunshots are heard within the patron's room.

Another situation may arise in which the hotel has the privilege of entrance for the protection of the guest. Assume that because of sounds coming from the patron's room, or the fact that he has not been heard of for a substantial period of time, the hotel fears that he may be sick and require medical attention. At some point, the law will recognize that there is a privilege to enter to take care of the guest rather than to take the position that since the patron's door is closed there is nothing that the hotel can and should do about it. Again, it is a matter of reasonableness. At some point it becomes clear that the fact that a man's life may be at stake will far outweigh the right which that man would otherwise have against strangers invading the privacy of his room.[2]

(*c*) **Protection of other patrons.** If the hotel has knowledge or reason to believe that acts are being committed within the

---

[2] As to entry into a patron's room to provide medical care, see § 2:5.

Intentional Torts and Death Claims

rooms of a patron which will be dangerous to other patrons of the hotel, the hotel has the right to enter or break and enter to prevent such harm. For example, it may reasonably appear that there is a fire in the rooms of a patron. It is obvious that the hotel will have the right to enter in order to protect other patrons, regardless of whether the fire is accidental, incendiary, or has been set by a guest seeking to commit suicide.

The hotel should seek to gain permission to enter the rooms, but this is not required when it reasonably appears that there is no time to delay over such matters.

(d) Protection of hotel. If the hotel has knowledge or reason to believe that acts are being committed or events are taking place which will harm the building or plant of the hotel, it has a privilege of entry. For example, when a guest in a room below complains that water is coming through the ceiling and walls, and water is pouring out from under the door to the apartment on the floor above, it is clear that the hotel must be allowed the privilege to enter to prevent the doing of harm to its building.

(1) Cleaning and maintenance. The hotel has the right to enter the room at such times as are reasonable for the cleaning and maintenance of the property. Ordinarily the guest has no objection to this but that fact is immaterial. That is to say, assume that the guest is an eccentric who for one reason or another does not want his rooms ever cleaned. In spite of such objection, the hotel has the right to enter to clean in order to maintain the condition of the rooms, to avoid offending the neighboring guests, and to avoid the possibility of violating health and sanitation laws.

(2) Enforcement of regulations. The hotel may enter the guest's room in order to enforce its regulations when it knows that they are being violated and the rules in question are designed to prevent criminal or immoral conduct or conduct which is offensive to other guests.

(e) Prevention of crime. The hotel will ordinarily have an employee or detective who is sworn as a peace officer or policeman. In such case, he may of course exercise the same authority that any other officer has of entering or breaking and entering without a search warrant when there is reason to believe that a crime is being committed within the closed rooms. If there is no such officer, the hotel will have nonetheless a right of entry

to prevent a felony by force to the same extent that an ordinary individual would have such a right, and undoubtedly should have a greater right because of its supervisory liability.

The hotel should also have a privilege of entry in order to prevent crimes such as gambling and prostitution, where, under the local law, the hotel may be subjected to criminal penalties if its premises are used for such purposes. The hotel therefore has the right to enter the premises in a reasonable manner and to a reasonable extent to determine that no one is engaged in conduct which would impose liability upon the hotel or cause its building to be closed as a nuisance.

(*f*) *Overlapping aspects.* From the brief statement above made it is apparent that many situations may arise in which more than one element may justify the entry by the hotel. For example, a guest has carelessly started a fire by smoking in bed. If the fire is not checked there may be harm to the guest, to other guests, to the hotel building, and in fact to the buildings of neighboring property owners. It is clear that the interest of protecting all these persons has become so great that it is absurd to refuse to permit the hotel to enter the guest's room merely because the guest, even though perhaps unconscious, does not open the door and let the hotel in. Otherwise stated, the great and obvious dangers involved give rise to a privilege to violate the right of privacy which would otherwise be respected.

(*g*) *Manner of exercising privilege to enter rooms.* When the hotel enters under the authority of an exception, it must still do so in a manner which is reasonable under the circumstances; namely, what is reasonable in the light of the time, the purpose of the entrance, and the consequences of delay. For example, a plumber making a routine check of all water fixtures should limit himself to the ordinary day hours, and should speak to the guest by phone or at the guest's door before entering, and should come back at a later hour if the guest is bathing at that time. In contrast, assume that a water main within the guest's room had burst or that clouds of smoke were billowing from the guest's room. The hotel would not be required to come back at a later time nor wait until it was able to obtain permission of the guest.

(*h*) *Protection of hotel from liability.* The hotel can protect itself from liability for violation of privacy in the various situations above listed by (1) appropriate regulations, and (2) appropriate clauses in leasing or rental agreements, if any.

(1) Regulations. As part of the general power of the hotel to regulate and manage the enterprise, the hotel can adopt a general regulation which informs the guests or other patrons that the management reserves the right to enter the premises with or without the consent of the patron when the representative of the hotel entering the premises, or directing another employee to do so, shall reasonably believe that such action is necessary for the protection of the patron or other patrons, the protection of the hotel property, or the prevention of crime. If proper notice is given of this regulation,[3] as by posting on the door of the guest's room, the hotel would undoubtedly be protected because the guest or patron by continuing to stay in the hotel without objection to the terms of the regulation would be deemed to have impliedly consented thereto.

As long as the hotel acted in a reasonable manner under the circumstances, it would be deemed within the scope of such implied consent and its entry would be lawful on the basis of such consent, as contrasted with the privilege which the hotel would claim in the absence of consent.

(2) Lease term. If there is a renting agreement covering the accommodations furnished the guest, patron, or tenant, and so on, it should also contain a provision which in effect would declare what is included in the regulation above described.

§ 8:13. Public privilege.

(a) Generally. Opposed to the right of privacy is the privilege of newspapers, radio and similar media to publish and inform people about things which are in the public eye.

To the extent that a person is a public figure, he may be made the subject of news coverage or semi-fictional treatment. In this connection it is immaterial whether he has intentionally done the acts which made him newsworthy, as in the case of a writer, an explorer, or a candidate for office; or whether he is the victim of circumstances, as in the case of a person involved as a victim of a crime, or the relative of the victim or the criminal.

(b) Lapse of time. The lapse of time may affect the privilege of publicity so that a person who has reformed or who was the victim of a crime many years ago may not be brought again into the public limelight. However, the mere lapse of time does not necessarily close the doors on the past if there is still a genuine public interest to be served by calling attention

---

[3] See Chapter 19.

to the lesson which could have been learned from the past or re-informing the public of matters of which it has probably forgotten.

(*c*) *Liability of hotel.* The hotel owes to its guests a supervisory duty of protecting them from newspaper reporters and others seeking to violate their right of privacy. Hence, whenever a hotel employee assists a newspaper reporter in getting into the guest's room, and so forth, the hotel runs the risk that it is liable for such violation of the guest's right of privacy. The right of the hotel in this respect can rise no higher than the newspaper's reporter. Therefore, if the facts are such that the reporter is committing a violation of the right of privacy, the hotel which assisted in such violation may probably be liable also on the theory of vicarious or supervisory liability.

The circumstances, however, may be such that the hotel will not be liable on the ground that the employee who cooperated with the reporter was acting outside of the scope of his authority,[4] although it must be remembered that if the hotel had reason to know that the given employee might commit such acts, the hotel is liable by virtue of its supervisory liability, even though the employee was acting outside the scope of his employment at the time.[5]

§ 8:14. Private privilege of investigation.

When a person applies for a position of trust, whether in private employment or government service, he must be regarded as agreeing that such investigation shall be made of his private or public life as shall be relevant to his possession of the qualities required for such position. Hence the investigation made for that purpose cannot be deemed an invasion of his privacy.

Similarly, when a person is a party to a lawsuit or a claimant, there arises a right of those adverse to him to make any investigation within the general area of the issues involved or relating to matters affecting his credibility.

> *The facts:* The plaintiff was involved in an automobile accident. She made a claim against the other driver's insurer. The latter had a private detective make an activity check on the plaintiff. This involved following her during the day when she left the

---
[4] See §6:3.
[5] See §5:4.

Intentional Torts and Death Claims 115

house in her automobile, noting where she stopped, and taking some motion pictures of her. Several times, because of traffic conditions, the investigator came sufficiently close to the plaintiff that she became aware that she was being followed. She began to worry about such conduct, became very nervous, had frequent nightmares and hallucinations which required medical treatment. Her attorney asked the insurance company whether it was making a check on the plaintiff. The insurer denied that it was so doing. When the investigator was asked, he admitted that he was following the plaintiff, but stated it was for a legitimate purpose and that he was privileged against disclosing the identity of his client. The plaintiff then sued the detective for an injunction to stop making the surveillance and to recover money damages for the invasion of her privacy and the intentional infliction of emotional distress. Was she entitled to relief?

Decision: No. The detective may observe and photograph the plaintiff while in public and such acts were not invasions of her right of privacy, for at such time she had voluntarily submitted herself to public observation. Furthermore, it was proper for the detective to follow her, for when a person makes a claim against an insurer for personal injuries, the insurer has the privilege of observing the activities of the claimant, for the sound social purpose of detecting fabricated claims. The activity was therefore lawful, and the emotional distress caused the plaintiff had not been intentionally inflicted nor was it the result of conducting the investigation in an unreasonable way. Furthermore, the fact that the insurer had denied making any activity check or that the detective had refused to disclose the identity of his client did not prevent the detective from making a reasonable investigation in a reasonable manner. [Forster v. Manchester, 410 Pa 192, 189 A2d 147 (1963)].

D. Death claims

§ 8:15. Effect of death.

Under the common law, death terminated all claims and duties. Accordingly, if either the plaintiff or the defendant died, the cause of action ended or, as it was termed, abated. This was so even though the tort in question consisted of the very act which caused the death. The common law has in general been changed to provide for the continuation of tort rights and tort liabilities in spite of the death of the wrongdoer or the victim and to create a new cause of action or a new element of damages to cover the "death" aspect of the tort.

The statutes variously provide for an action for wrongful death, a surviving tort action, and a survival tort action. In some states, both wrongful death and surviving and survival statutes have been adopted. Such statutes create separate causes of action although frequently provision is made for the trial or prosecution of all claims in one action.

The facts: Two drivers were involved in an automobile collision. Both died from the injuries sustained. The administrator of the estate of one brought an action for wrongful death against the administratrix of the estate of the other driver. It was claimed that this action could not be brought because (1) there was no statute authorizing the survival of causes of action in favor of the personal representative and (2) the cause of action for wrongful death did not survive the death of the alleged wrongdoer. The only statute applicable declared that "all personal causes of action survive against the personal representative of the deceased tortfeasor." Were these defenses valid?

Decision: No. There was no question as to whether a cause of action survived to the plaintiff in the action for the wrongful death, for the reason that the cause of action for wrongful death is a new cause of action created by statute and is not a cause of action held by the decedent which survives his death and is not "inherited" by the wrongful death action plaintiff. With respect to the death of the tortfeasor, the action for wrongful death was a "personal cause of action" which by the express statement of the statute survived the death of the tortfeasor and subjected his estate to liability. The fact that the legislature said "all" and made no express exception barred any other conclusion. [Ivey v. Wiggins, 276 Ala 106, 159 So2d 618 (1964)].

§ 8:16. Wrongful death action.

(*a*) *Generally.* This action is brought to recover damages on behalf of persons, such as the members of the family of the decedent, who have sustained loss as the result of his death. This form of statute was adopted in England in 1846, where it was known as Lord Campbell's Act. This name has become descriptive of this type of statute and hence an American statute will frequently be referred to as a Lord Campbell's Act.

Generally, such statutes cover death by any tortious misconduct of the defendant, whether negligent or intentional, for which he would be liable if sued by the decedent had the injury not been fatal.

(*b*) *Nature of action.* The action is generally brought by the personal representative or a special fiduciary appointed for the purpose of bringing the suit. The damages recovered in such action are distributed to the beneficial class specified by the statute, either in general terms of persons sustaining a pecuniary loss by the death or in terms of relationship, as the spouse, children, and parents of the decedent. The recovery does not become part of the estate of the decedent and his creditors cannot share in it in any way.

The damages recoverable in such action are (1) the medical and hospitalization expenses of the decedent and funeral expenses, and (2) the present worth of the money loss which has been sustained by the survivors who have been deprived of receiving future expectable benefits from the decedent.

(c) *Defenses.* Whether by express provision of the death action statute or by judicial decision, no action may be brought for a wrongful death unless the decedent could have brought the action had he lived. The plaintiff is therefore subject to any defense which could have been raised against the decedent.

There is a conflict of authority whether the existence of a family immunity as between the decedent and the defendant bars a suit by the plaintiff in the death action. Complex variations arise in terms of the effect of the contributory negligence or other fault of a member of the beneficial class or his death prior to the commencement of an action.

§ 8:17. Surviving action.

Some statutes provide that an action commenced by the victim of the tort does not abate with his death. Instead, provision is made for its being continued after his death, as by the personal representative of his estate. The damages recovered are initially the same tort damages that the decedent could have recovered had he remained alive. In addition, since the extent of harm has been aggravated by the resulting death, the damages to be recovered are increased to that extent. Recovery in such action is for the benefit of the decedent's estate.

§ 8:18. Survival action.

A number of states have statutes which permit the personal representative to bring the same tort action which the decedent could have brought had he survived. This is in effect the counterpart of a surviving action which was brought by the injured person and then continued after his death by his personal representative, the cause of action surviving the death. Under the survival action statute, no action was brought by the injured person, but instead an original action is brought by the personal representative.

As the survival action is so related to the surviving action, the damages recovered are the same and the recovery is likewise part of the estate of the decedent.

As the survival action enforces the cause of action which the decedent had, it necessarily follows that any defense which could have been raised against him were he alive and suing for his injuries may also be raised against the plaintiff in the survival action.

Chapter 9. NEGLIGENCE

§ 9:1. The interest protected.
§ 9:2. Elements of negligence.
    (a) Generally.
    (b) Necessity of fault.
    (c) Effect of compliance with statute or ordinance.
§ 9:3. Duty owed to the plaintiff.
§ 9:4. The reasonable man as the test of negligence.
    (a) Generally.
    (b) The imaginary man.
    (c) Variable character of the standard.
    (d) Administrative difficulty.
§ 9:5. Degrees of care.
§ 9:6. The actor as one of the circumstances.
§ 9:7. Foreseeability.
    (a) Generally.
    (b) Exact harm.
    (c) Improbable possible harm.
§ 9:8. Action in an emergency.
§ 9:9. Omission to act.
    (a) Generally.
    (b) Duty to act.
        (1) Control over others.
    (c) Rescue and aid of others.
        (1) Relationship requiring aid.
        (2) Defendant causing need for aid.
        (3) Harmful aid.
§ 9:10. Community conduct.
§ 9:11. Violation of statute or ordinance.
    (a) Generally.
    (b) Declaration of pattern of reasonable care.
    (c) Contemplated harm.
    (d) Intention to benefit injured person.
    (e) Registration and license laws.

§ 9:12. Significance of violation of statute.
    (a) Generally.
    (b) Party involved.

§ 9:13. Proof of negligence.
    (a) Generally.
    (b) Presumptions.

§ 9:14. — Res ipsa loquitur.
    (a) Generally.
    (b) Defendant's possession.
    (c) Comparative knowledge of the parties.
    (d) Effect of res ipsa loquitur.

§ 9:1. The interest protected.

The law gives to everyone the right to be protected from harm caused by the negligence of others. Thus, if the negligence of the defendant causes the plaintiff to be physically injured, the plaintiff may recover for the injuries which he sustains from the defendant's acts. The same is true when the defendant's negligence has caused damage to the plaintiff's property. These are general principles applicable to all kinds of persons, whether or not a hotel, and to all kinds of harm, such as harm from fire resulting from the negligent manufacture of an electrical unit, harm from an explosion resulting from negligence in the supplying of gas, harm from poisoning arising through the negligence of the pharmacist in compounding a prescription, harm from the negligent operation of an automobile, and harm from the defective condition of the hotel premises.

In many instances harm caused by negligence involves an actual physical injury to person or property caused by an actual physical impact or contact. In other instances, such elements of physical harm or physical contact may be lacking and the legal consequences may be more difficult to determine.

§ 9:2. Elements of negligence.

(*a*) ***Generally.*** Liability for negligence arises when (1) the hotel, or any other defendant, violates a duty (2) of reasonable care (3) owed by him to the plaintiff (4) which causes (5) the plaintiff to sustain loss or damage. This means that the plaintiff must prove that the defendant (1) failed to exercise that degree of care which a reasonable man would exercise under the circumstances to avoid reasonably foreseeable harm, and (2) such failure to do so has been the proximate cause of the harm sus-

Negligence   **121**

tained by a person (3) to whom the defendant owed the duty of reasonable care. In short, the defendant has been careless in a way and to an extent condemned by the law and such carelessness has harmed the plaintiff.

(*b*) *Necessity of fault.* Conversely stated, the defendant, in the absence of some special element, is not liable for harm which he has inflicted if such harm is sustained in spite of the exercise of due care. That is, there is no liability when there is a true "accident," as that term is used in the law as meaning an occurrence for which no one is legally responsible because it could not have been avoided through the exercise of reasonable care.

The mere fact that a harm occurs or that the premises or conduct of the hotel are not accident-proof does not establish that the hotel was negligent.

> *The facts:* A customer fell in the defendant's store. The store employees testified that the place where the customer fell had been swept clean only shortly before, using a push broom made of an oil-treated cloth. A third person who happened to be in the store, as well as the employees, testified that there was nothing slippery on the floor. Was the plaintiff entitled to recover?
>
> *Decision:* No. The mere fact that a plaintiff was injured on the premises does not establish that there has been any negligence. Consequently, recovery is not allowed merely because harm has been sustained. [Miller v. F. W. Woolworth Company, 238 Ark 709, 384 SW2d 947 (1965)].

(*c*) *Effect of compliance with statute or ordinance.* The fact that the defendant has complied with all applicable statutes and ordinances does not determine that he has exercised due care. Such standards ordinarily only relate to specific matters, such as a minimum limitation that must be observed, and do not replace the duty to exercise due care. This means that in addition to observing statutes and ordinances, a person must also exercise reasonable care.

§ 9:3. Duty owed to the plaintiff.

There is no liability for conduct in the abstract as distinguished from conduct which is a breach of a duty to the plaintiff or injured person. Otherwise stated, in order for there to be liability for negligence, it is necessary that there be a duty which the defendant owed to the plaintiff and which he has violated by conduct unbecoming a reasonable man.

The duty owed to the plaintiff may be owed to him as an individual or a class, such as a class of pedestrians, purchasers, patrons, guests, and so forth.

Actually the concept of duty is little more than judicial doubletalk. It is merely a way of drawing a circle around the conduct of the defendant and saying that persons within that circle are protected from his conduct while persons beyond the area of that circle are not protected. Thus, the concept of "duty" performs the task of the elevatorman who determines when the elevator has enough passengers and shuts out the others. If the law believes it desirable that you recover damages it says that there is a duty owed to you; if it does not wish you to recover, it concludes that there is no duty owed to you.

> *The facts:* A pregnant mother was on the sidewalk. Her very infant child was in the street when a truck negligently came down upon him. She attempted to warn the driver and the child but was helpless. The shock caused her to suffer actual physical and mental harm. She sued the driver for the harm to herself and the infant child. Was the defendant liable for the harm she sustained as a result of the shock?
>
> *Decision:* Judgment for the plaintiff. His negligent conduct had breached a duty of care owed to the mother. [Dillon v Legg, 68 Cal2d 728, 69 Cal Rptr 72, 441 P2d 912 (1968), reversing Maya v Home Ice & Fuel Co., 59 Cal2d 295, 379 P2d 513 (1963) in which on identical facts, judgment was entered for the defendants on the ground that although the harm sustained by the mother was the result of the driver's negligence, there was no liability for her harm because the driver owed her no duty; the court stating that legal responsibility for one's act must stop at some point, otherwise liability would run into infinity. Hence, the only duty owed by the driver was to persons in the street; not to a person on the sidewalk who was not struck by the defendant driver, nor exposed by him to the peril of such striking, nor put in fear of personal injury to herself.]

§ 9:4. The reasonable man as the test of negligence.

(*a*) *Generally.* Liability for negligence is based upon the failure to use due care. This in turn is defined as that degree of care which a reasonable man would exercise under the circumstances to avoid harm which is reasonably foreseeable. This in turn calls for a consideration of a number of points.

(*b*) *The imaginary man.* The reasonable man whose behavior is made the standard is an imaginary man. In a given case which is tried before a jury, the reasonable man becomes the ideal man as he appears to the composite or combined minds of the twelve jurors.

This reasonable man is not any one of the jurors nor an average of what the jurors would do. The law is not concerned with what the jurors would do in a like situation, for it is possible that they may be more careful or less careful than the abstract reasonable man. Likewise it is not what is done in the community, for again, the community may live above or below the standard of the reasonable man.

Sometimes, in order to avoid confusion with a "perfect" man, reference is made to an "ordinary" reasonable and prudent man. And attention is directed that "in applying the universally accepted standard of care: that of the ordinary, reasonable and prudent man under the circumstances, the term 'ordinary' should be given its true meaning by not requiring the conduct of an extraordinarily careful person. Such an 'ordinary' man is not necessarily a supercautious individual devoid of human frailties and constantly preoccupied with the idea that danger may be lurking in every direction about him at any time. We appreciate that to require such constant apprehension of danger from every possible source would indeed be beyond normal conduct and would be too exacting a standard."[1]

(*c*) *Variable character of the standard.* By definition, the standard is a variable standard for it does not tell you specifically in any case what should have been done. This flexibility is confusing to the student, to the lawyer, to the hotel, and to everyone; in the sense that you never know the exact answer in any borderline case until after the lawsuit is over. From the standpoint of society, however, this very flexibility is desirable because it is obviously impossible to foresee every possible variation that might arise in the facts and even more impossible to keep such a code of conduct up-to-date. Imagine how different the reasonable man must act while driving today's automobile on today's superhighways than he did when he drove a model T more than a half century ago.

(*d*) *Administrative difficulty.* But these very elements of abstractness and flexibility that make the reasonable man concept desirable also create administrative difficulty. This is so

---

[1] Whitman v. W. T. Grant Co., 16 Utah2d 81, 395 P2d 918 (1964).

because it is obviously difficult for the twelve people in the jury or anyone else to think of a reasonable man's standard in the abstract as unrelated to what the jurors themselves personally do or know. There is a strong tendency for a juror to say: "The defendant acted like a reasonable man because he did just what I would do."

In addition to this problem of self-identification, there is the equally obvious probability that each juror will have his own belief as to what a reasonable man would do; still further: that every jury will have its own opinion on that matter. For example, if the question was whether the defendant drove negligently because he was driving at a high rate of speed, a jury composed of persons who are approximately 25 years of age would undoubtedly accept as reasonable a higher rate of speed than would a jury the average age of whose members was 60.

§ 9:5. Degrees of care.

In principle, there are no degrees of care. That is to say, the standard is always that care which a reasonable man would exercise under the circumstances. The law, however, is stated in many jurisdictions in terms of degrees of care, such as slight care, ordinary care, or utmost care; and conduct which falls below the required standard is variously described as slight negligence, negligence, and gross negligence; and even willful and wanton misconduct. For the most part, these differing labels are merely a matter of name calling for the purpose of emphasis. For example, it is obvious that a person carrying a bottle of nitroglycerin must take more precautions than a person carrying a shotgun and many more precautions than a person carrying a shovel on his shoulder. To emphasize these distinctions, it is often said that these three cases call for the exercise of the utmost care, ordinary care, and slight care. Actually, the heart of the matter is that each person must exercise that degree of care which a reasonable man would exercise under the circumstances of carrying an object which could easily cause death to many persons, an object which could cause serious injury or death to one or a few persons, and an object which might cause harm to only one person.

Contrary to what has just been said, in many states there are statutes which make distinctions in terms of degrees of care, as in the case of guest statutes, statutes relating to crimes as manslaughter by automobile, and comparative negligence statutes.

§ 9:6. The actor as one of the circumstances.

Individual peculiarities or limitations of the actor are ordinarily immaterial and do not require or permit any deviation from the standard of care which the reasonable man would observe. That is, if your reaction time is no longer as fast as it was you must allow yourself more time in which to react. Otherwise stated, this slower reaction time is one of the surrounding circumstances which the reasonable man in your place would bear in mind so as to prevent the realization of reasonably foreseeable harm. Otherwise stated, greater care must be taken to be "reasonable" because you are more accident prone because of your slower reaction time.

In a few instances, the law exempts certain classes of persons from adhering to the standard of a reasonable man. Thus children and aged persons are generally only required to exercise that degree of care which could be reasonably expected of persons of their age, intelligence, and experience.

§ 9:7. Foreseeability.

(*a*) *Generally.* The word "foreseeability" emphasizes that the standard applied in determining whether conduct is negligent is based on foresight — and not hindsight. Thus, whether a risk was involved and whether the risk was unreasonable are matters to be determined not in the light of the fact that harm was actually inflicted but in the light of what appeared before the harm was inflicted.

(*b*) *Exact harm.* It is immaterial that the exact harm was not foreseeable as long as harm of the general character sustained could have been reasonably foreseen.

> *The facts:* A guest was sitting on a wooden stool in the bathroom. Part of the ceiling fell on her head. In the excitement she jumped forward and severely injured her knee against the tub. Her head was not injured. When she sued the hotel, the defense was made that it was not liable for the injury to her knee because it could not be foreseen that a falling ceiling would result in a knee injury caused by striking a tub, rather than an injury to the head.
>
> *Decision:* The defense was not valid. If the hotel had been negligent in allowing the guest to occupy premises in which there was a wet ceiling it would be liable if the condition of the ceiling was such that it could be reasonably foreseen that the ceiling would fall. The fact that the exact pattern of harm or of

the conduct of a guest after being hit could not be foreseen did not relieve the hotel from liability. It was sufficient that a reasonable man could foresee that a guest might in fright react to the falling ceiling in such a way as might aggravate the harm. [Danner v. Arnsberg, 227 Or 420, 362 P2d 758 (1961)].

(c) *Improbable possible harm.* The fact that there is a mathematical possibility that harm may be sustained is not sufficient to impose liability. It must be shown that there is such a reasonable probability of harm that a reasonable man would take steps to guard against it; rather than ignore the peril as one too unlikely to guard against.

> *The facts:* The country club constructed a golf course on gently rolling ground. At various points it built open wooden weather shelters. These had gabled roofs which peaked approximately 10' from the ground. The plaintiff took shelter from a rain storm in the shelter near the 16th green. It was the highest point within a radius of 200' with the exception of the 16th green, some 87' away, which was 7 1/2' higher than the shelter. Lightning struck the shelter and injured the plaintiff who sued the country club on the ground that the club was negligent (1) in placing the shelter at a high point, which made it more likely that it would be struck by lightning, and (2) in failing to provide lightning protective equipment for the shelters. At the trial the evidence showed that lightning would be more likely to strike a higher point than a lower point, but that the probability of being struck by lightning when under the shelter was less than when standing out in the open.
>
> *Decision:* Judgment for country club. There was merely a bare possibility that lightning would ever strike this shelter. The danger was therefore so remote that no duty was imposed upon the country club to exercise any care to prevent the causing of harm by lightning. [Davis v. Country Club, 53 TennApp 130 381 SW2d 308 (1963)].

In appraising the harm potential of a situation, the proprietor of a public place such as a hotel has the right to assume that the guest will exercise ordinary care to protect himself from harm. If reasonable care on the part of the guest would avoid the harm, the realization or sustaining of harm ceases to be reasonably foreseeable. That is, the hotel will be acting as a reasonable man if it assumes that the mathematically-possible harm will not come to pass because it is foreseeable that the patron will so act as to avoid the harm.

Negligence

§ 9:8. Action in an emergency.

One of the circumstances which must be recognized in determining the reasonableness of the actor's conduct is the period of time in which he has to think, and act, and the peril which he believes to be involved. Hence, when he is required to act in an emergency, it is natural that the law does not require him to exercise the same degree of intelligent choice as when he has time to wait and consider the alternatives involved; provided of course that the emergency did not arise from his negligence or other fault. More simply stated, an actor is not negligent when he acts in the way in which a reasonable man might act when confronted with a similar emergency, even though the actor in fact did that which was not the best thing to do.

§ 9:9. Omission to act.

(a) *Generally.* In general, tort liability for negligence is predicated upon acting in a particular way which exposes others to an unreasonable risk. The difference between an act and an omission is not easy to determine in many instances. For example, assume the facts are such that the reasonable man at the intersection in question would reduce speed and would signal the making of a left-hand turn. Assume that the defendant does not reduce his speed and does not signal a turn. Has he been guilty of a negligent act or a negligent omission? From the one point of view, he is guilty of an act of commission — that of driving in a way in which a reasonable man would not have driven. At the same time, the wrongness of his conduct lies in his omission to do certain acts, namely, reduce speed and signal the turn. In short, many negligent acts are negligent because there are certain omissions. In view of the foregoing, the concept of an "omission" has value only when we consider the case in which the defendant did nothing at all and the claim is made that he should have done something.

(b) *Duty to act.* The term "omission" has no significance in the law unless there is a duty to act. Thus, a person is not liable for not having done something when he was under no duty to do it, even though it would have been lawful for him to act or he had a right to act.

(1) Control over others. Ordinarily there is no duty upon the defendant to control the conduct of third persons so they do not harm the plaintiff. As an exception to this statement there is liability for failure to control the conduct of others when the defendant stands in certain relationships to such other persons as would give him the right to control their conduct. For example, a hotel is liable for failure to take reasonable steps to maintain order on its premises and to prevent unlawful acts. Likewise, a parent who has knowledge that his child has a gun or other dangerous instrument and that the child is inclined to cause harm therewith is liable to the plaintiff who is injured by the child, when the parent fails to take steps to prevent the harm by taking the instrument from the child.

(c) **Rescue and aid of others.** The general rule is that there is no duty to aid or rescue another person and hence no tort liability for harm to him for failing to do so. Thus you may stand idly by and watch another person bleed to death or drown although with no risk to yourself you could have easily saved him.

(1) Relationship requiring aid. The harshness of this rule has been modified in certain areas where the parties in question are not strangers but stand in some relationship which the law deems sufficiently close to require the taking of active steps by the one to rescue the other. Thus, an employer owes a duty to rescue an employee who is injured in the course of his employment. Likewise, as discussed in § 2:5, a hotel must take reasonable steps to provide medical care for a stricken patron.

(2) Defendant causing need for aid. When the defendant has been responsible for bringing about the situation which imperils the plaintiff, there is to some extent a duty upon him to extend aid, particularly when he was at fault in so exposing the victim to harm. This in effect parallels the criminal liability imposed by the hit-and-run driver legislation.

(3) Harmful aid. Whether or not a duty initially exists to come to the aid of another, it is clear that once the defendant does come to the aid of the plaintiff he will be liable to the plaintiff if through his negligence he puts the plaintiff in a worse condition than that in which he found him, or causes the plaintiff to refrain from taking any steps for his protection by causing him to rely on the defendant's assistance.

The fact that the rescuer is liable if he negligently puts the victim in a worse condition than that in which he found him may open the door to fraud. That is, the victim of an unidentified wrongdoer, such as a hit-and-run driver, or of an uninsured motorist, may find it highly profitable to claim that his harm was the result of the maladministration of the doctor who stopped to rescue him. In order to prevent this kind of fraud a number of states have adopted "good Samaritan" statutes which bar recovery against the rescuer in the absence of proof of willful or wantonly-inflicted harm.

§ 9:10. Community conduct.

What is customarily done by people or what is done within a given industry or trade is not the test of whether conduct is reasonable. That is, if the conduct is unreasonable if done by one person, it does not become reasonable because everyone is guilty of the same careless conduct.

There is, however, a line of cases which regards the community or industry practice as significant. Of course, as a practical matter, it should be recognized that when the actor has acted the way in which everyone else acts, there is a fair chance the jury will jump to the conclusion that he has acted in a reasonable manner, rather than condemn everyone for being guilty of negligence. Moreover if the hotel acts in a way which has proven safe for the community at large there is ordinarily no reason to foresee that harm will result, and consequently to so act was not negligent.

§ 9:11. Violation of statute or ordinance.

(a) Generally. If the actor violates a statute or ordinance he is of course subject to whatever penalty is imposed for such violation. Assume that in the course of violating the statute or ordinance he harms another person. Does the fact that he was violating a statute give the injured person any greater right than if there had not been a violation? There is no clear answer to the question, which depends upon the nature of the conduct prohibited by the statute or ordinance, the class of persons whom the lawmaker intended to benefit thereby, and the particular rule of law followed by the given court.

(b) Declaration of pattern of reasonable care. The statute or ordinance may be so drafted as to make it clear that it declares that which is required of a reasonable man. In such cases there is no difficulty in concluding that a person

violating the statute or ordinance is guilty of negligence, since by definition he has failed to live up to the official standard of due care. Thus, the manufacturing and selling of gliders and glider parts which do not comply with the federal safety statutes is in itself negligence, as the violation of a statute designed to protect persons or property is a negligent act.

(c) *Contemplated harm.* In order to impose liability for a breach of a statute it is necessary that the harm which is sustained belong to the class which the lawmaker sought to eliminate by the adoption of the statute or ordinance. For example, a statute prohibiting the sale of fireworks is intended to protect from physical harm from explosion or fire and therefore the illegal vendor of fireworks is not liable when a child purchasing the fireworks becomes ill from eating them. Similarly, a requirement that railroad locomotives have spark arresters is designed to prevent fire and hence the railroad is not liable when a cinder blows into the plaintiff's eye from a locomotive which is not equipped with a spark arrester.

> *The facts:* A statute required that air vent shafts on hotel roofs have a parapet at least 30" high. The defendant hotel had ones only 27" high. The plaintiff was a guest of a registered guest of the hotel. She placed a mattress on top of parapet. When she sat on it the parapet collapsed and she fell into the shaft and was injured. She sued the hotel claiming that its breach of the statute as to the height of the parapets constituted negligence. Decide.
>
> *Decision:* Judgment for the hotel. The statute requiring parapets was designed to protect from the hazard of stumbling and falling into unguarded air shafts and not to provide safe seats. Moreover the fact that the parapet was only 27" high had nothing to do with the harm as it would have occurred equally under the facts if the parapet had been 30" high. [Nunnely v. Edgar Hotel, 36 Cal 2d 493, 225 P2d 497 (1951)].

Similarly the fact that the hotel has violated the ordinance requiring handrails on its stairs did not impose liability upon it when the plaintiff while walking down the stairs was struck by an unknown person who was falling down the stairs; for in such case the harm sustained by the plaintiff was clearly not the hazard which the lawmaker had in mind and against which it intended to guard when it adopted the ordinance.

(d) *Intention to benefit injured person.* When it is clear that the statute or ordinance was not intended to protect the

Negligence

injured person or the class to which he belongs, the violation of the statute or ordinance does not give the victim the right to sue, in the absence of conduct which would otherwise enable him to do so. So it has been held that an ordinance requiring property owners to remove snow and ice from sidewalks does not give a pedestrian injured by a sidewalk fall the right to sue the homeowner, but merely imposed a duty upon homeowners to assist the city in performing its general duty to the public to keep streets open. Similarly, the fact that a person violates a speed limit intended to conserve gasoline as a wartime measure does not thereby automatically make him liable as negligent to a person whom he injures while so doing.

> *The facts:* A club held a dance at the hotel. One of its members, the plaintiff, became visibly intoxicated. Without regard to his obvious condition the hotel continued to serve him drinks. At the end of the evening the hotel confined the plaintiff in the men's room to keep him out of trouble while the other guests were departing. He crawled through a window and out onto the adjoining roof. The roof was fenced but when he came to an opening in the fence he went out on an outer ledge and thereafter either fell or jumped down some 35' to the roof of a hotel kitchen and was injured. He claimed that the hotel was liable for the injuries he sustained because it had violated the statute making it unlawful "to sell, furnish or give any liquor ... to any person visibly intoxicated," and that its selling of the liquor to the plaintiff when he was so intoxicated was in itself negligence. The hotel defended on the ground that (1) the statute was designed to protect third persons from harm because of the intoxicated condition of the patron; (2) the plaintiff had been contributorily negligent in voluntarily becoming drunk; (3) the plaintiff was drunk before he entered the hotel; and (4) the furnishing of liquor to the plaintiff was not the proximate cause of the harm which was sustained.
>
> *Decision:* Judgment for plaintiff. The statute was aimed at guarding against the consequences of excessive drinking, thus protecting the person supplied the liquor from harm to himself as well as protecting others from harm caused by him. The fact that the plaintiff had voluntarily drunk the liquor did not constitute contributory negligence because the statute referred generally to furnishing drink to persons who were visibly intoxicated, without any qualification as to how they became that way. It was unimportant whether the plaintiff had become intoxicated before or after arriving at the hotel for the conduct prohibited by the statute was merely the furnishing of liquor to one who at the time of such furnishing was intoxicated, without reference to

when such intoxication arose. The harm which was sustained was not so unforeseeable in its sequence of events or so freakish that the furnishing of the liquor could not be regarded as a substantial cause of the plaintiff's harm. It was therefore a proximate cause of that harm even though the exact manner in which the harm would be sustained or the exact nature of the harm could not have been foreseen. The plaintiff was therefore entitled to recover damages without proof of negligence or fault beyond that of violating the statute. [Majors v. Brodhead Hotel, 416 Pa 265, 205 A2d 873 (1965)].

(*e*) *Registration and license laws.* The breach or violation of a law relating to the licensing or registration of automobiles or drivers does not constitute and is not evidence of negligence. This for the reason that such laws are intended to raise money for the state and not to protect persons. Furthermore, the fact that the vehicle is or is not registered or licensed has no effect on the way that it is operated. The same is true although the operator is unlicensed. Otherwise stated, the injury of the plaintiff is not the natural and probable consequence of the breach of the statute and therefore such breach is neither negligence nor evidence of negligence.

> *The facts:* The defendant, while driving an illegally registered automobile, ran into the plaintiff. It was claimed that the violation of the statute constituted negligence. Was this correct?
>
> *Decision:* No. Negligence does not exist in a vacuum, but only with respect to someone who is exposed to unreasonable risk by the negligent conduct. While the defendant was guilty of a crime toward the government in driving the automobile without proper registration, the fact had nothing to do with the occurrence of the accident, which would have happened under the circumstances even if the automobile had been properly registered. There was accordingly no rational causal relationship between the non-registration of the automobile and the plaintiff's harm, and it was therefore improper to consider the violation of the statute in connection with the question of liability for such harm. [Falvey v. Hamelburg, 347 Mass 430, 198 NE2d 400 (1964)].

§ 9:12. Significance of violation of statute.

(*a*) *Generally.* When the plaintiff is within the class which the statute or ordinance is designed to protect and sustains the type of harm contemplated by the statute, it is generally

Negligence

held that the fact of the violation constitutes negligence in itself, or negligence per se as it is called. In such case, the actor is deemed negligent in the absence of evidence establishing that he was justified or excused in his conduct.

In some states, the principle is not carried so far and the breach as above described is regarded merely as evidence of negligence. That is, it is one of the factors which the jury is to consider in determining whether there was negligence; as opposed to their being required to hold that it was negligence. Some of the states take a middle position and hold that the violation of the statute in such case gives rise to a rebuttable presumption of negligence, which means that in the absence of reasonable proof to the contrary, it is concluded that there was negligence.

(*b*) *Party involved.* In general terms, it is immaterial whether the statute or ordinance is violated by the defendant or the plaintiff. That is to say, the violation of the statute or ordinance generally has the same effect whether the conduct examined be that of the alleged negligence of the defendant or the alleged contributory negligence of the plaintiff.

§ 9:13. Proof of negligence.

(*a*) *Generally.* The fact that damage has been done or that there has been an accident does not prove or indicate that anyone has been negligent. Thus the fact that the plaintiff fell on the hotel steps does not prove that the hotel was negligent, even though the steps show some signs of wear. This principle applies regardless of whether the harm occurs within the "hotel" proper or in or about other facilities operated by the hotel, such as a swimming pool.

In general, anyone claiming that another person is negligent has the burden of proving that fact. This means that the plaintiff has the burden of proving that the defendant was negligent and that the defendant has the burden of proving that the plaintiff was contributorily negligent. As an exception to this statement, some states require the plaintiff to disprove any element of negligence on his part.

While the plaintiff ordinarily has the burden of proving what took place, the plaintiff is not required to produce evidence as to every detail for some matters can be inferred or deduced by the jury.

The facts: Husband and wife, aged 80 and 79, respectively, were guests in the hotel. The electrical wiring was defective and when a heater was plugged in, it short-circuited the system and blew the fuse, making the guests' room totally dark. The husband saw the wife standing just before the lights went out, heard a falling crash when the lights went off, and then heard his wife cry in pain, and groping toward her in the dark found her on the floor. Neither the husband nor anyone else saw the wife actually fall. The jury found that the wife had fallen because of the darkness and did not fall because of her age or physical condition. The hotel appealed.

Decision: Judgment for wife. The fact that there was no direct evidence of what happened did not prevent the jury from concluding, as it had done, that the harm was caused by a fall which was caused by the fault of the hotel in maintaining the defective wiring system. Moreover, the fact that the wife had not stood still in the dark did not make her contributorily negligent as a matter of law. [Mutterperl v. Lake Spofford Hotel, 106 NH 538, 216 A2d 35 (1966)].

(b) Presumptions. In the proof of his case, a party may be aided by various presumptions. For example, when a suit is brought for the wrongful death of another, there is a presumption that the decedent was exercising due care at the time he met his death. Or if goods are taken from a bailee there is a presumption that they were taken because of the bailee's fault. These are rebuttable presumptions in that the truth may be shown to be contrary to that which is presumed, but in the absence of such proof the presumption is final.

§ 9:14. — Res ipsa loquitur.

(a) Generally. Although the fact that there is a harmful occurrence or accident ordinarily does not prove that anyone is negligent, there are certain instances when the very nature of the occurrence so clearly suggests the fault of someone that it is proper to infer that there was negligence if there is no further proof. That is, the Latin phrase res ipsa loquitur tells us that in such case "the thing speaks for itself."

To illustrate, if a warehouse is in the exclusive possession of one enterprise and a large crate or barrel falls from a window on the top floor, the occurrence so strongly smacks of a fault of the warehouse that the law permits the jury to infer that the warehouse company was negligent from the very fact that the occurrence happened. In this illustration, it is to be noted that

Negligence

the very nature of the occurrence is such that it would not ordinarily happen except for the negligence of the warehouse as it had exclusive possession of the building and the negligence involved was necessarily that of the warehouse or its employees. Likewise, the facts involved are clearly outside of the control of the pedestrian who is injured on the street below; hence there is no possibility that he was contributorily negligent. This principle of allowing the thing to speak for itself has been applied in a variety of cases such as falling elevators, collapsing buildings, the explosion of boilers, and the escape of water, gas, and electricity.

(*b*) *Defendant's possession.* In many cases the defendant was in exclusive possession of the premises involved when the rule of res ipsa loquitur has been applied. In many jurisdictions it is held or regarded that the exclusive possession of the premises by the defendant is essential to the operation of the rule. To a limited degree, the limitation is logical in that it serves to identify the defendant as the one whose negligence caused harm to the plaintiff, as opposed to the negligence of a third party.

By the better view, however, possession of the premises is merely a particular application of and not an essential condition to the rule. Otherwise stated, the more modern jurisdictions regard it as sufficient that the facts indicate the existence of negligence on the part of the defendant, without regard to possession, or at least that it is sufficient that the defendant had possession of the premises at the time that he acted, as contrasted with the later time when the plaintiff sustained harm.

The facts: The decedent was a guest in a hotel owned by defendant no. 1 and leased by it to defendant no. 2. A fire of unknown origin began in the first floor, spread through the elevator shafts to the fourth floor. The door and window of the decedent's room were open, which created a draft and pulled the fumes from the fire into the decedent's room and asphyxiated her. No harm was done in other rooms on the floor in which the doors and windows were closed. Suit was brought because of the decedent's death against both defendants no. 1 and no. 2. It was claimed by the plaintiff that the fire was the result of their negligence in the absence of a satisfactory explanation to the contrary.

Decision: Judgment for both defendants. The plaintiff had sought to apply the concept of res ipsa loquitur so that the fact of the harm could be the basis for proof of fault. This principle could not apply as to defendant no. 1 because he, as landlord, had no control over the premises and therefore could not be deemed negligent for failing to take precautions. Moreover, even the mere fact of the occurrence of harm does not establish negligence under the rule of res ipsa loquitur; which rule merely allows the jury to infer that there was negligence, when from human experience or from the evidence in the case it appears that the occurrence is one which would not normally occur unless someone had been negligent. The fact that a fire occurred did not necessarily indicate negligence. [Snyder v. Hollingbery, 141 CalApp2d 520, 297 P2d 485 (1956)].

(*c*) *Comparative knowledge of the parties.* In many situations in which the principle of res ipsa loquitur is applied it appears to be the fact that the defendant has more knowledge of the cause of the harm or the better means of obtaining such knowledge. A few courts have apparently made the superior knowledge of the defendant or the lack of knowledge of the plaintiff a condition to the application of the principle of res ipsa loquitur. This is unsound, as the only condition is that the circumstances are such that they bespeak of negligence on the part of the defendant.

(*d*) *Effect of res ipsa loquitur.* The principle of res ipsa loquitur merely permits the jury to draw or make an inference of negligence from the circumstances. It does not require that they do so.

In a few states, the concept of res ipsa loquitur is held to be more than just a permissible inference and instead to amount to a presumption. This means that if the defendant does not come forward with evidence to overcome the presumption, the jury must conclude that he was negligent.

Chapter 10. CONTRIBUTORY NEGLIGENCE AND ASSUMPTION OF RISK

§ 10:1. Negligence of plaintiff.
    (a) Generally.
    (b) Proximate cause.
    (c) Concurrent cause relationship.
    (d) Volitional conduct distinguished.

§ 10:2. Contributory negligence of particular persons.
    (a) Guest's visitor.
    (b) Children.
        (1) Duty of care.

§ 10:3. Effect of contributory negligence.
    (a) Common law.
        (1) Last clear chance.
    (b) Comparative negligence.

§ 10:4. —Nature of defendant's conduct.
    (a) Generally.
        (1) Willful tort.
        (2) Greater negligence.
        (3) Absolute liability.
    (b) Breach of statute.

§ 10:5. Imputed contributory negligence.
    (a) Generally.
    (b) Family relationship.
        (1) Claim of party at fault.
        (2) Claim of innocent spouse or child.
        (3) Damage to property owned by husband and wife.
    (c) Bailments.

§ 10:6. Assumption of risk.
    (a) Nature as a defense.
    (b) Assumption of risk by conduct.
    (c) Knowledge of risk and its consequences.
    (d) Acceptance of least hazardous alternative.
    (e) Assumption of risk as contrary to public policy.
    (f) Relation to contributory negligence.

§ 10:7. Determination of contributory negligence.
    (a) Generally.
    (b) Particular applications.
        (1) Familiarity with premises.

§ 10:1. Negligence of plaintiff.

(*a*) *Generally.* A plaintiff is guilty of contributory negligence when he is negligent and such negligence is one of the causes of the harm he sustains. That is to say, it is not the negligence of the defendant alone which causes the plaintiff harm: his own negligence contributes thereto.

In general terms, the standard of conduct which the plaintiff must observe is the same as that which is imposed upon the defendant. This means that the plaintiff must exercise that care which a reasonable man would take to protect himself from harm from reasonably foreseeable risks or hazards.

> *The facts:* The guest wanted to remove a brief case from the right hand side of the front seat of his auto. To support himself he placed his left hand on the center door pillar of the right hand side of the car. The bellboy closed the rear door of the car without noticing the guest's hand. One of the guest's fingers was smashed by the closing door and was thereafter amputated. The guest sued the hotel.
>
> *Decision:* Judgment for the hotel. The guest had been negligent in placing his hand on the pillar for such pillars are not intended to be used as hand supports. His contributory negligence barred recovery. [Giles v. Pick Hotels Corp. (CA6th) 232 F2d 887 (1956)].

(*b*) *Proximate cause.* The concept of causal relationship discussed in Chapter 7 with respect to conduct of the defendant is likewise applicable in determining whether the plaintiff's conduct affects the defendant's liability. Thus it is held that the fact that a motel unit is rented for an immoral purpose has nothing to do with whether the patrons may recover from the motel operator for harm caused by a defective heater; since the immoral purpose of the patrons was not a cause of the harm sustained. That is to say, the circumstances which merely lead a hotel patron to be at the point where he sustains harm do not constitute a "cause" of the patron's harm.

(*c*) *Concurrent cause relationship.* When the doctrine of contributory negligence is applicable, both the plaintiff and the defendant are at fault and the fault of each has been a cause of the plaintiff's harm. If the defendant's fault was not a cause of the plaintiff's harm, we would not speak of contributory negligence. In such case, we would merely say that the defendant was not liable because his negligence had not in fact caused any harm, while the plaintiff's negligence had not "contributed" to his harm but was the sole cause of his harm.

(*d*) *Volitional conduct distinguished.* The mere fact that the guest's voluntary conduct is the initiating cause which starts the sequence of events causing harm does not bar recovery if the guest's conduct was not negligent. For example, where a guest was injured when she stood on top of or near a retaining wall of a lawn area, which wall thereupon collapsed, liability of the hotel based on its negligent care of the premises was not barred merely because the guest's act had caused the sequence of events to start; where the lawn area was intended for the use of the guests, as shown by the fact that the hotel had placed chairs on the lawn, the top of the retaining wall was level with the lawn, and there was nothing distinctive about the wall which would suggest to guests that they should not step on it. Under such circumstances the guest was not contributorily negligent and the harm sustained should have been reasonably foreseeable to the hotel.

Likewise the fact that it was the plaintiff's voluntary acts which put him at the particular place at the particular time where he sustained injury does not in itself establish contributory negligence.

> *The facts:* On New Year's Eve the plaintiff was at the defendant's tavern at 2:20 A. M. The celebration was in full swing. Two drunken celebrants weaved across the floor and began fighting. In the course of so doing they knocked the plaintiff from her chair. Ignoring this fact they continued their fighting; in the course of which the plaintiff was kicked and stepped on. She sued the tavern for failing to maintain proper supervision. The latter made the defense that the plaintiff was contributorily negligent in being present at that time and under the circumstances of the party. Was this defense valid?
>
> *Decision:* No. The mere fact that the plaintiff had gone into a crowded party where drinking obviously would be taking place did not constitute contributory negligence. There was no reason to foresee that a fist fight would start or that if it started it would not be stopped before any harm was done to innocent bystanders. [Miller v. Staton, 64 Wash2d 837, 394 P2d 799 (1964)].

§ 10:2. Contributory negligence of particular persons.

(*a*) *Guest's visitor.* While the rule of law is the same that the visitor of the guest is barred by the visitor's contributory negligence, there may be a difference in the fact situation; namely lack of familiarity with the premises. In the case of the guest who has been in the hotel for a sufficient period of time, there is the definite element that he has become aware of the dangerous condition which caused him harm or would have become aware of it had he exercised due care: the conclusion being that knowing of the peril or carelessly failing to learn of it, the guest has been contributorily negligent and this negligence bars his recovery.

In the case of the guest's visitor, there is more likelihood that the visitor either has never been on the premises before or has been there so few times that the visitor cannot be deemed to have learned of the condition which caused him harm nor be deemed negligent for failing to have done so. These conditions are factors which will impress the jury, although as above stated the general rule of law remains the same for both the hotel's guest and the guest's visitor.

(*b*) *Children.* In many states the age classification of the criminal law is followed by analogy and it is held that a child under the age of 7 is conclusively presumed to be incapable of contributory negligence; a child between 7 and 14 is presumed to be incapable of contributory negligence but evidence may be introduced to show that in fact the child had sufficient capacity; and after 14 the child has capacity to be contributorily negligent. The border years of 7 and 14 are not followed in all states, and there is a wide variety of the years which are observed.

The effect of the above triple classification, regardless of what years are the cut-off points, is that if the child is in the youngest age-bracket it is immaterial what he does, for in no case will the defendant be able to avoid liability on the ground that the child was contributorily negligent. In the middle age-bracket, the defendant must carry the burden of convincing the jury that the minor in fact had sufficient capacity to be negligent and therefore contributorily negligent. In the final age-bracket, the minor is treated as an adult and the burden is upon him to show that he lacked the capacity to be contributorily negligent.

Some jurisdictions treat the matter as a question of fact in all cases. Some hold that this test does not apply to a child of tender years, varying up to 3 to 7 years; the child below that age being deemed as a matter of law unable to be contributorily negligent.

(1) Duty of care. If the child has the capacity to be contributorily negligent, the question then arises whether the child exercised due care. The reasonable man test is not applied in the case of a child. Instead there is a flexible "reasonable child" rule. Specifically, it is held that a child is only required to exercise that degree of care which could reasonably be expected under the circumstances of the case from an ordinary child of like age, intelligence, and experience.

§ 10:3. Effect of contributory negligence.

(a) Common law. Apart from statute, the contributory negligence of the plaintiff may have either no effect at all or may bar him from recovering anything from the defendant hotel. With respect to the first alternative, the contributory negligence of the plaintiff is immaterial when the last clear chance doctrine is applicable or when the defendant's conduct represents such a greater wrong as in the case of an intentional tort, that it imposes liability upon him in spite of the plaintiff's negligence. As a variant of this category is the situation in which the plaintiff, because of his age or other incapacity is regarded as not capable of contributory negligence; in which case, conduct which would bar the ordinary plaintiff has no effect.

The second alternative, namely that contributory negligence bars any recovery, is the one that we most commonly associate with contributory negligence. By the common-law doctrine, any contributory negligence of the plaintiff totally bars his recovery regardless of how insignificant it might be; assuming of course that the defendant's conduct was not worse than negligent, and so on, as described in § 10:4.

In many instances, the harshness of the rule of the common law has undoubtedly been avoided by the jury by unofficially and illegally allowing the negligent plaintiff to recover because the jury felt that the defendant's negligence was so much greater. Undoubtedly, in some instances, the jury has allowed recovery and made a reduction or discount to offset the extent to which the plaintiff was negligent.

> *The facts:* An action was brought for the wrongful death of a driver, in a state following the common-law rule of contributory negligence. The jury agreed that each juror should write on a piece of paper his opinion of the degree or extent to which he thought the defendant had been at fault. The foreman of the jury was then to add these estimates and divide the total by twelve. If by the average the defendant was more than 50% responsible for the collision, it was agreed that a verdict should be returned in favor of the plaintiff; otherwise in favor of the defendant. The jury foreman determined by the above method that the defendant was 47% responsible and returned a verdict in favor of the defendant. A new trial was sought by the plaintiff. Should a new trial be granted?
>
> *Decision:* Yes. It is wrong for the jury to make a comparison of negligence in a common-law state in which the doctrine of comparative negligence is not recognized. It is also wrong for the jury to make its decision by chance or quotient, without regard to whether the question is one of liability or the amount of damages. [Clark v. Foster, 87 Idaho 134, 391 P2d 853 (1964)].

(1) Last clear chance. As a limitation to the above stated effect of contributory negligence, it is ordinarily held that although the plaintiff's negligence contributed to the harm sustained by him such contributory negligence has no effect if the defendant had the last clear chance to avoid the harm to which the plaintiff was exposed. The exact scope of the doctrine varies greatly from state to state and in some it is rejected by name although in substance it is recognized.

(b) Comparative negligence. In a number of states, statutes have been adopted which expressly authorize the jury to determine the relative extent of negligence of each party and to reduce the plaintiff's recovery proportionately to the extent of his negligence. In some instances, the statutes specify a percentage by which the plaintiff's recovery is to be reduced in the event of his contributory negligence. Some statutes apply to negligence cases generally and some only to particular kinds of cases.

There is of course difficulty in administering a comparative negligence statute although the difficulty is in many instances more imaginary than real for in many instances the jury, whether authorized by statute or not, will, as above described, make just such an apportionment.

§ 10:4. — Nature of defendant's conduct.

(a) Generally. Assuming that there is negligence of the plaintiff which contributes to the harm he sustains, a recovery may nevertheless be had in the following situations:

(1) Willful tort. When the defendant intends to harm the plaintiff, as in the case of an assault or battery, the plaintiff's contributory negligence cannot be raised as a defense by the defendant.

(2) Greater negligence. Where the distinction is recognized between ordinary negligence and gross negligence or reckless conduct, the fact that the plaintiff was negligent is immaterial where he was only guilty of ordinary negligence whereas the defendant was guilty of such greater degree of negligence.

(3) Absolute liability. When the liability of the defendant is absolute, so that it is immaterial whether he is at fault, it is generally held that there is liability even though the plaintiff has also contributed to his harm by his own negligence.

(b) Breach of statute. A plaintiff is not excused from the consequences of his contributory negligence by the fact that the defendant was guilty of a breach of a statute or ordinance. The law does not make any distinction between ordinary negligence and negligence which involves or consists of the breach of a statutory or ordinance duty. Hence, liability for negligence based on such a violation is barred by ordinary contributory negligence.

§ 10:5. Imputed contributory negligence.

(a) Generally. In some instances the law will carry over the fault of one person so as to bar another from recovering if the original party could not do so. This is described technically as imputing the contributory negligence of one person to another.

The instances in which such imputation is recognized are limited, and ordinarily one person is not bound or affected by the contributory negligence of another. With respect to hotels, the principle may be applied with respect to claims of members of a family group and in the loan or rental of hotel automobiles.

(b) *Family relationship.*

(1) Claim of party at fault. When a wife or child sustains a non-fatal injury, the husband or parents may have a cause of action against the wrongdoer for the loss sustained by them as actual payments, such as medical expenditures, and the value of future services and so forth. This claim is in addition to the claim of the wife or child who is the person actually injured. When the negligence of the husband or parents has contributed to the injury sustained by the wife or child, the husband or parents are barred by contributory negligence from recovery on the cause of action which they would otherwise possess.

(2) Claim of innocent spouse or child. The fact that the husband or parents were guilty of contributory negligence does not bar the innocent wife or child from recovery on the tort claim for the damages actually sustained. With the virtual disappearance of any concept that husband and wife are regarded as one, the fact that either husband or wife is negligent does not in itself bar the other from bringing suit for the injuries caused by the defendant's negligence.

The fact that a child may recover damages for the harm caused him does not enable his parents, who were guilty of contributory negligence, to share in the recovery and therefore benefit by their own wrong. Any money recovered on behalf of the child is ordinarily not paid into the pockets of its parents but is held as a trust fund for the benefit of the child.

(3) Damage to property owned by husband and wife. As an exception to the rule that the contributory negligence of one spouse does not affect the right of the other, it is held that it does have that effect when the recovery would be shared jointly by the spouses because it would constitute community property or represent damages for harm to property held as tenancy by the entireties.[1] For example, where husband and

---

[1] Reference is here made to two forms of co-ownership between spouses. Tenancy by the entireties is of common-law origin and is most common in the east and northern midwest. Community property is of Spanish origin and is more common in the southwest although statutes have extended it to other states. See, generally, Anderson and Kumpf, Business Law, (9th ed, South-Western Publishing Co., 1972) chapter 28.

wife owned an automobile as tenants by the entireties, and the automobile was damaged because of the negligence of the husband and another driver, the negligence of the husband bars the wife from recovering damages for such injury, since the husband would share in damages compensating for the harm to the property owned in that manner.

(*c*) ***Bailments.*** The mere fact that a bailee has possession of the bailor's goods does not require that the bailee's negligence be imputed to the bailor. Hence when the hotel loans or rents a car to a guest or patron, the hotel is not bound by his negligent operation which contributed to the harm caused the car, so as to bar the hotel from bringing suit against the wrongdoing third person for such damage.

In a number of states there are statutes which provide that a person lending or renting a car to another is liable for the acts of the person driving the automobile with his consent, without regard to any question of whether the permittee was an agent or employee. There is a conflict of authority whether the contributory negligence of such a permittee is imputed under such a statute to the bailor.

§ 10:6. Assumption of risk.

(*a*) ***Nature as a defense.*** The assertion that the plaintiff has assumed the risk is advanced as a defense to the claim of the plaintiff. In the absence of a statute abolishing the defense of assumption of risk, a plaintiff cannot recover if it is concluded that he assumed the risk the realization of which caused the harm of which he complains.[2]

(*b*) ***Assumption of risk by conduct.*** In most instances, the assumption of risk is predicated upon the fact that the plaintiff voluntarily entered into some relationship with the defendant and is deemed to have assumed as an incident thereto the risks attendant upon such relationship, such as the risks of employment, the risks of being a spectator at an automobile race track, and so on.

(*c*) ***Knowledge of risk and its consequences.*** In order to establish that there has been an assumption of risk, it is necessary to show that the plaintiff knew of the risk in question and of

---

[2] In many instances, assumption of risk is used to refer to contracts which limit the liability of one of the contracting parties.

the harm which could foreseeably flow therefrom. Conversely stated, if the trier of fact, ordinarily the jury, concludes that the plaintiff had no knowledge of the risk or that he had no knowledge of the possible consequences of a recognized risk, the defense of assumption of risk cannot be raised.

Whether or not the plaintiff had knowledge of the risk and of its significance is to be determined in the light of the knowledge of a reasonable person of the plaintiff's age, sex, and experience. Where matters of general knowledge are involved, the plaintiff cannot disclaim that he has the knowledge possessed by all reasonable persons, such as knowledge of the danger of open furnaces, unguarded elevator shafts, tall ladders, slippery surfaces, and so on. Similarly a person who has been employed at a given place or in a particular trade for a substantial length of time will be deemed to have knowledge of the risks involved therein and the possible consequences of such risks.

The net result of the foregoing is that it is only in the case of the unusual risk that the defendant must present actual proof of the plaintiff's knowledge of the risk and the possible consequences. With respect to the ordinary risks the plaintiff will be deemed to have such knowledge and the defendant may assume that he has.

(*d*) *Acceptance of least hazardous alternative.* The fact that the plaintiff has accepted one of two alternative courses of action does not mean that in the eyes of the law he has assumed the risk of the course followed, provided the alternative chosen presents the smaller risk or threat of loss. To illustrate, when there is an almost certainty that a person's goods will be destroyed by a fire negligently caused by the defendant and there appears to be only a small risk involved in attempting to rescue such goods, the plaintiff is not to be regarded as assuming the risk of a rescue because he makes the choice of what appears to be the lesser of two evils and attempts to rescue the goods.

(*e*) *Assumption of risk as contrary to public policy.* In some instances, the assumption of risk doctrine is not applied because it would defeat public policy. For example, when a statute requires that an employer or an owner of public buildings provide safety appliances, fire fighting equipment, and so on, the public policy underlying the statute is not to be defeated by allowing the application of the doctrine of assumption of risk. So it has been held that the fact that the employee or the member of the public continues to work or be present on the premises does not constitute an assumption of the risk involved in the violation of the statute.

(*f*) *Relation to contributory negligence.* The term "assumption of risk" is used loosely to describe a number of different situations. In some instances, it is used loosely as an equivalent of contributory negligence. For example, the plaintiff who walks carelessly into the street without looking for approaching traffic is sometimes said to assume the risk of such conduct. In many instances, this use of the term is not important for the result is the same whether the plaintiff be regarded as having been contributorily negligent or as having assumed a risk: namely, the plaintiff cannot recover in either case.

The difference between contributory negligence and assumption of risk is difficult to define in a way that is meaningful. It may be said that contributory negligence is following a line of conduct which a reasonable man would recognize as exposing the plaintiff to undue risks: whereas assumption of risk is following a line of conduct which exposes the plaintiff to a risk but which is not so undue as to amount to contributory negligence. This meaning may perhaps be better illustrated: a painter going up the side of a wall to paint the building is exposing himself to a certain degree of risk greater than that to which he would be subject if he remained on the ground. As he is knowingly exposing himself to such risk, he may be regarded as having assumed the risks involved. If, however, he goes up without having made any inspection of the scaffolding, although he knows that no one else has checked or inspected it, he would be guilty of contributory negligence in not taking the steps which a reasonable man would take to avoid the realization of risks which he could foresee.

§ 10:7. Determination of contributory negligence.

(*a*) *Generally.* Whether the plaintiff is guilty of contributory negligence presents a question of fact for determination by the jury when the facts are such that reasonable men could differ as to the conclusion to be drawn from them or when the facts themselves are in dispute. In the event that both the facts and the conclusions to be drawn from them are clear and reasonable men could not disagree thereon, the question of contributory negligence is determined by the judge as a question of law.

These are the same criteria which determine whether the jury or the judge determines the negligence of a defendant. These are also the same principles applicable to any issue involving negligence or contributory negligence and are not limited to cases involving hotels, and their guests or patrons.

(*b*) **Particular applications.** The fact that a guest taking a bath steps off of the bath mat in the center of the tub and slips when standing on the porcelain does not in itself constitute contributory negligence and the matter must be submitted to the jury for its decision. Similarly it has been held that the question of contributory negligence should go to the jury where the plaintiff did not notice the film of water left on the tile floor after a toilet had been repaired, because of which film he slipped and fell; where the plaintiff did not notice a 1 1/2" pipe running across the sidewalk which was of the same color as the sidewalk and over which the plaintiff fell; where the plaintiff entered a dimly-lit hall and did not perceive an object on the floor or a stairway, and fell; where the plaintiff who was a guest at a summer bungalow colony hotel caught his foot in a hole in the handball court and fell; and where a roomer sat on the banister of a second floor porch which broke causing him to fall to his death.

(1) Familiarity with premises. The contributory negligence of the plaintiff will often be established by proof that the patron was so familiar with the long-existing conditions of the premises that it was clear that the harm could not have been sustained by the patron without his being indifferent to the existence of the known danger and thus contributorily negligent.

> *The facts:* The plaintiff patronized the defendant's beer tavern and fell when her heel caught on the door threshhold, which was raised about 3/4" to 1" above the floor level. This occurred on the fourth time she had gone through the door that night, and the plaintiff had been at the tavern from two to five times a week for the preceding four to five years. The plaintiff sued the tavern for harm caused by improper construction.
>
> *Decision:* Judgment for tavern. The patron having crossed the same threshhold so many times necessarily must have known its construction and have been aware of any danger created thereby. The patron was therefore deemed to have failed to guard against a known danger by stepping over the threshhold. Assuming that the defendant was guilty of negligence in maintaining this construction, the plaintiff was barred by contributory negligence. [Wesson v. Gillespie, ... Tex ..., 382 SW2d 921 (1964)].

Familiarity with the premises is not an essential element of contributory negligence and the plaintiff is barred although he had never seen the place before, if the circumstances otherwise warrant the conclusion of contributory negligence. So it has been held that the plaintiff, though stopping at the motel for the first time, was barred from recovering when she fell when leaving the motel because she ignored the drop down to the level of the ground, where neither the lighting nor the color of the walk had changed since she had stepped from the walk to the door only 30 minutes before.

II. Particular Situations

Chapter 11. LIABILITY FOR CONDITION OF PREMISES

A. General principles

§ 11:1. Nature of liability.
   (a) Generally.
   (b) Absence of implied warranty.
      (1) Assurance of safety.
   (c) Relation to hotel season.
      (1) Assumption of risk.

§ 11:2. Invitees.
   (a) Generally.
   (b) Who are invitees.
      (1) Pecuniary benefit.
      (2) Assurance of safety.
   (c) Duty to invitees.
   (d) Knowledge of conditions and dangers.
      (1) Repairs and renovations.
         (i) Warning during repairs.
   (e) Duty to retire area from use.
   (f) Warning of danger.
      (1) Non-discoverable dangers.
      (2) Obvious danger.
   (g) Government employees as invitees.
      (1) Policemen and firemen.

§ 11:3. Licensees.
   (a) Generally.
   (b) Duty owed to licensees.
      (1) Discovery.
      (2) Avoid harm.
      (3) Warn.
         (i) Particular applications.

§ 11:4. Scope of invitation or license.
   (a) Area involved.
   (b) Purpose.
   (c) Status outside of scope of invitation or license.

§ 11:5. — Guest's visitor.
   (a) Generally.
   (b) Purpose.

§ 11:6.   Trespassers.
    (a) Generally.
    (b) Duty owed to trespasser.
        (1) Duty to warn.
        (2) Right to eject.

§ 11:7.   Stranger off of hotel premises.

§ 11:8.   Liability of hotel to children.
    (a) Children properly on premises.
    (b) Trespassing children.

§ 11:9.   Burden of proof.
    (a) Generally.
        (1) Preponderance of evidence.
    (b) Res ipsa loquitur.

B. Particular causes of injury

§ 11:10. Nature of defect or condition.
    (a) Generally.
    (b) Lease of hotel.

§ 11:11. Design or construction.
    (a) Generally.
    (b) Uncommon construction.
    (c) Construction protecting from acts of third persons.

§ 11:12. Floors.
    (a) Generally.
    (b) Floor of room.
    (c) Weather conditions.
    (d) Banquet accommodations.
    (e) Act of third persons.
    (f) Contributory negligence.

§ 11:13. Walks and walking areas.
    (a) Generally.
    (b) Foreign substances.
    (c) Weather conditions.
    (d) Informal traffic routes.
    (e) Contributory negligence.

§ 11:14. Doors and halls.
    (a) Generally.
    (b) Instructions of hotel.
    (c) Revolving doors.
        (1) Physical defects.
        (2) Conduct of others.

Liability for Condition of Premises   **155**

§ 11:15.   Stairs, ramps, and guardrails.
      (a) Generally.
      (b) Construction.
            (1) Guardrails and handrails.
            (2) Concealed stairs and steps.
      (c) Maintenance.
      (d) Stairs open for general use.
      (e) Contributory negligence.

§ 11:16.   Lighting of premises.
      (a) Generally.
      (b) Contributory negligence.
            (1) Absence of alternative route.
            (2) Instructions of hotel.
      (c) Guest turning on light.

§ 11:17.   Elevators.
      (a) Generally.
      (b) Maintenance by independent contractor.
      (c) Open elevator shaft.

§ 11:18.   Windows and screens.

§ 11:19.   Furniture.
      (a) Generally.
      (b) Hidden defects.
      (c) Res ipsa loquitur.
      (d) Contributory negligence.

§ 11:20.   Electrical and gas appliances and fixtures.

§ 11:21.   Plumbing fixtures.
      (a) Generally.
      (b) Bathtubs.
      (c) Contributory negligence.

§ 11:22.   Falling objects.
      (a) Generally.
      (b) Inspection of premises.
      (c) Time for repair.
      (d) Contributory negligence.
      (e) Res ipsa loquitur.

§ 11:23.   Fire.
      (a) Generally.
      (b) Fire safety statutes.
      (c) Persons benefited.
      (d) Escape harm.

§ 11:24. Contagion and disease.

§ 11:25. Rodents and vermin.
    (a) Rats and mice.
    (b) Insects.

A. General Principles

§ 11:1. Nature of liability.

(*a*) *Generally.* A person may be injured because he falls on a foreign substance on the hotel floor; because of a hole, crack, or other defect in the floor; because a stairway is defectively lighted; because the elevator door does not work properly; and so on. In determining whether the hotel is liable for the harm sustained because of the defect of the premises, the classification between guests and non-guests is ignored and distinctions are made in terms of invitees, licensees, and trespassers; and adjoining property users.

More simply stated, the rules governing the hotel's liability for injuries caused by the condition of the premises are the same as in the case of any other occupier of land. That is to say, a hotel is not a business which is distinct from all others; and with respect to liability for the condition of the premises, the liability of the hotel is substantially the same as other business proprietors to their business invitees and other persons on their premises. In short, no distinction exists between hotels and other public places in the matter of precautions to be taken for the protection of persons invited to enjoy the facilities furnished.

Furthermore, the liability of the hotel is not predicated upon a breach of contract but upon the breach of tort law which imposes upon any occupant of land certain duties with respect to third persons coming onto the premises. There are definite limits to this liability, as is the case with other occupiers of land, and the hotel is not an insurer of the safety of its guests or patrons.

The hotel must exercise reasonable care to keep the premises within its possession in a reasonably safe condition without regard to whether it is a hotel or a landlord with respect to the injured person. Likewise it is immaterial in this respect whether the injured person is a guest, tenant, lodger, or patron.

(*b*) *Absence of implied warranty.* The hotel does not make any implied warranty that its premises are safe for its guests;

for that would in effect make the hotel an insurer of the perfect condition of the premises. Hence, when the guest was injured because a bathtub collapsed when a leg of the tub had become loosened and fallen down, the guest could not recover by the mere proof of that fact but had to establish the negligence of the hotel — namely that it had not used due care to avoid reasonably foreseeable harm.

(1) Assurance of safety. In contrast with the foregoing, where the hotel expressly assures the patron that the premises or the articles of furniture in his room are safe, such statement constitutes a warranty that they are fit for their normal and intended use.

(*c*) **Relation to hotel season.** If the hotel holds itself out to serve the public, the degree of its liability is not altered by the fact that the hotel's regular season has not begun or is over. For example, it has been held that a motel was liable for failing to properly light a walkway although its season had not yet begun and although the injured guest and his family were the only guests then at the motel.

(1) Assumption of risk. When the hotel is in fact not yet ready for guests because the season has not yet opened or has closed, it may be well for the hotel to make it clear to the guest that in effect he is taking "pot luck" at the hotel because of that fact. If the guest is receiving a reduced rate, there is not too much difficulty in telling him about the actual conditions; although if there is no rate reduction he will not be too happy about not getting what he feels is his money's worth. If the hotel does, however, disclose the true situation to the guest and he voluntarily accepts the situation, he assumes the risk and the hotel will not be liable to the extent of the risks made known to him.

§ 11:2. Invitees.

(*a*) **Generally.** The significance of being an invitee is that the hotel owes a greater duty of guarding the invitee against harm than it does the licensee or the trespasser, as will be discussed in this and in the sections which follow. Again this is not law which is peculiar to hotels but is part of the general body of tort law applicable to all occupiers of land.

(*b*) **Who are invitees.** Invitees include the guests and patrons of the hotel, that is, persons provided lodging; persons patronizing any of the services which the hotel may offer to the public; persons performing services, or delivering materials or goods to the hotel.

(1) Pecuniary benefit. In many instances a person is held to be an invitee because his presence on the premises will or may result in financial gain to the hotel.

> *The facts:* The plaintiff was shopping in the drugstore on the first floor of the hotel building. Access to the store existed both from the street and through the hotel lobby. The store rented its space from the hotel and paid a rental calculated as a percentage of all sales. The plaintiff left the store, went into the lobby, and sought to leave by the hotel door. The door was locked but this was not apparent nor did anything appear which would suggest that the door was locked. The plaintiff's hand slipped from the push plate on the door when it did not open and broke through the glass pane of the door, causing severe injury. The plaintiff sued claiming that the hotel had been negligent. The hotel defended on the ground that the plaintiff was merely a licensee to whom no duty was owed to make the premises safe.
>
> *Decision:* In view of the fact that the hotel benefited financially from purchases made at the store and that the store was designed to permit access for hotel guests, the plaintiff, in coming to the store and in leaving through the hotel lobby was an invitee and not a licensee. [Krensky v. Metropolitan Trust Co. 4 IllApp2d 14, 123 NE2d 345 (1954)].

(2) Assurance of safety. The majority of courts do not make pecuniary benefit to the hotel the test of whether there is an invitation. Instead the test is whether the entrant should regard the occupier as assuring him that the property is safe, in which case he is deemed an invitee. Accordingly, if the hotel would provide free facilities for a civic improvement meeting or a political rally, or for a free lecture or educational program, or a live broadcast, a person coming on the hotel premises to take part therein or to be part of the audience would be an invitee because such a person could reasonably expect that the premises would be safe for him and would not expose him to harm.

Persons coming on premises to use facilities have sometimes been held invitees on the theory that there was some advantage to the defendant, in terms of good will, in their coming on his premises. In addition, such classification could be sustained on the theory that the proprietor had assured them that the place would be safe for their use. Likewise a person attending as a guest at a party given by the hotel is a business invitee of the hotel for the purpose of determining the hotel's liability to him for harm arising from the condition of the premises.

The basis on which these distinctions are made is that in some situations a reasonable man would recognize that he is given merely the right to take the premises as he finds them, in which case he is a licensee; in other cases, the reasonable man would recognize and would expect that the premises have been made safe for him to use, in which case he is an invitee. This is a distinction which can be more readily felt or sensed than expressed in words, for it is obviously reasoning in a circle: whether greater precautions must be taken depends upon whether a person is an invitee; but whether he is an invitee depends upon whether it should be realized that greater precautions are to be taken. To some extent the confusing circle can be clarified by recognizing that a person is an invitee if his presence is encouraged or welcome as distinguished from being merely tolerated, as in the case of a licensee.

(c) *Duty to invitees.* With respect to invitees, the hotel must take reasonable steps to maintain its premises in good condition; must make reasonable inspection of the premises to disover defects; and must warn of any defects known to the hotel and proceed to repair or remedy them with due diligence. If it fails to make such inspection of its premises it is liable for injury caused by defects which a reasonable inspection would have disclosed.

> *The facts:* The plaintiff went to the hotel merely to have dinner. In the lobby she tripped over an electric cord which ran to a desk lamp. She claimed that the hotel was negligent in allowing the cord to run loose on the ground. The hotel denied that it was liable to her because she was not a guest.
>
> *Decision:* The plaintiff was an invitee since she was there for the purpose of having dinner in the hotel's restaurant. The hotel therefore owed to her the duty of any proprietor to its business invitees, namely, the duty to use due care in making the premises safe. If the location of the wire on the floor was negligent under the circumstances, the hotel was accordingly liable to the plaintiff. [Coston v. Skyland Hotel, Inc. 231 NC 546, 57 SE2d 793 (1950)].

The duty on the hotel of providing accommodations that are reasonably safe for use is a continuing duty and the hotel retains possession of the accommodations for this purpose even though the guest is in physical control of his rooms while he is a guest. The same is true whether the patron is a lodger or a boarder.[1]

There is however, no duty to make the premises 100% free from harm, nor is the hotel liable for unknown defects which could not be reasonably discovered; all of which follows from the fact that the standard required of the hotel is merely the observance of reasonable care.

(d) **Knowledge of conditions and dangers.** When it is sought to hold the hotel liable for some defect relating to the floor, stairs, and so forth, such as a physical defect therein, or the presence of some foreign substance thereon, or a slippery condition as a result of washing or waxing, it is necessary to show that the hotel or its authorized employee created the condition, or, if arising by the fact of a third person, that either (1) the hotel or its authorized employee knew thereof, or (2) the condition existed for such a length of time that it may be deemed that the hotel or its authorized employee must have known thereof, in which case the hotel is said to have constructive knowledge. Otherwise stated, liability depends upon the fact that the hotel either caused, or knew or should have known of the harmful condition and did nothing.

In the absence of such real or constructive knowledge of a condition caused by a third person, or an accident, there is no liability. Thus the hotel is not liable where the invitee slipped and fell on water on a lavatory floor, in the absence of any proof that the hotel knew of the condition or that the condition had existed for such a length of time that the hotel could be deemed charged with knowledge of the condition; for the mere existence of such condition at the time the plaintiff sustained harm does not establish knowledge thereof by the hotel.

(1) *Repairs and renovations.* Particular care should be exercised by the hotel when repairs or renovations are made so that there is a complete restoration or finishing of the premises and that no holes, slots, bolt heads, and so forth, be left from the earlier condition or the repair work. This is particularly so where the work is done by the hotel's own employees, for in such case the hotel has knowledge of the condition, through the knowledge of its employees, and therefore is clearly negligent if it permits the premises to remain in a condition which is dangerous.

---

[1] As to liability when a landlord-tenant relationship exists, see chapter 12.

Liability for Condition of Premises 161

(i) Warning during repairs. Reasonable care must be taken during the course of making repairs to warn of any continuing, non-obvious peril or to warn of the fact that the repairs have not been completed and the premises are not yet safe to use.

> *The facts:* A very elderly mother and her son were guests at the motel. For no apparent reason the toilet in their unit overflowed and the tile bathroom floor was covered with water. A maintenance man was called and promptly came. In the course of his repairing he talked to the mother. He then left without telling the mother that he was going out to get a mop and bucket to finish cleaning up. The mother went into the bathroom and slipped on the wet tile and was injured. The defendant claimed that the mother had walked into an obvious danger and that the court should hold as a matter of law that the motel was not liable.
>
> *Decision:* The question must go to the jury to determine whether there was a breach of duty by the motel and contributory negligence by the mother, for the failure of the maintenance man, when he left the room to get a mop and bucket, to warn that the danger still existed and that he had not finished could reasonably be regarded by a jury as being a breach of the motel's duty to give warning of the presence of a danger which might not be obvious, particularly since the departure of the maintenance man would suggest that everything was then safe. [Worth v. Reed, 79 Nev 351, 384 P2d 1017 (1963)].

(e) **Duty to retire area from use.** When the hotel discovers or learns of the existence of some defect or harmful condition which may foreseeably cause harm, it is under the duty to take action. Just what is to be done depends upon the immediacy of the foreseeable harm. If there is reason to foresee that there will be sufficient time to make repairs before any harm can occur, the premises involved may be allowed to remain in use. If, on the other hand, there is reason to believe that harm may be sustained before there would be time to make necessary repairs, the hotel is negligent if it fails to retire from use the portion of the premises involved, as by moving the tenant out of the room, roping off the area, and so forth. Accordingly, where there was the reasonable possibility that the ceiling might collapse as the result of water leakage before the ceiling could be repaired, the hotel was negligent where it did not rope off the area, if in a public part of the hotel, or remove the guest from the room in which the defective ceiling was located.

(*f*) **Warning of danger.** When the hotel has knowledge, actual or constructive, of a condition of danger of which the guest or patron is not likely to know, or to perceive, the hotel is liable to the guest or patron if it fails to give him warning of such condition or defect, in consequence of which the guest or patron is injured.

(1) Non-discoverable dangers. When the condition is one of which the hotel does not have knowledge and reasonable examination would not disclose the existence of the defect, it is not liable to the guest or patron who sustains harm in consequence thereof. For example, the hotel was not liable when a bench collapsed when the plaintiff stood upon it and the only explanation was merely that the bench had become weak with age but there was no visible sign or other indication which a reasonable examination would have shown that the bench was in any way defective or unsafe.

(2) Obvious danger. At the other end of the fact situation spectrum from the dangers which cannot be discovered by reasonable examination are those conditions which are obvious to anyone exercising reasonable care. In such case, the hotel is not liable to the guest or patron who is injured in failing to perceive the obvious danger and act accordingly. In such case, even if the hotel be deemed negligent, the plaintiff is barred from recovering because he had been contributorily negligent in walking into an obvious danger; or, by exposing himself to the obvious peril, had assumed the risk of harm arising therefrom.

Illustrative of the foregoing, it has been held that there is no requirement of posting signs warning that it is dangerous to jump off a wall of a patio pool into the adjoining ocean, where it is obvious that between waves there is hardly any water by the wall, and from the construction of the wall it is clear that the wall does not constitute a platform for diving into the ocean. Likewise there is no duty to warn a guest of the obvious fact that there is no bath mat in the tub and that the smooth, shiny tub may be slippery when wet.

As the duty to warn is predicated upon the premise that the hotel has superior knowledge, it is obvious that there is no obligation to warn of matters within the common knowledge of everyone, as that when it is raining heavily there may be water on the marble lobby floor and that wet marble may be slippery.

Liability for Condition of Premises 163

(g) ***Government employees as invitees.*** In many instances, public employees, inspectors, and officers are entitled by law to enter the premises and hotel building. In general, such persons have the status of invitees. The classification of government employees as invitees must be regarded as resting upon the fact that the hotel as a reasonable man must recognize that such employees are likely to come upon his premises and that in many instances they are required to do so.

As the corollary of the duty of the public employee to appear on the defendant's premises is the necessary duty of the defendant to receive the public employee in a manner which will not be harmful to him.

(1) Policemen and firemen. Policemen and firemen, at least when acting in an emergency, are generally deemed merely licensees to whom no special duty is owed. Some courts hold that when a fireman or policeman appears in the line of his official duty but not in an emergency situation, he is to be treated as a business invitee. Sometimes the necessity of classification is avoided on the ground that the hazard was one as to which the fireman had assumed the risk as an incident to his profession and that as the facts creating the hazard were obvious to him, no question could arise as to whether a warning had to be given to him.

> *The facts:* The defendant had gasoline storage tanks on its property. These had small safety or breather valves to permit the release of air pressure. They were not adequate to take care of the greater pressure which would arise in case of a fire. This was known to the defendant, together with the fact that in case of a fire, such pressure would cause the tank to explode. A fire broke out and because of the insufficient valves a tank blew up and rocketed out into the street where it killed a fireman. An action was brought for his death against the defendant on the ground that it maintained its premises in a dangerous condition, because of the insufficient valves, and had failed to warn the firemen of the peril. The defendant claimed that the firemen took the risk of explosion of gasoline tanks and that there was neither sufficient time to warn the firemen nor reason to foresee that the tank would fly out in the street if it exploded.
>
> *Decision:* The fact that a person is a fireman does not mean that he assumes the risk of every hazard. Where there is a hidden trap condition of which the owner has knowledge, the owner cannot avoid liability on the ground that the injured person was a

fireman. The fact that there was no opportunity to warn did not relieve the defendant of the liability which arose because of his maintenance of the premises in a negligent condition, but merely made it impossible to escape from liability for the consequences of such negligence. [Bartels v. Continental Oil Co . . . Mo . . . , 384 SW2d 667 (1964].

§ 11:3. Licensees.

(*a*) ***Generally.*** A licensee is a person who comes into the hotel with the latter's permission to do so and the license is granted solely for the accommodation of the licensee. For example, a person who comes into the hotel to get a drink of water or to use its toilets is a licensee. Similarly, a peddler newspaperboy, or veterans' poppy vendor whom the hotel permits or tolerates on the premises is a licensee.

Persons visiting the hotel, in the sense of visiting its officials or officers, as distingushed from persons visiting guests, are "licensees" even though they have been invited. Likewise, firemen and policemen are generally treated as licensees although other public officers are treated as invitees; as discussed in the preceding section.

(*b*) ***Duty owed to licensees.*** As the licensee receives all the benefit from his presence on the premises, the law requires only a minimum degree of care to be taken on his behalf and does not put the hotel to any inconvenience to make things safe for him.[1a]

(1) Discovery. If the licensee has a license to enter at different times or if several persons have been given a license, the hotel is under a duty to take reasonable steps to insure that it will discover the presence of the licensees in the hotel in order to avoid harm to them. For example, if the hotel has given a license to post lobby advertising, as listing the current movies or stage shows, the hotel must be alert to detect the presence of its licensees in time to avoid causing them harm. As a practical matter, this is not a particularly significant obligation because the hotel must observe all persons in its building by virtue of its supervisory liability.

(2) Avoid harm. Once the presence of a licensee becomes known to the hotel, it is required to refrain from any conduct which would expose the licensee to harm. There is however, no

---
[1a]See Supplement p. 473.

duty to take affirmative action to make the place safer than it was before.

(3) Warn. The hotel must warn a known licensee of any dangerous activity or condition of the property which is of such a nature that the licensee is not likely to be aware of it in the absence of a warning. This duty extends to all such activities or conditions without regard to whether they are engaged in or created by the hotel itself or by other third persons on the premises, and without regard to whether the dangers are the result of the natural condition of the land or of artificial conditions created by man.

The duty to warn only exists if the danger is known to the hotel. Otherwise stated, it is not required in the case of a licensee to make any investigation to learn of the existence of dangers which are not actually known to it. Conversely, there is no duty to inform the licensee of known conditions or hazards that are apparent and obvious to any reasonable man entering upon the premises.

(i) Particular applications. Illustrative of these principles, it has been held that a licensee cannot complain that he was not warned that all the rooms of the hotel were not on the same level; with the result that in going from a television viewing room to the movie room he fell in the dark because of the difference in such levels. Likewise, a shopper, stopping in the hotel lobby to rest, cannot hold the hotel liable when a dog suddenly ran into the lobby and bit her.

And as further illustration, where a hotel allowed a stranger to use a second floor balcony to watch a parade, the stranger was not a guest in the hotel but only a licensee, and when he was injured by the collapse of the balcony floor, the hotel was not liable to him as the hotel only owed him the duty of refraining from willfully causing him harm and was not under any duty to keep the premises in good condition and free from defects.

§ 11:4. Scope of invitation or license.

(a) Area involved. The invitee holds the status of such only with respect to the area to which the invitation extends and all stairs and ways necessary for the use of the covered area, and all facilities incidental to or provided for use in connection with the covered area. Hence a person entering the hotel proper and non-hotel facilities as a patron is an invitee not only with respect to the use of the particular premises but also with respect

to the door and stairs by which he enters and leaves. Elevators, escalators, telephone booths, and toilets provided for the convenience of the patrons are likewise within the area protected by the invitation.

A license likewise extends a right to use not only the exact area involving the exercise of the license but also such areas as are necessary or incidental for passage to and from the area of use.

(*b*) *Purpose.* Both the invitee and the licensee enter for a particular purpose which is approved by the hotel. It is assumed by the hotel that both will do the act or particular acts as to which their privilege extends and will not engage in any other act, and above all, will not engage in any illegal activity.

(*c*) *Status outside of scope of invitation or license.* If the invitee or licensee goes outside the scope of his invitation or license, he is ordinarily merely a trespasser for such time as he is outside of the physical area covered by the invitation or license. In some instances, the invitee is regarded as reduced to the status of a licensee, rather than that of a trespasser. Illustrative of the loss of preferred status, if either the invitee or the licensee goes into the private office of the hotel, or the engine room, or any other place which is closed to them, they are trespassers while they are in that area and have no greater duty owed to them while they are there, than the duty which is owed to a trespasser.

> *The facts:* A transient was assigned a cot in the Y.M.C.A. at 12:50 a. m. He was given permission to use the locker room shower. He was later found drowned in the swimming pool. The pool was lighted all night. The plaintiff sued the Y for the transient's death for failing to safeguard the transient.
>
> *Decision:* Judgment for Y.M.C.A. The proprietor of a lodging house or hotel is not required to anticipate that guests will go beyond the area in which they have a right to be. There was no reason to foresee that the guest, with permission only to take a shower, would go through the door into the swimming pool which was plainly lit through the night. Since there was no reason to foresee the presence of the guest outside the area of invitation, the defendant was not negligent in not safeguarding the transient outside of such area, or by failing to lock the door to the pool, failing to maintain a guard on the pool through the night, or failing to warn the transient of the pool. Moreover, as the pool was plainly visible, the decedent necessarily knew what he was entering. [Jefferson v. Young Men's Christian Association, 354 Pa 563, 47 A2d 653 (1946)].

The concept of scope of invitation applies not only to area of use but also to nature of use. For example, the hotel's obligation that a chair be reasonably safe as a chair does not include any undertaking that it be safe as a stepladder.

The conduct of the invitee or licensee beyond the scope of his invitation or license may be of such an extreme nature that the hotel will be justified not merely in requiring the invitee or licensee to return to the proper scope of the invitation or license, but may go further and revoke the license or invitation, and direct that the person leave the hotel, using such force as should be necessary in order to compel him to do so.

§ 11:5. — Guest's visitor.

(*a*) *Generally.* For obvious reasons, the scope of the invitation to the visitor of a guest of the hotel is co-extensive with the right to visit but does not carry with it the right to go into areas of the hotel beyond that needed to make the visit. The visitor has by the invitation the right to use only the lobby, elevators, stairways, and the hallway on the floor in which the guest has his room or apartment, and the area of the guest's room or apartment. If the visitor goes beyond this area he becomes a licensee and may be even merely a trespasser.

> *The facts:* A visitor went to see a guest in the hotel. Learning of the absence of the guest, the visitor stopped in the television viewing room and then the movie room of the hotel. In going from the one room to the other, she fell because of the difference in the level between the rooms. She claimed that as an invitee, the hotel owed her the duty to make the premises safe or to warn her of the danger of the different levels between the rooms.
>
> *Decision:* The visitor was not an invitee at the time. She had gone beyond the scope of her invitation and was merely a licensee, and as such, she was owed no duty except that of refraining from willfully causing her harm. [Steinberg v. Irwin Operating Co. (Fla) 90 So2d 460, 58 ALR2d 1198 (1956)].

(*b*) *Purpose.* The unlawful purpose of the visitor may likewise destroy the invitation so as to make the visitor merely a licensee or a trespasser. This doctrine is not always followed so that it has been held that the liability of the hotel for the death of the visitor resulting from the negligent maintenance of the hotel's elevator was not barred by the fact that at the time of the fatal injury the visitor was going to visit a prostitute who was a registered guest in the hotel.

§ 11:6. Trespassers.

(*a*) *Generally.* A person is a trespasser when he enters the hotel or any part thereof where he has no right to be. He may be a person who has no right to be anywhere in the hotel or one who has no right to be in the particular place in question. Moreover, he may be a person who had a right to be present, but that right has been terminated for one reason or another.

> *The facts:* The plaintiffs were not married. They registered at the defendant's lodging house as husband and wife. Early that evening a fire broke out. In escaping by way of a roof, the plaintiffs were injured. The defendant claimed that it was not liable because the plaintiffs were trespassers as the result of their falsely registering, in violation of a local statute, and because their object was illicit relations.
>
> *Decision:* The defendant was liable as he did not exercise the care required toward invitees. The fact that the plaintiffs falsely registered and presumably had an illegal purpose did not destroy their character as invitees to whom the defendant owed a duty of reasonable care. [Cramer v. Tarr, (DC) 165 FSupp 130 (1958)].

(*b*) *Duty owed to trespasser.* Subject to certain exceptions, the hotel owes to a trespasser only the duty of taking no steps to harm him once the hotel becomes aware of the presence of the trespasser.[1b] Thus the hotel is not required to make its land or buildings safe for trespassers nor to anticipate that trespassers might come onto their property and be harmed by its condition or by the use to which the hotel is putting it.

(1) Duty to warn. There is a conflict of authority whether the hotel, upon becoming aware of the presence of the trespasser, is under a duty to take affirmative action to warn the trespasser of any dangerous condition or dangerous activity.

(2) Right to eject. The fact that the hotel, when it becomes aware of the presence of a trespasser, must act in such a way that it does not expose him to harm does not mean that the trespasser cannot be ejected. In this connection, the defendant may use such force as is necessary under the circumstances to eject the trespasser, and is not liable to him, even though the trespasser is thereby harmed. Thus the hotel may inflict inten-

---

[1b]See Supplement p. 473.

tional harm in the course of and for the purpose of ejecting the trespasser, although in all other respects it must exercise due care to prevent harm to him.

§ 11:7. Stranger off of hotel premises.

The hotel as the occupier of land owes a general duty to so use its premises as to avoid reasonably foreseeable harm to third persons off of the premises. Thus the hotel must be managed in such a way that it does not constitute a nuisance with respect to neighboring properties. Similarly, the hotel must make periodic inspections of its building and of such additions and extensions as signs and television towers, to maintain such property in good condition. In contrast, if the hotel fails to do so, it is negligent and is liable for the harm caused a pedestrian when part of the building, or a sign, or a TV tower falls into the street and injures a passerby.

§ 11:8. Liability of hotel to children.

(*a*) *Children properly on premises.* The standard of care which the hotel owes to a child is the same as an adult; namely, reasonable care under the circumstances. Obviously, however, more things must be done to assure the safety of a small child than of a child in its teens, and again of an adult. At the same time, the hotel does not become responsible for the child guest as though it were a nurse or a babysitter.

> *The facts:* A mother and her child of three were guests at a hotel. The mother left her room for a few minutes. During this interval, the child leaned against the screen in the window. The screen had not been fastened and pushed out when leaned against by the child, causing the child to fall through the window. Suit was brought for the harm thus sustained by the child. The hotel claimed that it was not liable because the mother had not watched the child properly.
>
> *Decision:* Judgment against the hotel. A hotel should foresee the possibility that small children will lean against screens in windows. The hotel was therefore under a duty to use reasonable care that the screens were securely fastened or hooked so that they would not open when a small child merely leaned against them. By failing to fasten the screen in question, the hotel had violated this duty and was liable for the harm sustained. The mother was not negligent in leaving the child in the room nor in not checking whether the screen was fastened because she had the

right to assume that the screens in the windows would be fastened. [Crosswhite v. Shelby Operating Corp. 182 Va 713, 30 SE2d 673, 153 ALR 573 (1944)].

The hotel must remember that children will behave like children and that their search for games and adventure will lead them into hazards that would not exist for, and which would not be sought by, adults. The hotel accordingly must exercise due care to eliminate all "game traps" that the children may create for themselves.

> *The facts:* The hotel had a number of mattresses piled up near an open window in the hall. The plaintiff was aged seven and was the son of a guest in the hotel. Unknown to anyone, the plaintiff fell through the open window and was injured. The hotel claimed that because of the plaintiff's improper conduct, the plaintiff was merely a trespasser to whom the hotel owed only the duty of refraining from intentionally causing harm.
>
> *Decision:* The hotel, knowing that children were on its premises, must anticipate that certain situations would present an attraction to children and that they would not be able to appreciate the danger involved. That they voluntarily engage in such dangerous activity does not make them merely trespassers and the hotel remains under the duty owed to guests of exercising due care to protect such children from harm. [Roberts v. Del Monte Properties Co. 111 CalApp2d 69, 243 P2d 914 (1952)].

(b) *Trespassing children.* Contrary to the rule that the hotel is not required to anticipate the trespassing of others,[2] it is generally held under one form of terminology or another that under certain circumstances the hotel should foresee that certain things or conditions on its land, such as a swimming pool or an amusement device, will attract trespassing children onto the hotel property. When such is the case, it is generally held that the hotel must take reasonable precautions to protect the children from harm. This doctrine was in many states originally called the "attractive nuisance" theory, on the basis of the analysis that the children are attracted to the land by what is to them an attraction, but which is in fact a nuisance in the sense of being a hazard to them.

In general terms, the trespassing child rule applies only where the possessor of the land knows or has reason to know that children will trespass thereon; that they will encounter condi-

---

[2] See § 11:6.

tions which are likely to harm them, which potential for harm will not be recognized by them because of their youth; and the utility of keeping things in their hazardous condition is greater than the disutility of taking steps to prevent the sustaining of harm by the trespassing children. In any case, the decision of the court involves the balancing of the two considerations of protection of children and protection of the freedom of the hotel to use its property as it chooses. These standards are manifestly not precise and the decisions have wavered greatly in trying to reach a practical and desirable compromise between the conflicting objectives involved.

§ 11:9. Burden of proof.

(*a*) *Generally.* The guest, patron, or other party plaintiff, has the burden of proving that he has sustained harm because of the negligence of the hotel, that is, the latter failed to exercise due care, and that such a breach of duty by the hotel was the proximate cause of the harm sustained by the plaintiff. Accordingly, when it is claimed that the hotel is liable because it had knowledge of the condition of the premises, the burden is on the plaintiff to show that the defendant hotel had knowledge of the condition.

(1) Preponderance of evidence. The plaintiff must persuade the jury by a preponderance of the evidence that the harm was caused by the hotel's negligence. Accordingly, where it was merely a guess whether the guest may have fallen out of the hotel because of a defective condition of the window, or because he was intoxicated or leaned too far out, the burden of proof has not been met and there can be no recovery.

(*b*) *Res ipsa loquitur.* In some instances the plaintiff is aided in carrying his burden of proof by the application of the rule of res ipsa loquitur[3]. This principle has been held applicable where a guest was injured by the rush of boiling water and steam from a shower or was harmed by the escape of illuminating gas while the guest was asleep; although there is some contrary authority as to the shower case.

The principle, however, has no application when the fault which is the cause of the harm may with equal logic be blamed to the act of a third person or to another guest and could have

---

[3] See § 9:14.

occurred regardless of how much care had been exercised by the hotel. For example, the principle is not applicable when a guest was injured because he fell on a drinking glass which was on the stairs, for the glass could have been negligently left there by a fellow guest or a child a minute before, and under circumstances where the hotel obviously was not negligent.

Res ipsa loquitur likewise is not applicable to breaking furniture. Hence it does not apply when a bathtub collapsed when used because a leg of the tub had become loosened and had fallen. The rule of res ipsa loquitur is not applicable when a step collapses from dry rot and the motel company is not liable where reasonable inspection had been made of the premises.

B. Particular causes of injury

§ 11:10. Nature of defect or condition.

(*a*) *Generally.* Ordinarily it is not of particular significance whether the defect or condition causing harm is the result of defective construction of the hotel or poor management.

(*b*) *Lease of hotel.* When the hotel property is leased by its owner to the operating hotel company, it becomes necessary to distinguish between structural and operational defects. In harmony with general principles relating to landlord and tenant, it is held that the fact that a lessee operates the hotel does not shield the owner of the hotel building from liability arising from structural defects of which the owner had or should have had knowledge.

> *The facts:* Defendant no. 1 purchased a building which was being used by defendant no. 2 as a hotel. Defendant no. 1 leased the hotel building to defendant no. 2. There was a fire in the hotel in which the guest died. The plaintiff sued both defendants for damages for the death, claiming negligence of the defendants through (1) failing to provide outside fire escapes, closed stairways, sprinkler systems, and fire alarms, and in (2) failing to provide sufficient watchmen, or (3) to give an alarm when the fire was discovered, and (4) in permitting combustible materials to accumulate in the halls. The defendants denied liability.
>
> *Decision:* Defendant no. 1 knew or had the opportunity to know when she purchased the hotel that it had the structural defects described under (1) in the preceding paragraph. Defendant no. 1 also knew that the building was used as a hotel for a large num-

ber of persons and benefited financially by its being so used, as this was the source for the rents paid to defendant no. 1. Under these circumstances, the duty rested upon defendant no. 1 to take reasonable steps to make the premises physically safe for the tenants. Having failed to do so, it would be liable for the death of a guest caused by such structural defects, even though operational negligence by defendant no. 2 also contributed thereto. Only defendant no. 2 was liable on the basis of (2), (3), and (4), since such acts related to the operation of the hotel, in which operation defendant no. 1 took no part. [Irwin v. Torbert, 204 Ga 111, 49 SE2d 70 (1948)].

§ 11:11. Design or construction.

(*a*) *Generally.* In the absence of a building code, zoning restriction, or other similar provision, there is no limitation upon the type of construction which the hotel may build nor its design nor materials. Although not controlling, the fact that the design of the defendant's hotel or the material used was common within the hotel industry is admissible to show the hotel was not negligent in having that type of construction or using that kind of material. For example, it is held that the use of terrazo for a walk is not in itself negligence when measured by the general standard of building construction practiced in the area. Similarly, the use of marble in stairs cannot be deemed negligent for such material is commonly used for such purpose. And this is nonetheless so even though marble and terrazo when wet will be slippery.

The community use of a particular design or substance is relevant in determining the foreseeability of harm. Thus it has been pointed out frequently that thousands of persons must have walked on the same material without anyone ever being hurt. With this community experience in mind, it can be recognized that the hotel in using the material which has proven safe in so many instances has no reason to foresee that harm will befall anyone and therefore is not negligent in making use thereof.

(*b*) *Uncommon construction.* The fact that the design or construction of the hotel is not customary or standard does not by itself establish negligence. There must be proof that a reasonable man would foresee that the design was such as to expose patrons of the hotel to an unreasonable risk of harm. The mere fact that the mathematical probability of possible harm is increased is not sufficient. For example, it is not negligent to have a split level cocktail lounge or a difference in level between two adjoining rooms open to the public. While the fact that the floor is not at the same level throughout does introduce the possibility that someone might fall down the step or steps between the two levels, it is not probable that such will occur without the negligence of the falling patron. Hence the reasonable man and the law both conclude that the presence of steps does not create a reasonable probability of harm and therefore harm is not "foreseeable."

(*c*) *Construction protecting from acts of third persons.* The fact that the hotel might have been so constructed as to afford greater protection from assault by third persons does not establish that the hotel was negligent in not being so designed. Thus it has been held that it is not negligent for a motel to have the doors of the rooms open on a courtyard or in failing to have the motel enclosed, as against the argument that the guest's assailant was enabled to enter her room because of such construction and the absence of an enclosing fence.

§ 11:12. Floors.

(*a*) *Generally.* The hotel stands in the same position as any other proprietor or occupant of property with respect to the duty owed to persons invited on the premises. Thus the hotel must exercise reasonable care to keep its floors free from defects, foreign objects, or harmful substances used in washing, cleaning, or construction. If for any reason the floor is not free from such conditions, the hotel must exercise reasonable care to inform or warn its invitees of the condition in question, unless it is so obvious that the hotel may assume that the invitee as a reasonable man will perceive the condition himself.

But to establish liability, negligence of the hotel must be shown and the mere fact that there was a foreign substance on the floor and that the plaintiff fell because of it, does not impose liability on the hotel. Moreover, no liability arises for a fall because of a foreign substance on the floor unless the presence of this substance was the act of the hotel or its employee or had been there so long that it could be reasonably concluded that the hotel knew of its presence. For example, the mere fact that the toilet in a common lavatory was running over and there was water over the floor does not in itself establish that the hotel or its employees had knowledge of that condition.

(*b*) *Floor of room.* Because of the duty to clean a room for an incoming guest, the duty to provide a safe floor is perhaps

Liability for Condition of Premises 175

greater in the case of the incoming patron than of a person moving at large through the hotel. So it has been held that the incoming guest could recover from the hotel when she stepped on a needle in the floor of her room, where the floor had not been cleaned properly, of which fact the guest had complained to the hotel and it further appeared that the floor was generally unclean.

(c) *Weather conditions.* When the weather has produced the hazard which causes harm, the question of liability turns upon whether the hotel exercised reasonable care in maintaining the premises in a safe condition in spite of the weather. If it failed to exercise such care to prevent the entry of the elements, such as the entry of water upon the floor, it is liable for harm sustained as the result of such negligence. But the hotel is not required to mop the floor continually to make it as safe as possible nor is it an insurer that no harm will result because of the weather-caused condition.

> *The facts:* The foyer of a cocktail lounge was slightly over 4 feet wide and led from the outside door. The latter did not close tightly so that rain water seeped in and lay on the floor. There was no outside canopy to reduce the hazard of incoming rain water. The floor of the foyer was 100% vinyl. On the day in question it had been raining and at the time in question it was still raining slightly. Water lay on the foyer floor but could not be seen easily because of the dim light. No porter was on duty that day although ordinarily one was present.
>
> The plaintiff entered the lounge, did not perceive the water and slipped and fell. She sued the insurance company of the lounge. The defendant denied liability on the ground that the cocktail lounge did not guarantee that no one would be hurt on the premises. At the trial, it was testified to by witnesses that pure vinyl was slippery when wet and that it could not be manufactured to include a non-slip aggregate. The floor was waxed with a non-slip wax although it would have been inexpensive to place a mat of rubber or similar material in the foyer to prevent slipping.
>
> *Decision:* Judgment for plaintiff. By allowing the rain water to enter and stand on the dimly lit, pure vinyl floor, the cocktail lounge created a trap and hence was liable when a customer fell because of the slippery condition of the floor. [Hesse v. Marquette Casualty Co. ... LaApp ..., 170 So2d 173 (1965)].

(d) *Banquet accommodations.* The fact that banquet accommodations may require the placing of objects or platforms with respect to which the guests must step around or step down does not constitute negligence when the condition so created is perfectly obvious to anyone exercising reasonable prudence.

> *The facts:* A speaker's platform was placed at one end of the hotel's banquet hall. It was approximately 10 inches high and was pushed up close to the wall but stood away some 14 inches because radiators and five or six pilasters projected into the room. The plaintiff was attending the banquet to accompany her husband who was the master of ceremonies. The plaintiff, in walking on the speaker's platform slipped off the back edge of the platform and into the space between it and the wall. Near where she fell there was a small serving tray standing on the floor in the open space between the platform and the wall. The plaintiff claimed that the hotel was liable because it was negligent in creating a step-down and failing, by use of contrasting colors or in some other way, to warn or mark the open space between the platform and the wall.
>
> *Decision:* The hotel was not negligent in providing a platform which necessarily was above the level of the floor and required a step-down. There was no need to give any warning of the open space situation by contrasting colors or in any other way, because it was obvious and the presence of the tray standing in the open space was a further indication to everyone of the presence of the space. [Jones v. Pinehurst, Inc., 261 NC 575, 135 SE2d 580 (1964)].

(*e*) **Act of third persons.** It is immaterial whether the condition of the premises is the consequence of the act of third persons. That fact does not relieve the hotel from liability on the theory that another or intervening cause is the cause of the plaintiff's harm.

For example, where the hotel knew that the workmen of a contractor working on the front of the hotel were tracking old mortar through the hotel cafeteria, the hotel owed patrons of the cafeteria the duty of taking greater precautions against the presence of foreign substances, namely, the old mortar, on the cafeteria floor.

(*f*) **Contributory negligence.** Liability for defects in or the condition of floors is denied when the guest in the exercise of reasonable care could have perceived that there was a hazard against which reasonable care should have been taken by the guest. Thus a guest can not recover from a hotel when he slips and falls on grease on a bathroom floor where the presence of the grease was obvious and the eyesight of the guest was normal.

Similarly, a person coming into a hotel in the early morning and seeing the floor being washed with a washing compound, must recognize the fact that the wet marble floor will be slippery, and must act accordingly, and is therefore barred when she falls because of her failing to do so.

In some cases it will be obvious that the guest has been contributorily negligent. In other cases, the court cannot determine the question as a matter of law but must submit it to a jury to evaluate under all the circumstances. For example, where a film of water was left on the tiled floor of a motel bathroom after the toilet had been repaired by a plumber, and the plaintiff entering the bathroom fell thereon and was injured, it is a question for the jury to determine whether the guest had been contributorily negligent; this for the reason that a film of water on a tiled floor is not particularly visible.

§ 11:13. Walks and walking areas.

(*a*) *Generally.* The responsibility of the hotel for walks and walking areas outside of the hotel building itself is in general the same as that of the hotel with respect to floors within the building. As a practical matter, however, there is the greater likelihood that acts of third persons or the operation of the weather may enter into the problem and produce a different result, although not changing the legal principles themselves.

(*b*) *Foreign substances.* The liability for foreign substances on walks and walking areas is the same as with respect to floors of the hotel building.

> *The facts:* The hotel did not have lodging accommodations for two guests. It was arranged that the guests should room at another building operated by the hotel and should eat at the hotel. The hotel automobile furnished free transporation between the two buildings. One guest alighted from this automobile in front of the hotel. He slipped and fell on grease in the driveway and was injured. He sued the hotel.
>
> *Decision:* Judgment for the hotel. The mere presence of grease does not establish liability, because the hotel had only the duty of using reasonable care to make the premises safe for its guests, as they were merely invitees. The fact that the grease was on the driveway did not permit the application of res ipsa loquitur since the event was not of such a nature that it would ordinarily happen only if someone were negligent. Therefore the plaintiff was required to prove negligence in either the placing of

the grease on the driveway by the hotel or its employees, or in the fact that the grease had been there for such a long time that the hotel must be deemed to have known of its presence and to have been negligent in allowing it to remain. As there was no evidence as to negligence of the hotel nor the time when the grease had been placed on the driveway, the hotel was not liable. [Goldman v. Hollywood Beach Hotel Co. (CA5th) 244 F2d 413 (1957)].

(*c*) *Weather conditions.* A hotel must exercise reasonable care to maintain its outside walks and walking areas safe for use in spite of weather conditions. Hence a winter resort hotel is liable where it permits snow and ice to accumulate on a walk leading from the public walk to the hotel, for as to the ordinary hotel area the resort has the same duty to keep the premises safe as any other hotel. There is no such duty of course with respect to the area actually used for ski runs or the approaches to the ski slopes because it would be obviously impossible to maintain them at all times in a safe condition, and persons entering such areas assume the risk that they might slip and fall as the result of ice or snow.

The hotel is only required to exercise reasonable care in keeping walking areas free from snow and ice. While the snow is continuing it is obvious that reasonable latitude must be allowed the hotel for the law does not impose the absurd requirement that the hotel constantly be sweeping and mopping while it continues to snow. Once the snow definitely is over, however, the standard of care requires that reasonable steps be taken to make the premises safe for patrons.

> *The facts:* Snow was falling throughout the morning. The motel owner swept the snow away from in front of the office two times before 8 A.M. The snow continued. About an hour later, the plaintiff left her room and went to the motel office for travel information. She fell on level snow in front of the office, which snow was between 1/4 inch and 1 inch deep. She sued the motel.
>
> *Decision:* Judgment for motel. The motel is only required to exercise reasonable care in protecting from snow, ice, and water. There was no evidence that the motel had been careless in failing to keep the area clear and consequently it could not be held liable. [Carter v. Davis, . . . NM . . . , 392 P2d 594 (1964)].

(*d*) *Informal traffic routes.* When the hotel knows or has reason to know that its patrons are following certain routes over

Liability for Condition of Premises

its premises, the hotel must act to make such informal routes safe for use, or to post adequate warning of non-observable dangers, or to close off such areas as is necessary to break up the given traffic flow. This is merely a particular aspect of the general duty owed to its invitees to take reasonable steps to make safe for their use all parts of the hotel premises which are open to them.

The facts: The plaintiff and her husband were guests at the motel. To get to the beach they walked across two shuffleboard courts located between the motel and the beach. The two courts were separated by a 2 inch x 4 inch piece of lumber fastened in the cement. This strip was painted black, as were all marking lines on the court. The wife apparently did not see the dividing strip and was tripped by it. She sued the motel for the injuries sustained. The trial court held that as a matter of law the plaintiff could not recover. She appealed.

Decision: The court had acted wrongly in determining that the wife could not recover. In view of the location of the shuffleboard courts, it was not unexpectable that guests would walk across them to get to the beach. The case should therefore have gone to the jury to determine whether the black strip constituted a trap for persons so crossing the courts and the trial judge could not determine as a matter of law that the plaintiff was barred. [Miceli v. Lifter (Fla) 161 So2d 253 (1964)].

(*e*) **Contributory negligence.** The patron or other plaintiff may be barred from recovering from the hotel because of the condition of walks and walking areas where such claimant is guilty of contributory negligence.

The facts: A row of concrete bars were set along the curb of the parking area as a barrier to keep cars from running onto the walking area. The bars were 5 inches to 6 inches high, with openings for pedestrians approximately every 3 feet. A patron tripped over one of the bars. She brought suit against the insurer of the enterprise for the harm which she sustained.

Decision: Judgment for insurer. The plaintiff had fallen over a barrier which was obvious to anyone taking the trouble to look. There was no element of the absence of sufficient light, so as to make the barrier constitute a trap for the unwarned. The plaintiff consequently could not be allowed to say that she had exercised due care. She was barred by her negligence. [Murphy v. Newark Ins. Co., ... LaApp ..., 170 So2d 248 (1965)].

Whether the plaintiff was contributorily negligent may be affected by the degree of illumination provided by the hotel.

It may be that because of the inadequate lighting so afforded, the plaintiff is not able to perceive the peril which exists and therefore cannot be deemed to be exposing himself to a known or obvious peril. Otherwise stated, what might be an obvious or patent defect in the premises in the daytime is not necessarily such at night and if the lighting is not adequate it is possible that the plaintiff will not be charged with negligence in exposing himself to the peril. For example, it has been held that an uncovered crawl or access hole in a concrete slab alongside of a motel walk was not a patent defect at night in the absence of sufficient illumination to reveal the existence of the hole.

Ordinarily it is a question for the jury whether the plaintiff is barred by contributory negligence. For example, whether the guest of the motel was guilty of contributory negligence in falling over a 1 and 1/2 inch pipe running across the sidewalk which was of the same color as the sidewalk is a question for the jury.

> *The facts:* The walk leading from the motel rooms was one step lower than the floor of the rooms. The outside walk was different in color and texture from the floors of the motel rooms. The guest went in and out of the rooms three times on the first day and on the morning of the second day fell down the step in leaving the room. The walk and step area was at the time well-lighted by daylight. The guest sued the motel.
>
> *Decision:* Judgment for the motel. The mere construction of the walk at a different level was not negligent and the difference in appearance between the motel floor and the walk, and the area's being well-lighted eliminated any elements of maintaining a trap or dangerous condition of which notice was required. Moreover the condition was not unknown to the guest who had used the way three times on the preceding day. Under the circumstances the only conclusion that could be made was that the guest must have been inattentive and therefore her harm was caused by her own negligence. [Wainwright v. Thomas (DCSC), 250 FSupp 963 (1966)].

§ 11:14. Doors and halls.

(*a*) ***Generally.*** A hotel must use reasonable care to provide its invitees with doors and halls which are reasonably safe in that they are lighted, free from obstructions, and, where significant, are properly marked with guiding signs. In some instances, this duty is made more specific by fire safety protection statutes which specify the exact physical characteristics

Liability for Condition of Premises

as to the lighting, marking, number, condition, and so forth, of doors and halls.

> *The facts:* The guest walked along the unlighted second floor hall of the hotel and fell over a mattress which the hotel employee had left in the hall. The guest sued the hotel.
>
> *Decision:* Decision for the guest. The hotel was required to keep passageways reasonably well lighted and free from obstructions so that guests could pass without danger to themselves. [E. Goldin v. Lipkin (Fla) 49 So2d 539, 27 ALR2d 822 (1950)].

(*b*) *Instructions of hotel.* Liability of the hotel is more readily found in such cases when the particular hall or door is used because the guest is requested or directed to do so by the hotel but the guest is not warned of the existence of a particular danger therein. For example, when the hotel suggests that a guest use a side exit, the hotel is liable when it fails to warn the guest that there is no light and no guardrail around the platform around the side exit doors, and in consequence of which conditions, the guest falls from the platform and is injured.

(*c*) *Revolving doors.* Guests are sometimes injured by revolving doors. This may be the result of third persons improperly using the door or the result of a defect in the door itself.

(1) Physical defects. When there is a physical defect in the door which is the cause of the harm, the case is governed by the general principles applicable when guests or invitees sue the hotel for harm caused by the physical plant.

(2) Conduct of others. Frequently, the revolving door injury arises when a perfectly safe door is improperly used. That is, when a third person, whether a guest or not, rushes through the revolving door or purposely gives it a shove to make it spin faster.

Generally the question of liability is one for the jury, liability being dependent upon the hotel's failure to exercise reasonable care in the maintenance and operation of the door. Accordingly, there was a question for the jury whether negligence of the hotel existed when there was a temporary boarding up of one of the panels of glass of the revolving door, with the result that a third person pushing through the door could not see the guest who was then injured by the sudden turning of the door. Likewise, it has been held for the jury to determine whether a hotel should have taken any special precautions or have provided a special doorman to prevent the excessive spinning of the revolving door during the Saturday evening after a football game during which time there was much carousing in the main lobby.

It must be remembered that the significance of the statement that the question of the hotel's negligence is a question for the jury has two-fold significance: first, it is not an open and shut question, that is, a question of law, as to whether the hotel is or is not negligent; and second, the jury will be sustained if on the facts involved they conclude either that the hotel was or that it was not negligent, when as in the above case the view of the guest was blocked by the temporary boarding or the rapid spinning of a door was possible because a temporary special doorman had not been provided.

> *The facts:* The landlord rented part of the ground floor to a drug store. The patron entered the landlord's area, then went into the drug store, and when leaving the drug store was injured by the door. All doors were automatic and opened upon approach. All doors were marked plainly as "In" or "Out." With the first set of doors the signs were at eye level and the In door was the left-hand door of the pair of doors. When the patron left the store she assumed that the left hand door was also the In door and left by the right hand door. This was in fact the In door and when she touched it, it opened toward her and she was thrown back some five feet and injured. The In and Out signs for these two doors were above eye level and there was surrounding advertising material which distracted from them. The patron claimed that this variation in construction between the two pairs of doors and the presence of the distracting advertising was negligence. The patron sued both the landlord and the tenant drug store.
>
> *Decision:* Judgment for defendants. There is no rule of law that requires door arrangements to be uniform throughout a building and a patron must exercise reasonable care to determine which door to use and cannot assume uniformity of arrangement.
>
> The presence of the signs was immaterial since the patron did not claim that she attempted to identify the proper door, only to be distracted by the advertising signs. To the contrary, she acted on the basis of an assumed uniformity of construction and, not looking for a sign, could not have been distracted by the advertising. [Platz v. Kroger Co., 110 GaApp 16, 137 SE2d 561 (1964)].

§ 11:15. Stairs, ramps, and guardrails.

(*a*) *Generally.* The hotel is under the same duty of reasonable care with respect to stairways and ramps as in the case of the premises generally. The hotel must use reasonable care to see that stairs and ramps are properly constructed and maintained for the protection of invitees.

(*b*) *Construction.* The fact that stairs are not made of the safest materials does not show that the hotel is negligent where the materials used are not inherently dangerous and are commonly so used. Thus the hotel is not liable because its stairs were made of marble, since marble is not inherently dangerous, although other substances are safer.

Likewise, the fact that there are irregularities or imperfections in stairs, or that step risers are higher than usual, does not in itself establish negligence.

(1) Guardrails and handrails. It is not negligent for a hotel to fail to put up handrails and guardrails. This is particularly true where some other safety factor is present, such as solid walls on both sides of the stairs in question. Statutes and city ordinances, however, frequently require guardrails.

The hotel, however, is liable when it permits a trap-like condition to exist which would tend to deceive a person exercising reasonable caution. For example the hotel is liable where a two-section stairway had a guardrail on the upper well-lighted portion but did not have a guardrail on the lower half, which was dimly lit so that the absence of a guardrail could not be detected readily.

In any case, the guest who is injured by the absence of handrails must show that such factor was the proximate cause of his injury. Likewise, when it is claimed that the handrails were too short, such fact is immaterial unless it can be shown that the shortness of the handrail was a proximate cause of the injury in that the plaintiff was unable to check his falling because he could not reach the short handrails.

The hotel may avoid liability to the guest by showing that the guest had no right to be at the place at which he fell because of the absence of or the condition of the guardrails, or had otherwise gone beyond the scope of permitted activity.

The facts: The platform at the end of a diner was surrounded by a railing. The plaintiff was a patron at the diner. He left the diner, placed his hands on the railing, and leaned over to see where his friend had parked. The railing broke and the plaintiff fell and was injured. He sued the diner.

Decision: Judgment for diner. First, there was no evidence that the diner had been negligent. There was no evidence as to why the railing had broken and liability could not be based upon the mere guess or conjecture of what might have been the reason. Secondly, the plaintiff had exceeded the scope of the diner's invitation to him when he leaned on the railing and took the chance that it would support him. Hence no duty owed to him was violated by the diner with respect to the railing. [Paquette v. Bradley, 348 Mass 326, 203 NE2d 555 (1965)].

(2) Concealed stairs and steps. The hotel will be liable to a person who is injured because stairs or steps were so constructed as to be concealed to a person exercising reasonable care, so that he is not aware of their presence until he is right upon them. This is particularly true where the stairs or steps are not lighted so that the patron must grope for the light switch in the dark, thereby exposing himself to the danger of falling down the unknown stairs or steps before he is able to turn on the light and become aware of their presence.

(c) Maintenance. Distinct from the case of no railings, which is obvious to the reasonable man, is the case where the hotel has erected railings but has failed to maintain them in a safe and secure condition, which condition generally is not obvious to the reasonable man. In the no-maintenance case, the fact that the hazard is not ordinarily visible means that the hotel should be aware that it is leading others into a trap if it fails to maintain the railings with reasonable care, or if it does not, without warning the guests of the hidden peril.

(d) Stairs open for general use. In order to allow recovery, it is necessary to show that the stairs and ramps in question were intended to be used by the guests or the public at large. Obviously there can be no liability of the hotel when the patron enters an area in which he was not intended to be, as, for example, where he uses cellar stairs where he had no right to be.

The fact that elevators are available does not withdraw all stairways from public use. Accordingly, the fact that the guest could have ridden on the elevator does not bar recovery from the hotel where the guest used a stairway which, from its characteristics, reasonably appeared to be intended for use by the patrons of the hotel.

(*e*) ***Contributory negligence.*** The guest may be barred by voluntarily entering stairways and ramps where there is an obvious or known danger, the risk of which he assumes; or where because of the inadequate lighting, the guest knows that he is not able to know whether there is any unusual hazard present. The question is generally one for the jury to determine.

In some cases, however, the negligence of the plaintiff may be so clear that his contributory negligence may be determined by the judge alone as a matter of law, without submitting the question to the jury. Such has been held where the plaintiff fell because the first riser of the stairs was eleven inches high, although the area was well lighted; the rationale being that a reasonable man would have perceived the situation for a reasonably prudent man would not expect all stairways to be exactly alike, nor that every stairway would be built with the steps at just the right height for his stride, and would consequently be on the lookout for such variations.

§ 11:16. Lighting of premises.

(*a*) ***Generally.*** A hotel is liable for harm to its invitee when through the hotel's negligence as to lighting, an invitee falls and is injured. The same is of course true when because of inadequate lighting the invitee cannot see a defect negligently allowed to exist, or is unable to see a foreign substance or object negligently left on the floors.

(*b*) ***Contributory negligence.*** Liability of the hotel may be barred because under the circumstances the invitee is deemed guilty of contributory negligence in entering an area where he knows there is no lighting or that the lighting is inadequate. For example, when a mountain top hotel maintains a lighted pathway in the night, a guest is barred by his contributory negligence when he leaves the pathway and walks into the dark, unlighted area. Likewise, it is held that a guest is guilty of contributory negligence when he walks through his room in the dark, when light switches were readily available, and in the dark strikes a chair which, unknown to him, had been placed there by the hotel.

But in contrast, a visitor to a roomer living on the second floor of a rooming house is not contributorily negligent as a matter of law when she attempts to go down unlighted stairs, where they were in the same darkened condition as when she went up them at the beginning of the visit; the question should be submitted to a jury.

In many of the lighting cases, the plaintiff finds himself in a dilemma with contributory negligence being a bar under either alternative. Thus the plaintiff who falls over a chair in his room is faced with the conclusions that (1) if the room were lighted, the plaintiff would be contributorily negligent in failing to perceive and avoid hitting an object as large as a chair; but (2) if the room were not lighted, and the plaintiff did not turn on the light switch where readily available, he also was contributorily negligent in seeking to go through the dark. When under any alternative, the conclusion is reached that the plaintiff must be barred by contributory negligence, it necessarily follows that he may be so declared as a question of law.

(1) Absence of alternative route. In a given case, the fact that there is no alternative route which is better lighted or safer to travel is a factor in holding that the guest is not guilty of contributory negligence when he makes use of the one route: otherwise he would in effect be imprisoned until daybreak. To illustrate the foregoing, assume that the elevator is not running and the only other available course of travel is a dimly-lit stairway. Here the use of such stairs has been held not to be contributory negligence.

Whether a guest is contributorily negligent in not using an alternative way depends, of course, upon whether he has knowledge of the existence of that alternative way. If in the exercise of due care he does not recognize or know that there is an alternative route, his conduct must be viewed in the light that there is no alternative.

(2) Instructions of hotel. There is also authority that contributory negligence does not arise when the guest enters upon the unlighted route at the direction or suggestion of the hotel. For example, the fact that the guest voluntarily used the dimly-lit stairs did not constitute contributory negligence when the elevator was crowded and its operator suggested that the guests use the stairs. Similarly, the fact that the plaintiff walked into a dimly-lighted lavatory was not in itself contributory negligence where she was directed to use it by the hotel clerk, for she had the right to assume that it was safe for use.

(*c*) *Guest turning on light.* The character of the guest's conduct as contributory negligence or not may often be affected by whether he failed to turn on a light or to obtain a flashlight or other supplementary light. Thus it has been held that a guest was guilty of contributory negligence when he groped down the hall in search of a toilet, following printed instructions, but failing to obtain a light to guide him on the way. Likewise, a guest following oral instructions that the toilet was in the basement was guilty of contributory negligence when the guest failed to turn on the light switch which was readily accessible from the top of the stairs, and instead descended the dimly-lit stairs until he fell.

When, however, the guest trips over an object on the floor, such as a rolled up bath mat, at the very moment he is entering the room in order to turn on the light, he is not necessarily guilty of contributory negligence, and the question must be submitted to the jury to determine whether in view of all the surrounding circumstances he is to be deemed guilty of such negligence.

§ 11:17. Elevators.

(*a*) *Generally.* The elevator, when operated by a hotel employee, must be operated in a non-negligent manner, but the mere fact that the elevator was stopped two inches above the floor does not establish negligence. The hotel has the duty to use reasonable care to furnish properly working and safe elevators for its invitees. In view of the high danger in defective elevators, the hotel must take such care as is commensurate with such foreseeable harm. Thus it may be said frequently that the hotel is held to a very high degree of care although the sound analysis is that in order to avoid the great foreseeable harm the hotel must do much more to make the elevators safe than would be the case with respect to ordinary equipment, furniture, and so forth.

(*b*) *Maintenance by independent contractor.* The fact that the hotel exercises due care in selecting an independent contractor to maintain and service its elevators does not excuse the hotel from liability and the contractor in such case does not insulate the hotel from liability. As it cannot delegate the duty to take care of persons on the premises, the hotel remains liable even though it exercised due care in selecting the independent contractor. The hotel, therefore, remains liable for the breach of the duty to its invitees.

In many jurisdictions today, the injured party, assuming that he would ordinarily have the right to bring suit against the hotel, may also bring suit against the contractor.

(*c*) *Open elevator shaft.* When the elevator door is open but the car is not at the door opening, such facts constitute negligence. If the plaintiff has ordinary vision and there is sufficient lighting to reveal the fact that the car is not at the door, the plaintiff cannot recover if he walks through the open elevator door and falls down the shaft.

If, however, the plaintiff has defective sight or is blind, or the lighting is so poor at the time that the absence of the car cannot be detected, there is authority that the plaintiff is not deemed contributorily negligent if he relies upon the fact that the shaft door is open as indicating that the elevator car is at that point. By other authority, the plaintiff in such case would be guilty of contributory negligence by walking boldly in through the open door without groping with his foot to verify the presence of the car.

§ 11:18. Windows and screens.

The mere fact that there was no screen or grill on a window, which fact was readily apparent to an adult, did not establish that the hotel was negligent with respect to an adult guest who fell through the widow.

Although the purpose of screens in windows is not primarily to keep persons from falling out, the hotel should foresee that when rooms are rented to persons with a small child, there is the likelihood that the child will lean against the screen. Hence there is the duty on the hotel to use reasonable care to securely fasten the screens. Consequently, when it has failed to do so and a child of three years is injured when it leans against the unfastened screen and falls out of the window, the hotel is liable for its negligence in failing to fasten the screen in a reasonable manner.

> *The facts:* The wall of a motel room facing the courtyard was glass running from the floor to the ceiling. An infant guest, just under the age of 7, seeking to run into the courtyard, ran into the glass wall, broke it, and was severely cut. On several prior times, other guests had collided with the glass paneling but apparently no harm had been sustained. The glass paneling was of a kind

in common use although other kinds were available which would not break so readily. The motel claimed that it was not liable because it was not negligent in using a kind of glass which was common in the motel industry, and furthermore that the child was barred by contributory negligence.

Decision: Judgment for the child. The motel owed a high duty to its invitees who were children and as the child was under 7 years of age she was not guilty of contributory negligence. The motel was not initially negligent in installing the kind of glass but with the history of prior collisions and the knowledge that children would be on the premises, the motel was under a duty to take some steps to protect children from the possibility of harm from collision and fracture of the glass, as by giving warnings, placing markings on the glass, or by putting guards in front of the glass. Having failed to do so, the motel was liable for the consequence of its negligence. The court recognized that there was a conflict of authority but held that the fact that the plaintiff was a very young minor increased the motel's duty sufficiently to impose liability. [Wauch v. Duke Corporation (DCNC), 248 FSupp 626 (1966)].

§ 11:19. Furniture.

(*a*) ***Generally.*** A hotel is liable to guests and patrons for harm sustained by the collapse of chairs and furniture if the hotel has failed to make reasonable periodic examination of the furniture. The liability rests on negligence and hence the hotel is not liable if it had made reasonable and periodic inspection of the furniture to check whether it is safe for use. Ordinarily a guest cannot recover from the hotel where she stood on a bench and it broke, where there was no defect which was visible nor which could be ascertained by reasonable inspection, for the hotel is not the insurer against the breaking when in the course of ordinary wear the item of furniture just wears out.

There is no liability when the condition of the furniture is obvious. Thus the fact that there was no guardrail on the top of a double bunk bed supplied to parents of a six-year-old and a four-year-old child was not negligence in itself and such a bed was not a dangerous instrumentality.

Furniture accidents generally present questions of fact for determination by the jury. Consequently, where a patron is injured because the wooden stool had no rubber pads or other device to keep it from slipping on the marble floor, the situation is one which presents questions which should go to the jury to determine whether there was a dangerous condition of which the patron could not have had knowledge and therefore should have been informed.

(b) *Hidden defects.* When the defect which causes the harm is unknown to the hotel and reasonable investigation would not disclose its existence, there is no liability on the hotel when the hidden defect in fact causes harm. This is particularly true of a defect which gradually appears as a normal incident to ordinary use and wear of the furniture. So it has been held that the mere fact that a guest is injured by a rusty nail protruding from a redwood chair by the swimming pool side does not establish liability of the hotel without the proof of some negligence, even though it is claimed that the hotel knew or should have known of the existence of the nail.

(c) *Res ipsa loquitur.* There is a conflict of authority as to whether the rule of res ipsa loquitur applies. That is, whether the jury will be permitted to infer that the hotel was negligent from the mere fact that the furniture broke or collapsed and harm was sustained. In some instances, the application of the principle is denied on the ground that the hotel did not have exclusive possession and control of the furniture at the time. This view is particularly likely to be held where the furniture is moved, or unfolded, or set up by the guest before it is used by him, as in the case of a folding chair, and then collapses. This contrasts with the factual situation where all that the guest does is sit down on a stool which is bolted to the floor and the bolts give way causing the collapse of the stool.

In other cases, the principle of res ipsa loquitur is applied either by name or in substance as in reaching the conclusion that the fact that a folding bed snapped shut upon the guest showed that the hotel was negligent in the performance of its duty to furnish a safe bed.

(d) *Contributory negligence.* The guest is barred by his contributory negligence when he makes use of furniture which is obviously defective or makes a clearly inappropriate use of sound furniture. Illustrative of the latter, a guest who weighs 227 pounds, and is an experienced traveler and a frequenter of hotels, is contributorily negligent when he uses a luggage rack for a chair when the rack is obviously not made for and is not suitable for such purpose.

The facts: The guest discovered that there was something wrong with the folding bed in her room because it had a tendency to fall down when being lowered. In spite of efforts of the hotel to repair the bed, it still had this tendency. The guest continued to use the bed. Some time later she was injured when the bed fell on her. She sued the hotel.

Decision: Judgment for the hotel. The guest was guilty of contributory negligence when she continued to expose herself to the use of the known defective bed. [Duncan v. Chelsea Hotel Co., 326 IllApp 241, 61 NE2d 769 (1945)].

But every non-intended use of furniture is not necessarily contributory negligence.

The facts: In the early morning, a guest of the motel stood on a dressing-table stool to turn on the air conditioner, the controls of which were 81 inches from the floor. The guest was 5 feet 2 inches tall and weighed 107 lbs. The stool broke and she was injured. The motel claimed that she was guilty of contributory negligence in using a stool for a stepladder and in failing to call a motel employee to make the adjustment to the air conditioner.

Decision: Judgment for guest. It was not unreasonable for the guest, in view of her size and weight, to use the stool for a stepladder, even though that was not the purpose for which it was designed, since there was no reason to foresee that it would not sustain her weight for a limited period of time. Likewise she was not contributorily negligent in attempting the adjustment herself when it only required the flipping of a switch. [Nettles v. Forbes Motel, ... LaApp ... , 182 So2d 572 (1966)].

§ 11:20. Electrical and gas appliances and fixtures.

The hotel is liable to its invitee when its failure to use reasonable care in the construction or maintenance of electrical or gas appliances and fixtures is the proximate cause of harm to the invitee.

Thus the hotel is liable where a gas burner knob had no stopping pin, with the result that it could be turned in a continuous circle without it being apparent when the gas really was turned off. The hotel is liable when a gas appliance, such as a heater, is connected with a defective or prohibited kind of hose, with the result that gas leaks and fills the room, leading to an explosion which injures or kills the guest.

§ 11:21. Plumbing fixtures.

(*a*) **Generally.** The hotel is liable to its invitee when its failure to use reasonable care in the installation, construction, or maintenance of plumbing fixtures is the proximate cause of harm to the invitee.

> *The facts:* The plaintiff took a shower at the hotel. The mixing valve handle of the shower was very difficult to move. By applying great force the guest moved the handle toward hot, but under such force the handle suddenly moved to extreme hot and the guest was scalded by the rush of boiling water and steam. The guest sued the hotel.
>
> *Decision:* Judgment for guest. The hotel had been negligent in failing to maintain the shower valve in such condition that it could be used reasonably. In view of the fact that extreme harm could result from a defective shower control, the burden was on the hotel to exercise a degree of care proportionate to the probable harm that might occur. The fact that it was the act of the guest in turning on the shower which had led to the harm, is immaterial, for the use of the shower was foreseeable and intended by the hotel. [Parsons v. Dwight State Control Co., 301 Mass 324, 17 NE2d 197, 118 ALR 1099 (1938)].

(*b*) **Bathtubs.** In the absence of reason to know the contrary, an invitee has the right to assume that the bathtub has been cleaned and is safe for use. Conversely, the hotel is liable if the incoming guest slips in the tub because of grease left there after the departure of the former guest in that room. That is, when the hotel provides accommodations for a new guest it must make a reasonable inspection of the premises before it turns them over to him and it is liable to the guest for negligence if it permits a surface scum to remain on a bathtub because of which the plaintiff fell and was injured.

> *The facts:* The guest slipped and fell on a white substance similar to plaster of Paris which was on the bottom of a bathtub in the defendant hotel. She sued for the injury sustained. Was the hotel liable?
>
> *Decision:* No. There was no evidence that the hotel knew of the condition nor that the condition had existed such a length of time that it could be assumed that the hotel in the exercise of reasonable care would have learned of its existence. [Ferrara v. Sheraton McAlpin Corp. (CA2d) 311 F2d 294 (1962)].

There is authority that the hotel is not liable when the presence of such grease or scum was detectable at the bottom of the tub even from the slightest examination.

A motel is not liable for negligence in failing to provide a mat for a combined tub and shower bath or in failing to supply

Liability for Condition of Premises 193

more than two handrails or racks or a ribbon bottomed tub, or in failing to warn the guest that the tub was slick and hazardous.

When the hotel guest using a shower bath turned on a porcelain handle which broke causing injury, the rule of res ipsa loquitur applied to permit an inference of negligence of the hotel where the room was not occupied by anyone other than the guest and the bathroom had been serviced that day by hotel employees.

(*c*) *Contributory negligence.* When harm is caused the guest solely because of the guest's own fault, there is of course no liability of the hotel. To illustrate, when the guest was severely burned in the shower as the result of her unexplained failure to turn on the cold water, the harm was the result of the guest's own fault and barred recovery by her, although it is also held that the hotel has the burden of seeing that the water will not come out of the shower scalding hot.

A guest who is less agile because of an arthritic condition must take a greater degree of care in exposing herself to danger as by sitting in a tub of hot water without checking the temperature, and consequently is barred by her contributory negligence when she sustained serious burns from the unusually hot water because she could not get out of the tub quickly enough.

§ 11:22. Falling objects.

(*a*) *Generally.* An invitee may be injured by a falling object, such as a window shade, chandelier, part of the ceiling, glass from the transom of a door, and so forth. If the hotel knows that there is some defect in the ceiling, transom glass, or any elevated object, the hotel is naturally liable for the harm so caused when there is reason to foresee that if the defect is not corrected it may result in the fall of some object and the harm of persons lawfully on the premises.

In some instances, it is held that the rule of res ipsa loquitur applies to aid the plaintiff in the proof of the negligence of the hotel.

(*b*) *Inspection of premises.* If the hotel does not know of the defect of the premises, it may be liable on the ground that it was negligent in not making a reasonable periodic inspection to determine whether its premises were in good condition. Whether the hotel will be liable in spite of the fact that it makes a periodic, reasonable inspection depends largely upon the nature of the harm involved and the circumstances of the particular case.

(c) *Time for repair.* If the hotel does not have a reasonable time in which to repair the premises, such as a defective ceiling, and injury is sustained before a reasonable time has elapsed, there is no liability provided harm was not reasonably foreseeable. If the hotel as a reasonable man should have recognized that harm was reasonably foreseeable, it should not have allowed that part of the premises to be used or occupied, and if it did, it is liable for the harm sustained.

(d) *Contributory negligence.* A guest cannot hold the hotel liable for harm from a falling object when he is himself guilty of contributory negligence. But the mere fact that he voluntarily occupies a room in which the ceiling is cracked does not in itself constitute such negligence. This for the reason that there is no logical probability that a ceiling will fall merely because it is cracked.

(e) *Res ipsa loquitur.* In a number of cases it has been held that res ipsa loquitur is properly applied to authorize the jury to infer that the hotel was negligent when part of the ceiling fell on the guest; particularly when this took place while the guest was sleeping. As the rule of res ipsa loquitur does not declare that there was negligence, but merely permits the jury to make such inference, the court should also submit to the jury the details of inspections of the premises made by the hotel; in order that the jury can appraise such inspections to see if they amounted to the exercise of reasonable care, thus excluding the inference that the hotel had been negligent.

> *The facts:* That patron was shopping in a self-service store when she was injured by flying glass from a carton of soft drinks which fell from a stack behind her and shattered. The patron sued the store and the soft drink company which bottled and delivered the carton. The plaintiff claimed that the cartons had been stacked negligently and that they were also improperly stacked in such a way that customers could remove cartons from the bottom instead of only from the top. There was no evidence as to who stacked the cartons, but there was evidence that several different companies stacked cartons of soft drinks in the same place. Immediately after the fall of the carton, the plaintiff noticed another customer and her son within 2 or 3 feet of the stack.
>
> *Decision:* Judgment against the plaintiff. The fact that harm was sustained did not show that there was negligence. The principle

of res ipsa loquitur could not be applied because it was possible that the cause of the occurrence was the act of one of the other bottling companies or of a customer, as well as of either of the defendants. [Graham v. Fex-X, Inc. (TexCivApp) 384 SW2d 785 (1964)].

§ 11:23. Fire.

(*a*) *Generally.* The hotel owes a duty to its invitees to exercise reasonable care under the circumstances to protect them from harm by fire. As in the case of negligence liability generally, the plaintiff has the burden of showing that the hotel was negligent in respect to the fire and that such negligence was the proximate cause of his harm. At the same time, it is obvious that because of the harm that fire can do, together with the great probability that a hotel fire will be extremely dangerous to human life, a reasonable man would be very careful with respect to fire in connection with a hotel.

(*b*) *Fire safety statutes.* The violation of the fire safety statute is generally regarded as evidence or proof of negligence, and when such negligence is the proximate cause of the guest's harm, the hotel is liable for such harm. Statutes requiring fire exits and free access ways are deemed to impose duties a breach of which by the hotel constitutes negligence on its own part.

In harmony with the general rules of proximate cause, no civil liability arises from the breach of a fire safety statute unless that breach is a cause of the plaintiff's harm.

> *The facts:* The fire safety laws required that rooming houses (1) have hand fire extinguishers in the hallways, and (2) that either there be a fire ladder on the outside of the building or that the inside staircase satisfy certain safety requirements. The defendant rooming house failed to maintain fire extinguishers as required. There was an outside fire escape, but it did not meet the statutory requirements as to handrails or the angle of the ladder to the ground, and the inside staircase did not satisfy the statutory requirements.
>
> The plaintiff was a roomer in the defendant's rooming house. The rooming house caught on fire. The plaintiff was awakened from sleep by the shouts of people and was injured when he jumped from his second-story room to the ground. He sued for his personal injuries and the loss of his belongings which were left in the room, basing his claim on the defendant's negligence. The defendant proved that by the time the plaintiff awoke, the

hallways were all in flames and that it would have been impossible to reach a fire extinguisher in the hall had there been any. It also showed that it was impossible to reach the outside fire escape because of the spread of the fire.

Decision: The fact that the defendant had violated the statute did not impose liability unless such violation was the cause of the plaintiff's harm. As the fire had so spread that the plaintiff could not have made use of a hand extinguisher in the hall, had there been one there, nor made use of the fire escape, if the fire escape had complied with the statutory requirements, it could not be said that it was the failure to comply with the statute which caused the plaintiff's harm, for such harm would have occurred on the facts of the case even if the defendant had fully complied with the statute. Hence, the breach of the statute was not a cause of the plaintiff's harm and the defendant was not liable for such harm. [Lee v. Carwile, ... LaApp ..., 168 So2d 469 (1964)].

Statutes also may constitutionally provide that in case of fire the hotel must notify all persons in the hotel and do everything in the hotel's power to notify and save the guests.

The fact that a guest knows that the hotel has violated the fire safety statutes does not in itself bar the guest for contributory negligence or assumption of risk. Hence no presumption of contributory negligence arises from the fact that a guest registered at a hotel not equipped with fire extinquishers and fire escapes as required by statute, although the guest died in a subsequent fire because of the absence of such equipment.

(*c*) **Persons benefited.** The duty of the hotel under fire safety statutes is broader than protecting guests; for such statutes are intended to protect boarders and lodgers as well.

(*d*) **Escape harm.** If the hotel is liable for harm caused by fire, it is also liable for harm sustained in the guest's attempt to escape from the fire. However, contributory negligence and assumption of risk may enter into the picture to bar recovery. For example, a guest is barred by contributory negligence when she attempted to escape from the fifth floor by means of a rope made of bed sheets and the rope came apart while she was descending.

§ 11:24. Contagion and disease.

The act of holding out the hotel to serve the public is a representation to the public that the hotel is a reasonably safe place in which to stay. Hence the act of accepting a guest is a representation to him that the hotel has no knowledge that the guest's room may be infected as a result of the prior guest's illness.

If the hotel guest knows or has reason to know a fact which would put a reasonable man upon inquiry as to the condition of the premises, the guest, by registering in the hotel assumes the risk thereof, and he cannot recover damages for the harm sustained by him. Where the knowledge of the guest is no more than knowledge of a mere rumor, no obligation of inquiry falls upon the guest.

§ 11:25. Rodents and vermin.

(*a*) *Rats and mice.* A hotel is liable for the harm caused a guest by rat bites when the hotel was negligent in failing to take measures to exclude or destroy the rats. Thus the hotel has been liable where it did nothing to oppose the rats and there were numerous ratholes along the baseboard of a guest's room.

The fact that the hotel is located in a highly industrialized area, next to a main set of railroad tracks, and charged low rates for its rooms, does not lessen the duty of the hotel to protect its guests from rats. But the mere fact that a guest in a motel is bitten by a mouse does not establish that the motel was guilty of negligence. And even though a statute declares that "the owner of every dwelling shall be responsible for keeping the entire building free from vermin," a hotel is not absolutely liable to a guest who is bitten by a rat but is liable only if the hotel knew or should have known of the presence or likely presence of a rat.

(*b*) *Insects.* The fact that a guest is bitten by an insect in the guest's room does not in itself establish that the hotel was negligent nor does it warrant the application of the doctrine of res ipsa loquitur.

Chapter 12. LIABILITY FOR CONDITION OF LEASED PREMISES

§ 12:1. Hotel relationship as a real estate lease.
    (a) Generally.
    (b) Nature of real estate.
    (c) Classification of tenants.
    (d) Liability of parties to real estate lease.

§ 12:2. Landlord's liability to tenant.
    (a) Generally.
    (b) Permittees of tenant.
    (c) Disclosure of known hazards.
        (1) Exceptions.

§ 12:3. Landlord's liability to third persons.
    (a) Non-liability of landlord.
    (b) Condition existing at time of leasing.
    (c) Subsequent conduct of tenant.
        (1) Limitations to exception.
    (d) Public admission premises.
        (1) Area of liability.
        (2) Limitations to exception.

§ 12:4. Liability of landlord for retained part of land.
    (a) Generally.
    (b) Standard of care.
    (c) Persons protected.
        (1) Tenant's knowledge of condition.

§ 12:5. Landlord's agreement to repair.
    (a) No repairs made.
        (1) Non-liability not changed.
        (2) Liability created.
    (b) Negligent making of repairs.
        (1) Independent contractor.

§ 12:1. Hotel relationship as a real estate lease.

(a) Generally. As discussed in Chapter 2, the relationship between the hotel and its patron may be that of landlord and tenant. When that is the case, the relative rights and duties of hotel and patron are the same as those of any other landlord and

Liability for Condition of Leased Premises

tenant. That is to say, their rights and duties are to be found in the general law relating to real estate leases and landlord and tenants, in statutes governing that relationship, and in the terms of the agreement or lease executed by the parties.

In order to emphasize that the hotel has the status of a landlord rather than that of a common-law inn, and that the patron is a tenant of real estate, rather than a guest in a hotel, the terms "landlord" and "tenant" will be used in this chapter to identify the hotel and its patron.

(*b*) *Nature of real estate.* In the eyes of the law the terms "land" and "real estate" are defined as the earth itself and everything which is imbedded in or attached to the earth, whether naturally or by act of man. From this broad definition, it follows that the hotel building is "land" or "real estate." It therefore follows that half of the building is land or real estate, as is just one floor, as is a suite of rooms, as is just one room. The patron of the hotel who stands as a tenant with respect to any part of the building is consequently a tenant of real estate and the agreement between him and the hotel is a lease of real estate.

(*c*) *Classification of tenants.* From the broad definition above made, it can be readily seen that no distinction is made in terms of the purpose for which the tenant has made his lease. Thus the principles here considered are applicable to both the residential tenant who is living in the hotel and the commerical tenant who has rented a store or office space in the hotel.

In terms of practical operation there may be differences. For example, the residential lease will undoubtedly make greater provision for cleaning and similar services than would the commercial lease. For the most part these practical differences will not affect the equal application to both kinds of leases of the general principles of landlord and tenant law discussed in this chapter.

Moreover, the principles are equally applicable where the proprietor or manager of the hotel has rented the entire hotel building from its owner. Thus the "hotel" may be both a tenant as to the building owner and the landlord as to its tenants.

(*d*) *Liability of parties to real estate lease.* As a lease by definition is the transfer of possession of real estate, and as possession of real estate is ordinarily the basis for imposing tort liability with respect to the condition of the premises,[1] it follows that the starting point in the tort law with respect to landlord and tenant is that liability for tort rests upon the tenant who is in possession; and the landlord who is not in possession is not liable to anyone. This conclusion is confirmed by the fact that the lease in transferring possession to the tenant gives the latter an exclusive possession, so that thereafter the landlord does not have any right to go upon the premises, even for the purpose of making repairs, except to the extent that the lease expressly reserves him the right to reenter.

§ 12:2. Landlord's liability to tenant.

(*a*) *Generally.* In the absence of statute or an express term of the lease to the contrary, the tenant takes possession of the premises on a "tenant beware" basis and the landlord is not responsible for its condition. In a number of states and cities, statutes and ordinances have been adopted to impose upon the landlords the minimal duty of making the premises tenantable or in a safe condition.[1a] Such legislation is construed as creating a tort liability in favor of the injured person in case of their breach. Under such laws, the fact that the tenant knows that the landlord is guilty of a breach does not bar recovery on the theory of assumption of risk, for it would be contrary to public policy to permit the landlord to escape liability on such a basis.

(*b*) *Permittees of tenant.* When the landlord owes a duty to his tenant, it ordinarily extends to any person on the premises with the permission of the tenant.

(*c*) *Disclosure of known hazards.* When the landlord has actual knowledge of the existence of a hazard on the rented premises which hazard is hidden and therefore not likely to be discovered by the tenant in time to remedy it before he sustains harm, it is generally held that the landlord is under the duty to inform the tenant of the hazard. If he fails to do so, the tenant, or others entering the premises with the permission or upon the invitation of the tenant, who are injured by such concealed hazard may recover from the landlord for the damages thus sustained.

The duty of disclosure exists not only when the landlord has actual knowledge of the hazard but also when he has knowl-

---

[1] See Chapter 11.
[1a] See Supplement p. 474.

Liability for Condition of Leased Premises

edge of such facts as would put a reasonable man upon inquiry, that is, he has "notice" of the hazard. But, in the absence of contrary statutory provision, the landlord is not required to make any investigation to discover defective conditions, even though he benefits from the lease and would be required to make such inspection in the case of persons whom he invited as invitees.

(1) Exceptions. The landlord is not required to inform the tenant of defects or conditions when it is apparent that the tenant actually knows of them at the time of the execution of the lease or it is reasonably to be expected that he will learn of them when he goes into possession in time to protect himself from harm. And clearly the landlord's nondisclosure has no significance after the tenant has been on the premises such a length of time that it is obvious that he has learned of the condition in question.

> *The facts:* The plaintiff was a resident in an apartment hotel. There was a wet slippery spot in the hallway which had been there for a long time and was caused by the dripping of an overhead water pipe. The plaintiff knew of the spot and had passed it daily for several months. The plaintiff while walking down the hall talking to a companion fell on the spot. She sued the hotel. Decide.
>
> *Decision:* Judgment for hotel. The relation between the apartment hotel and a resident was merely that of landlord and tenant. The landlord owes only a duty of being non-negligent with respect to the condition of the premises retained in his possession. Hence contributory negligence on the part of the plaintiff would bar recovery. Here the plaintiff was contributorily negligent because she knew of the presence of the spot in the hallway and walked right into it, even though a safe route existed to walk around it. The fact that she was distracted by talking to her companion did not alter the fact that she was clearly contributorily negligent. [Manes v. Hines & McNair Hotels, 184 Tenn 210, 197 SW2d 889 (1946)].

The duty of the landlord to provide safe premises extends only to such places or areas as it was intended or contemplated that the tenant could properly be. The fact that the plaintiff may be a child of such tender years that he is legally incapable of being contributorily negligent does not avoid this limitation upon the landlord's liability.

> *The facts:* The plaintiff, aged 3, had lived all his life in the apartment house owned and operated by the defendant. In front of

a cellar window of the apartment house there was an unguarded window well 37 1/2" deep, 4" wide, extending 2' from the side of the building. There was a ridge aroung the rim of the well some 5 3/4" wide and approximately 4" above the ground level. About 18" from the well there was a paved concrete walkway 4' wide. The minor plaintiff returning by himself from a nearby playground walked along the unpaved area next to the concrete walk and fell down the well. The plaintiff sued the landlord for failing to guard or cover the window well. Was the defendant liable?

Decision: A tenant was an invitee with respect to the concrete walk provided by the landlord. When an invitee left the area to which the invitation extended, he was merely a licensee or trespasser to whom the landlord owed no duty of making the place safe. The child of the tenant had no higher status than the tenant and therefore could not recover because of hazards arising outside of the area of invitation. [Barnes v. Housing Authority of Baltimore, 231 Md 147, 189 A2d 100 (1963). (The court was impressed by the fact that the child must have known of the open well and the danger of falling in it, for he knew the playground area and the way home, and had lived there all his life and therefore assumed the risk in deviating from the concrete walkway.)].

§ 12:3. Landlord's liability to third persons.

(*a*) *Non-liability of landlord.* Distinct from third persons claiming under the tenant, such as his guests and family, are other third persons having no relation to the tenant. After the landlord surrenders possession of the leased premises he is generally not responsible to such third persons for the condition of the premises thereafter existing. Likewise, the landlord is not vicariously liable for the conduct of the tenant which amounts to a nuisance.

(*b*) *Condition existing at time of leasing.* As an exception to the general rule of non-liability of the landlord to strangers, it is held that he is liable for harm caused them by a private nuisance which existed on the land at the time that he leased the premises to the tenant. Likewise, he is liable for harm from hidden hazardous conditions existing when the property was leased which in the normal course of ordinary wear and tear cause harm. So it is held that the landlord is liable for the damage resulting when a lease is made of a store with a defective sign which overhangs the street, and in the course of time the sign collapses and injures a person on the sidewalk.

Liability for Condition of Leased Premises

Similarly, there is liability when the landlord leases a house and there is a rotten cellar grating in the pavement which, at a later time, collapses under the weight of the plaintiff and causes him to sustain injuries.

> *The facts:* A landlord leased premises to the tenant. At the time there was a defective drain spout which permitted rain water to flow onto the sidewalk. By the lease, the tenant agreed to make all necessary repairs to the premises. He failed to do so, and the plaintiff while passing on the sidewalk, fell because of such rain water which had frozen and was injured. The plaintiff sued the landlord, who denied liability on the basis that the tenant had undertaken to make the repairs. Was this a defense?
>
> *Decision:* No. The landlord was liable initially because the condition amounted to a nuisance and as landlord he was responsible for the harm caused by the nuisance existing at the creation of the lease. The fact that as between him and the tenant there was a duty on the part of the tenant to repair and eliminate the condition did not affect the landlord's duty to the public. The landlord was therefore liable in spite of the tenant's agreement to repair. [Updegraff v City of Ottuma, 210 Iowa 382, 226 NW 928 (1929)].

(c) Subsequent conduct of tenant. As an exception to the rule that the landlord is not liable for harm caused by the tenant's use of the premises, it is sometimes held that the landlord is liable for harm caused by the tenant in making a use of the premises when the landlord has leased the premises to be used for that purpose and the harm is the foreseeable result of such activity even when conducted in a reasonable manner.

On this theory it has been held that a landlord leasing land to a quarry company for the purpose of permitting the latter to remove stone contemplates that the tenant will blast and that there will be an irreducible minimum of hazard to third persons.

(1) Limitations to exception. The exception here considered is necessarily subject to the limitations that the landlord is not responsible (a) when the use made of the premises goes beyond that authorized by the lease or (b) when the hazard which causes the harm to third persons arises only because of the unusual or negligent way in which the tenant performs the work and it would be reasonably possible to have conducted the activity in a way which would not have caused harm.

(*d*) **Public admission premises.** When the premises leased to the tenant will be used by him for the admission of the public at large, it is apparent that if the premises are in a defective condition there is the risk of harm to a substantial number of people. The duty of the landlord is correspondingly increased to offset this greater foreseeability of harm. This consideration is increasingly valid when the lease of the premises to the tenant contemplates the admission of the public within such a short time that it is obvious that the tenant will not be able to make any inspection and repair of the premises, or when the duration of the lease is so short, as the renting of a building for one dance, that it is not reasonable to expect that the tenant will bother making repairs.

In the foregoing cases, it is held that when the landlord rents a building such as a store, a theater, or a hotel, he must make a reasonable investigation of the premises and repair defects which would cause harm to the public before he transfers possession to the tenant. If he fails to do so and a member of the public is harmed by a defect which he could have discovered by a reasonable investigation or by a defect which was known to him but which he neglected to repair, the landlord is liable to such third person.

In general, no distinction is made in terms of whether a large number of members of the public will be present at any one time, as in the case of a theater, or a relatively small number, as in the case of a gas station. Likewise, no distinction is made in many states as to whether the purpose of the presence of the public is for amusement or business. In a few states, however, the exception is held to apply only to large attendance cases and to amusement cases.

(1) Area of liability. Since the liability imposed upon the landlord in the class of cases here considered is predicated upon the foreseeability of harm to the general public, it follows that the liability of the landlord is limited in terms of the particular part of the premises which is to be opened to the public.

(2) Limitations to exception. The lessor is not an insurer in such case, and hence is not liable for defects which a reasonable investigation would not disclose. Likewise, he is not liable for a condition which is so obvious to anyone coming onto the premises that it is reasonable to believe that members of the public will recognize the existence of the hazard and will avoid being harmed thereby.

Liability for Condition of Leased Premises 205

The facts: The United States purchased a tract of land which had been used as a restaurant and then executed a lease back to the restaurant operator, the original owner, for a period of years. While this lease was in effect, a patron of the restaurant who had been going to it for 15 years, fell because of a loose brick when stepping from the restaurant door; the bricks being piled in front of the door to serve as steps. She sued the United States under the Federal Tort Claims Act, which allowed such suits and imposed upon the United States the same liability as that to which an ordinary individual would be subject. The patron claimed that the Government as landlord was liable for having leased the premises in a dangerous condition.

Decision: Judgment for United States. The liability of the landlord to a business invitee of his tenant is based upon the superior knowledge of the landlord who is therefore subjected to the duty of warning the invitees who cannot discover the peril by themselves. This principle could not apply where it was obvious that the patron must have known the actual condition of the premises in view of having gone to the restaurant for 15 years. Moreover, the condition of the bricks outside the door of the restaurant was an obvious condition and did not constitute a trap. Hence no liability existed on the part of the United States for failing to warn the patron of the condition in question. [Weaver v. United States, (CA10th), 334 F2d 319 (1964)].

If by the terms of the lease the tenant agrees to repair the premises and further agrees that the premises will not be opened to the public until the repairs have been made, the landlord is not liable unless, as a reasonable man, he should have realized that the tenant would in fact not make the repairs or could not do so within the time intervening before the date of the opening of the premises to the public. If the agreement of the tenant to repair does not indicate that the premises will remain closed until the repairs are made, the mere agreement of the tenant to make the repairs does not relieve the landlord of his liability under this public admission exception.

§ 12:4. Liability of landlord for retained part of land.

(*a*) *Generally.* When the landlord leases parts of a building to different tenants, he may remain in control and in possession of certain areas enjoyed by all, which areas benefit all the tenants. For example, the roof, stairs and elevators, basements, and sidewalks ordinarily remain in the possession of the landlord.

(b) Standard of care. With respect to such retained portions, the lessor must exercise due care to discover such defects as reasonable investigation would disclose and to exercise such care to keep the area in a safe condition.

The facts: The apartment house hotel had a garden fronting on the public pavement which was made of terrazo. The garden was at a higher level than the pavement and when it was watered the excess water would seep through the retaining wall of the garden onto the terrazo pavement and meander in an irregular path toward a drain and collect in a depressed area in the pavement. This made the pavement leading to the lobby door continually wet without regard to the weather conditions. This could have been avoided by proper waterproofing of the retaining wall of the garden or by a construction of drainage channels along the wall. The condition of the pavement was known to the apartment house manager both because of its obvious character and the fact that complaints had been made by other tenants, one of whom had fallen because of it.

The plaintiff was another tenant in the apartment house who slipped on the wet pavement just outside of the front lobby entrance. The apartment house defended on the ground that everyone knows that wet terrazo is slippery and therefore the tenant had assumed the risk of the wet condition.

Decision: This was not the case of an occasional or incidental wet surface but was the maintenance of a continuing hazardous condition as the result of a defective control of the drainage which could have been remedied by a properly constructed retaining wall or drainage channel. It was a condition of which the defendant landlord had knowledge, and the areas involved were within the control and power of the defendant to correct and eliminate. As the apartment house failed to take any corrective action but merely allowed the hazardous condition to continue, it was liable to the tenant who was injured through its neglect. [Nevoso v. Putter-Fine Bldg. Corp. 18 AppDiv 2d 317, 239 NYS2d 504 (1963)].

The landlord, however, is not an insurer of the retained portions and is not liable for a condition created therein by the tenant or by a third person. Moreover, the tenant or other person injured may be barred on the theory of contributory negligence. He may also be barred on the basis of assumption of risk if, with knowledge of the danger involved, he exposes himself to the hazard.

The facts: The plaintiff tenant rented the first floor of a duplex from the defendant. There was a driveway from the house to the garage. The surface of the driveway was chipped and cracked and weeds had grown in the cracks. The driveway had been in this condition for 19 years before the plaintiff rented the first floor. Eight months after going in possession as tenant, the plaintiff tripped while walking on the driveway. The tenant claimed that the landlord was liable because he had not given any warning of the condition of the driveway. Was the landlord under a duty to give such warning?

Decision: No. With respect to an area of the premises retained by a landlord and used in common by different tenants or by a tenant and the landlord, a tenant has the status of an invitee. But even as to an invitee, there is no duty to warn of obvious conditions and dangers, particularly where the injury was not sustained until the tenant had been in possession for a substantial period of time, such as eight months. [Jackson v. Land, ... Okla ... , 391 P2d 904 (1964)].

(c) *Persons protected.* The duty to maintain the retained portion of the premises in a safe condition runs to the tenants of the landlord and to all persons claiming under them, such as their invitees, guests, and employees. Thus a customer patronizing a store leased to a tenant is regarded as an invitee of the landlord with respect to the portion of the premises under the control of the landlord, for the reason that he has an interest in the success of his tenant. The landlord's duty with respect to retained areas does not extend to persons who are merely trespassers or intruders on the premises.

(1) *Tenant's knowledge of condition.* The fact that the plaintiff was on the premises by virtue of a tenant's permission does not result in the conclusion that if the tenant is barred because of his knowledge of a defect, his invitee or licensee must also be barred. Otherwise stated, the tenant may be barred by his contributory negligence or his assumption of risk, but this does not bar his invitee from claiming the benefit of the rule stated in the preceding section.

§ 12:5. Landlord's agreement to repair.

(a) *No repairs made.* There is a conflict of authority as to the effect of a landlord's agreement to repair when no repairs are made.

(1) *Non-liability not changed.* By the earlier view, the fact that the landlord makes such an agreement does not impose

liability upon him in situations in which none would otherwise exist. Accordingly, if under the principles discussed in this chapter it would be concluded in a given case that the landlord was not liable to the tenant or to a third person injured, the same conclusion would be reached although the landlord had contracted to repair the given defect or condition which, not being repaired, caused the injury sustained.

Under this view, the liability for the breach of the covenant or contract to repair is merely a liability for breach of contract which may be enforced by the tenant. Likewise, the damages recoverable for such a breach extend only to the cost of making the repairs or the loss in rental value because of the lack of the repairs. Damages for injuries sustained as the result of the breach are not recoverable.

(2) Liability created. By the modern trend, the landlord who agrees to repair the premises becomes liable if he fails to make the repairs, not only for his breach of contract, but also for the harm sustained by the tenant and others because of his failure to make the repairs. The duty recognized in these states runs to the benefit of the tenant, his family members and guests, his invitees, and to any persons on the land standing in the position or under the right of the tenant.

The obligation of the landlord by this view is not an absolute obligation. It only requires that the landlord act in a reasonable manner after he has discovered the dangerous condition or has received notice about it from anyone.

(b) *Negligent making of repairs.* The division of authority above noted exists only where the landlord does not begin to perform any of the promised repairs. If he does undertake or begin to make the repairs, he must do so in a reasonable manner and may be sued by anyone for damages sustained as the result of his making the repairs in a negligent manner.

(1) Independent contractor. If the landlord does not personally do the repair work but hires an independent contractor for that purpose, the landlord is charged with the negligence of the contractor, at least where the work is done on the premises retained by the landlord and the landlord was under a duty to the plaintiff to make repairs.

Chapter 13. LIABILITY FOR THE HOTEL AUTOMOBILE

§ 13:1. Particular aspects of motorist's duty of care.
    (a) Generally.
    (b) Standard of care.
    (c) Fit driver.
    (d) Safe vehicle.
    (e) Vehicle under control.
    (f) Lookout for others.
        (1) Anticipation of others.
        (2) Obscured vision.
    (g) Warning to others.

§ 13:2. Nature and use of vehicle.
    (a) Generally.
    (b) Physical nature of vehicle.
    (c) Emergency vehicles.

§ 13:3. Duty to persons on the highway.
    (a) Generally.
    (b) Persons under a disability.
        (1) Contributory negligence of person under disability.
    (c) Children.

§ 13:4. Expectable conduct of others.
    (a) Generally.
    (b) Limitations.
        (1) Effect on duty to maintain lookout.
        (2) Known misconduct of others.

§ 13:1. Particular aspects of motorist's duty of care.

(*a*) *Generally.* With the increasing use by a hotel of automobiles the question of liability for collision becomes increasingly important. For the sake of simplicity, the word "motorist" will be used in this chapter to refer to the hotel employee driving the vehicle in order to emphasize the fact that we are here concerned with general rules of tort law and not rules limited to hotels.

The importance of this chapter lies in the fact that the hotel may be vicariously liable for the negligence of its driver employee as described in Chapter 9.

(*b*) **Standard of care.** It is impossible to state just what a motorist must do in all cases in order to exercise due care. It is this very impossibility of prediction or of codification which has led to the adoption of the concept that the conduct in each case shall be considered on its facts and in the light of the general standard of conduct of a reasonable man. Otherwise stated, the inability to establish precise standards has led to a flexible rule that can be applied in all cases Nevertheless, the duty to exercise due care tends to divide into particular major areas or elements which are here considered.

Initially we start with the basic premise that there is no liability merely because someone is hurt. Thus, the motorist is not liable for harm he inflicts if in all respects he has exercised due care. It is of course true that the automobile has a high potential for inflicting harm and can be a dangerous thing in the hands of the improper driver. Ordinarily, however, this does not give the automobile the legal status of a "dangerous instrumentality." This label is reserved for things such as dynamite and wild animals, which by their very nature *ordinarily* have a high potential of harm, and because of which the law ordinarily imposes an absolute liability for harm caused without regard to fault. Although the automobile can be dangerous, the plaintiff still must prove fault.

The fact that the automobile has a potential of danger is merely one of the circumstances which the reasonable man must recognize in determining what care is to be taken to avoid foreseeable harm.

(*c*) **Fit driver.** It is negligent for a person to drive an automobile when he is not physically and mentally fit to do so. For example, if a person is subject to a condition or disease which may cause him to blackout or become unconscious, it is negligent for him to drive an automobile. Consequently, if he blacks out while driving he is liable for any harm which he causes while in that condition.

There is also authority that a motorist who falls asleep while driving is negligent as a matter of law when he fails to show any excuse or justification for his falling asleep, and the fact that he did not have any warning that he was going to fall asleep is not a sufficient excuse.

> *The facts:* The driver of an automobile suddenly told his companion "I feel sick" and fainted. The car ran into another automobile. The driver had no prior history of fainting and had been

in good health prior to the seizure. A guest in the car sued him for the injury she sustained in the collision. Was he liable for the harm done?

Decision: No. The sudden and unforeseen event of the driver's fainting spell was an accident. A driver does not guarantee that something may not happen which would incapacitate him where he has no reason to know that he might be subject to such incapacity. [Cohen v. Petty, 62 AppDC 187, 65 F2d 820 (1933)].

(d) Safe vehicle. The defendant is negligent if he goes upon the public highway in a vehicle which he knows or has reason to know is unsafe. For example, it is negligent to drive on a public highway with brakes which are defective. In such a case, a reasonable man would recognize that there is the possibility of being required to stop while driving at a substantial speed and that, as his car could not stop within the shorter range of a properly-equipped car, he would thereby be exposing other persons to greater risk.

(e) Vehicle under control. The automobilist must have his vehicle under control at all times so as to be able to avoid collision with pedestrians and other vehicles properly using the highways. This concept may be stated more specifically in some states as requiring that the driver exercise such control that the vehicle may be stopped in time to avoid collision or be able to stop within the distance that the driver can see ahead of the car. In some instances the concept is stated in terms of sufficient control as to be able to stop quickly.

The speed of the vehicle which is permitted, apart from speed limits, accordingly varies with visibility, time of day or night, strength of headlights of the driver's automobile, condition of the road, weight of the vehicle, and so on; all being factors which would affect the distance which the plaintiff could see ahead to be on the lookout for danger or his ability to stop within the area in which he can see.

(f) Lookout for others. A driver must maintain a continuous lookout in order to be aware of the presence of other persons or their property, so that he can make use of his ability to stop the automobile over which he has been maintaining proper control. After all, being able to stop within a given distance has no meaning unless the driver is also aware of what is on the road so that he can determine whether there is any need to stop within the given distance ahead of the car.

(1) Anticipation of others. In some cases, the duty to maintain a lookout for others rises higher, to a duty to anticipate the presence of others. This is largely a question of degree. The reasonable man will in all cases maintain a lookout to determine the presence of those who might be on the road, but in some situations he will look to determine the presence of those whom he realizes will be on the road.

To illustrate, he will expect the presence of persons and vehicles at crossings; the presence of persons at bus and trolley stops; the presence of persons crossing streets when school, football games, and theater shows let out; and so on.

(2) Obscured vision. The fact that the vision of the driver is obscured is a factor which determines whether the driver has exercised reasonable care. If the view of the intersection is blocked by a parked truck, it is negligence for the driver to sail through the intersection as though he had a clear view from a mile away.

In this connection it is immaterial whether the vision of the driver is obscured by conduct which is itself illegal, as by the illegal parking of another vehicle too near the corner or by the illegal erection of a billboard on the corner lot. It is likewise immaterial whether the obscurity is an act of nature or of man, such as dense mist or clouds of smoke.

(g) Warning to others. As a corollary of the duty of the motorist to look out for others is his duty to warn others of his presence, as by blowing his horn or changing his lights from low to high beam. The giving of a warning is not a substitute for other aspects of exercising due care, and the negligent driver does not escape liability by sounding his horn if it is too late for the victim to save himself from the peril which the negligent driver has already created.

§ 13:2. Nature and use of vehicle.

(a) Generally. The nature and use of a vehicle does not alter the basic principles that the driver must exercise the care of a reasonable man under the circumstances. The nature and the particular use of the vehicle are merely circumstances which the reasonable man must consider in determining whether he is taking reasonable care against reasonably foreseeable harm.

(b) Physical nature of vehicle. The driver of the larger vehicle or the heavily-loaded vehicle must recognize that he will or may have greater difficulty in stopping than a smaller or lighter car driven at the same speed. Likewise, the driver of a heavily-loaded passenger car in which the rear window is obscured must recognize the greater hazard which arises because of the restriction of his vision of rear traffic.

The reasonable man must bear in mind all such physical characteristics whether permanent or temporary, which at the time of operating the vehicle affect the care which he should exercise. Hence a motorist or truck driver is under the duty to know the essential characteristics or operational behavior of his vehicle, and he may be guilty of negligence when he does not.

> *The facts:* A truck driver employed by a trucking company was sent with a truck to pick up a loaded trailer from an oil corporation. He entered the premises of the oil corporation under a canopy which was clearly marked "Clearance 12 ft," which sign the plaintiff saw on entering. He received the trailer and attached it to the truck and then left by the same gate and canopy. He did not know the height of the trailer and took it for granted that if the trailer was too high for the canopy, the guard at the gate would warn him. The front end of the trailer was actually 1/2" too high for the canopy and pulled the canopy down on the cab, injuring the driver, who then sued the defendant oil company. Was it liable?
>
> *Decision:* No. The oil company performed its full duty to the plaintiff when it marked the canopy with the clearance height. The plaintiff in driving a trailer "had a duty to himself and to the public to know the machine he was operating and the size of the trailer." He was therefore guilty of contributory negligence when without knowledge he proceeded under the canopy. Moreover, this duty could not be discharged by relying upon the oil company's gate guard to inform him if he was not clearing the canopy. [Clark v. Cit Con Oil Corp. ... La ..., 150 So2d 784 (1963)].

(*c*) *Emergency vehicles.* Public and private vehicles used in emergencies are subject to the duty of using reasonable care. Thus, police and fire cars, ambulances, and private automobiles going to the hospital must all be driven with reasonable care. On the one hand, the fact that the vehicle may be a government vehicle or that it is used for emergency purpose does not relieve it from liability for negligence. On the other hand, the only duty of care is the general duty of exercising reasonable care. Sometimes the court will state the rule as requiring special care, as though there were a different legal standard. Actually the rule is still the ordinary rule of using reasonable care under the circumstances, but as the circumstances have changed to embrace an emergency, it is apparent that what must be done to be reasonable care has also changed.

In a number of states, the question of the liability of the emergency vehicle has been regulated by statute. In general, such statutes restate the duty of the emergency vehicle driver to exercise due care although their provisions are variously interpreted in the different states.

§ 13:3. Duty to persons on the highway.

(*a*) *Generally.* A driver is under the duty to exercise due care with respect to persons on the highway, such as pedestrians, workers, traffic officers, and persons repairing or using other motor vehicles. In general, the duty owed to all such persons is the same, although in the case of persons whose job requires them to be and stay on the highway, the driver is required to recognize that they must necessarily be where they are and thus expose themselves to a continuing and greater risk than the ordinary pedestrian. Specifically, the driver as a reasonable man will anticipate that the workman repairing the street or the traffic officer is the more likely to be in the street in a place of danger and that he is likely to stay in that general area. Accordingly, the driver must exercise such care as would be taken by a reasonable man to avoid harm to such persons.

(*b*) *Persons under a disability.* The driver must exercise toward all persons the care of a reasonable man to avoid harm. If he has no knowledge or reason to know that a person in the highway is under a disability, the driver need only act in the same manner as in the case of any other pedestrian.

If, however, the driver knows or has reason to know of the disability, he must act in the way in which a reasonable man with such knowledge would act to avoid harm. Hence the driver must recognize that the blind man will not see his headlights, that the deaf man will not hear his horn, and that the intoxicated person might not be aware of anything. If the driver fails to act as a reasonable man under such circumstances, when he has knowledge of the disability, he is negligent.

(1) Contributory negligence of person under disability. The person on the highway is not automatically guilty of contributory negligence by going onto the highway with a disability.

The fact that the person is under a disability does not bar him from going on the highway. However, he must exercise the care of a reasonable man suffering from his disability. For example, a person who is lame must not voluntarily place himself in a position from which only a physically sound person would be able to extricate himself. When the person under the disability fails to act as a reasonable man under his circumstances, he is guilty of contributory negligence.

(c) **Children.** The driver owes to children the same duty of care as to any other persons: that of a reasonable man under the circumstances. The exact content of what a reasonable man would do, obviously, is varied, in view of his knowledge of the expectable behavior patterns of children. Thus, the driver must anticipate that children may act the way children do and must expect that they are likely to be found in certain areas or at certain times. He must also recognize that children will be less likely to be aware of their peril or to take adequate steps for their own protection. The reasonable man must anticipate that they will dart out from behind parked automobiles and thus must be alerted by the sudden appearance of a ball rolling out into the street. The driver cannot rely on the fact that a child is accompanied by an adult person, for he must still recognize that the child may suddenly leave the adult and expose himself to danger.

The driver, by contrast, is not under any duty to anticipate the presence of children where there is no reason to expect them.

The facts: The defendant made a visit and parked his car. The people he visited had a number of children, the youngest, fifteen months old, was able to crawl but could not walk. When the defendant left his friends he returned to his car, talked to two of the older children for ten to fifteen minutes, started the car and went to drive away. In moving away he ran over the fifteen-month old child who had been underneath the car. In order to get under the car the child had had to crawl through the back door of the house a distance of 45' to 60' during the time the defendant was talking to the other children and to get under the car without his brothers and sisters seeing him. Was the defendant liable for the child's death?

Decision: No. There was no reason to anticipate the presence of the child underneath the automobile. The driver of an automobile is only required to exercise reasonable care. This does not require him to look underneath and around his automobile to locate children when he has no reason to expect they would be there. [Rose v. Nevitt, 56 Wash2d 882, 355 P2d 776 (1960)].

§ 13:4. Expectable conduct of others.

(*a*) *Generally.* A driver may assume that other drivers and pedestrians will respect traffic laws and will themselves exercise reasonable care. Thus, there is no liability on the part of the initial driver when he assumes that an approaching car is yielding the right of way to him, as it is required to do, but a collision results because the other car does not do so. Likewise, a driver has the right to assume that a pedestrian will not cross against a red light and into the face of his oncoming automobile. If that occurs, the driver is not liable.

(*b*) *Limitations.* The rule above stated is subject to the limitations that the reasonable man will recognize that other persons do not always obey the law and act with reasonable care. As reasonable men, we know that there are certain trouble situations where there is a high probability that someone will not live up to the proper standards. In the words of the cartoonist, we know that there are situations in which "They'll do it every time."

(*1*) *Effect on duty to maintain lookout.* As the reasonable man will anticipate the possible negligence of others, his lookout will extend to look for such conduct. For example, when the driver sees that he has the green light at the intersection he cannot shut his eyes to everything else and gun through the intersection. He must still recognize that pedestrians or vehicles may be crossing against the red light and must maintain a lookout which extends to the "fringes" of the intersecting street in order to see if there are any pedestrians or drivers who appear likely to be improperly entering the intersection.

As a further example, a reasonable man should anticipate that children playing on the sidewalk with a ball may run out into the street to retrieve the ball; that pedestrians will cross in the middle of the block; or that an animal, an older person, a person with a physical handicap, or a person who at the time is obviously intoxicated, may act in such a way as to call for a greater exercise of care if harm is to be avoided.

If the driver is aware of the misconduct of another person within sufficient time to avoid harm but fails to act, (a) he cannot recover from such other person for his own harm, and (b) the facts may be such that the other person may recover from the driver under the doctrine of last clear chance.[1]

---
[1] See § 10:3.

(2) Known misconduct of others. When the driver is in fact aware that other persons are walking or driving illegally or in a negligent manner, he must modify his own conduct to avoid reasonably foreseeable harm. This means that the other persons acting improperly are not "outlaws" who can be run over by the driver to punish them for their misconduct. Even though they are in the wrong, the driver must still act with reasonable care to avoid harm.

Chapter 14. LIABILITY AS TO SOLD PRODUCTS

§ 14:1. The problem.

§ 14:2. Theories of liability.
    (a) Generally.
    (b) Comparison of theories.
        (1) Failure to warn or give instructions.
        (2) Damages recoverable.

§ 14:3. Express warranties.
    (a) Generally.
    (b) Nature of express warranty.
    (c) Form of express warranty.
        (1) Conduct.
        (2) Signs and labels.
    (d) Time of making express warranty.
    (e) Opinions and value.
        (1) Hotel expert.

§ 14:4. Other warranties.
    (a) Generally.
    (b) Warranties of ownership.
    (c) Identity of goods.
    (d) Warranty of fitness for a special purpose.

§ 14:5. Food and drink.
    (a) Nature of the transaction.
    (b) Warranty of fitness for consumption.
        (1) Natural product exception.
        (2) Regular business of the hotel.
        (3) Allergy of patron.
    (c) Negligence.
    (d) Willful tort.
        (1) Liability for act of employee.

§ 14:6. Drugs, cosmetics, and preparations.
    (a) Generally.
    (b) Criminal liability of hotel.
    (c) Warranty of fitness for purpose.
        (1) Regular business of hotel.
        (2) Allergy of patron.

Liability as to Sold Products　　　　　　　　　　　　　　**219**

　　　　　(d) Negligence.
　　　　　(e) Willful tort.
　　　　　(f) Fraud.
§ 14:7.　Merchandise and sporting goods.
　　　　　(a) Generally.
　　　　　(b) Statutory regulation.
　　　　　(c) Warranty of fitness for purpose.
　　　　　　　　(1) Regular business of hotel.
　　　　　　　　(2) Allergy of patron.
　　　　　(d) Other bases of liability.
§ 14:8.　Restriction or avoidance of liability.
　　　　　(a) Generally.
　　　　　(b) Business organization.
　　　　　　　　(1) Disclosed character of concessionaire.
　　　　　(c) Contract limitation of liability.
　　　　　　　　(1) Limitations on waiver.
　　　　　(d) Liability insurance.
　　　　　(e) Proximate cause.
§ 14:9.　Who may sue the hotel.
　　　　　(a) Generally.
　　　　　(b) Injury to buyer.
　　　　　(c) Injury to buyer's family, household, and guests.
　　　　　　　　(1) Recovery allowed under the Code.
　　　　　　　　(2) Recovery allowed under general law.
　　　　　　　　(3) Recovery denied.
　　　　　(d) Injury to buyer's employees and to strangers.
　　　　　　　　(1) Generally.
　　　　　　　　(2) Recovery allowed.
　　　　　　　　(3) Recovery denied.
§ 14:10.　Remedies of hotel when sued.
　　　　　(a) Generally.
　　　　　(b) Knowledge of occurrence.
　　　　　(c) Pendency of action.
　　　　　　　　(1) Notice to insurer.
　　　　　　　　(2) Notice to hotel's supplier.
　　　　　(d) Payment of loss.
　　　　　　　　(1) Suit against hotel's supplier.
　　　　　　　　(2) Suit against remote distributor or manufacturer.

§ 14:1. The problem.

Patrons and guests of the hotel may be harmed by the food or beverages they eat and drink; or by products sold in the hotel's store; or by products used in the hotel beauty shop or barber shop. To what extent is the hotel liable for the harm caused by such products? As a further complication, the product may be purchased by one person for the use of another. When the latter person is harmed by the product, may he sue the hotel, although he had never made any contract with the hotel?

Because of its virtual universal adoption, this chapter is written on the basis of the Uniform Commercial Code unless otherwise indicated.

§ 14:2. Theories of liability.

(*a*) ***Generally.*** In general, the plaintiff's cause of action will rest upon one of four theories: (1) breach of warranty, (2) negligence, (3) fraud, or (4) strict tort liability.[1] Under modern systems of pleading, the plaintiff in most states will be allowed to aver any two or all four of these grounds in the alternative, and then recover on any theory which proves to be supported by the facts.

In most instances, it is easier for the plaintiff to prove breach of warranty than either negligence or fraud; and in most instances it is easier for him to prove negligence than fraud. This is seen by considering the elements which must be shown under each theory.

(*b*) ***Comparison of theories.*** In the action for breach of warranty, the plaintiff is only required to establish that there was a warranty, that it was broken, that he was harmed, and the extent of his harm.

In contrast, in the action for negligence, the plaintiff must in a sense go into the enemy's camp and show that the defendant was guilty of conduct which fell below the standard of care which a reasonable man would exercise. In many instances, the plaintiff will find it impossible to do this because he will not be able to show what the defendant did in connection with the particular item he has purchased, or the lot of which the item was a unit, or because the witnesses will generally be employees of the defendant who will be unwilling to testify against their employer and who will therefore state that they did not see what happened or do not know. In most instances the hotel will be able to show that it had exercised due care in that it had purchased the product from a reliable manufacturer and merely resold it without having any reason to know of any defect.

---

[1] See Supplement p. 474.

The action for fraud requires the plaintiff to go into the defendant's mind and prove that the defendant had the necessary mental state to constitute fraud, in addition to proving all the other elements of the cause of action for fraud.

In fact, it has been the difficulty of proving a case for negligence or for fraud which has caused the law to gradually expand so as to permit recovery for breach of warranty.

(1) Failure to warn or give instructions. Liability may arise because of the failure of the vendor to give warning of the nature or defects of the commodity sold. Depending upon the mental state of the vendor, this may be regarded as negligence in failing to take steps to prevent foreseeable harm or actual fraud in concealing the character of the goods in order to effect a sale.

> *The facts:* A shipment of bottled soft drinks received by the hotel had been dangerously overcharged. A number of bottles had exploded while in the custody of the hotel or in the possession of its guests. When the plaintiff guest ordered a soft drink through room service, the hotel sent up a bottle taken from this shipment. The guest was injured when the bottle exploded. The hotel claimed it was not liable. Decide.
>
> *Decision:* If the hotel through past experience with the product knows that it carries the potential of harm, the hotel is liable when it continues to serve or sell the harmful product. The hotel knew, through the repeated explodings, that this shipment of bottles was overcharged. Consequently the hotel was liable to the guest injured by such an exploding bottle when it permitted room service to deliver him a bottle from the dangerous shipment. It was further negligent in not warning him of the hazard connected with the shipment from which the particular bottle was taken. [Soper v. Enid Hotel Co. ... Okla ..., 383 P2d 7 (1963)].

Similarly a supplier of equipment has the duty of giving adequate instructions in its use and is liable for the failure to do so, when such failure results in harm to the buyer or other lawful users of the equipment. But, as in any other case, the person injured may be barred by his own fault or negligence.

> *The facts:* The defendant sold and installed an incinerator in a school cafeteria. A school employee loaded the incinerator heavily with empty paper milk cartons. The cartons apparently did not start burning and the employee opened the door of the incinerator to see what the trouble was. There was a sudden intense burning of the paper containers and the employee was

burnt before she could close the door. She sued the defendant on the ground that he had failed to give instructions in the use of the incinerator.

Decision: Judgment for defendant. An incinerator is merely a type of stove, and everyone knows that if the door of a stove is opened, the rate of burning is intensified because of the entry of a larger quantity of air. A seller or supplier is not under any duty to give warning as to matters which are of common knowledge. The injury of the plaintiff was caused by her own carelessness and not the failure to give instructions. [Parker v. Heasler Plumbing Co., ... Wyom ... , 388 P2d 516 (1964)].

(2) Damages recoverable. Basically the damages which the plaintiff can recover tend to be the same whether the action is for breach of warranty, negligence, or fraud. There are a number of exceptions and variations to this statement but the general trend can be said to be in the direction of allowing the plaintiff to recover all that he has lost through the defendant's wrongful conduct.[1a]

As a modification to this statement, there is the possibility that in the negligence and the fraud cases, when the conduct of the defendant appears extreme and highly improper, the jury may award the plaintiff not only compensatory damages, to compensate him for his actual loss, but also punitive or exemplary damages, which are additional damages which the defendant is required to pay in order to punish him or make an example of him because of his outrageous conduct.

§ 14:3. Express warranties.

(a) Generally. We do not ordinarily think of the hotel as being liable for breach of warranty, but to the extent that the hotel sells food, drink, drugs, or merchandise of any kind, it is in the position of a seller and therefore can be held liable whenever a seller can be held liable, provided the person making the warranty had authority to speak on behalf of the hotel and bind it with respect to the sales transaction.

(b) Nature of express warranty. An express warranty is any statement relating to the goods which forms part of the basis for the sale. Otherwise stated, it is a statement which leads the buyer to make the purchase because he believes the statement to be true. If the customer asks the hotel druggist what is good for removing spots, the druggist makes an express war-

---

[1a] As to strict tort damages, see Supplement p. 475.

ranty when he says: "This product is good for that," and hands the customer a can of some fluid. The statement of the druggist constitutes an express warranty that the contents of the can is a substance which will work as he has declared. Assuming that the druggist is or is deemed the hotel employee, the hotel would be liable for the harm to the customer's clothing if it should turn out that the contents of the can were harmful to clothing since "good for spots" would to a reasonable man have the meaning that it was effective to remove the spots but not harmful to the fabric from which they were removed.

(c) *Form of express warranty.* No express form of words is required to constitute an express warranty. That is to say, the salesman is not required to say, "We warrant," "We stand in back of," "We guarantee," or any similar expression. The simple statement of fact that the product "is" or "does" is a warranty although it is not said that there is any warranty and even though the hotel's agent may mentally have the intent that no warranty should exist.

The express warranty may consist of spoken words: for the sale ordinarily made by a hotel will not require a writing in order to be binding.[1b]

(1) *Conduct.* The express warranty may be based upon conduct. For example, in the illustration above given of the spot remover, assume that the customer asked the druggist for something good for spots and then the druggist without saying a word, handed the customer a can. It is obvious that the act of handing the can to the customer is an expression by the druggist that this is a can of such substance as is requested by the customer; and therefore his action constitutes an express warranty that the contents of the can is good for removing spots.

(2) *Signs and labels.* An express warranty may be made by placing goods on a counter under a sign which bears a particular statement. For example, assume there is a sign on a table on a counter which says "Jones' Cleaner — Good for removing spots from clothing." If this sign refers to a display of tin cans, the effect thereof is to state to a reasonable man that what is in the tin cans is Jones' Cleaner and so forth. By the mere act of putting the cans on a display with this sign, the hotel makes a statement to all customers as to the nature of the

---

[1b]When the transaction is for a price of $500 or more a writing is required under the Code.

contents of the can and is therefore bound by an express warranty to that effect.

It is immaterial whether the sign in the above situation was made by the hotel or was furnished by the manufacturer of the product. The hotel by using the manufacturer's or distributor's advertising materials adopts them as its own, just as though it had said the words itself, and is therefore liable for the statements which orginated with the manufacturer or distributor.

From the foregoing it naturally follows that when the label on the can which the hotel sells contains various statements as to what the contents are and will do, that the hotel by its act of selling the can, with that label thereon, is appearing to back up the words on the label; and its act of selling therefore constitutes an express warranty that the contents of the can are everything that the label states them to be. The fact that the hotel has no actual knowledge of the contents of the can and has no reasonable way of checking thereon is immaterial.

> *The facts:* The customer purchased frankfurters from a supermarket. They were contained in a sealed plastic bag and were manufactured by a manufacturer of good reputation. There was no evidence of negligence but when the customer ate the frankfurters he was cut by pieces of glass. The customer sued the supermarket. It defended on the ground that it was merely a middleman and that it could not have known what was in the sealed container.
>
> *Decision:* Judgment for customer. The fact that a vendor is merely a middleman and cannot tell anything about the product because it is in a sealed container does not affect its liability as a seller of foods. He therefore remains liable for breach of warranty when, in effect, he has assumed the risk of selling products without being able to examine their actual condition. [Sams v. Ezy-Way Foodliner Company, 157 Maine 10, 170 A2d 160 (1961)].

(d) *Time of making express warranty.* It is immaterial whether the express warranty is made before, during, or after the sales transaction. For example, a statement made by the hotel to a worried or puzzled customer who phones back to the hotel a few hours later is binding as an express warranty when it is a statement on behalf of which the customer relies. To illustrate, if no warranty had been made as to whether the can of spot remover would remove spots from silk, we might have the purchaser phoning the hotel's store later on and asking

"Are you sure that this stuff removes spots from silk?" To this the store replies, "Yes, it will." This is a statement relating to the nature of the goods which constitutes an express warranty and it is immaterial that it was made after the sale.[2]

(*e*) *Opinions and value.* The fact that the hotel recommends a particular article, or expresses an opinion as to its merits or value does not constitute an express warranty. This is for the reason that the customer should recognize that this is just "sales talk" and hence that he cannot rely on it or treat it as though it were a statement of fact.

(1) Hotel expert. If the customer of the hotel is relying upon the opinion or judgment of the hotel and the hotel is an expert in the field of the particular commodity, the hotel's statement as to quality, merits, or value can be an express warranty. This situation will not arise ordinarily but could arise in connection with a resort hotel which has a sport shop. For example, if the hotel's ski shop is run by a person held out to be an expert, and a beginner asks the expert's advice as to what to buy, the expert's statement of why a particular article should be purchased is an express warranty that it has the value or merits that the expert states. Moreover, in such a situation an implied warranty will also arise that the article would be reasonably fit for the purpose for which it was furnished.

§ 14:4. Other warranties.

(*a*) *Generally.* Whenever a hotel sells any goods to a buyer it is regarded as thereby automatically guaranteeing the buyer certain things. This is described technically by saying that certain warranties are implied. Ordinarily these warranties create no problem for the hotel. It is important, however, to recognize their existence for the occasional case in which they may be significant.

(*b*) *Warranties of ownership.* When the hotel sells any commodity it thereby warrants that the buyer will receive the title to the commodity and that there will not be any encumbrance upon the property. This means that if the goods sold by the hotel are stolen goods the buyer has the right to sue the hotel and the innocence and good faith of the hotel are no defense.

---

[2] In non-Code states, the warranty made after the sale is completed is not binding on the theory that there is no consideration to support it.

Similarly, the items sold the buyer may be subject to a claim in favor of a creditor, manufacturer, or distributor, of the hotel. If the buyer does not acquire a title clear of such outstanding claims, the hotel is liable to the extent of loss sustained by the buyer.

In most instances, these problems do not arise because the method of financing will be such that the creditor's claim disappears from the goods when purchased by the ultimate customer, or because the amount involved is so small that it is not worth disputing. The problem could arise when the hotel's sport shop sells expensive equipment or when the hotel, in the process of renovation, sells a bulk of its old furniture to a second-hand dealer or otherwise disposes of it.

(*c*) *Identity of goods.* A number of warranties arise to assure that the buyer will get just what he ordered. Thus there is a warranty that the goods which the buyer receives will conform to any statement as to what goods are or will do. Likewise there is a warranty that the goods will conform or match the description, sample, or model on the basis of which the customer made his purchase.

(*d*) *Warranty of fitness for a special purpose.* Ordinarily the hotel will not be liable because the article purchased does not meet some special or peculiar need of the buyer, distinct from the ordinary use to which such things are put. The exception could arise, as in the case of the hotel drug store in which the buyer relies on the store's superior skill and judgment in telling him what he needs. When this situation arises, the hotel is bound by a warranty that the goods purchased by the customer will satisfy such particular purpose of the buyer.

§ 14:5. Food and drink.

(*a*) *Nature of the transaction.* When the hotel sells food and drink it is immaterial whether the sale is made for consumption in the dining room or the purchaser intends to take the purchase with him. In both cases it is treated as a sale of goods under the Code.

(*b*) *Warranty of fitness for consumption.* When the hotel sells food or drink it automatically makes a warranty or guarantee that the food and drink are fit for human consumption. If it is not so fit, there is a breach of warranty for which the seller is liable.

(1) Natural product exception. No breach of warranty arises when the harmful object found in the food or drink was of such a nature that it could be expected to be present in the food, as an oyster shell in oysters, a chicken bone in chicken, and so forth. Here recovery is denied on the theory that the consumer should anticipate the presence of bones, shells, and so forth, which were part of the natural state of the food prior to its preparation.

Moreover, in some instances the bone or shell is of such size that a reasonable man must necessarily have been aware of its existence; with the result that the consumer is deemed contributorily negligent by the fact that he proceeded to eat or drink in spite of the presence of such foreign object.

(2) Regular business of the hotel. In order for the warranty above described to arise, it is necessary that the hotel regularly engage in the business of selling food, although it is immaterial in what manner it does so; that is, whether it is in a private restaurant, a diner, a beach house, and so forth.

If the hotel does not regularly sell food but merely does so in a given instance it is not liable for the harm caused the buyer in the absence of negligence or willfully-inflicted harm through the supplying of known dangerous food. For example, assume that the hotel does not sell food ordinarily but to accommodate a guest who arrives late at night or guests who are trapped in the hotel in a snow-storm, the hotel sells food which it purchases for the particular occasion or which it ordinarily provides only for some of its employees. In such situations, the hotel is merely a casual seller and the patron who buys food is taking pot luck; if the luck is bad, he can hold the hotel responsible only for negligence or willful harm, but not for breach of warranty.

(3) Allergy of patron. The food supplied by the hotel to the patron may be normal food in that it would ordinarily not harm anyone. The patron in question is harmed, or made very ill, or even killed by the food, because this patron has a particular allergy to something about the food. If the allergy is an unusual or relatively unusual allergy the hotel is not liable for the harm caused this particular patron.

(c) **Negligence.** Regardless of whether the hotel engages in the sale of food regularly or not, it is liable to a patron when the hotel is negligent in the purchase, preparation, or serving of the food because of which the patron is harmed. For example, the hotel patron might be made sick because the meal he purchases contained food which had spoiled because the hotel's cook carelessly allowed the food to stand an unreasonably long time without refrigeration.

(*d*) **Willful tort.** If the hotel would serve a patron with a food or a drink which was harmful in character and did so with the intention of producing harm, or playing a practical joke, the hotel is liable for any harm which results. To illustrate, the hotel, in order to rid itself of a pest or for the purpose of driving away the patronage of a particular person or class of persons, purposely feeds the patron food which was unfit to eat with the intent of making him sick thereby so that he would not come back again. If it can be shown that the hotel acted with the intent to cause harm, it will be liable for any harm which in fact follows from the eating of the food, even though the harm actually sustained went beyond the range intended by the hotel.

To illustrate, the hotel had only intended to make the person mildly sick, but this mild sickness aggravated a condition of the patron's stomach which was unknown to the hotel. Here the hotel will be liable for the additional harm, both physical and pain and suffering which the patron sustains.

(*1*) *Liability for act of employee.* There is a possibility that when the harm is willfully caused, the hotel may not be liable on the theory that its employee in doing an act to cause harm intentionally was acting outside the scope of his employment and his actions would not impose liability on the hotel.

If the harm was caused by the hotel employee as a personal practical joke on the patron or because of a personal dislike or animosity toward him, the hotel will ordinarily not be liable. In contrast, if the employee of the hotel did the act for the purpose of advancing the interest of the hotel, as by getting rid of the patron whom the employee knew the hotel wanted removed, the modern rule of law will hold the hotel liable, although some of the older cases would regard the employee as going outside of the scope of his employment in such case, and thus not subjecting the employer-hotel to liability for his act[3]

In any case, the hotel is of course liable if the employee, in causing harm to the patron, is acting under orders given by a superior employee of the hotel who has authority to give

---

[3] See § 6:3.

orders which would bind the hotel. Likewise the hotel will be subject to supervisory liability, as contrasted with vicarious liability above considered, if the hotel knew of the employee's habit of playing such practical jokes and did nothing to stop him or was negligent in hiring an unfit person.[4]

§ 14:6. Drugs, cosmetics, and preparations.

(*a*) *Generally.* The hotel may sell or furnish patrons or guests with drugs, cosmetics, and preparations. These may be directly applied to the patron as in the case of the beauty shop or barber shop, or they may be sold in containers to the customer with or without adequate labeling thereon.

(*b*) *Criminal liability of hotel.* State statutes may prohibit certain sales or sales under certain conditions, as prohibiting sales to minors or sales at certain hours. In addition to state statutes, federal legislation may be applicable where the goods consist of misbranded or adulterated foods, drugs, cosmetics and therapeutic devices. The federal statutes embrace such legislation as the Pure Food, Drug and Cosmetic Act, as amended; the Color Additive Acts of 1958 and 1962; and the Drug Industry Act of 1962.

(*c*) *Warranty of fitness for purpose.* In most cases, the hotel is liable where the preparation or drug causes harm to the patron, in consequence of the fact that the act of selling the product gives rise to a warranty to the buyer-patron that the product is fit for its ordinary use or purpose. When that is so, the hotel-seller is liable for breach of warranty without regard to whether it was careless or not, and without regard to whether it knew or had reason to know that the product was in any way defective or harmful.

(*1*) *Regular business of hotel.* In order for a warranty of fitness for purpose to arise it is necessary either (a) that the hotel has regularly engaged in selling such products, in which case an implied warranty of fitness arises, or (b) the hotel has made some statement which serves as an express warranty that it is fit for use.

With respect to the element of regularly engaging in business, the situation is the same as in the case of foods. Hence, if all drug stores are closed and the hotel as a favor to the guest sells

---

[4]See § 5:3.

him a patent medicine which the desk man finds in the first aid kit or in the house physician's closet, there is no warranty that the product is fit for any purpose.

(2) Allergy of patron. The hotel is not liable for harm which results from the buyer's particular allergy. Again the situation is the same as in the case of the sale of food and drink.

(*d*) **Negligence.** If the hotel had been negligent in the keeping, handling, or dispensing, or use, of the drug or preparation, it is liable for its negligence in the same way in which it would be liable in the food and drink case.

(*e*) **Willful tort.** If the hotel sells the patron a preparation or drug with the intention of causing him discomfort, annoyance, harm, or pain, it is liable for all the consequences which proximately flow from the doing of such act. Here the situation is the same as in the willful tort inflicted through the serving of food or drink. Likewise the problem is the same as to tort liability of the hotel for the acts of its employee.

(*f*) **Fraud.** In the case of the sale of a drug or preparation, the factual situation of the willful tort may also take the form of fraud. Here the sale is made to the patron by means of false statements as to the product, the object being to get the patron's money or to get rid of the product in question, as opposed to any desire to cause the patron loss or harm. To the contrary, the hotel in such a situation would ordinarily hope that no harm would result so that its fraud would not be discovered.

If it can be shown that the hotel was guilty of fraud, and that the patron sustained harm through the fraud, even though it was merely the losing of the good money which he paid, the hotel is liable for such harm. To constitute fraud it must be shown that the hotel made a false statement as to a material fact either (1) knowing that the statement was false and intending to deceive, or (2) not knowing whether the statement was true but being recklessly indifferent to whether it was or not and to the consequences which might flow from its being false.

The same question arises as in the case of willful torts generally, with respect to whether the hotel is liable for such an act of its employee.

§ 14:7. Merchandise and sporting goods.

(*a*) *Generally.* The hotel may run a store in which it sells ordinary merchandise or commodities or a particular kind of merchandise, such as sporting goods. Here the product is the same as could be purchased in any ordinary store of the kind in question not associated with a hotel. Obviously the hotel which so engages in the selling business is liable the same as though selling were its only business, and its liability with respect to the goods it sells must be the same as in the case of any other merchant of similar products.

(*b*) *Statutory regulation.* The hotel-seller, as in the case of any other seller of commodities, may be subject either generally or specifically with respect to particular products to various regulatory ordinances and statutes. With respect to federal statutes, the hotel, subject to the nature of the product may be liable under the Fur Labeling Act of 1921, the Textile Fibre Products Identification Act of 1958, the Hazardous Substances Labeling Act of 1960, or the Flammable Fabrics Act of 1953.

(*c*) *Warranty of fitness for purpose.* When the hotel regularly sells the merchandise in question, there is the usual implied warranty of a vendor that the merchandise is fit for the ordinary purpose for which it is sold.

(1) Regular business of hotel. If the sale of the product or class of products in question is not regularly engaged in by the hotel, no implied warranty arises as to fitness for ordinary purpose, and any liability of fitness must rest on some other theory.

(2) Allergy of patron. The problem is the same here as in the case of the sale of food and drugs discussed above.

(*d*) *Other bases of liability.* The hotel, whether it regularly engages in the business of selling the product or line of products in question may be liable to the injured person for negligence, willful tort, or fraud. The principles governing these theories are the same with respect to merchandise and sporting goods as in the case of the sale of drugs, cosmetics, and preparations.

§ 14:8. Restriction or avoidance of liability.

(*a*) *Generally.* The hotel may restrict or avoid liability by taking certain precautions with respect to an individual sale or as to the manner of doing business generally.

(*b*) *Business organization.* The easiest way for the hotel to avoid liability for breach of warranty is to operate its store as a concession and to show by signs on the premises that the store is owned and operated by the concessionaire rather than by the hotel. When the independent character of the concessionaire is made public, the hotel stands in the same position as does the landlord of any other store property to a customer who deals with the tenant who has rented the store property. That is, the tenant and the concessionaire are independent persons for whose acts the landlord-hotel is not liable.

(1) Undisclosed character of concessionaire. If a reasonable man looking at the hotel store would not see any sign or indication that the store was not run by the hotel itself, the above rule would not be applied. That is, if the store appears to be run by the hotel itself, the hotel is estopped or denied the right to claim that only the concessionaire is liable, and instead, is held liable as though it were in fact the hotel's own store.

(*c*) *Contract limitation of liability.* In general, the hotel, when it sells any article, may include in the transaction a provision reducing its liability to a stated amount or limiting its liability to the doing of certain things, as to replacing defective parts free, or providing free labor for repairs.

Implied warranties are waived by such terms as "as is," "with all faults," or other language which to the ordinary man has the meaning that there are no implied warranties. If there is a written contract, a warranty of fitness can only be waived by a conspicuous statement therein to that effect. All implied warranties of fitness are excluded by a statement such as "there are no warranties which extend beyond the description on the face thereof."

> *The facts:* The plaintiff purchased a used automobile from the defendant. The written contract stated: "Car is sold as is. No warranty." A few days after this, the car did not run and the seller repaired the car for the buyer. The car did not stay in a running condition and the buyer sued the seller for breach of warranty, claiming that (1) there was an implied warranty that the car was fit for use and (2) when the defendant returned the

car after having repaired it he thereby made a further implied warranty that it was then fit for use.

Decision: Judgment for defendant. No implied warranty of fitness arose in connection with the sale because the contract by its express terms excluded any warranty. The fact that the seller took the car back for repairs, or that the repairs were made, did not constitute a waiver by the seller of the "no warranty" clause nor did his returning the automobile as having been repaired constitute a warranty that from then on it would be fit for use. [Yanish v. Fernandex, 156 Colo 225, 397 P2d 881 (1965). (The court also held, as is likewise held in many states, that no warranty of fitness arose in connection with the sale of used or secondhand goods.)].

Implied warranties are also waived as to any defect which the buyer could have discovered by reasonable examination, when, either he makes the examination and fails to notice the defect, or waives the right to make the examination.

(1) Limitations on waiver. Under the Code a limitation of liability in a given case may be void because it is deemed to be unreasonable or unconscionable. In some states, special statutes may also declare that waivers as to particular classes of merchandise or consumer goods are void.

Furthermore there may be liability for fraud even though warranties have been waived.

The facts: The buyer purchased a tractor and scraper as new equipment of current model. The written contract stated that the seller disclaimed all warranties and that no warranties existed except as were stated in the contract. Actually, the equipment was not the current model but that of the prior year. Likewise, the equipment was not new but had been used for 68 hours as a demonstrator model and then the hour meter had been reset to zero. The buyer sued the seller for damages. The latter defended on the ground that all liability for warranties had been disclaimed.

Decision: The seller had knowingly sold the equipment under the misrepresentations that it was new and that it was the current model. This was fraudulent and the disclaimer of liability for breach of warranty did not affect the liability of the seller for his fraud. [McInnis v. Western Tractor & Equipment Co., 63 Wash2d 652, 388 P2d 562 (1964)].

(d) Liability insurance. The most practical solution for the hotel is to carry product liability insurance. That is, insurance

which provides coverage against loss or liability resulting from harm caused by any food, drink, drugs, and other articles sold by the hotel. This generally may be obtained either as a separate policy called product liability insurance, or as part of a general risk of business policy, or as part of a general policy protecting the hotel against public liability.

(*e*) *Proximate cause.* In a given case, the hotel may be shielded from liability because the jury finds that the commodity which caused the harm to the buyer was tampered with in some way or adulterated by a third person. If this conclusion is reached by the jury it necessarily follows that the seller-hotel is not liable for the harm.

14:9. Who may sue the hotel.

(*a*) *Generally.* Assuming that the hotel is liable for harm caused by the use or consumption of something which it has sold, the question then arises as to who may bring suit against the hotel. This question is complicated in terms of who has purchased the article from the hotel and who has been injured.

(*b*) *Injury to buyer.* In the most simple situation, the buyer from the hotel is himself harmed. For example, the customer purchases food and is made sick thereby. In such case, assuming the existence of a warranty or other basis for liability, the buyer may sue the hotel for the damages which he has sustained.

(*c*) *Injury to buyer's family, household, and guests.* The person actually purchasing from the hotel may not be the one injured. Instead the person injured is a member of the buyer's family or of his household, or is his guest. In such case, the buyer cannot sue for the injuries sustained by such person because a person can only sue for the harm actually done to him. The question then arises whether the person actually injured can sue the hotel when he was not the hotel's customer. The common law refused to allow such a stranger to the contract to sue for a breach by the seller-hotel of its obligations. This concept has gradually been abandoned as follows:

(*1*) *Recovery allowed under the Code.* In states which have adopted the Code, the injured third person, when he is a member of the buyer's family or household or is his guest, may sue for the harm caused by the hotel's breach of the warranty arising from the sale by the hotel to the buyer, when harm to such other person should have been reasonably foreseen by the hotel if the goods purchased by the buyer were defective in any way.

In such case, recovery is limited to personal injuries sustained by the third person and does not extend to property damage. By way of illustration, the hotel guest buys a package of dye in the hotel drug store for his adult daughter. Because of a defect in the dye, the dress which the daughter dyes is ruined. Under the Code the father could not sue for the ruined dress which he does not own as he has not sustained any loss. The daughter who has sustained the loss through the damage to her dress cannot sue under the Code either because the injury sustained is property loss and not personal injury.

(2) Recovery allowed under general law. Independently of the Code, many states allow recovery by the family member, household member, or guest of the buyer. Thus where personal injury is sustained the same result is reached in these states as under the Code. Recovery as allowed under this rule is broader than that under the Code as recovery is allowed under the general rule for damage to property as well as to person, whereas the Code is limited to recovery for personal injuries. The fact that a state has adopted the Code does not prevent this broader recovery under general law.

This right of the third person to sue is recognized generally, on the theory that privity of contract is no longer required, either generally in all such cases, or at least when the article purchased was a food, drink, or drug.

(3) Recovery denied. In some states, recovery by the third person is denied on the broad general ground that privity of contract is always required and its absence bars suit by a stranger, or on the particular ground that it bars recovery in the particular case, as because the harm sustained was to property, where suit is brought under the Code; or that the product was not a food, drink, or drug.

(d) **Injury to buyer's employees and to strangers.**

(1) Generally. The Uniform Commerical Code expressly refrains from regulating such situations as the suit of a buyer's employee against the hotel-seller or a suit by a total stranger against the hotel-seller. The question of the liability of the

hotel in such case is therefore governed by general or non-Code law.

(2) Recovery allowed. In a number of states, the buyer's employee and the stranger will be allowed to recover from the hotel. In some states this right to recover will be limited to claims arising with respect to foods, drugs, beverages, and dangerous instrumentalities.

(3) Recovery denied. In some states, the hotel is not liable to the buyer's employee or the total stranger, on the ground that such other person is not a party to the contract which binds the hotel as seller. That is, the third person is not in privity of contract with the hotel and therefore cannot enforce any rights which arise under the contract with the hotel.

§ 14:10. Remedies of hotel when sued.

(a) *Generally.* When the hotel might be sued by a buyer there are certain steps which it can take to protect itself before any action is brought against it, after an action has been brought against it, and after it has paid any claim or judgment against it.

(b) *Knowledge of occurrence.* As soon as the hotel has knowledge that there is anything wrong or any event which might give rise to liability, both its attorney and the insurer on its public liability or products liability should be notified as soon as possible. In addition, the hotel should make every effort to gather evidence as discussed in Chapter 23.

(c) *Pendency of action.*

(1) Notice to insurer. Once an action has been brought against the hotel, notice of that fact must ordinarily be given promptly to the hotel's liability insurer. Likewise, process, pleadings, and any other papers served upon the hotel in the action must be forwarded to the insurer.

(2) Notice to hotel's supplier. If the hotel is sued for a breach of warranty for which the hotel's supplier is liable over to it, as discussed under subheading (d) which follows, the hotel may give such seller written notice of the lawsuit. In this notice, the hotel may state that the hotel's supplier may defend the action against the hotel and that if the supplier does not do so he will then be bound by any determination of fact made in the

action against the hotel when such facts come into dispute in a later action brought by the hotel against the supplier to recover the damages that the hotel has been required to pay its customer. In Code states, if the hotel's supplier fails to appear and defend the action he is bound by the questions of fact so determined in the first action and cannot reopen the questions so decided when he is thereafter sued by the hotel.

(**d**) **Payment of loss.** After the hotel has paid the amount recovered against it by its customer, it may then turn around and sue the seller and any prior distributor and the manufacturer of the product to the following extent:

(1) Suit against hotel's supplier. As the hotel and its supplier are the parties to a contract of sale in which the hotel is the buyer, the hotel has all the remedies against the supplier which any buyer has against his seller. The hotel may therefore hold its seller liable for breach of warranty, negligence, strict tort and fraud, under the same principles which determined whether the customer could sue the hotel on those theories.

In this case, the damage which the hotel has sustained is the amount which it has been required to pay to its purchaser, together with the possible addition of punitive or exemplary damages where the supplier's conduct was particularly outrageous, willful, or high-handed. If the hotel can show a loss of business in consequence of the supplier's breach, recovery may also be had for such element of damages.

(2) Suit against remote distributor or manufacturer. In this case, the hotel is not a party to any contract with the remote distributor who sold the goods to the supplier who supplied the hotel, nor with the manufacturer who has made the goods. The problem is therefore the same as in the case of a suit against the hotel brought by the employee of the customer of the hotel or by a total stranger. The same principles considered in connection with that class of suits governs here.

In some states the rule is followed that since there is no privity between the hotel and such remote persons there can be no recovery by the hotel. In others, recovery is allowed without regard to the absence of privity of contract, particularly where the remote party has conducted general or widespread advertising in which he has sought to appeal directly to the ultimate consumer rather than merely to the wholesaler or dealer who actually purchases the goods from him.

In virtually all states, the hotel may sue the remote defendant when food, drink, drugs, or a dangerous instrumentality is involved. The right to sue a remote party is rapidly expanding to permit suit without regard to the kind of goods involved.

Chapter 15. LIABILITY AS TO SUPPLIED PRODUCTS

§ 15:1. The problem.

§ 15:2. Liability of bailee.
    (a) Standard of care.
    (b) Reasonable care.
    (c) Unauthorized use.
    (d) Modification of liability by contract.

§ 15:3. Liability of bailor.
    (a) Generally.
    (b) Known defect.
    (c) Unknown defect.
    (d) Fault of bailee.
    (e) Waiver of defenses as against bailor's assignee.

§ 15:4. Liability to third persons.
    (a) Liability of bailee.
    (b) Liability of bailor.

§ 15:1. The problem.

The hotel may rent or borrow automobiles, tractors, boats, sporting equipment, and so on from a holding corporation, another hotel, or a supplier. The hotel in turn may rent or loan such articles to its patrons. The relationship that arises when there is a renting or a lending of such items is a bailment. Various questions may arise as to the liability of the parties to the bailment to each other and with respect to third persons.

The problems here considered are similar to those considered in Chapter 14 which arise when there is a sale. But here there is only a rental or lending and different principles of law apply.

As the questions now considered are part of the general law of bailments,[1] reference will be made to the parties as bailor and bailee; bearing in mind that when the hotel obtains possession of the property from another, the hotel is the bailee; when it

---

[1] As to bailments generally, see Anderson and Kumpf, Business Law (9th ed 1972 South-Western Publishing Co.) Chapters 28, 29.

transfers possession to a patron, the hotel is the bailor and the patron is the bailee.

§ 15:2. Liability of bailee.

(a) *Standard of care.* A bailee is required to exercise reasonable care of the bailed property and must not make an unauthorized use of it. If he conforms to this standard he is not liable for loss caused by an act of God, namely a natural phenomenon which is not reasonably foreseeable; the act of a third person, whether willful or negligent; or an accident, defined as an occurrence for which no one is legally responsible.

(b) *Reasonable care.* The bailee must exercise that care which a reasonable man would exercise in the situation to prevent reasonably forseeable harm.

In some instances it is stated that the bailee must exercise either slight, ordinary, or great care, depending upon the extent of his benefit from the bailment. This is misleading, since the true test is the care which a reasonable man would take, and the nature of the bailment and the bailee's benefit therefrom are merely circumstances that the reasonable man will consider in determining what specific steps to take. The significant factors in determining what constitutes reasonable care in a bailment are the time and place of making the bailment, the facilities for taking care of the bailed property, the bailee's knowledge of its nature, and the extent of the bailee's skill and experience in taking care of goods of that kind.

(c) *Unauthorized use.* If the bailee makes an unauthorized use of the property he is liable for any harm which befalls regardless of the care which he otherwise exercises.

(d) *Modification of liability by contract.* A bailee's liability may be expanded by contract. A provision that he assumes absolute liability for the property is binding, but there is a difference of opinion as to whether a stipulation to return the property "in good condition" or "in as good condition as received" has the effect of imposing such absolute liability.

Bailees by contract provisions may generally limit their liability for negligence. Modern cases hold that a specialized commercial bailee, such as a parking garage, cannot limit liability for its willful or negligent conduct.

§ 15:3. Liability of bailor.

(*a*) *Generally.* The bailor may be liable to the bailee when a defect in the bailed goods causes damage to the bailee or his property. The extent of this duty varies in terms of whether the bailor benefits from the bailment and the relative discoverability of the defect.

(*b*) *Known defect.* If the defect in the bailed property is known to the bailor he must in all cases inform the bailee of its existence. If he fails to do so, and loss is caused thereby, he is liable to the bailee.

(*c*) *Unknown defect.* If the bailor does not benefit from the bailment, as when he loans his car to his friend for the convenience of the latter, he is not liable for harm caused by any defect which was not known to him.

If the bailor benefits from the bailment, as when he charges rental, he is under the duty to take reasonable steps to discover defects and to make the property safe for use by the bailee, particularly when from the circumstances of the case it is apparent that the bailee will make immediate use of the property without having any opportunity to make an investigation or repairs of his own. If the bailor fails to do so and a defect which he could have reasonably discovered causes the bailee harm, he is liable to the bailee. In some states this liability is described in terms of an implied warranty that the goods be reasonably fit for their intended purpose.

If the unknown defect is by its nature such that a reasonable investigation would not have disclosed its existence, as when it would be necessary to take the automobile apart to find the defect, the bailor is not liable for the harm caused by the defect regardless of the nature of the bailment or his benefit therefrom.

(*d*) *Fault of bailee.* In any case, if the bailee knows of the defective condition of the bailed property, he is barred by his contributory negligence or assumption of risk if, in spite of that knowledge, he makes use of the property and sustains injury because of its condition. For example, if you know that the brakes are bad on the car you borrow or rent, you cannot hold the bailor liable when you are thereafter injured by the condition of the brakes.

The facts: The owner of a truck rented the truck to a dump man. While it was being used by the employee of the dump man, the emptying or dumping lever stuck, causing a back injury of the employee. The employee sued the owner of the truck, claiming that the latter was negligent in failing to have the truck equipped with a rope and pulley attached to the dumping lever in order to make it easier to operate. The defendant proved that the employee had been doing this kind of work for six days and that he had operated the lever without any harm just before the time when it stuck. Was the owner liable to the employee?

Decision: No. Assuming that there was negligence in not supplying a rope for the lever, this was an omission which was obvious to anyone using the lever on the truck. If the use of the truck without such a rope constituted an exposure to hazard, the employee was contributorily negligent in exposing himself to that hazard, for it was necessarily obvious to anyone using the truck that there was no rope attached to the dumping lever. [Chamblis v. Walker Construction Co., 46 IllApp2d 287, 197 NE2d 83 (1964)].

(*e*) *Waiver of defenses as against bailor's assignee.* Under the Uniform Commercial Code,[2] the bailee to a certain extent may waive as against assignees of the bailor's interest any defenses that he would otherwise have against his bailor-lessor.

§ 15:4. Liability to third persons.

(*a*) *Liability of bailee.* When the bailee injures a third person with the bailed property, as when a bailee runs into a third person while driving the bailed or rented automobile, the bailee is liable to the same extent as though the bailee were the owner of the property.

(*b*) *Liability of bailor.* The bailor is ordinarily not liable to a third person. Unless the bailee is acting as the employee or agent of the bailor, the fault or negligence of the bailee is not imputed to the bailor.

The bailor is liable, however, to the injured person: (1) if the bailor has entrusted a dangerous instrumentality to one whom he knew was ignorant of its dangerous character; (2) if the bailor has entrusted an instrumentality such as an automobile to one whom he knew to be so incompetent or reckless that injury of

---

[2] 1962 Text. See 2 Anderson on the Uniform Commercial Code § 9-206, supplement.

third persons was a foreseeable consequence; or (3) if the bailor has entrusted property with a defect that causes harm to the third person when the circumstances are such that the bailor would be liable to the bailee if the latter were injured because of the defect.

The facts: A customer rented an 18 foot outboard motor boat from the defendant who assured him that it was suitable for crossing to specified nearby islands. There was a patch on the hull of the boat which had been put on some seven years before. Dry rot had penetrated the area around the patch but this was unknown to all parties. The customer set out on the proposed trip at about 7 p.m. with his ten-year-old son and two adults. In the course of the trip, the patch, as was later determined, lifted up because of the dry rot and the boat began to fill with water. There was nothing in the boat with which to bail out the water. The passengers, in the effort to level the boat which was tilting because of its filling with water, went to one side, which caused the water to shift to that side, throwing all but the customer into the water. The customer seeing his son in the water jumped in after him. The boat continued on by itself and was later discovered undamaged on a nearby beach. One of the adult guests drowned and the survivors were rescued by a tanker. The boat rental agency was sued for the death of the passenger who had drowned. It claimed that it was not liable (1) generally, and was not liable in particular because (2) the passenger had been thrown into the water because of his negligence in rushing with the other passengers to the same side of the boat, and (3) immediate rescue had been made impossible because of the negligence of the customer in unnecessarily jumping out of the boat to rescue his son who was wearing a lifejacket, and that such negligence was a superseding cause which broke the chain of any liability running to the defendant. Was the defendant liable?

Decision: Yes. The agency was liable because the dry rot condition could have been readily discovered by tapping the patched area soundly. There was accordingly liability to the customer and persons in the boat. The fact that the passengers had done the wrong thing in going to the one side of the boat or that the customer had exercised bad judgment in jumping out of the boat at night, rather than attempting to rescue the passengers from the boat, did not affect this liability of the defendant because such actions were merely reactions to an emergency condition which the defendant's negligence had created, and therefore did not destroy the proximate causal relationship of his negligence to the death of the passenger. [Adler v. University Boat Mart, Inc., 63 Wash2d 334, 387 P2d 509 (1963)].

Chapter 16. LIABILITY FOR GUEST'S PROPERTY

A. Property entrusted to hotel

§ 16:1. The problem.
    (a) Generally.
    (b) Theories of liability.

§ 16:2. Strict liability of hotel.
    (a) The hotel as an insurer.
    (b) Practical significance of rule.
    (c) Rationale for strict liability of hotel.
    (d) Retention of key by guest.
    (e) Negligence liability.

§ 16:3. Exceptions to strict liability.
    (a) Act of God.
    (b) Act of public authority.
    (c) Act of public enemy.
    (d) Act of guest.
        (1) Limitation on exception.
        (2) Negligent conduct of guest.
        (3) Non-negligent conduct of guest.
        (4) Violation of regulations.
        (5) Violation of individual direction.
        (6) Retention of valuables.
        (7) Possession and display of valuables.
        (8) Failure to disclose value.
        (9) Intoxication.
    (e) Inherent nature of the property.

§ 16:4. What property is protected?
    (a) All property of guest.
    (b) Property for traveling.
        (1) Baggage.
    (c) Money.
    (d) Automobile.
        (1) Repairs
        (2) Property in automobile.
        (3) Salesmen's merchandise and displays.

Liability as to Guest's Property **245**

§ 16:5. When entrusting begins.
    (a) Generally.
    (b) Property entrusted to an employee.
        (1) Authority of hotel employee.
    (c) Token or symbolic delivery to hotel.
    (d) Property left in the hotel building.

§ 16:6. Effect of departure of guest.
    (a) Generally.
    (b) Departure without intent to return.
        (1) Cut-off point.
    (c) Departure with intent to return.
    (d) Temporary absence with intent to retain guest status.

§ 16:7. — Agreement as to property.
    (a) Generally.
    (b) Creation of agreement.
        (1) Authority of employee.
    (c) Property to be held.
    (d) Property to be delivered or shipped.
    (e) Mail and property to be forwarded.

B. Other property situations

§ 16:8. Property retained by guest.
    (a) Generally.
    (b) Property worn by guest.

§ 16:9. Property found in room.

§ 16:10. Transportation of property by or for hotel.
    (a) Generally.
    (b) Hotel employees.
    (c) Independent contractor.

§ 16:11. Property of person not a guest.
    (a) Generally.
    (b) Standard of care.
    (c) Property of non-guest.
        (1) Liability-limiting statute.
    (d) Property of intended guest.
        (1) Intent to become guest immediately.
        (2) Person not actually becoming guest.
        (3) Liability-limiting statute.

§ 16:12. — Patron of non-hotel enterprise.
    (a) Generally.
    (b) Restaurant.

(1) Supervisory liability.
    (i) Limitation of liability.
(2) Bailment liability.
    (i) Existence of bailment.
    (ii) Extent of liability.
    (iii) Limitation of liability.

§ 16:13. Liability of boarding house.
(a) Generally.
(b) Bailee liability.
(c) Dual capacity of hotel.
(d) Liability-limiting statute.
(e) Effect of deposit of property with boarding house.
(f) Liability for acts of others.
(g) Property.

C. Particular losses

§ 16:14. Persons causing loss.
(a) Status of hotel.
(b) Strict liability.
(c) Negligence liability.
    (1) Unknown cause.
(d) Contract or absolute liability.

§ 16:15. Loss by fire.
(a) Generally.
(b) Strict liability.
(c) Negligence liability.
(d) Contributory negligence.

§ 16:16. Burden of proof.
(a) Generally.
(b) Proof of defenses.
(c) Prima facie proof of an exception.

D. Modification of liability

§ 16:17. Contract modification of liability.
(a) Limitation of liability.
    (1) Hotel's negligence.
    (2) Reasonable amount.
(b) Increase of liability.

§ 16:18. Limitation of liability by regulation.
(a) Generally.
(b) Nature of regulation.

Liability as to Guest's Property 247

        (c) Notice of limitation.
            (1) Content of notice.
        (d) Waiver of limitation.

        E.   Statutory limitation of liability

§ 16:19. General pattern of statutory regulation.
        (a) Generally.
        (b) Notice.
            (1) Place of posting.
            (2) Actual knowledge of guest.

§ 16:20. Extent of liability under statute.
        (a) Maximum limitation.
            (1) Special contract or declaration of excess value.
        (b) Change of theory of liability.
        (c) Cause of loss.
        (d) Time to which applicable.

§ 16:21. Property to which statute applicable.
        (a) Generally.
        (b) Ordinary baggage and clothing.
        (c) Ordinary money, watches, and jewelry.
        (d) Surplus money, watches and jewelry.
        (e) Salesmen's merchandise and displays.
        (f) Pattern of statutes.

§16:22. What constitutes delivery or deposit.
        (a) Generally.
        (b) Particular applications.
        (c) Hotel receipt.
        (d) Authority to receive property.
        (e) What constitutes a metal safe.
        (f) Waiver.

        F.   Damages recoverable

§ 16:23. Direct and consequential damages.
        (a) Generally.
        (b) Consequential damages.

§ 16:1. The problem.

(*a*) *Generally.* The liability of the hotel for loss of or damage to property of a guest varies in terms of the location of the property and the presence and intent of the guest. For example, the property may be physically on the person of the guest, as his watch; it may be in his room when he is present, or in his room when he is absent from the room, as in the case of a suitcase; or it may be property which the guest has entrusted to the hotel, and which may be in the hotel's checkroom, as an overcoat, or in the hotel's safe, as money or jewelry, or stored with the hotel. Again the property may be in the possession of a third person operating or cooperating with the hotel in a variety of ways, such as a next door parking lot which is independently operated but which handles the cars of the guests as a business accommodation to the hotel.

(b) Theories of liability. In some cases, the liability of the hotel may be substantially the same as an insurer or a common carrier; in others, it is merely a bailee held only to the duty of exercising reasonable care; and in others, it has no duty beyond exercising reasonable care to keep the premises clear of thieves and persons of known dangerous propensities. In some instances, a contract or absolute liability concept has been adopted, in order to meet the case of the wrong done by the hotel's employee when liability of the hotel cannot be based upon either a vicarious or a supervisory liability.

In general, the degree of loss is immaterial. Thus the question of liability remains the same whether the guest's property has disappeared or whether it has been damaged. For example, the legal principles are the same whether the guest's coat has disappeared completely from the checkroom or whether when it is produced there is a cigarette burn or inkstain on it.

To a large degree, many of the problems considered in this section are avoided by the adoption of statutes limiting the liability of the hotel.[1]

§ 16:2. Strict liability of hotel.

(a) The hotel as an insurer. When property is entrusted by the guest to the hotel, and no contractual or statutory limitation is applicable, it is generally held that the hotel is absolutely liable for any loss or harm to the property unless the hotel is able to show that the loss or injury resulted from (1) an act of God; (2) an act of public authority; (3) an act of a public enemy; (4) the act of the guest or a person whose conduct is imputed to the guest, or (5) the inherent nature of the goods. By statute,

---

[1] See §§ 16:19 et seq.

the exceptions may be expanded, as by exempting the hotel when the loss was caused by a fire not begun by it.

(*b*) ***Practical significance of rule.*** The rule of law above stated reverses the customary rule that the defendant is innocent until proven guilty: to the contrary, it declares that the hotel is guilty and bound to pay unless the hotel can show that there is a proper reason why it should not do so. The rule is also significant in that it means that in the wide range of situations in which no one can prove what happened, the hotel will lose because it will not be able to show that an excusing cause was operative. In order to excuse the hotel from liability under this rule there must be no other factor present as a cause for the harm other than one or more of the excepted causes. If there is negligence or willful fault of the hotel the exceptions to the rule are not operative. Conversely, the fact that the hotel is free from fault is immaterial under this rule of strict liability. Thus the hotel may have exercised the highest degree of care, but if the loss has been sustained, the hotel is nevertheless liable, unless one or more of the exceptions be applicable.

(*c*) ***Rationale for strict liability of hotel.*** Historically the rule of strict liability was designed to wipe out the common situation in which the innkeeper and the local highwaymen were working as partners to victimize the unwary traveler whose ill fortune brought him to stay at the inn. This original reason can no longer be said to be the basis for the rule. Nevertheless, sound reasons exist which justify its continuance. When the guest entrusts property to the hotel, it is obvious that the hotel is in the much better position to explain what has happened to it than is the guest. Moreover, the hotel is the one which has the control over its employees and is the better able to prevent harm occurring to the goods. Significantly, in the modern era, the hotel is able to obtain liability insurance to cover the loss at a smaller cost and with less inconvenience per unit value of coverage than if each guest were required to take out separate property insurance.

(*d*) ***Retention of key by guest.*** The fact that the guest has a key to his room does not lessen the liability of the hotel with respect to the guest's property in the guest's room. The key is given to the guest merely to assure his privacy and does not indicate that responsibility has been made to pass from the hotel to the guest.

(e) *Negligence liability.* In some jurisdictions, the view is taken that the hotel is not liable as a virtual insurer of the property entrusted to it but is merely obligated to exercise due care and is merely a bailee with respect to such property. This is of course the case where the owner is a residential patron and not a guest. In some such cases, the relationship is openly described as a bailment; in others, the hotel is said to be an insurer, but the court then excuses it from liability under circumstances which would excuse a bailee, so that it is clear that the court in fact is applying bailment law. Likewise it is not infrequently stated that it is a special kind of bailment. That is to say, it is held that the hotel, although a bailee, must exercise more than ordinary care, or the highest degree of care, or extreme diligence to protect the goods of the guest.

§ 16:3. Exceptions to strict liability.

(a) *Act of God.* An act of God is a natural phenomenon which is not reasonably foreseeable; such as the bolt of lightning, the sudden tornado, or the flash flood. Conversely, if the act of nature is foreseeable it is not an act of God and the hotel is not excused from liability. For example, a hurricane is not an act of God when the news media have been predicting its arrival in the area for several days. Likewise a flood crest moving down the river is not an act of God when its existence and possible arrival in the hotel's city was known a day or more before the city was actually flooded.

(b) *Act of public authority.* The property of the guest may be taken from the hotel by an act of public authority. Police, health inspectors, food inspectors, and the like may claim the property of the guest is stolen, infected with a parasite or a contagious germ, or is adulterated or otherwise harmful. Likewise a sheriff executing on property of the guest may take it from the hotel. In such cases, it is an excuse that the hotel surrendered the property to the person acting under authority of a government.

In so doing, the hotel is protected without regard to whether the action of the public authority was properly taken. Its duty to its guest does not require the hotel to dispute the right of a public authority to take the property.

(c) *Act of public enemy.* The word "public" is here used to describe a government so that public enemy is not a person wanted by the F. B. I. and so forth but is a person in the military force or a saboteur of a foreign government which is at war with the United States.

> *The facts:* The guest entrusted his property to the hotel. During the night the property was stolen from the hotel in spite of the careful protection given the property by the hotel. The guest sued the hotel which claimed it was not liable because the robbers were public enemies and that fact excused the hotel.
>
> *Decision:* A robber is not a public enemy since he does not act under the authority of an enemy government which is at war with our government. The hotel was therefore liable. [Johnston v. Mobile Hotel Co. 27 AlaApp 145, 167 So 595, cert den 232 Ala 175, 167 So 596 (1936)].

(d) *Act of guest.* The hotel is not liable if the loss is the result of the negligence of the guest or of someone, such as his servant, whose fault is imputed to the guest. Such negligence, however, is not a bar to recovery unless it contributed to the loss or made it possible. Moreover the negligence must exist while the guest stands in that relation to the hotel. Otherwise stated, negligence of the guest before becoming such or after the guest's relationship has terminated has no effect.

(1) Limitation on exception. In some jurisdictions, a rule of what in effect is comparative negligence is applied with the result that minor or slight negligence on the part of the guest does not bar recovery by him. Furthermore, some states apply a last clear chance doctrine, so that the hotel remains nonetheless liable if it had a reasonable opportunity to protect the guest's property and to protect it from his negligence but fails to do so.

Illustrative of the latter, it has been held that the negligence of the guest in failing to lock his room did not bar recovery where although the guest negligently left without closing and locking his door, the hotel's employees noticed this but delayed more than an hour before doing anything about it, within which time property of the guest disappeared from his room.

(2) Negligent conduct of guest. As in all cases, the question of what is negligent depends upon the circumstances of the situation. When the negligence of the guest is established, it is no defense that it was customary for everyone to be careless in the same way.

The facts: The guest went to the powder room and left her coat unattended in spite of the fact that there was no attendant in the powder room and a sign of the hotel warned not to leave coats unattended. It was stolen. She sued the hotel.

Decision: Judgment for the hotel. The conduct of the guest was clearly negligent and that negligence contributed to her loss. Moreover the fact that the sign of the hotel gave clear warning against leaving the coats unattended in the powder room was important in showing that the conduct of the guest was in disregard of her property. The fact that it was customary for everyone to be negligent in the same way as the guest did not make her conduct any the less negligent. [Corrigan v. San Marcos Hotel Co., (CA9) 182 F2d 719 (1950)].

(3) Non-negligent conduct of guest. A variety of acts have been held not to constitute negligence, although the doing of such acts had some element of foreseeable harm. Thus it has been held that there was no negligence on the part of the guest which barred his recovery when the guest shared a room with a stranger who stole the property; put his suitcase on the bellboy's bench while waiting for a room, although he did not tell anyone that he had so placed it; left his room key on a rack in the office desk; and did not stop to pick up his baggage until several days after it had arrived.

The failure of a guest to lock his door does not, in the absence of statute, affect the liability of the hotel. Likewise there is no negligence in going to sleep in a room in which the guest knows the lock is defective or the locking device is one which can be opened from the outside.

(4) Violation of regulations. Reasonable regulations for the disposition of property are binding upon a guest when he has knowledge thereof. Consequently, if he fails to obey a regulation and such disobedience contributes to his loss, he is barred by his conduct.

If the misconduct by the guest does not contribute to the loss, it has no effect. The knowledge of the guest need not be actual, and it is sufficient that a printed copy of the notice has been posted conspicuously in the guest's room.

(5) Violation of individual direction. A reasonable direction given the guest by the hotel must be complied with. Consequently where the noncompliance contributes to the harm or causes the harm of the property, the hotel is not liable therefor.

(6) Retention of valuables. In most states and to a large degree statutes regulate the effect of the guest's retaining possession of his property, rather than depositing with the hotel for keeping in its safe. In the absence of an applicable statutory provision, a guest is not negligent in failing to turn over valuable property to the hotel, although the guest knows that the hotel has a safe for such property.

(7) Possession and display of valuables. It is ordinarily held that the guest is not guilty of such negligence as bars recovery when he carried with him large amounts of money or jewelry or displayed or made a show thereof when in public. Hence the fact that the guest wore valuable diamonds in public or flashed a large roll of money in the barroom is not in itself such negligence as automatically bars recovery from the hotel.

(8) Failure to disclose value. In the absence of any statute there is a division of authority as to whether a hotel guest is as a matter of law required to disclose at least the general nature and value of the contents of a suitcase, parcel, or sample case deposited by him with the hotel management, or whether as a matter of law the hotel is required to make inquiry. In many cases, an iron safe statute imposes upon the guest the requirement of stating the value of the property left for safekeeping to the extent that the guest is limited to recovering a specified maximum amount when no greater value is declared by him.[2]

When the general character of the property is apparent or known to the hotel, as that a coat is fur or that a case contains jewelry, there is likewise authority that there is no need to declare its value to the hotel. This is for the reason that the hotel, knowing of the general nature of the property, has the burden of asking further questions of the guest if it desires to know more about it.

In some instances, however, where the character of the property, as coming within the character of "valuables" is unknown; or ordinary property, such as a trunk, contains a jewelry case; or the property, although known to be valuable, has an unusually great value; it is held that the hotel is not liable for the full value of the property but only for the apparent or "ordinary" value of the property as though it had been the kind of property that it appeared to be. That is, in such cases the failure to disclose the

---

[2]See § 16:20.

actual or true value or character of the property bars recovery for the full amount thereof.

Apart from a requirement of disclosure based upon statute, the trend is to require the disclosure of the value of property in order that the hotel may take proper care thereof, and it has been held that the failure to inform the hotel of the exceptional value of the property was itself contributory negligence.

(9) Intoxication. When the guest had been drinking to the point of becoming intoxicated, there is a conflict of authority whether such fact constitutes contributory negligence which bars recovery. In any case, it has been held that the hotel is not relieved from liability for its employee's theft merely because the guest from whom the property was stolen was intoxicated at the time.

(*e*) **Inherent nature of the property.** The hotel is not liable when the damage to the guest's property is merely the result of the natural or inherent characteristic of such property to spoil, rot, dry out, or decay. Likewise the hotel is not liable to the guest when the property consists of an animal of such vicious character that it injures itself.

§ 16:4. What property is protected?

(*a*) **All property of guest.** By the majority view, the hotel stands in the special insurer-like relation to all property of the guest which is brought into the hotel and which the hotel permits to be brought in, whether at the time of the arrival of the guest or subsequently thereto.

(*b*) **Property for traveling.** On the theory that a guest is a transient or traveler, there is a minority view that only property used in traveling or in some way related to journeying is within the special protection of the hotel. The theory is that as the excess property is not used in connection with traveling the guest is in effect making the hotel be a special kind of warehouseman. This is unfair to the hotel which only holds itself out to serve a "traveler's" needs. Hence it is held by this view that the strict liability does not apply to the additional property as to which the hotel is made to play the part of a warehouseman.

(1) Baggage. The traveling property to which strict liability is limited by the latter view is sometimes described as "baggage." In general terms, baggage includes anything

which is usually taken by a traveler for his use, convenience, or entertainment. It thus ranges from trunks to clothing and jewelry and watches.

The test of what is baggage varies with the individual guest and the test is not what a reasonable man would take on a trip but rather what would a person with the social and economic background of the guest take with him, as well as such significant elements as the personal tastes of the guest, the length of his travels, and whether he is alone or with his family or others.

Baggage, on the basis of the above definition, does not include merchandise, tableware, sheets, and firearms.

(c) *Money.* Whether money of the guest is to be brought within the protection of the hotel's high degree of liability is disposed of in the same way as is done with other property. Consequently, in jurisdictions which recognize all of the guest's property as within the area of the hotel's liability, such strict liability applies to money. In contrast, in jurisdictions in which only baggage comes within the hotel's strict liability, only such amount of money is covered as is reasonably necessary for traveling expenses, although much leeway is permitted in providing for the protection of money even though it is not needed for an immediate and actual use.

(d) *Automobiles.* Authorities conflict as to whether the strict liability rule applies to a guest's automobile. Generally such liability will only be imposed when the car is turned over to the custody and control of the hotel by its surrender to a hotel employee with actual or apparent authority to so receive it. An important factor in some of the cases imposing strict liability is that the wrong was committed by the hotel's employee, the court being influenced by a concept of supervisory liability or of contractual undertaking to protect the car from the acts of the hotel and its employees.[3]

When the automobile is left in an unguarded lot some courts will find strict liability of the hotel provided the lot had been designated by the hotel for the use of the guests and the guest had informed the hotel that he had so parked his car. In contrast, other courts refuse to find strict liability where the guest parked his car on the unguarded lot and retained possession of the keys.

---

[3] See § 5:4.

The facts: A guest drove up to the hotel and gave the keys to a uniformed employee to park the car. The employee took the car for a ride, damaged it, and stole some things from the glove compartment. The hotel claimed that it was not liable for the unauthorized act of the employee.

Decision: Judgment for guest. The hotel was subject to strict liability for the safety of the guest's automobile turned over for safekeeping to an employee with apparent authority to receive the car. [Bidlake v. Shirley Hotel Co. 133 Colo 166, 292 P2d 749 (1956)].

In contrast with the rule of strict liability, some courts hold that the hotel has only the duty of reasonable care with respect to the guest's automobile or that it is merely a bailee thereof. For example, when the guest's automobile was parked in the hotel's garage and the guest was assured that the automobile would be locked and that the car and its contents were safe, it has been held the hotel was merely a bailee and the burden was upon the guest to show negligence of the hotel when the contents of the car were stolen; although this raised questions of the propriety of storing the car in the place in which it was stored and of the adequacy of the watchman service.

The conclusion that the hotel is merely a bailee or has only the duty of a bailee is particularly likely to be held where the hotel does not retain possession of the guest's car but delivers it to a concessionaire in charge of parking for the hotel or to a neighboring independent parking lot which co-operates with the hotel.

Ordinarily the conclusion that the hotel is merely a bailee carries with it the conclusion that reasonable care is all that is required and that if reasonable care be exercised no liability of the hotel can arise. There is authority, however, that even when the car is deemed to be merely a bailment to the hotel, there may be absolute liability of the hotel on the theory of the breach by the hotel of an implied term of the bailment contract. So it has been held that when the guest's automobile is stolen from the hotel parking lot by a bellboy of the hotel who was off duty at the time, the effect is a misdelivery of the automobile by the hotel, which although it stands in the position of a bailee, is liable for the loss arising from such "breach of contract," without regard to whether it acted in good faith or was negligent.

No problem arises when the harm is done to the guest's automobile by the negligence of an employee acting within the scope of his employment, for in such case all jurisdictions will impose vicarious liability upon the hotel. Hence the hotel is liable for the negligence of its employee in parking a guest's automobile on a public street and leaving the keys in the ignition; after which the car disappeared.

It is believed that the trend of the law will be in the direction of holding the hotel liable only as a bailee with respect to harm caused by third persons. This conclusion will come to be accepted when it is recognized that the analogy between today's automobile and yesterday's horse is not valid. The horse required shelter, feed and water, and had to be confined. Only slight mistreatment or neglect could impair the usefulness of the horse. Today's automobile does not require such nurturing. The guest as a reasonable man should recognize that if the hotel provides parking facilities it should not be held to any higher degree of liability than the man who runs only a parking lot or garage.

With respect to harm caused by the hotel's own employees, the hotel will probably be treated as a bailee unless there is a proper basis for vicarious or supervisory liability. Contrary to this conclusion some courts will in effect make the hotel absolutely liable for the conduct of its employees whether within or outside of the scope of their employment by finding that it is a part of the contract with the guest to return the car in its original condition. The subject should be regulated by statute.

While all of this growth of law is taking place, the hotels should individually adopt regulations defining their liability with respect to automobiles.[4]

The liability insurance coverage of the hotel should be reviewed to make sure that its protection with respect to guests' automobiles is adequate.

(1) Repairs. The making of repairs is not a normal incident to providing accommodations for a transient and hence is not part of the hotel's functions. Consequently a hotel is not liable for the misconduct of a repairman directed by it to repair the guest's car as requested by the guest. In the absence of negligence on the part of the hotel in failing to exercise due care in the selection of a competent repairman, the hotel is not subject to any liability for the negligence of the repairman or the harm which follows as the result of the defective repair work.

---

[4]See § 19:2.

(2) Property in automobile. When the hotel has knowledge or reason to know that the automobile entrusted to it contains baggage or clothing, it is liable for their loss to the same extent as for the loss of the automobile. The theory is that the hotel should anticipate that a person who is a traveler will have such items of property in his car and therefore a holding out to take care of the car must be construed as a holding out to take care of its contents as well.

In any case, the creation of a bailment as to the car is likewise a creation of a bailment as to those articles which are customarily associated with a car, such as a spare tire, a jack, and tools for changing a tire, and so forth. This is so without regard to whether the hotel has any knowledge or notice of the fact that such articles are within the car.

(*e*) *Salesmen's merchandise and displays.* The courts which hold that the hotel owes its special duty with respect to all property brought to the hotel by the guest apply this rule to samples and displays brought by a salesman and the stock of goods which he hopes to sell.

The courts which limit the rule of strict liability to actual baggage hold that as to the salesman's goods only a duty of care of a bailee is owed, whether the goods are kept by the salesman in his room or are put in a special display or salesroom.

§ 16:5. When entrusting begins.

(*a*) *Generally.* Assuming that the owner of baggage is a guest of the hotel either because he has already become such or is shortly about to do so, it is also necessary to show, before the hotel's liability for the guest's property arises, that there has been some delivery of the property into the custody or control of the hotel. Obviously when the guest registers in a hotel no liability exists yet for the guest's property which is in the guest's taxi, or which is down at the railroad station, and so forth. It is therefore necessary to determine at what moment the guest's property is deemed to come within the hands of the hotel so that liability arises on the part of the hotel for the care of the goods.

(*b*) *Property entrusted to an employee.* When there is an actual physical delivery of property into the possession or control of an employee of the hotel, there is of course such custody of the hotel as gives rise to the hotel's duty with respect to the property.

(1) Authority of hotel employee. When the fact of delivery to an employee is relied upon to establish the beginning of the hotel's duty as to the guest's property, it necessarily follows that the employee must have had authority to receive the property on behalf of the hotel. Conversely stated, if the property is delivered by the guest to someone who has no authority to act for the hotel there is, in the eyes of the law, no delivery to the hotel and the hotel's responsibility for the property does not arise.

(c) Token or symbolic delivery to hotel. A delivery to the hotel may take place although the actual property is not delivered to it. The delivery may be made of a token or symbol which is of such a nature that the person holding the token has the power to control the property. Hence the delivery of a railroad baggage check or the delivery of keys to a car is such a delivery of the "property" that the hotel is liable as such with respect to the property.

> *The facts:* The guest drove up to the hotel. When he inquired about parking his car, the bellboy took the keys and gave the guest a claim check, and then told the room clerk to call a private garage which had an arrangement with the hotel to provide parking facilities. Unknown to anyone, another bellboy took the key to the car and then took and wrecked the car. The guest claimed that the hotel was liable as hotel with respect to the car.
>
> *Decision:* Judgment for the guest. The duty of the hotel as to the car came into being when its authorized bellboy took the keys to the car. Thereafter the hotel owed the guest the duty of a hotel because it was in possession of the car when it had the keys, even though it never obtained the actual possession of the car itself. [Zurich Fire Ins. Co. v. Weill (Ky) 259 SW2d 54 (1953)].

(d) Property left in the hotel building. Instead of placing his property or baggage in the hands of an employee of the hotel, the guest may merely put the property down on the floor, as in the hotel lobby; or he may put it in an area or a corner designated as a checkroom or baggage room, although there is no attendant or employee of the hotel in charge; or the guest may leave the property in his room. In each of these three situations there are the common characteristics that the place of leaving the property is physically within the hotel building; the hotel does not know that the guest has left his property at the particular place; and the hotel does not have actual physical possession of such property.

On the theory that all property within the walls of the hotel is to be protected, this unknown property of the guest is generally covered and the hotel owes to it the strict liability of a hotel even before it has any knowledge of its presence. This conclusion may be reinforced in some instances by the fact that the place of deposit of the baggage was specifically designated for that purpose by the hotel, even though the hotel did not station any employee at that place and had no knowledge that the guest had left his baggage at that place. For example, leaving the baggage in a room marked "baggage room" or a room which is designated by a sign as the place where baggage is to be left, is obviously the leaving of property with the hotel.

Regulations of the hotel and statutes may of course limit this strict liability. Moreover in the case of property other than baggage, there is a view that the liability of the hotel only arises if there is a bailment or the property is in the guest's room.

§ 16:6. Effect of departure of guest.

(a) *Generally.* The effect of the physical departure of the guest on the existence of the hotel's strict liability for property depends upon whether the guest's intention is to return or to leave permanently.

(b) *Departure without intent to return.* When the guest leaves finally, whether voluntarily or because compelled to leave by the hotel, the special liability of the hotel ceases. If the hotel still has property of the guest in its possession thereafter, the liability of a hotel is merely that of a bailee.

(1) *Cut-off point.* The special liability of the hotel does not cease the very moment that the guest leaves the hotel. It continues for a reasonable period of time allowed the guest in order to remove his property from the hotel. For example, where the guest intends to come back with an automobile which he is going out to rent, the holding of the guest's property until he returns with the car continues the status of the hotel, as far as the goods are concerned, for a reasonable time to allow the guest to go for the car and return.

In some states, however, the view is taken that the strict liability of the hotel terminates the moment the guest leaves; the law not providing for the continuance of the strict liability status for a reasonable time thereafter. By this view, the liability of the hotel is thereafter merely that of a gratuitous bailee, responsible only in the case of fraud or gross negligence.

(c) ***Departure with intent to return.*** The fact that a guest who in all other respects is finally departing has the intention of returning does not continue the strict liability of the hotel. If any property is left with the hotel, as with instructions that the guest will send for the property or will stop at a subsequent day for it, the liability of the hotel is merely that of a bailee, either gratuitous or for hire depending upon whether it is being compensated therefor.

This rule is particularly applied where the guest has paid his bill in full in order to avoid liability for another day's rent although he intends to return that night and become a guest again. For in such case, as the guest has terminated the relationship so that he will not be required to pay any more money, it is unreasonable to expect that the strict liability of the hotel should continue after the relationship of hotel-guest has been so terminated, for the purpose of benefiting the former guest.

When the guest enters into a special contract with the hotel for the care of his property while he is gone, as in the case of the traveling salesman, the liability of the hotel is merely that of bailee for hire, and negligence must be shown to establish liability.

(d) ***Temporary absence with intent to retain guest status.*** The mere fact that the guest is not physically present in the hotel does not of course affect the hotel-guest status, when in all other respects the guest is still in possession of his accommodations and is being billed by the hotel at the ordinary guest rate.

The relationship also continues when the guest is temporarily away from the hotel but the hotel makes some adjusted charge against him during his absence for holding his property until his return. Accordingly the property of the guest in such a situation although held in the baggage room of the hotel is still within the protection of the strict liability of the hotel.

§ 16:7. — Agreement as to property.

(a) ***Generally.*** The guest relationship may be finally terminated but it may be agreed by the guest and the hotel that the hotel should hold or store the property of the guest for a specified or an indefinite period or until instructions are forwarded by the guest; or to ship or forward the property.

(b) ***Creation of agreement.*** Such agreements do not arise by implication. The hotel has the right to expect that the guest will remove all his property with him and therefore the guest must expressly inform the hotel that he has not removed all of his property and the hotel must in turn expressly agree that it will do some act relating thereto.

(1) Authority of employee. As in the case of any other act of an employee, the hotel is not bound by such an agreement made with a guest unless the employee has authority, real or apparent, to enter into such an agreement. And this is so whether or not the agreement calls for payment by the guest.

> *The facts:* A guest was leaving a hotel permanently. The hotel clerk agreed to take care of the guest's personal baggage in the office until the guest would call for it. Through mistake it was delivered to the wrong person. The former guest sued the hotel.
>
> *Decision:* The hotel was not liable because it owed no duty with respect to the baggage because the clerk had no authority to make any agreement with a guest which would run indefinitely beyond the time when he ceased to be a guest. [Booth v. Litchfield, 201 NY 466, 94 NE 1078 (1911)].

(c) Property to be held. If the agreement requires the hotel to hold the property of the departed guest but the hotel does not receive compensation for the storing or keeping of the guest's property, it is merely a gratuitous bailee, liable only for fraud and gross negligence. If the hotel receives a payment or other benefit for the service it is a bailee for hire and is liable only for failure to exercise due care.

It is interesting to note that in the case of property to be held, the courts tend to take whichever view will favor the hotel which is helping out the patron but getting nothing in return at that time. That is to say, in contrast with the conclusion above stated, there is authority that if there is a limitation of liability statute, the relationship in the held property case is that of hotel and guest, with the result that the statute is applicable and the hotel's liability is less than even a bailee's. To illustrate where a guest leaves property stored with the hotel as an accommodation to him and with the intent to return, the hotel still remains in the position of hotel-guest, with the consequence that a liability-limiting statute continues to apply and limits liability for a loss sustained during such storage period.

(d) Property to be delivered or shipped. The hotel may agree with the departing guest to send his property on to a carrier.

Liability as to Guest's Property 263

This agreement is binding and is deemed supported by consideration in the form of the benefit which the hotel derives from the patronage of the guest. In such case, the strict liability of the hotel continues, although the guest relationship has otherwise terminated, until the goods are delivered by the hotel to the place or to the carrier as agreed.

Statutes limiting the strict liability of a hotel ordinarily can have no application to reduce the liability in the delivery situation here considered, for the practical reason that such statutes speak in terms of depositing property in a safe or of using locks or doors of the guest's room; conduct which does not arise in the situation here discussed.

(*e*) ***Mail and property to be forwarded.*** A promise by the hotel to forward to a departing guest any mail or packages which should thereafter arrive is binding upon the hotel. The clerk at the desk has authority to make such agreeement. In this situation it is held that the hotel has the status of bailee and is not subject to the strict liability of a hotel. As a hotel benefits from the agreement, in that good will is maintained or developed, the relationship is deemed a bailment for mutual benefit, with the consequence that the hotel is held to the standard of ordinary care.

§ 16:8. Property retained by guest.

(*a*) ***Generally.*** A hotel is liable as a hotel for the property of its guest even though the guest has retained possession and control of his property. Stated in general terms, the property of a guest is deemed "within" the hotel for the purpose of determining the hotel's liability even though it is actually in the possession of the guest within the hotel. Hence the strict liability of the hotel exists although the guest is wearing or has kept with him in his room his clothing, jewelry, money, suitcase, and so on.

(*b*) ***Property worn by guest.*** There is some authority that clothing and jewlery actually worn by the guest is not protected by strict liability. This is particularly likely to be true when the guest has put down any of such property as on a chair and left it unattended.

> *The facts:* The guest left her mink coat in an unattended cloakroom in the hotel, as she had done many times before. No charge was made for the use of the cloakroom which was intended for the convenience of dining room guests. The cloak-

room was accessible from both the dining room and the lobby. The guest did not inform the hotel that she had placed her coat there. When the coat disappeared she claimed that the hotel was liable as a bailee because of negligence in failing to have an attendant present and in failing to post a sign warning guests that property was left at their risk.

Decision: Judgment for hotel. No bailment arose from the mere leaving of the coat in the unattended cloakroom, as a bailment does not arise unless there is a delivery of personal property into the possession of another under an agreement express or implied that the property be returned to such person or delivered to a third person as specified in the agreement. The coat in the cloakroom was not in the possession of the hotel since it did not have control of it, in the form of an attendant or a locked door, for anyone could walk up and take the coat; particularly when the hotel did not even know that the coat was there.

The hotel was not negligent in failing to have an attendant or in failing to post a warning sign since no such duty rests upon the hotel. Moreover the guest was thoroughly familiar with the fact that the coat was accessible to anyone from the dining room or the lobby and she had accordingly assumed the risk involved in leaving the coat there. [National Fire Ins. Co. v. Commodore Hotel, Inc., 259 Minn 355, 107 NW2d 708 (1961)].

§ 16:9. Property found in room.

Personal property which is found in a hotel room which had been rented to a transient is to be held by the hotel for the true owner, even though the hotel had promised the subsequent guest who turned it in that he could get the property back if the owner was not found by the hotel.

The facts: The hotel maid, while cleaning the room after a departing guest, picked up a diamond broach, which she thought belonged to the guest, and placed the broach on the dresser in a piece of tissue paper. The new guest to whom the room was rented turned the broach in to the hotel with the understanding that if the hotel could not find the true owner, the hotel would return the broach to him. When the hotel was unable to locate the owner, the guest demanded the return of the broach.

Decision: Judgment for hotel. When property is found in the room of a transient guest after his departure, the hotel has the right to keep possession of it awaiting the return of the true owner. As the hotel cannot impair the title of the true owner, it cannot agree to surrender the property to the later guest, and its promise to do so is not binding. [Flax v. Monticello Realty Co. 185 Va 474, 39 SE2d 308 (1946)].

§ 16:10. Transportation of property by or for hotel.

(*a*) ***Generally.*** The hotel may furnish transportation to and from the hotel, whether as a free accommodation or charging therefor. The service may be furnished by the hotel using its own employees or the hotel may have made an agreement with or have given a concession to an independent contractor.

(*b*) ***Hotel employees.*** When the service is provided through the use of the hotel's employees the hotel should be subject to the rule of strict liability as soon as the property of the intended guest is given to the hotel driver or is placed upon the vehicle to come to the hotel. Apart from the presence of a greater time and distance interval between that moment and the time and place when the intended guest will actually be registering, there is no significant difference between the intended guest's handing his suitcase to the hotel bus driver at the railroad station or handing his suitcase to a porter in the lobby, when in both instances it is clearly his intention to proceed to the registration desk and obtain accommodations if possible.

When the transportation is furnished the outgoing guest from the hotel to the depot or other terminal point, the same conclusion should be reached as to the nature of the hotel's liability. For again, there is only the difference as to time and space between the case of the hotel porter's carrying the guest's bag from the hotel down to the corner bus stop and the hotel employee taking the guest's bag to a more distant railroad or air terminal.

(*c*) ***Independent contractor.*** In contrast with the operation of the transportation service by the hotel's employees, the hotel may make a contract with an independent contractor to do so. In such case, the hotel is liable for the property of the guest transported by such carrier, as against the contention that there is no liability because an independent contractor is involved. This is particularly so where the hotel makes it appear to the public that it is furnishing the transportation and that the persons involved are the hotel's employees.

There is, however, a conflict of views as to the extent of the hotel's liability. Some cases have held that the hotel acts as an ordinary bailee and therefore is only liable if due care is not exercised; that is, if there is negligence. By other cases, it is held that the strict liability rule applies on the theory that the property is under the control of the hotel, through its agent, even though the latter in fact is an independent contractor. Some courts take the position that the hotel is to be regarded as acting as a common carrier in such a situation and that accordingly it is liable as a common carrier. The latter conclusion has for all practical purposes the same result as though a hotel were held to the strict hotel liability for there is no practical difference for the purpose of the present problem between the insurer-like liability of a hotel and that of a common carrier.

§ 16:11. Property of person not a guest.

(*a*) *Generally.* The hotel is not subject to the strict liability for property except with respect to persons who are its guests. Accordingly, as to persons who are merely licensees or invitees its liability exists only in terms of its negligence. If the non-guest has actually delivered property to the hotel, the hotel is liable as a bailee.

(*b*) *Standard of care.* If the hotel receives a benefit from the bailment it is held to the standard of a bailee for hire. If the bailment is solely for the benefit of the owner of the property and it is done merely as a courtesy or accommodation by the hotel without any expectable benefit therefrom, except at most the creation of good will, the hotel is merely a gratuitous bailee and is not required to go out of its way to take care of the property. This is frequently stated legalistically by declaring that the hotel is only liable in such case if it is guilty of gross negligence and is not liable for ordinary negligence.

It is not always easy to define what is designated by these "labels" of gross and ordinary negligence. A practical working definition is that gross negligence is so bad that even a volunteer getting nothing for his trouble should still not commit such act. For example, it is gross negligence for a hotel to give the property of a leaving guest to a total stranger without asking him to identify himself or establish his authority to take the property of the guest. If, however, the hotel placed the baggage of the guest behind the registration desk where no one except hotel employees could be expected to be present, the hotel would have exercised ordinary care even though it was in fact possible for a thief to enter and steal the baggage at the moment when the desk clerk went into the inner office.

(*c*) *Property of non-guest.* If a person stops at a hotel and leaves property in the care of the hotel or merely uses its checking service, the hotel is merely a bailee, owing the duty of care only, when the patron does not intend to become a guest and in

Liability as to Guest's Property

fact does not do so. For example, a person merely attending a banquet or a wedding held at a hotel and leaving his automobile with the hotel employee does not create a hotel-guest duty. Under such circumstances, the patron never intends to and does not become a guest of the hotel and the hotel's obligation as to his property is merely that of a bailee.

Non-guests of a hotel attending a banquet or dance at the hotel are only bailors when they check their hats and coats at the hotel checkroom.

Similarly where the visitor left a ring with the hotel clerk to give to a guest there was merely a bailment; although the hotel was held liable when the ring was lost, on the theory that it had been negligent. And where a non-guest sent property to a hotel to be held by the latter, the hotel did so as a bailee, and not receiving any compensation therefor, was merely a gratuitous bailee.

(1) Liability-limiting statute. The conclusion that the hotel is merely a bailee as to the non-guest patron may work to the advantage of the patron in a given case. To illustrate, in the case of the patron attending the wedding ceremony, it has been held that as the hotel was merely a bailee, a statute which would otherwise limit the strict liability of the hotel could have no application to the situation of leaving a car with the hotel, with the consequence that the full value of the car could be recovered from the hotel when it disappeared, even though the patron had done nothing to comply with the statute so as to preserve the full liability of the hotel under the statute.

(d) *Property of intended guest.* A person may enter a hotel with the intention of becoming a guest and entrust his baggage to a hotel employee while he asks at the desk if there are accommodations or registers, and so forth. If the person in fact registers as a guest, it is held that the liability of the hotel extends backward to the moment that the person had entrusted his property to the hotel employee, even though at that moment he was not yet a guest.

(1) Intent to become guest immediately. In order for the rule just discussed to apply, it is necessary that the person have the intent to become a guest immediately. If he leaves his property with the intention of coming back later and to register at that time, he is not deemed a guest of the hotel as to either his

person or his property until he makes such later contemplated registration.

(2) Person not actually becoming guest. The situation may arise in which the intended guest leaves his property with the hotel but then does not register as a guest, for example, because there are no accommodations available, or any other reason. In such case, as the guest-hotel relationship never arises, it is held that the hotel was merely a bailee during the time the prospective guest's property had been in its care.

> *The facts:* An applicant was informed that the hotel had no accommodations. It was agreed with the clerk that the applicant could leave his bag at the hotel and the hotel would notify him if there was a vacancy. When the hotel did not call the applicant, he secured a room elsewhere and later returned for his bag. The bag could not be found. The hotel claimed it was not liable as it was merely a gratuitous bailee and was therefore liable only for gross negligence.
>
> *Decision:* The bailment was for the mutual benefit of the parties, and consequently the gross negligence rule did not apply, because the hotel had the prospect of immediate economic gain if it had space available, even though in fact it was never realized because no vacancy arose. [Kleckner v. Hotel Strand, 60 Pa Super 617 (1915)].

(3) Liability-limiting statute. By way of contrast, when there is a statutory limitation of liability, there is authority that the relationship is hotel-guest; a conclusion which is reached in order to protect the hotel which is doing the patron a favor. So it has been held that where a person had frequently stopped at a given hotel, she stood in the guest-hotel relationship with respect to goods left at the hotel in anticipation of its providing accommodations for her although in fact the hotel was unable to do so and secured accommodations for her at another hotel. Consequently, the liability-limiting statute still applied.

§ 16:12. — Patron of non-hotel enterprise.

(a) Generally. When the hotel engages in a supplementary or auxiliary business, the liability which it owes with respect to the property of the patrons of such other business is the same as though the hotel was not running a hotel. Thus the hotel is held merely to the standard of due care and if the patron actually entrusts his goods into the hotel's possession while acting in such

other business, there is merely a bailment of a gratuitous or a mutual benefit nature, depending upon the particular circumstances of the case.

(*b*) *Restaurant.* With respect to patrons of the hotel's restaurant who are not hotel guests the hotel does not owe the ordinary hotel duties. Instead, the extent to which it is liable for the property of its patrons is based, according to the circumstances of the case, upon bailment law or upon the law governing proprietors of public places.

(1) Supervisory liability. The proprietor of a restaurant owes the duty to persons to exercise reasonable care under the circumstances to avoid the presence of persons who are likely to cause harm to its patrons and their property. This is not an insurer's liability and the restaurant proprietor is not liable unless, in the exercise of reasonable care, he knows or has reason to know of the dangerous character of a person on the premises and failed to take reasonable action to cause his eviction or arrest.

(i) Limitation of liability. The restaurant may attempt to limit its liability by signs declaring that it is "not responsible for loss" or that "hats and coats of patrons are at their own risk." Such signs have no significance for the reason that if the restaurant fails to exercise the degree of reasonable care above noted, the restaurant is held liable in spite of such signs. That is, the law regards such signs as invalid as contrary to public policy when the restaurant has been negligent with respect to its duties. Conversely, if the restaurant has properly performed its duties it is not liable for loss and the signs in such case are therefore unnecessary.

The only practical effect that the signs can have is that by bringing home to the mind of the patron the risk which he may be running, the signs may make it easier to prove that the patron was guilty of contributory negligence in leaving his property in an exposed place or that he assumed whatever risk was involved in so doing.

(2) Bailment liability. If the restaurant is a bailee it is liable for harm resulting to the property because of its negligence or willful misuse of the property.

(i) Existence of bailment. In order to constitute the restaurant a bailee it is necessary to show that the patron's prop-

ety was delivered into the possession of the restaurant or its employees with the understanding that the same property would be returned to the patron. That is to say, the property must be left in a checkroom from which the property can be taken only by producing a check, token, or by the patron's identifying himself; or by physically handing the property to an employee whose duties include receiving such property. Conversely stated, no bailment arises, and hence the liability of the restaurant is merely as a proprietor of a public place, when the property is not delivered into the restaurant's possession but is merely left on a chair or hung on hooks in the restaurant. It is immaterial in this respect whether there is any sign requesting that the patrons hang their hats and coats on the hooks; a sign which states they must do so; or no sign at all. The reason for this conclusion that the sign has no effect is that the hat and coat hung on the hook are within the reach of everyone who passes by and are therefore not in the possession of the proprietor — possession being an essential element of a bailment.

(ii) Extent of liability. Ordinarily a bailee is not liable where the loss is caused by an act of God; an accident; or the act of a third person, whether willful or negligent. In contrast, it is liable where harm results from its own negligence or from its willful misuse of the property. When the restaurant is a true bailee with respect to its patron, there is no reason why non-liability should not continue with respect to acts of God and accidents.

With respect to the acts of third persons, the restaurant-bailee would be under a double duty; (a) as restaurant, the duty to exercise reasonable care to exclude dangerous persons, and (b) as bailee, the duty to exercise reasonable care to avoid harm by third persons. Since what is reasonable care is determined in the light of all the circumstances, the bailee must take into consideration that it is a restaurant and that dangerous persons may be visiting or frequenting the restaurant. The net result is that as bailee the same degree of care is owed the patron's property as that under the duty owed as a restaurant.

(iii) Limitation of liability. Assuming that a bailment exists, as when there is an actual leaving of a hat and coat in a guarded checkroom, what is the effect of a sign which says "not responsible for loss," or other similar exclusions? It would ap-

pear that in view of the fact that one of the surrounding circumstances is the fact that the bailee is also a restaurant, the bailee-restaurant should not be allowed to impose on its liability as bailee any limitation which would reduce its liability as a restaurant. Hence it should be concluded that the superior duty as a restaurant prohibits any limitation which reduces or destroys the restaurant-bailee liability for its own negligence.

§ 16:13. Liability of boarding house.

(a) *Generally.* The liability of a boarding, lodging, or rooming house is not the same as the strict liability of a hotel. There is, however, some degree of conflict in the law as to just what that lesser degree of liability is.

For convenience of discussion, the term "boarding house" and its related terms will be used to refer also to lodging and rooming houses, unless the text makes it clear that only boarding houses are involved.

(b) *Bailee liability.* Generally the boarding house has the same duty to exercise reasonable care as the bailee for hire. As in all cases, what is reasonable care is determined in the light of all the surrounding circumstances, one of which circumstances being the extent to which the boarding house has the right to exercise control over the property of the boarder.

In some cases, the boarding house is said to have merely the duty to exercise care and hence is liable only for gross negligence.

Ordinarily no distinction is made in this connection between the boarding house and the lodging house, although there is some authority that the latter owes a lesser degree of care.

(c) *Dual capacity of hotel.* A hotel may stand in a hotel-guest relationship to some patrons while it stands as a boarding house as to others. In the absence of a prohibitory statute, there is nothing to prevent such dual capacity, with the consequent variation in the nature of the liability of the hotel with respect to the different patrons.

(d) *Liability-limiting statute.* Generally, liability-limiting statutes apply only with respect to property as to which the hotel would otherwise be under a strict and unlimited liability. Other statutes are held to apply to both hotels and boarding houses and to establish an equality as to the liability of such enterprises.

(e) **Effect of deposit of property with boarding house.** The deposit of property of the patron with the boarding house does not alter the relationship of the parties. The boarding house remains a bailee, although now the circumstances determining whether due care has been exercised are expanded to include the fact that the boarding house is in possession, and that the boarder is relying upon the boarding house to take protection of the property.

Generally the bailment of property so deposited by the boarder is regarded as a bailment for hire, the rent paid by the boarder furnishing the consideration. When the courts regard the boarding house as merely taking possession of the guest's property as a favor to him, some courts will hold that the boarding house is merely a gratuitous bailee and consequently is liable only for gross negligence.

(f) **Liability for acts of others.** The boarding house is liable for the negligent acts of its employees committed within the course of their employment when harm is caused thereby to a boarder's property. With respect to willful acts, such as theft, of the boarding house employees, it is held that there is no liability, unless the boarding house was negligent in employing the particular person. That is to say, liability for the employee's act of theft depends upon whether the boarding house knew or should have known that the hiring or continuance in employment of the particular employee would expose the property of its patrons to unreasonable risk.

The boarding house is likewise liable for the negligence and willful acts of other boarders and of guests when it fails to exercise reasonable care in excluding persons of such criminal tendencies as would expose other boarders to harm from their presence.

(g) **Property.** The coverage of property under the boarding house's liability is less extensive than that of the hotel; although there is coverage of such classifications as baggage, clothing, jewelry, and automobiles.

§ 16:14. Persons causing loss.

(a) **Status of hotel.** The significance of the identity of the person causing loss turns upon whether the hotel is subject to strict liability or whether it is merely a bailee subject to the duty to use reasonable care under the circumstances.

(*b*) **Strict liability.** When the hotel has the strict insurer-like liability with respect to property it is immaterial whether the loss or damage is caused by its own employees, other guests, strangers, or unknown persons; for none of these constitute an excepted cause which exempts the hotel from liability. Moreover, when the hotel is unable to prove the identity of the person causing the loss it merely means that it has failed to establish that the loss was caused by one of the excepted causes.

(*c*) **Negligence liability.** If the hotel is liable as a bailee it is ordinarily not liable if the loss was caused by an employee acting outside the course of his employment: or another guest, a stranger, or an unknown person; for a bailee is ordinarily excused from liability for the act of a third person. In contrast, the hotel is liable, although a bailee, where the loss is due to (1) the negligence of its employee, in whole or in part, where the employee was acting within the course of his employment, whether by harming the property thereby or by enabling a third person to cause negligent or willful harm to the property, or (2) the negligence of the hotel in hiring or retaining in its employ a person whom it should have foreseen was likely to cause harm to the property or to steal it, or to enable others to do so, or (3) the negligence of the hotel in permitting persons to stay on the premises or near the property whom it should have reasonably foreseen were likely to cause harm to the property or to steal it.

In the first case, the negligence of the employee is imputed to the hotel-bailee and it is bound by its employee's negligent actions within the scope of his employment. In the second case, the employee is acting outside the scope of his employment but the hotel-bailee is liable for its own negligence as a bailee and as a proprietor of a public place. In the third case, there is no question of course of employment and the hotel is liable merely for breach of its supervisory duty and as bailee in permitting guests and other persons to remain on the premises when it should foresee that they would cause harm.

(1) Unknown cause. If the liability of the hotel is merely that of a bailee, the fact that the cause is unknown means that the bailor-owner has failed to carry his burden of proof of showing that the bailee-hotel was negligent in its treatment of the bailed property. If the jury is convinced in such cases that the hotel exercised due care, the case must be decided in favor of the hotel even though it cannot be determined just what happened.

(*d*) *Contract or absolute liability.* If the theory is adopted that there is a contract duty to protect the property, such duty is absolute and the identity of the wrongdoer is immaterial.

§ 16:15. Loss by fire.

(*a*) *Generally.* The liability of the hotel for the loss of a guest's property by fire depends upon the theory of liability which is followed, and upon the cause of the fire; with the possible modification of the results by a statute exempting the hotel from liability.

(*b*) *Strict liability.* When the strict liability rule is applied, the fact of loss by fire does not excuse the hotel; for mere fire loss is not one of the excepted causes which exempts the hotel. Accordingly, the hotel is liable for loss from an accidental fire or a fire of unknown cause.

If, however, the hotel is able to show that the loss was caused by an excepted cause, then the fire is merely a link in a chain of events for which the hotel is not liable. That is to say, the hotel is not liable if it can show that the fire was caused solely by an act of God, such as lightning striking the hotel; the public authority, such as a health inspector ordering the destruction of the property because it was infected with a dangerous contagious disease; the act of a public enemy, as a foreign military force or saboteur setting fire to the hotel; an act of the plaintiff guest, as by careless smoking in bed, and setting fire to his room; or, the highly inflammable character of the property, causing it to catch on fire under circumstances under which ordinary property would not do so.

In some states statutes exempt the hotel from liability for fire when the hotel had exercised due care. Some courts hold that a fire merely establishes a prima facie case of negligence, which the hotel may overcome by proof of due care.

(*c*) *Negligence liability.* When the hotel is merely a bailee, it is not liable if the fire was caused by an act of God, a negligent or willful act of a third person or by an accident. In contrast, the bailee-hotel is liable if the fire resulted from its failure to exercise due care or the negligence of its employee. Negligence liability may also be based upon its neglect as the proprietor of a public place to run the hotel in a non-negligent manner as by exercising reasonable care to keep out of the hotel criminals who may be reasonably expected to cause harm.

(**d**) ***Contributory negligence.*** If the guest is guilty of contributory negligence, that is, negligence which has contributed to the loss by fire, he is barred from recovering from the hotel, regardless of the theory on which the hotel's liability is based.

§ 16:16. Burden of proof.

(*a*) ***Generally.*** When there has been a loss of or damage to the property of the patron of the hotel, the patron has the burden of proving such facts as will entitle him to relief whether he proceeds on the theory of strict, negligence, or contract liability. The distinction between the three lies not with respect to who must first move with proof, but instead, the extent to which proof must be presented by the property owner. If strict or contract liability exists, the plaintiff need prove only the hotel-guest relationship with respect to himself and the property and that loss has been sustained with respect to the property. In the case of negligence liability, the plaintiff must show the existence of the hotel-guest relationship or the making of the bailment, the fact of harm to the property, and further that such harm was caused by the willful or negligent conduct of the hotel.

(*b*) ***Proof of defenses.*** Once the plaintiff establishes that he was a guest of the hotel and that his property sustained harm or loss, the burden is upon the hotel to show that the loss was caused only by excepted causes. It has sometimes been said that when loss of property is shown and the hotel cannot explain the loss a presumption arises that the hotel was negligent. This is a somewhat misleading statement. What should be said is that if the hotel-guest relationship exists, the hotel is liable for loss unless it shows that the cause was only one or more of the excepted causes. This goes beyond a presumption of negligence for by the strict liability rule above recognized it is immaterial whether the hotel was negligent. The significant fact is that the hotel has not shown, in the assumed case, that the loss was caused by one of the exceptions and therefore it is held liable without regard to whether it was negligent.

If the hotel is held merely to the liability of a bailee, whether generally, or in the particular case because a bailment exists, the correct statement is that the proof of the bailment and of the loss places upon the bailee the burden of showing that it exercised due care and made no unauthorized use. Consequently, the burden of going forward with the evidence rests upon the hotel. If it fails to do so, it has not carried the burden of proof and the jury will be told to enter a verdict in favor of the patron against the hotel.

(c) *Prima facie proof of an exception.* When the hotel comes forward with evidence which makes out a prima facie case that the loss was due to an excepted cause, the burden is then upon the guest to come forward with evidence which either disproves the hotel's evidence or which establishes some additional factor which overcomes the effect of the exception: such as the fact that the hotel was also negligent and that the loss was the result of the combined operation of the excepted cause and of the negligence of the hotel.

§ 16:17. Contract modification of liability.

(a) *Limitation of liability.* In the absence of a statute a hotel may reduce its liability which would otherwise exist, subject to two qualifications:

(1) Hotel's negligence. The hotel cannot limit or affect its liability for loss caused by its own negligence. Thus a clause on a checkroom stub or ticket stating that the hotel was not responsible for loss, or that the property was left at the owner's risk, and other similar expressions have no effect when the loss is caused by the negligence of the hotel.

(2) Reasonable amount. A limitation of the hotel's liability cannot declare that the hotel will not be responsible for any loss or that its maximum liability will be one dollar per item lost, and so forth. To the contrary, the limitation cannot reduce liability below such an amount which would still be reasonable compensation for the loss sustained.

(b) *Increase of liability.* A hotel may by express contract assume the liability of a hotel as to persons who are not guests, but merely lodgers, boarders, or invitees. As to such persons the hotel would merely be a bailee in the absence of such an agreement.

§ 16:18. Limitation of liability by regulation.

(a) *Generally.* The hotel may limit its liability, subject to two qualifications, by adopting a rule or regulation which declares that its liability is limited. This differs from the limitation of liability which rests upon the contract of the parties, in which the facts are such that it can be held that the guest or other person has agreed to the terms of the contract, including the limitation of liability. In contrast, the limitation by rule or regulation is in substance a one-sided declaration, that is, a statement by the hotel of "this is the way I'm running things, if you do not like it, go elsewhere."

(*b*) *Nature of regulation.* The hotel may, in the absence of statute, adopt a regulation that money and valuables must be deposited in the hotel safe and that the hotel is not responsible if this is not done. Whenever proper notice is given of such a regulation, it binds the guest who consequently cannot recover from the hotel when money is stolen from his room.

Such regulations are strictly construed and must be explicit as to the effect of failure to deposit in the hotel safe. For example, when the regulation in the notice merely states that the guest "may" deposit their valuables in the hotel safe, such regulation is construed as merely offering such service to the guests but not as indicating that if they fail to make use of that service they are barred from suing the hotel for loss.

The limitation of liability established by rule or regulation must allow the guest to recover an amount which is reasonable and cannot limit liability for the hotel's negligence. These qualifications are the same as in the case of a contract limitation of liability.[5]

(*c*) *Notice of limitation.* When the limitation of liability is claimed upon the basis of a rule or regulation, the hotel must show that the guest had been informed of that limitation. In the ordinary case, this is done by the posting of notices of the limitation. It may also be done by orally informing the guest of the limitation.

(1) Content of notice. A notice of limitation of liability must make it very clear that the hotel is limiting its liability. Anything short of this does not constitute a notice which is effective to limit liability. Hence the hotel's liability is not affected by a mere request to guests to take certain precautions with respect to their property or by a notice which informs

---

[5] See § 16:17.

the guests of certain dangers or hazards that exist in certain situations.

(*d*) *Waiver of limitation.* When the facts are such that a limitation by regulation would otherwise be effective, it still may be shown that in the given case the hotel had waived the limitation; thus restoring the liability of the hotel to what it would be in the absence of any such regulation limiting liability.

Such a waiver can only be effectively made by an agent or employee of the hotel who has the authority to speak on behalf of the hotel in such matters. If he does not have such authority, the waiver which he attempts to make has no effect.

> *The facts:* A regulation declared that persons to whom a room had not yet been assigned must either retain possession of their baggage or entrust it to a porter, and that if a person did not comply with such regulation, the hotel's liability would be limited. The hotel clerk at the front desk told the guest that he could ignore this provision as it would not be applicable to him. The guest did not comply with the regulation's provisions. When his property disappeared, he claimed that the hotel was liable as at common law. The hotel defended on the ground that the limitation limited its liability in such case.
>
> *Decision:* Judgment for hotel. The limitation regulation was applicable. The waiver of the provision which was made by the clerk did not bind the hotel and had no effect for the reason that the desk clerk did not have authority to waive noncompliance with the regulation. [Widen v. Warren Hotel Co. 262 Mass 41, 159 NE 456, 56 ALR 313 (1928)].

§ 16:19. General pattern of statutory regulation.

(*a*) *Generally.* In most states there is a statute which limits the liability of the hotel in some respect. These statutes may limit the liability of the hotel with respect to property delivered to the hotel for keeping in its safe, vault, or other safe place for deposit of property. In contrast, the statute may require that the hotel provide proper locks for doors, transoms, and windows; and penalize the guest who fails to make use of such locking devices by limiting the hotel's liability if the locking devices are not used by the guest.

Such statutes are generally valid, particularly when stated in terms of the guest's negligence. For example, it is held that a statute may validly bar the liability of the hotel for the valuables not deposited in the hotel safe, where the hotel and its employees were not responsible for the loss, on the theory that the statute merely made specific the exception of "negligence of guest" which existed under the common law — the statute in effect declaring that a guest was negligent if he failed to avail himself of the security of the hotel safe.

Liability-limiting state statutes are not applicable to hotels located in areas ceded to the national government and operated as national parks.

(*b*) ***Notice.*** Statutes limiting liability are generally not binding unless the guest is properly given notice of its provisions. Frequently the statute will regulate the kind of notice required in detail, as by specifying the words to be used in the notice, the size of type in which the notice must be printed, the number of notices to be posted, and the places where they are to be posted. Such provisions are held mandatory and must be complied with or the hotel's liability remains unchanged.

Conversely, when the statutory provisions have been satisfied, the limitation is effective, even though such compliance may not actually convey to the guest the full effect of the statutory provisions; the construction here given contrasting with a notice of a hotel regulation which must expressly inform the patron of the limitation on the hotel's liability.

The facts: A statute declared that whenever a hotel provided a "safe or other depository" for safekeeping valuables of the kinds specified in the statute, and "shall place, in a conspicuous position in the room or rooms occupied by the guests, a notice stating the fact that such ... depository is provided, in which such valuables may be deposited, the hotel shall not be liable for the loss of property not so deposited." The hotel, acting under this statute, conspicuously posted in the rooms a notice that "A safe is provided in this hotel for the safekeeping of the following property belonging to guests: ..." Property of the guest which came within the statute and the notice was kept by the guest in her room. When it was stolen, she claimed that the hotel was liable in spite of the statute and the notice, on the theory that the notice did not satisfy the statute as it did not inform the reader that if property was not deposited in the safe the hotel would not be liable for any loss.

Decision: The notice was sufficient because the statute did not require that it contain a statement of the provision limiting the liability of the hotel, but only of the "fact" that a safe was available for the use of the guests. Consequently, the notice was sufficient and binding on the guest and recovery was barred by the statute. [Platt v. New Irvington Hotel, 85 NJS 330, 204 A2d 709 (1964)].

(1) Place of posting. It is generally required that the notice be posted in a public place or in a particular room of the guest. A notice in the hotel office or a vestibule is deemed posted in a public or conspicuous place as required by statute where the notice is clearly in view of the guests.

> *The facts:* The statutory notice of limitation of liability was posted on the wall of the hotel office behind the registration desk and could be clearly seen by persons registering. The statute required that the notice be posted in a public place. The guest claimed that this posting of the notice had no effect because the space behind the registration desk was not a public place as guests and patrons of the hotel were not allowed behind the desk.
>
> *Decision:* The notice was in full view of members of the public at the registration desk. The notice was therefore posted in a public place, even though members of the public could not go up to the sign itself. [Goodwin v. Georgian Hotel Co., 197 Wash 173, 84 P2d 681, 119 ALR 788 (1938)].

A notice posted in an upper floor hallway does not satisfy a requirement of a posting in "public rooms"; and a posting on a bathroom door is not a posting on the "door of the sleeping room."

(2) Actual knowledge of guest. There is a conflict of authority as to the effect of actual knowledge of the guest of the limitation of liability. Some courts take the position that the statute must be satisfied with respect to the notice provisions, even though the guest in fact knows of the limitation. Other courts take the position that since the object of notice is to inform the guest, the statutory requirement is more than met if it is shown that the guest actually knew of the limitation provision. By this latter view, the fact that there was not a sufficient posting under the statute is immaterial when the guest in fact knew of the limitation.

§ 16:20. Extent of liability under statute.

(a) Maximum limitation. Statutes generally specify a maximum limitation above which the hotel is not liable and this limitation applies even when the money or property is received

by the hotel for deposit in the iron safe. For example, if the statute declares that the hotel is not liable for money left in the guest's room and not deposited in the hotel's iron safe, and that the maximum acceptable for deposit in the iron safe is $300, the guest can preserve the hotel's liability by depositing money in the iron safe but only as to the first $300 so deposited.

(1) Special contract or declaration of excess value. The problem faced by the guest where his money or property exceeds the maximum specified by the statute may be solved under some statutes by entering into a written contract with the hotel by which the hotel agrees under certain terms to hold the excess above the statutory maximum and to be liable therefor. Under some statutes it is sufficient that the guest declare the value when he deposits the property, or to inform the hotel of its unusual value.

When a statute requires that the guest expressly declare the value of property in order to hold the hotel liable for its actual value, this duty remains even though the hotel did not require the guests to make such declaration.

Moreover, there is no compliance with the exemption clause of such statute when the property is merely handed to a bellboy and he is merely told that it is valuable. Hence there could not be recovery beyond the statutory maximum although the bag contained more than $25,000 worth of diamonds, and even though the hotel had been negligent.

There is authority, however, that the fact the guest had not followed strictly the requirements of the statute with respect to property deposited with the hotel is not a defense to the hotel where over the years, it had followed a system which did not satisfy the statutory requirements and had not required guests to do so.

(b) Change of theory of liability. In contrast with statutes which merely set a maximum limit on the amount which may be recovered by the guest, some statutes change the theory on which the hotel may be held liable. For example, some statutes provide that the hotel shall only be liable for negligence, as though it were an ordinary bailee, and further that its liability for negligence shall be limited to a specified maximum in the absence of an agreement between the guest and the hotel placing a higher valuation on property entrusted to the hotel for safekeeping.

(*c*) *Cause of loss.* Assuming that the liability-limiting statute would otherwise apply, it of course does not apply when the hotel owner or operator steals the money or takes the guest's money from the safe and uses it for his own purpose.

The limitation statute may also expressly provide that it is applicable or that it is not applicable when the loss is caused by the theft or negligence of an employee of the hotel. In the absence of an express provision, some statutes have been held to apply, so that the limitation of liability is binding, even though the loss was caused by the fault of a hotel employee; but inapplicable where caused by the hotelkeeper.

(*d*) *Time to which applicable.* A liability-limitation statute does not apply from the very moment the guest enters the hotel until the moment he leaves.

Upon arriving at the hotel, the guest is allowed a reasonable period of time in which to learn from the notice provided by the hotel that there is a limitation of liability unless certain acts are done, such as depositing money and jewelry in the iron safe, and further, must be allowed a reasonable time in which to give the money and jewelry to the hotel for that purpose. If during this preliminary period loss is sustained, the hotel cannot claim the protection of the limitation statute.

Conversely, the guest who is leaving the hotel must be allowed a reasonable period of time in which to get his property together, and to obtain his property from the safe. In such case, the fact that he has his property with him, and therefore not on deposit in the safe, does not limit the liability of the hotel as would otherwise be the case by virtue of the limitation statute.

§ 16:21. Property to which statute applicable.

(*a*) *Generally.* It is ordinarily held that a statute limiting the liability of the hotel for property loss applies only to such property as comes within the rule that the hotel, with certain exceptions, is liable as an insurer for the goods of a guest. If the property in question does not come within this rule of strict liability, there is no reason for the limitation statute to apply since the liability of the hotel would then be restricted to a bailee's liability and as such could be still further restricted by a contract limitation or regulation imposed by the hotel.

On the basis of this analysis, a statutory limitation of liability of a hotel applies only with respect to the liability of the hotel toward a guest and not as to other third persons on the premises.

The facts: The boy and girl came to the hotel to be married and be present at a wedding reception to be held after the ceremony. On arriving at the hotel the boy entrusted his automobile, and the clothing therein, to the hotel doorman with express instructions to place it in a garage. The doorman left it on the street across from the hotel and locked it. The car was broken into and the clothing was stolen from it. The boy sued the hotel, which claimed it was only liable for the maximum amount stated in the statute.

Decision: Judgment for boy for actual amount of loss. Statutes limiting a hotel's liability apply only as to the hotel-guest relationship and are not applicable when the owner is not a guest. Hence, the case must be decided without the benefit of the statute. The relationship between the boy and the hotel was a bailment. When the hotel employee violated the undertaking to place the automobile in a garage, the hotel bailee was liable for the harm caused by the negligence of its employee. [Ross v. Kirekeby Hotels, Inc., 8 Misc2d 750, 160 NYS2d 978 (1957)].

(*b*) *Ordinary baggage and clothing.* When the statute does not make any express reference to baggage and clothing worn or carried by the guest, it is ordinarily held that the limitation statute is not applicable to them. If the statute expressly includes or excludes any of such property, the terms of the statute would of course be given effect.

(*c*) *Ordinary money, watches, and jewelry.* Many statutes also exempt ordinary amounts of money which the guest would be expected to carry with him to meet his ordinary needs and also watches and jewelry which the guest actually wears. If the statute does not make an express exception to such property, there is a conflict of interpretation; some courts holding that the statute does not apply to ordinary amounts of money, watches, and ordinary jewelry; while other courts hold that such property comes within the statute.

The facts: An iron safe statute declares that the hotel was not liable for money not placed in the hotel's safe. The guest had $60 in his room. It disappeared and he sued the hotel. When it denied liability on the basis of the statute, the guest showed that the amount was reasonable for his financial standing and his daily needs.

Decision: The statute applied to money and made no exceptions. It was therefore applicable to the guest's money even though it was reasonable in amount for him and was needed for his daily life. [Leon v. Kitchen Bros. Hotel Co., 134 Neb 137, 227 NW 823, 115 ALR 1078 (1929)].

(*d*) **Surplus money, watches and jewelry.** Iron safe statutes and similar statutes limiting the liability of the hotel apply to money, watches, and jewelry that are in excess of the guest's ordinary needs, or which are carried as samples or stock in trade, or which are not required by him for his ordinary daily needs.

In a given case it may be difficult to say whether the property in question should be regarded as ordinary or as surplus; and when this question is disputed the matter is determined by a jury.

(*e*) **Salesmen's merchandise and displays.** It is generally held that the statute applies to such property when the hotel would be under a strict hotel liability as to such goods in the absence of the statute. In contrast, in those states in which there is merely a duty of care with respect to property other than baggage, it is held that salesmen's goods are not covered by a statute which has the effect of limiting the strict liability of a hotel for baggage.

The statute may expressly refer to salesmen's goods, as by declaring that the hotel is not liable for merchandise or samples brought into the hotel unless it has been given notice that the goods are so brought in. If the statute requires that the hotel be given written notice, the statute must be strictly followed so that the statute is not effective when no such notice is given, even though the hotel knows of the facts which would be stated in a written notice.

(*f*) **Pattern of statutes.** Some statutes are confined to samples and merchandise brought into the hotel for sale; or to jewelry or valuables of small size; and some states may have several statutes or sections of the same statute each devoted to a particular category of property.

§ 16:22. What constitutes delivery or deposit.

(*a*) **Generally.** The depositing form of statute requires some delivery to or deposit with the hotel of the guest's property in such a way as to reasonably communicate to the hotel that the guest is entrusting his property to the hotel's care.

(*b*) *Particular applications.* What constitutes a sufficient delivery or deposit naturally varies with the nature of the property and the facilities of the hotel for safekeeping. It may consist of physically handing over the property to a hotel employee, as handing a locked suitcase or an envelope containing money. It may be putting the property in a place as directed by the employee, as when the guest hangs his coat on a row of hooks in back of the office desk as so directed and in the presence of the hotel employee.

The fact that property is given to the hotel for safekeeping is sufficient to bring the statute into play. It is not necessary for the hotel to prove that the property had actually been placed in the safe or safe deposit box.

(*c*) *Hotel receipt.* Unless a statute expressly requires that the guest obtain a receipt, there is no requirement that a receipt be issued by the hotel. That is to say, a delivery to or deposit with the hotel may be proven by the guest, thereby entitling him to recover the full value of the property, although he has no receipt to show for the deposit where none was issued by the hotel.

As a practical matter, if the hotel customarily issues receipts and this particular guest cannot produce a receipt it will obviously be difficult for him to convince the jury that he had in fact made a delivery of the property to the hotel.

(*d*) *Authority to receive property.* The person receiving the property from the guest must have authority to act on behalf of the hotel for that purpose. Otherwise there is no delivery to the hotel and the iron safe or deposit statute is not applicable. As in cases of agency generally, it is sufficient that the employee of the hotel have apparent authority to act on behalf of the hotel, whether in fact he does so or not. For example, a guest may reasonably conclude that an employee in charge of the office has authority to receive deposits of property and it is immaterial whether he in fact does have such authority.

Of course there is no deposit with the hotel when the guest merely entrusts the property to another guest, even though it is with the understanding that the other guest will deposit the property with the hotel, when in fact he does not do so.

(e) **What constitutes a metal safe.** Statutes providing for the deposit of property in the hotel's metal safe are liberally interpreted to permit the use of any comparably safe device. Thus a wall of safe deposit boxes similar in size and operation to those found in banks constitutes a "metal safe" and is "suitable" for the safekeeping of property, as those terms are employed in the statute limiting the hotel's liability for property.

(f) **Waiver.** The provisions of a liability-limiting statute may be waived by the hotel or its authorized employees. There is a conflict of authority as to whether the desk clerk has such authority.

F. Damages recoverable

§ 16:23. Direct and consequential damages.

(a) **Generally.** When the hotel is liable for the loss of property of its patron, the damages are measured by the value of the property at the time when the loss was sustained. When the property has a recognized value on a standardized or regular market, the problem of finding the value is not too difficult once it is established just what property was involved and its condition at the time of loss.

(b) **Consequential damages.** Generally the patron cannot recover from the hotel damages representing consequential losses which flowed from the initial loss of the property. For example, the fact that the patron was unable to make a certain sale to a third person, because the hotel had lost the property which was to be resold, does not entitle the patron to hold the hotel liable for the profit which the patron has lost through the defeating of his expectations.

> *The facts:* The guest was a jewelry salesman. He entrusted his sample case to a bellboy of the hotel to place on the airport bus of an independent taxicab company. At some point between the hotel and the airport the sample case disappeared. The guest's employer was indemnified by his insurer but the insurer then cancelled its policy as to the guest and the guest was then fired by his employer. No other insurance company would cover him as a jewelry salesman with the result that he was unable to get another job as such, although he had been a jewelry salesman for forty years. This shock induced a heart attack which confined him at home for several months. The guest sued both the hotel

and the taxicab company for the earnings which he lost, claiming $100,000, and pain and suffering, claiming $25,000.

Decision: Judgment for defendants. The harm for which recovery was sought was not for damage to the bailed property but was for harm sustained by the guest as a consequence of the loss of that property. The law does not allow recovery for the consequential damages sustained by the guest in the form of loss of earnings, illness, or pain and suffering. Moreover, the law does not protect the relational interests of the guest — in this case, his ability to obtain insurance coverage and employment — against interference which was not intentionally directed at causing such harm. Even assuming that the defendants had intentionally taken the jewelry sample case there was no evidence that their intention was to cause the guest to lose his insurance coverage or his employment. [Morse v. Piedmont Hotel Co. 110 GaApp 509, 139 SE2d 133 (1964)].

Chapter 17. CHECKS AND CREDIT CARDS

A. Checks and other commercial paper

§ 17:1. Definitions.
    (a) Generally.
    (b) Checks.
    (c) Drafts.
    (d) Trade acceptances.

§ 17:2. Accommodation parties.
    (a) Generally.
    (b) Rights of hotel against accommodation party.

§ 17:3. Acquisition of check by hotel.
    (a) Generally.
    (b) Check payable to the order of the hotel.
    (c) Patron's check payable to the order of cash.
        (1) Protection from theft.
    (d) Check payable to order of the patron.
        (1) Danger of blank indorsement.
    (e) Cash check of third person.
        (1) Requiring indorsement by patron.
    (f) Misspelling of name.
    (g) Verifying chain of title.
        (1) Bearer variation.

§ 17:4. Negotiation of check by hotel.
    (a) Generally.
    (b) Indorsement for deposit in hotel's bank.
    (c) Indorsement for transfer.
        (1) Limitation of liability.

§ 17:5. Liability to the hotel of parties on patron's check.
    (a) Generally.
    (b) Liability of other parties on patron's check.
        (1) Liability for original debt.

§ 17:6. Liability to the hotel of parties on check negotiated by patron.
    (a) Generally.
    (b) Liability of drawer.
        (1) Thirty-day presentment rule.
        (2) Notice of default to drawer.

Checks and Credit Cards **289**

   (3) Form and manner of giving notice of default.
   (4) Defenses against patron.
  (c) Liability of patron.
   (1) Liability as indorser.
§ 17:7. Liability on warranties on transfer.
  (a) Generally.
  (b) Liability on paper distinguished.
  (c) Warranties of unqualified indorser.
  (d) Warranties of qualified indorser.
  (e) Warranties of transferor by delivery.
  (f) Warranties of selling agent or broker.
§ 17:8. Liability of drawee bank.
  (a) Generally.
  (b) Acceptance or certification.
   (1) What constitutes an acceptance or certification.
§ 17:9. Execution of check or commercial paper by hotel officer, employee, or agent.
  (a) Generally.
  (b) Who are the parties.
  (c) Proper execution as representative of hotel.
   (1) Body of instrument.
   (2) Signature.
   (3) Irregular execution.
  (d) Parol evidence rule.
§ 17:10. Liability of hotel's bank to hotel.
  (a) Generally.
  (b) Failure or refusal to pay hotel's check.
  (c) Stopping payment.
   (1) Liability of bank to hotel.
   (2) Liability of hotel for improper stopping of payment.
§ 17:11. Effect of forgery, lack of authority, and fraud.
  (a) Generally.
  (b) Forged signatures.
   (1) Forged signature of other person.
   (2) Forged signature of hotel.
    (i) Conduct barring hotel.
    (ii) Examination of bank statement.
   (3) Ratification of forgery.
  (c) Unauthorized signature.
   (1) Authority by acquiescence.
  (d) Hotel check payable to an impostor.

  (e) Dummy payee checks drawn by hotel employee.
  (f) Alteration of checks.
    (1) Hotel as holder of check.
    (2) Hotel as drawer of the check.
    (3) Liability for increased amount.
  (g) Protection of hotel.

§ 17:12. Assumed name.
  (a) Generally.
  (b) Registration of trade name.
    (1) Penalty for violation of registration statute.
  (c) Signing of commercial paper.

§ 17:13. The dead patron's check.
  (a) Generally.
  (b) Common-law state.
  (c) Code states.

B. Credit cards

§ 17:14. Credit cards.
  (a) Generally.
  (b) Liability of true owner of card.

§ 17:15. — Liability of the impostor.
  (a) Criminal liability.
  (b) Civil liability.

§ 17:16. Liability of the hotel.
  (a) Unknown impersonation.
  (b) Known impersonation or reason to know.

A. Checks and other commercial paper

§ 17:1. Definitions.

(*a*) ***Generally.*** The check and the credit card are the two forms of non-money payment with which the hotel most frequently comes into contact in connection with its guests and patrons. When we look at the hotel as a buyer of supplies and materials, it may also make use of other forms of commercial paper such as promissory notes, drafts, and trade acceptances.[1]

---

[1] This chapter is based on article 3 of the Uniform Commercial Code.

(*b*) *Checks.* A check is an order drawn on a bank to pay a sum of money to the order of a named person, or to bearer, or to an impersonal payee such as "cash." The check may be in any form and may be handwritten, typewritten, or printed. When the guest makes a check on his bank payable to the order of the hotel, the guest is termed the drawer of the check, the bank on which the check is drawn is termed the drawee, and the hotel to which the check is made payable is the payee. When the bank indorses the check, the person who then acquires it by such indorsement is the indorsee.

A check is of course drawn on the assumption, as well as taken by the payee on the assumption, that the depositor-drawer has on deposit with the drawee bank a sum sufficient to cover the check. If there are not sufficient funds for that purpose, the drawer is both civilly and criminally liable.[2]

(*c*) *Drafts.* If the paper looks like a check but is not drawn on a bank, it is a draft or bill of exchange: both of these terms being separate names for basically the same kind of paper. A draft is technically defined as an unconditional order in writing addressed by one person upon another, signed by the person making it, requiring the person to whom it is directed, the drawee, to pay money to the order of a named person or to bearer. It is thus an order upon one person that the latter shall pay money to a third person.

In contrast with the check, the draft is not based on any assumption that the drawee is indebted to the drawer for the payment of the amount in question. To the contrary, the only premise is that the drawee will make payment on the due date. Just how the parties will work out their respective rights is a matter with which the law is not concerned.

(*d*) *Trade acceptances.* When the hotel purchases on credit, one of the ways in which the transaction may be handled is for the hotel to accept a trade acceptance drawn on it for the period of the credit term. More simply stated, the trade acceptance is a draft which a seller draws upon the hotel-buyer. The draft represents the purchase price of the goods, together with any additional items for which the hotel is liable. The trade acceptance provides for payment at the end of the credit term which has been agreed to by the hotel and the seller. The seller sends this trade acceptance to the hotel-buyer and the latter signs it,

---

[2] See § 21:8.

indicating that he has accepted it. The acceptance has the legal effect of making the hotel-buyer bound to pay the instrument according to its terms.

The transaction is conducted in this manner by the seller because when the hotel accepts the trade acceptance, the seller is in a stronger position to enforce his claim or to sell his rights to a third person than when there was merely a contract obligation of the hotel to pay.

§ 17:2. Accommodation parties.

(*a*) *Generally.* In order to give greater strength to a check, another person may sign it as an accommodation party. Whether he received consideration for so doing is immaterial. For example, the hotel may refuse to cash a check for a stranger unless someone it knows signs as a "co-party," thereby inducing the hotel to take the paper.

(*b*) *Rights of hotel against accommodation party.* If the check which the patron gives the hotel carries an accommodation signature, the hotel can recover from the accommodation party just as though he had been an ordinary party to the check. The fact that the hotel knows that he signed merely as an accommodation as a favor to the patron does not affect the right of the hotel to enforce payment from such person.

> *The facts:* The defendant signed a promissory note as a maker to accommodate the other maker of the note. The note was delivered to the payee and by him transferred to the plaintiff. The plaintiff sued the defendant. He raised the defense that he was merely an accommodation party and could not be sued alone, without joining the other maker.
>
> *Decision:* The fact that the defendant was a co-maker did not require the joinder of the other maker. As the plaintiff was a holder for value he could enforce the note in an action against the accommodation party alone even though he knew of the capacity in which such party had signed. [Reed v. Buck, ... Tex ..., 370 SW2d 867 (1963)].

§ 17:3. Acquisition of check by hotel.

(*a*) *Generally.* In most instances the check which the hotel acquires will be made to its order by the patron of the hotel. The check may however be payable to the order of "cash" or it

Checks and Credit Cards

may be a check made by someone else payable to the order of the patron. Different rules govern the acquiring of the check and affect its safekeeping in these differing situations.

No distinction is made between the case where the check is merely being cashed and the case in which the check is received for payment. Likewise no distinction is made in terms of whether the check is for the exact amount due or is a greater amount, the patron receiving cash for the difference.

(b) Check payable to the order of the hotel. No problem arises here for the hotel acquires the check when it is handed over to the hotel clerk or cashier by the hotel guest or patron.

(c) Patron's check payable to the order of cash. Here again the hotel acquires the check by the mere physical transfer of it to the hotel employee, as in the case of checks made payable to the order of the hotel.

(1) Protection from theft. The ownership of a check which is payable to the order of cash is transferred by a physical delivery alone, regardless of whether there has been a theft or loss of the check. This means that if a thief or a dishonest hotel employee pockets the check payable to cash he is able to take it and cash it at a bank. To protect itself, the hotel should guard "cash" checks to the same extent as money. It is also desirable to indorse the "cash" check to the order of the hotel's bank. This destroys the money-like character of the cash check and means that no one can become the owner of the check without first obtaining the indorsement of the hotel's bank.

(d) Check payable to order of the patron. The check tendered or offered to the hotel may be a patron's pay check or any other check made payable to the hotel's patron by someone else.

If the check is payable to the order of the patron, he must indorse the check and hand it to the hotel in order to make the hotel the owner of the check. He may make this indorsement either by merely signing his name on the back, which is called a blank indorsement; or he may write on the back "pay to the order of hotel," or "pay to hotel," and then sign his name, which is called a special indorsement in that it states specifically the person to whom the check is to go.

(1) Danger of blank indorsement. The check which is indorsed with only the payee's name is just the same as the check which is payable to the order of cash in so far as the question of transfer is concerned. That is, the check indorsed in blank may be picked up and used by the embezzling employee or the thief. In order to avoid such risk, the hotel when it receives a check with a blank indorsement should write above the indorser's signature the words "pay to *name of hotel.*" This makes the check specially indorsed to the hotel and no further transfer of it can be made without the hotel's indorsement to someone else.

(e) Cash check of third person. The patron may present to the hotel a check signed by a third person and calling for payment "to the order of cash." Such a check has the same effect as the cash check drawn by the patron as above described.

(1) Requiring indorsement by patron. Whenever this kind of check is tendered to and accepted by the hotel, the hotel should require the patron to indorse the check. This is not legally necessary to make the hotel the owner of the check. Its purpose is to make the patron a signing party, because he will then be liable to the hotel if the check is not paid and certain steps are thereafter taken.[3] Without any indorsement, the person transferring the check to the hotel would not be liable if the check is not paid by the bank.

(f) Misspelling of name. The name of persons on the check or the name of the hotel may be misspelled or improperly abbreviated. These irregularities should be avoided, but do not be troubled by their appearance: the defects may be easily cured. Under the Code, a person to whom a check is payable or indorsed may indorse it to his bank for deposit or transfer it to another person by indorsing the check either with the wrong or misspelled name or with his correct name. The bank or other person taking the check may require that it be indorsed in both the wrong name and the right name.

(g) Verifying chain of title. In the great majority of cases the check which the hotel receives will be made payable to its order and no question arises that it has acquired the check. Such question does arise, however, where the patron indorses to the hotel a check which initially was payable to the patron or

---

[3] See § 17:6.

Checks and Credit Cards 295

to a third person and thereafter indorsed to the patron. For example, the guest of the hotel may indorse his pay check to the hotel in payment of his hotel bill. Similarly a check may have been made payable to the order of a third person and indorsed by him to the guest and then indorsed again by the guest of the hotel.

These latter situations are of course relatively rare and except for the case of the guest's pay check would be more likely to arise in connection with drafts and in transactions between the hotel and persons other than guests and patrons.

Assuming that a case of multi-party paper as above described does arise, the important thing to remember is to verify that the paper has all necessary indorsements before the hotel takes the check or other commercial paper. To do this, start with the face of the paper. If it was payable to the order of a named person as "Pay to the order of A," the next step is to see that A has indorsed it. If he has indorsed it "Pay to B," and signed it, it is then necessary to determine that B has indorsed it. If B has indorsed it "Pay to C," and has signed it, it is then necessary that C have indorsed it. If C has indorsed it "Pay to Hotel," and has signed it, the title to the paper has been traced to the hotel and it is the holder. In contrast, assume that the paper on the face were made payable to the order of A and on the back appear the indorsements:

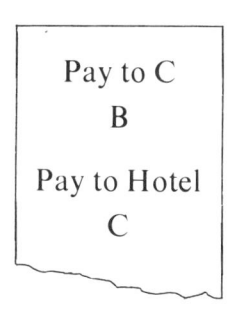

> Pay to C
> B
> Pay to Hotel
> C

In this case, the hotel would not be the holder, because A had not indorsed and delivered the check to anyone. The check would still belong to A and the hotel should obviously refuse to accept the check from C.

(1) Bearer variation. The above pattern of a chain of title may be varied because some indorser has merely indorsed his name and has not specified the person to whom the instrument was to be then payable. To illustrate, B has made the indorse-

ment by merely signing his name "B;" as compared with signing "Pay to C," and then signing "B."

If the paper has such a signature-only-indorsement, called a blank indorsement, it is immaterial that there is a gap in the chain of title before the next indorser. For example, the check is made payable to the order of A. On the back appear the indorsements:

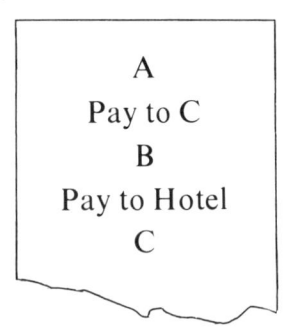

```
A
Pay to C
B
Pay to Hotel
C
```

In this case, there is no explanation on the check of how B ever acquired the paper. This is in contrast with the case where A has signed not merely his name but written "Pay to B" and then signed his name. Although you cannot tell from looking at the check how B acquired the paper, that is not important. Before B had the check in his hands, which he necessarily did in order to indorse it, the back of the check looked merely like this:

```
A
```

As long as the check looked like this, with the last indorsement blank, it had the effect of bearer paper so that anyone who acquired possession of it was the holder. Hence the analysis to the question here considered is that as long as the last indorsement was merely A's signature, anyone could become the holder of the check by obtaining physical possession of it. B necessarily acquired possession since he indorsed to C. This was a valid or lawful indorsement which made C the holder and C in turn indorsed to the hotel, making it the lawful holder. Accordingly, the fact that there is an apparent gap in the chain of title has no effect as long as the gap is between a blank indorsement and the next indorsement.

What has just been stated applies regardless of where the blank indorsement appears. For example, the paper which is payable to the order of A is indorsed:

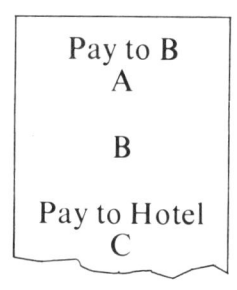

```
Pay to B
   A

   B

Pay to Hotel
   C
```

Here we have the gap between B and C, but the same principle above discussed is applicable, namely, C was lawful holder of the check when he had it in his possession to indorse it, and consequently the hotel became the lawful holder on his indorsement.

§ 17:4. Negotiation of check by hotel.

(*a*) Ordinarily the check which the hotel receives is deposited by it in its bank account. Where the check is received not as part of the ordinary patron-hotel transaction, it may be that the hotel will be indorsing the check to someone else.

(*b*) *Indorsement for deposit in hotel's bank.* When the hotel indorses its checks for deposit into its own bank and makes such deposit the relationship is ordinarily that of principal and agent. This means that as long as the agent bank exercises due care or reasonable care in attending to collection of the check, it discharges its duty to the hotel, even though the check in fact never is paid.

It also means that if the check is not paid by the bank on which it is drawn, the hotel's bank will charge back against the hotel's account the amount of this check which had not been paid.

(*c*) *Indorsement for transfer.* If the hotel sells part of its property, it may be that it will not deposit the purchase price in its own account but will be required by the terms of the agreement, or for any other reason, to indorse the check and hand it over to someone else.

(*1*) *Limitation of liability.* When the hotel negotiates or transfers a check to another person it becomes liable under certain circumstances for the payment of the check in the event that it is not paid by the drawee bank. Moreover, it becomes liable under certain circumstances for a breach of warranty that it has the right to negotiate or transfer the check, that all signatures on the check are genuine or authorized, that the instrument has not been altered, and that no defense is good as against the hotel.[4]

If for any reason the hotel is afraid that the check may not be honored by the drawee bank, it should make a qualified indorsement when it negotiates the check to another person. This may be done by the hotel by adding to its indorsement the words "without recourse." Thus, the indorsement would read:

> Pay to John Jones
> without recourse
> Sunset Hotel

These words "without recourse" bind the person taking the check from the hotel and subsequent parties so that they cannot hold the hotel for the payment of the check if it is not paid by the bank on which it is drawn.

If for any reason the hotel believes that there may be some circumstance which would otherwise constitute a breach of warranty as discussed in § 17:7, it should add "without warranties" to its indorsement. Thus the indorsement would read:

> Pay to John Jones
> without warranties
> Sunset Hotel

The hotel may also combine the two qualifying clauses as by declaring:

> Pay to John Jones
> without recourse and
> without warranties
> Sunset Hotel

While the foregoing is the law on the subject, it may well be that as a practical matter no one else will take the check from the hotel if it bears any of these clauses, since other persons may be suspicious that the addition of such clauses indicates that there must be something wrong which led the hotel to indorse in such a manner.

---

[4]See § 17:7.

Checks and Credit Cards 299

§ 17:5. Liability to the hotel of parties on patron's check.

(*a*) *Generally.* When a check is given to the hotel, certain persons are liable for the payment of the check. Apart from this liability on the check, the patron of the hotel is liable to it on his patron-hotel contract; and if the patron has intentionally passed a bad check, he may also be liable for fraud and for the crime of passing bad checks and obtaining property or money by false pretenses.

(*b*) *Liability of other parties on patron's check.* When the patron draws or writes his own check on his bank and makes it payable to the hotel, the only party liable on the check to the hotel is the drawer-patron himself. In such case, if the check is not honored by the patron's bank, the patron can be sued on his check.

(*1*) *Liability for original debt.* If the patron's check is not honored, he may also be sued on the original debt owed the hotel, for the giving of the check did not wipe out the original debt but only held back collection while it was being determined whether the check would be honored.

§ 17:6. Liability to the hotel of parties on check negotiated by patron.

(*a*) *Generally.* The situation may be slightly more complicated by having the patron indorse his pay check or any other check of a third person over to the hotel in order to pay his debt to the hotel. In this case, there are now two people on the check before it comes to the hotel: the third person, who is the drawer; and the patron of the hotel, who is the original payee of the check and becomes its indorser when he indorses it to the hotel.

(*b*) *Liability of drawer.* Although the hotel never dealt with the drawer in this case, the drawer is liable to the hotel and to any other holder of the instrument under certain circumstances.

(*1*) *Thirty-day presentment rule.* In order to hold the drawer of the check for its non-payment, the hotel must present the check to the drawee bank for payment within a reasonable time. Unless there is a good basis for allowing more time, the Code provides that this must be within thirty days if the check is both made and is payable in the continental United States.

(2) Notice of default to drawer. If the hotel makes proper presentment of the check to the bank for payment but the bank refuses to make payment for any reason, the drawer cannot be held liable for such non-payment unless the drawer is given prompt notice of such default. This means that notice of such default must be sent or dispatched to the drawer not later than midnight of the third full business day following the day on which the default occurs.

In some instances, a delay in giving such notice is excused. In some instances, total failure to give any notice is likewise excused. But in the great majority of cases it will be found that notice must be given as above described or the drawer cannot be held responsible for non-payment.

(3) Form and manner of giving notice of default. The notice given to the drawer telling him that the bank has refused to pay the drawer's check may be given in any reasonable manner and to any reasonable address — the standard being that reasonable steps are taken to insure that the drawer will get the notice. It is immaterial, however, whether he in fact does ever get the notice, provided that it was properly dispatched or given.

The notice of default may itself be oral, given over the telephone, in writing, or by a mailed letter. The essential elements are that it identifies the check in question and states that it has been dishonored by the bank by refusal to pay the check.

(4) Defenses against patron. If the patron of the hotel indorses his pay check to the hotel, it may happen that the employer-drawer when sued by the hotel raises the defense that the check was issued to the patron, its employee, by mistake, or that the employer had a counterclaim against the patron-employee in excess of the amount of the check. Can the employer refuse to pay the hotel because it has some such defense against the patron, its employee?

The answer to this question requires consideration of very technical rules which seek to establish that the hotel is a holder in due course. If it is a holder in due course, many defenses which the employer could raise against the employee-patron are cut off and cannot be raised against the hotel when it brings suit against the drawer. Some defenses can be asserted against the hotel by the employer-drawer even when it is a holder in due course, that is, under any circumstances. In very simplified terms, we may say that the hotel is a holder in due course whenever it takes the check as part of an ordinary payment for ordinary services or food rendered or goods sold to a patron.[5]

Consequently, in such case, most of the defenses that the employer of the patron could raise against the patron-employee have been cut off so that they cannot be asserted against the hotel. It may therefore be concluded as a practical matter that the drawer-third person will always be liable to the hotel provided that the hotel satisfied the time requirements as to presentment of the check to the drawee bank within a reasonable time and notice of default to the drawer within the three-day period.

(c) Liability of patron. The liability of the indorser-patron on the check drawn by a third person is the same as in the case when the patron draws his own check. In addition, the indorser-patron, by the act of transferring the check of the third person automatically makes certain guarantees or warranties which strengthen the position of the hotel in that these warranties are not subject to the requirement of presentment to the drawee and prompt notice to secondary parties, that is, to the drawer and other indorsers.

(1) Liability as indorser. As the payee has the status of an indorser, he is not only liable for the payment of the check but also makes certain warranties with respect to the claim represented thereby. In order to hold the indorser-patron liable on the check, it is necessary to present the check for payment within a reasonable time, but in the absence of evidence to the contrary, such time is deemed to be seven days after the indorsement was made.

---

[5]A holder in due course is a holder who takes the instrument for value; and in good faith; and without notice that it is overdue, or that it has been dishonored, or of any defense against or claim to it on the part of any person. UCC § 3-302. As against such a holder the following claims or defenses may not be raised: adverse claims of ownership to the paper, improper completion, ordinary contract defenses, nondelivery and conditional delivery of the instrument, duress which makes the paper voidable, fraud which induced the execution of the instrument, illegality which makes the instrument voidable. 2 Anderson on the Uniform Commercial Code §3-305:7 et seq.

In order to hold the payee-indorser for the non-payment of the check, he must be given notice of the bank's default in the same manner and in the same time as in the case of notice of default to the drawer of the bank's default.

> *The facts:* A debtor gave a promissory note to his creditor who indorsed it to another person who indorsed it to the plaintiff. When the debtor defaulted on the note, the plaintiff notified both indorsers of that fact. The notice sent to the first indorser did not reach him because it was sent to an old address taken from the bank's files. The bank used the current city directory to obtain the address of the second indorser, who in fact received the notice sent him. The bank had not used this directory to verify the address of the first indorser. The first indorser denied liability.
>
> *Decision:* Judgment for first indorser. The first indorser had not been "notified." He had in fact not received the notice and sending to an old address was not sufficient where the plaintiff had, through the use of the current city directory, access to up-to-date information with respect to such indorser's address. [Bank of America Nat. T. & S. Association v. Century L. & W. Co., 19 CalApp 197, 65 P2d 110 (1937). Although a note was here involved, the same principles apply to other negotiable commercial paper as checks and drafts.].

§ 17:7. Liability on warranties on transfer.

(*a*) *Generally.* Whenever a person makes a negotiation of a check or other commerical paper he thereby makes certain implied warranties. This means that in the eyes of the law he agrees that if certain facts are not so, he will pay for the damage which has been caused.

These warranties arise whether the person negotiating the paper is the patron, the hotel, or a third person.

(*b*) *Liability on paper distinguished.* It is necessary to distinguish liability for breach of a warranty from liability for the payment of the paper. The acceptor of a draft, the bank certifying a check, and the maker of a promissory note all bind themselves by the paper to pay the amount specified therein. The drawer of the draft or check and all unqualified indorsers likewise bind themselves to make payment of the paper provided the primary party, named in the preceding sentence, does not do so; the paper having been presented at maturity and proper notice being given of the default as described in § 17:6. The obligation of all of these parties is to pay the amount of the paper.

In contrast, the liability for breach of warranty is not to pay the paper but rather to pay the plaintiff the loss which he has sustained when he is not able to recover the amount of the paper for certain limited causes. The effect of the warranty is to act like a separate insurance policy that provides coverage in the event that the paper is noncollectable for certain reasons.

(c) *Warranties of unqualified indorser.* The implied warranties of an unqualified indorser may be enforced by his transferee and by any subsequent holder who acquires the paper in good faith. The warranties relate to:

(1) Good title. The transferor impliedly warrants that he has good title to the paper, which includes a warranty of the genuineness of all indorsements necessary to his title to the paper; or the alternate warranty that he is authorized to act for the person who has such good title.

(2) Rightful transfer. The transferor impliedly warrants that his act of transferring the paper is rightful; apart from the question of his title or authority to act.

(3) Signatures. The transferor impliedly warrants that the signatures on the paper are genuine or are executed by authorized agents.

(4) No alteration. The transferor impliedly warrants that the paper instrument has not been materially altered.

(5) Insolvency proceeding. The transferor impliedly warrants that he has no knowledge of the existence or commencement of any insolvency proceeding against certain parties namely, the maker or acceptor of the instrument, or against the drawer of an unaccepted draft.

(6) Defenses. The transferor also impliedly warrants that no defense of any party is good as against him.[6]

(d) *Warranties of qualified indorser.* A qualified indorser also makes the above implied warranties of an unqualified indorser with the modification that the warranty of "no defenses" is whittled down to a warranty that the indorser does not know of any such defense, rather than the broader warranty that no defense, known or unknown, exists. The implied war-

---

[6]Anderson and Kumpf, Business Law (9th Edition South-Western Publishing Co. 1972) Chapter 22.

ranties of the qualified indorser can be enforced by the same persons as in the case of the unqualified indorser.[7]

> *The facts:* A check was negotiated several times until it reached the plaintiff. When he learned that one of the signatures on the paper had not been authorized he sued a party who appeared as an indorser after the unauthorized signature but before the plaintiff. This defendant had indorsed without recourse. He raised the defense that the plaintiff had no right to sue him without first attempting to recover from the person whose signature was unauthorized.
>
> *Decision:* Judgment for plaintiff. There is no requirement that a party bring an unsuccessful lawsuit against another person before he sued the indorser on his warranty. If the plaintiff proved in the action against the indorser that the prior signature was unauthorized, the plaintiff would have established that there was a breach of warranty. He was not required to do this in a separate lawsuit against the person whose signature was unauthorized. [Union Bank v. Mobilia 43 (Pa) Erie County LJ 45 (1959). Note that the fact that the defendant's indorsement was without recourse did not affect the existence of the warranty of the validity of prior signatures.].

(*e*) **Warranties of transferor by delivery.** The implied warranties of a person who transfers commercial paper by delivery are the same as those made by a qualified indorser but they can be enforced only by the immediate transferee and then only if he had given consideration for the transfer. A subsequent holder cannot enforce such warranties regardless of his status or character.[8]

(*f*) **Warranties of selling agent or broker.** If a selling agent or broker reveals the fact that he is acting in such capacity, he only makes implied warranties of his good faith and authority to act. If he does not reveal such capacity, he is subject to all the implied warranties of any other transferor who would transfer an instrument in the same manner as he has done.[9]

§ 17:8. Liability of drawee bank.

(*a*) **Generally.** The drawee bank on which a check is drawn has no liability to the holder until it accepts or certifies the

---

[7]Op. cit., chapter 22.
[8]Op. cit., chapter 22.
[9]Op. cit., chapter 22.

instrument. This means that if the hotel takes a check from its patron the hotel cannot hold the bank named as drawee when it refuses to make payment on the check. The drawee bank has no liability on the check regardless of whether the bank has a good reason for refusing to make payment.

(*b*) *Acceptance or certification.* A check or draft can only be accepted by writing the acceptance or certification directly on the instrument itself. An oral acceptance or certification or one appearing in a different writing, as in a letter or a telegram, has no effect.

This means that the hotel is taking a calculated risk when it phones the bank on which the check is drawn, asks if it will honor the check, and then takes the check or cashes it on the strength of the bank's oral assurance. The bank is not bound by such oral assurance and can refuse to pay the check for any or no reason.

> *The facts:* A debtor gave his creditor a check in payment of the debt. The creditor asked a teller at the debtor's bank whether the debtor had sufficient funds to cover the check. The teller stated that the check was sufficiently covered. The creditor deposited the check in his own bank. Before the creditor's bank had collected the amount of the check from the debtor's bank, the debtor withdrew the entire balance of his account from his bank. The creditor sued the debtor's bank for the amount of the check.
>
> *Decision:* Judgment for debtor's bank. The drawee of a check has no obligation to pay the check unless it certifies it. The statement that there was sufficient money on deposit to cover the check had no binding effect. [Ewing v. Citizen's National Bank, 165 Ky 551, 172 SW 955 (1915)].

(1) What constitutes an acceptance or certification. In substance, both are the same and each is an agreement to pay. If it is a bank agreeing to pay the check drawn upon it, the term is "certification;" if any other drawee of a draft, it is an "acceptance." The acceptance ordinarily is made by the drawee's writing "accepted" on the draft and signing his name. Any other form of words expressing the same idea is effective and in fact the acceptance may consist of merely the drawee's signature without anything more. In the case of a bank, the certification will ordinarily be a stamp so stating with a date and the signature and title of the person making the certification on behalf of the bank.

§ 17:9. Execution of check or commercial paper by hotel officer, employee, or agent.

(*a*) *Generally.* In most cases, the check or draft is not executed by the "hotel" but by an officer, employee, or agent, acting for the hotel. Where the hotel is a corporation, this is obviously necessary because the corporation is not itself a living being capable of executing documents.

(*b*) *Who are the parties.* When commercial paper, such as a check or draft is executed by an officer, employee, or agent, the question may arise as to whether such officer, employee, or agent is bound by the instrument and is personally liable thereon. In some instances, it was the intent of the parties that he be so bound. For example, the third person dealing with the hotel may be unwilling to rely on paper executed by the hotel corporation alone and insist on having the personal obligation of the particular officer of the hotel as well. In other cases, it is clear that the officer, employee, or agent was never intended to be a party and that it was merely a mistake in writing or signing the paper which has made it appear that he was a party to the transaction.

(*c*) *Proper execution as representative of hotel.*

(1) Body of instrument. The problems here considered can be avoided by executing the paper properly. This means that any reference to persons in the body of the instrument should be to the hotel, such as "To the Smith Hotel: Pay to the order of . . . ," or "The Smith Hotel hereby promises to pay . . ." That is to say, the name of the officer, agent, or employee taking part in the transaction should not appear in the body of the instrument which specifies the obligations of the parties.

(2) Signature. With respect to the signing of the instrument, the name of the hotel should appear first followed by the word "By" and then followed by the signature of the officer, agent, or employee signing the instrument on behalf of the hotel. Thus the signature should read "The Smith Hotel, By John Smith, Treasurer."

There are other variations which are also proper in most states but the above is always recognized as creating an obligation only with respect to the hotel. Conversely, under such method of execution the person acting for the hotel is not liable if he has acted within the scope of his authority.

Checks and Credit Cards 307

(3) Irregular execution. If the method of execution above prescribed is not followed and the paper has been negotiated to another person there is the possibility and in many instances the certainty that the hotel will not be bound by the instrument and that instead the instrument will personally bind the officer, employee, or agent executing the paper. In some instances, both the hotel and the officer will be held bound.

The facts: A promissory note was executed on behalf of a corporation by Dornan, its treasurer and vice-president. The signatures were made in the following manner:

Corporate	Chet B. Earle Inc.	(Seal)
Seal	James G. Dornan	(Seal)

The holder of the note sued the officer on the ground that he was personally liable as a co-maker. He defended on the ground that he was merely an agent and was not personally liable.

Decision: A person whose name follows the name of the corporation is liable as a co-signer if the instrument does not show that he signed in a representative capacity, even though the words which would indicate that he signed in such a capacity were merely omitted inadvertently and even though the instrument bore the seal of the corporation. [Bell v. Dornan, 203 Pa Super 562, 201 A2d 324 (1964). The principle of this case is applicable to checks and commercial paper of any kind.]

The foregoing is based on the factual situation that the instrument has been negotiated to a third person who looking at the instrument cannot see from its face that the employee or officer was in fact such. Conversely, as between the improperly-signing officer or employee and the person with whom he dealt, the officer or employee can establish by evidence that in fact it had been intended by the parties that only the hotel was to be bound and that the officer or employee was merely signing in a representative capacity, although that fact had not been indicated by the face of the paper.

(d) **Parol evidence rule.** Commercial paper is subject to the parol evidence rule. This means that it cannot be shown by parol evidence or testimony that the obligation of the parties to the instrument is not what it appears to be from the instrument, as against the claim that it had been agreed before or at the time when the instrument was executed that it was to have a different effect than its wording shows.

The facts: The defendant, Snoweden, signed a note as maker for $10,000 and delivered it to the plaintiff, directing the plaintiff to loan $10,000 to a corporation, which was done by the plaintiff. When the plaintiff sued the defendant on the note, the latter objected on the ground that he had signed the note to accommodate the corporation which had received the money and that the plaintiff had assured him that as the corporation had adequate collateral for the loan of $10,000, the plaintiff would never look to the defendant for payment of his note. Was the defendant liable?

Decision: Judgment for plaintiff. The fact that the note was executed to accommodate another person did not affect the right of the plaintiff to recover thereon. As there was nothing on the face of the instrument which showed that the maker was not to be held liable, the parol evidence rule prohibited the contradiction of the face of the instrument by proof of any agreement inconsistent with the provisions of the instrument. [Snoweden v. Franklin National Bank, (CA5th) 338 F2d 995 (1964)].

§ 17:10. Liability of hotel's bank to hotel.

(*a*) **Generally.** Apart from the question of liability based upon conduct with respect to various kinds of commercial paper, the hotel's bank owes certain duties to the hotel, as it does to all of its customers. The hotel is entitled to recover from the bank for breach of such duties.

(*b*) **Failure or refusal to pay hotel's check.** A bank is under a common-law duty to its depositor to pay his check to the extent of money on deposit. If the hotel's bank breaches its duty to pay on or honor the check of the hotel, the bank is liable to the hotel for the damages caused thereby.

If the check is dishonored in the hands of the person to whom the hotel had made payment by check, the original debt for which the check was given revives and such other person may then bring suit against the hotel on the original obligation.

(*c*) **Stopping payment.** The depositor may stop the payment of a given check by an oral instruction or written notice. Under the Code an oral stop order is only binding on the bank for fourteen calendar days, unless confirmed in writing within the period. A written order is not effective after six months unless renewed in writing.

(1) Liability of bank to hotel. If the bank improperly makes payment after receiving the hotel's stop payment order,

the bank is liable to the hotel for the amount of the check; although it is possible that there may be a valid limitation of the bank's liability.

(2) Liability of hotel for improper stopping of payment. If the hotel stops payment on its check, the result is the same as though the check had never been issued. The debt for which the check was given remains unpaid and must be paid thereafter unless the hotel has a good defense or reason for refusing to make payment, such as that the goods purchased were never received, or were returned, or were not as warranted, and so forth.

The situation may be altered by the fact that the hotel's payee, the person to whose order the hotel had made the check, had negotiated the check in the meantime to a holder in due course. For example, the hotel pays its food supplier by check, the supplier indorses the check and cashes it at his bank. The supplier's bank having taken the check as part of a regular business transaction would ordinarily be a holder in due course. Assume now that the hotel on learning that the shipment was spoiled had notified its bank to stop payment on the check. In such case, while the hotel's bank can properly refuse to pay the supplier's bank, the supplier's bank is a holder in due course of the check and may require the hotel to pay the amount thereof, because the defense which the hotel has against its supplier is one of the defenses which cannot be raised against a holder in due course.

The net result is that the right to stop payment may be without value. The importance of making payment only after delivery of goods and after a reasonable examination thereof is obvious, for in such way the hotel will be able to protect itself by rejecting the goods and thus avoid the problem of the effect of stopping payment.

§ 17:11. Effect of forgery, lack of authority, and fraud.

(a) Generally. In a variety of situations the hotel will find that it is liable for the loss which has been sustained because some signature on the check is a forgery, or the instrument was executed without authority to do so, or fraud has in some way been practiced upon the hotel. In some of these situations, and in particular, in Code states, the trend is toward imposing liability on the hotel in all such situations.

(b) *Forged signatures.*

(1) Forged signature of other person. The person whose signature is forged is not bound by the check and therefore cannot be sued by the hotel. A few minor exceptions exist to this statement, but the application of the general rule means that the hotel is the loser insofar as that particular person is concerned.

(2) Forged signature of hotel. The hotel's bank may pay out money on what appears to be a check drawn by the hotel but which is in fact a forgery of the hotel's signature. When the hotel's bank does this, it cannot charge the hotel with the amount of such payment, because it is liable for such loss caused by the breach of its contract to pay only on the lawful signature of its depositor, the bank. For example, where an employee of the hotel forges the signatures of the officer or employees of the hotel who are authorized to sign hotel checks and then procures the cashing of such checks by the hotel's bank, the latter bank cannot deduct the amount of such payments from the hotel's bank account and must restore to such account any deductions it has made.

The duty of paying out on genuine signatures only of the depositor is an absolute duty on the bank and it is immaterial how skilled the forgery was or how carefully the bank had acted. Otherwise stated, it is not a question of whether the bank was negligent or careful, but merely a question of whether in fact the signature on the check was that of the bank's depositor.

(i) Conduct barring hotel. If the hotel has through negligence contributed to or made possible the forgery, it cannot hold the bank liable. Thus the hotel may be barred when it carelessly left its mechanical check writer and signature stamps accessible to unauthorized persons, by means of which the forger was able to duplicate the official signatures and then cash the checks for his own benefit.

(ii) Examination of bank statement. The hotel must examine its bank statement and its cancelled checks promptly and with reasonable care and notify the bank promptly of any forgery. If it does not do this, the bank is held to a lesser degree of care, so that the bank is not liable if it used ordinary care in making payment on the forged instrument. If the bank had not used ordinary care, the depositor can object to the forgery of his name but must do so within a year.

The facts: An attorney's secretary forged her employer's name to 41 checks totalling approximately $12,500. The forgeries were so skillful that an ordinary person could not detect the forgery even by making a comparison with the correct signature on the bank card. When the monthly bank statements and cancelled checks were received by the attorney, he would have the same secretary verify them, and only occasionally would he make a spot check or examination of them. Was the bank liable for payments made on the forged checks?

Decision: No. A bank depositor is bound by all facts which a proper examination of his cancelled checks and the bank statement would show. He is not relieved from this rule by the fact that the employee to whom he assigned the task of bank account reconciliation was the very person who was the forger. Thus the fact that he was deceived by his employee does not relieve him from his duty toward the bank. Hence when the latter makes payment on a series of forged checks because it had never been told that forgeries had been made, the depositor is barred from objecting to such payments or the deduction of the amounts of such checks from his account. [Clarke v. Camden Trust Co., 84 NJS 304, 201 A2d 762 (1964)].

(3) Ratification of forgery. As an exception to the rule that a person whose name has been forged is not bound thereby, is the qualification that he is bound if he approves or ratifies the forgery of his name. Thus, when nephew pays his hotel bill by forging uncle's name on a check, the uncle is not bound on the check or in any way obligated to the hotel; but if uncle ratifies the forgery, then he is bound by the indorsement made by the nephew. Whether the uncle has ratified the forgery depends upon whether his words or conduct indicate that he intends to or is willing to be bound by the forgery of his signature.

(c) Unauthorized signature. It may be that the check has been originally drawn by, or has since been indorsed by, one person acting in the name of another, but the acting person does not have authority to do so. Here the legal result is the same as though the unauthorized agent were making a forgery.

To some extent, the hotel may protect itself from loss arising from an unauthorized signature since it may verify with the principal that the act of the purported agent is in fact authorized. For example, the hotel might telephone the principal to check that the agent in fact is acting with authority.

While this is theoretically true, it may be difficult or impractical to follow this plan, for the reason that the sheer weight of the business flow may make it impossible to stop to take time out to try to track down the purported principal in question and to ask him whether the signature was authorized.

In the event that a letter is written to the apparent principal, the letter must inform him of all material facts necessary to identify the transaction. If a telephone call is used, a memorandum should be made and preserved of the time and date of making the phone call, the person and place to which the call was made, facts identifying the check in question, and all other significant details of the case.

(1) Authority by acquiescence. In addition to ratification, it is quite likely in the unauthorized signature case that there may be a history of past dealings in which the apparent principal had acted in such a way as to indicate that he approved the making of the unauthorized signatures. For example, if the hotel had been cashing checks on the basis of the patron's signing of the name of the patron's employer, and such third person-principal, although knowing or apparently knowing of such conduct, made no protest to the hotel, the hotel is justified in regarding the third person as having authorized the action by the signing party.

(d) *Hotel check payable to an impostor.* In contrast with a check of a patron or a third person given to the bank as payment, the situation may arise in which the hotel makes payment to a third person, and further, that the payment is made to that person because the hotel is deceived by him as to his identity. For example, Henry Jones does repair work for the hotel. Later on, the cashier of Jones stops in the hotel and falsely says to the hotel that he is Henry Jones and presents a copy of the bill to establish his identity. The hotel then issues a check payable to the order of "Henry Jones" but gives it to the cashier, still believing him to be Henry Jones.

In this situation of payment to an impostor, the check under the Code is binding upon the hotel just as though no such fraud had been present. This principle applies regardless of the manner in which the fraud is perpetrated, as by the impostor by himself either in person, by letter, or over the telephone; or by the impostor conspiring with an employee of the hotel to defraud it.

When this impostor situation arises, the hotel may stop payment on its check. This remedy of stopping payment is subject to the limitation that if the impostor has transferred the instrument to a good, honest holder,[10] and the hotel is unable to stop payment on the check before it reaches the hands of such a good holder, the hotel is bound by the giving of the check; which means that the hotel's bank can charge the hotel's account with the amount of the check.

(e) *Dummy payee checks drawn by hotel employee.* The business side of the hotel may be organized so that one employee prepares checks and another employee or the cashier of the hotel signs them. Of course, the theory on which the checks are prepared for signature is that money is due to the persons to whom the checks are so made payable. The employee preparing the checks to be signed may, however, have the different idea of including a bunch of dummy checks. For example, the laundryman Henry Brown is not owed any money. Instead, the employee makes out a check to the order of Henry Brown for $500 for laundry, then has the treasurer of the hotel sign the check, and the employee then indorses the check to himself, signs "Henry Brown" under this indorsement, and cashes or deposits the check in his own account. As variations of this theme, it may be that there never was a person called Henry Brown or that Henry Brown has died. It is also possible that the fraudulent intent of this employee is shared with others who with him conspire to defraud the hotel.

In all of these situations, the Code provides that when the scheming employee takes the dummy checks and cashes them for his benefit, the hotel is liable as against the claim that the indorsement was a forgery. This means that when the hotel's bank pays out on these checks, the payment by the bank is proper and the bank may therefore properly deduct the amount of the dummy checks from the hotel's account.

(f) *Alteration of checks.* The question of the effect of the alteration of a check may arise in two situations. The one is when the hotel becomes the holder of a check which has been altered. Here the question is whether the hotel can enforce the check according to its altered terms, or the original terms, or not at all. The other situation is the one in which the check which is altered is the check originally drawn by the hotel in payment of its debt or obligation. Now the question is

---

[10] Technically the person must be a holder in due course and the check must be negotiated to him by proper indorsement and delivery, or if the check is bearer paper, by delivery alone.

whether the hotel is liable for the full amount of the check as altered, the original amount, or nothing at all.

(1) Hotel as holder of check. When the hotel holds the check of another person which has been indorsed to it, and the check has been altered, the hotel will be able to enforce the check according to its original terms. Otherwise stated, the hotel will ordinarily be a holder in due course in that it has received the check as part of a legitimate business transaction and has acted in good faith, and such holders may enforce a negotiable instrument according to its original terms before the alteration was made.

To constitute an alteration under the Code it is necessary that there be (1) a material change to the instrument, (2) made by the person who is the holder of the paper, (3) with fraudulent intent. Any change made by a stranger to the paper, that is, a person who is not the holder thereof, has no effect; in which case the check can of course be enforced by the hotel according to its original terms.

(2) Hotel as drawer of the check. If the hotel's check is altered, the liability of the hotel is ordinarily not affected and the hotel is merely liable for the amount for which the check was originally drawn.[11] In consequence of this conclusion, if the hotel's bank pays the increased amount of the check, instead of the original amount for which the hotel is bound, the hotel's bank cannot charge the hotel's account with the difference between the original amount of the check and the raised amount. If the bank does so, it must restore the difference between the original and the raised amounts to the hotel's account; the bank in such case bearing the loss.

(3) Liability for increased amount. In two situations there may be liability of the drawer of a check for the increased instead of the original amount of the check. The drawer of a check, whether the hotel or any other person, is barred from objecting that its check has been altered if he was negligent and such negligence substantially contributed to the making of the alteration. Under these circumstances a holder in due course,

---

[11] If the holder of the check is not a holder in due course, the hotel is not required to make payment on its check, for as against such an ordinary holder a drawer is released from liability by an alteration of the check. As this situation does not arise with any frequency, the rule ordinarily applied is that the hotel remains liable to the extent of the check as originally drawn.

including any bank, may treat the check according to its face value and the negligent drawer is bound according to its altered terms.

> *The facts:* The employer told his employee to draw a check to the employee's own order for $10.10. The employee wrote the check with space to the left of the amount. After the employer signed the check, the employee filled in the spaces and thereby raised the amount of the check to $2,110.10. The employee cashed the check at the employer's bank, receiving this greater amount. The bank then charged the employer's account with such amount. The employer sued the bank for $2,100.
>
> *Decision:* Judgment for bank. The employer had been negligent in signing a check which because of the blank space could be easily increased to a larger amount. The employer was therefore bound by the increased amount. [Goldsmith v. Atlantic National Bank (Fla) 55 So2d 804 (1952)].

When the alteration had been made to the hotel's check, and the hotel's bank had charged the hotel's account with the increased altered amount of the check, the hotel may have lost its right to object by its failure to do so. Specifically it will be barred, which means that the bank will be allowed to charge the hotel's account with the increased amount, if the hotel fails to inform the bank that there has been an alteration after receiving the cancelled altered check and the bank statement. Here the hotel is barred under the same conditions as apply to prevent the hotel from objecting that the hotel's signature is a forgery, when such is the case.[12]

(g) *Protection of hotel.* The various situations in which the hotel may be liable make it essential that a hotel have adequate insurance coverage from the various risks involved. In those instances in which the loss is caused by the misconduct of employees, it is necessary that the hotel carefully consider job applicants and maintain careful continuing supervision of the office management.

With respect to the latter, particular care should be taken to prevent any check-writing equipment from being accessible to unauthorized personnel, to insure that checks are written in such a way that they cannot be easily altered by employees, and that cancelled checks and bank statements be promptly examined and any irregularities promptly reported to the hotel's bank.

---

[12] See § 17:11 (b).

In addition to notifying the bank, if the irregularities involve employees with respect to whom the hotel has fidelity insurance coverage, it is generally necessary that notice be given to the insurer whenever circumstances arise which show the existence of a loss covered by the policy. The failure to give such notice bars recovery from the insurer. A difficult question at times arises as to whether the circumstances are such that the employer has discovered an irregularity which should be reported, as distinguished from a mere suspicion that something may be wrong, as to which notice to the insurer is not required. In case of doubt, the safe rule is to notify the insurer.

§ 17:12. Assumed name.

(*a*) *Generally.* The use of an assumed name may or may not indicate misconduct. If the name of someone else is assumed for the purpose of signing his name with the intent to defraud, the act is forgery. If the identity of another person is assumed for the purpose of inducing the making of a check payable to the order of the person whose identity is assumed, the situation arises of checks payable to an impostor.[13]

The assumption of the name may, however, be perfectly innocent, as where the person who assumes the name does not intend to conceal his identity or to cause anyone to believe that he is someone else. For example, if the small hotel or other business run by John Jones is known as "Ye Olde Hostelry" and checks are signed in that name, no one is defrauded for everyone knows or can learn who is involved.

(*b*) *Registration of trade name.* When a business is conducted under an assumed or fictitious or trade name it is common for state statutes to require that such name be registered. This is ordinarily done by filing a paper in the city hall of the county seat and sometimes also with the state capitol, in which paper is set forth information showing the identity of the persons behind the enterprise. Generally the filing is accompanied by newspaper advertising that the paper has been filed.

The paper which is filed will customarily state the assumed name, the nature of the business, the principal place of business, and the names and addresses of the persons who are the

---

[13]See § 17:11.

owners or operators of the business. This paper is generally signed and sworn to by one or more of such owners or operators. When submitted to the government official, it is placed on file and indexed so that anyone who wants to find the true identity of the people behind the assumed name may look through the index and the files and find this information. Ordinarily this problem does not arise in connection with corporations which by their very nature and the terms of their charter or certificate of incorporation may use the specified "corporate name."

(1) Penalty for violation of registration statute. The doing of business under an assumed or fictitious name without having complied with an applicable registration statute is a crime for which both fine and imprisonment may ordinarily be imposed as the penalty. As an additional penalty, the person failing to register is generally barred from bringing any lawsuit to enforce his contracts made with other persons until proper registration is made.

The latter limitation ceases to operate once proper registration is made, and even without any registration being made, has no effect when the other person in fact knows who are behind the assumed name, or is bringing suit against the non-registering business; or when the latter sues the third person for a tort as compared with a breach of contract.

(c) Signing of commercial paper. Under the Code it is immaterial whether an assumed name or the true name is used. That is to say, the signing or indorsing of a check or other commercial paper in a trade name or in an assumed name imposes liability on the signer to the same extent, and in all respects has the same effect, as though the signer had used his own name.

§ 17:13. The dead patron's check.

(a) Generally. The patron of the hotel may make payment by check and then die thereafter while the check is still in the mail or in the hands of the hotel, or at the hotel's bank.

(b) Common-law state. Before the adoption of the Uniform Commercial Code, the ordinary answer was that when the person drawing the check died, the authorization found in the check also ended. The result was that the dead man's check had no value, except as evidence that he had owed that much money to the hotel.

(c) Code states. In states which have adopted the Uniform Commercial Code, the hotel should put the dead patron's check through for deposit and collection just as though he were alive. This is so because the dead man's bank can continue to act upon his check as long as it does not know of his death. Even after the bank learns of the depositor's death, it may continue for ten days to pay out on checks drawn by him unless ordered to stop by a person claiming an interest in the account, that is, by the executor, administrator, heir, and so on of the deceased depositor.

B. Credit cards

§ 17:14. Credit cards.

(a) Generally. From the standpoint of the hotel, the credit card does not present any problem. That is, it is entitled to rely on the credit card regardless of whether it is presented by its true owner or by a finder or thief who falsely represents that he is the person named in the card. This necessarily implies, as is the case, that the issuer of the card or credit-extending agency, such as the Diners' Club, is liable to third persons, such as the hotel, dealing with the possessor of the credit card whether or not such person is the lawful holder.

(b) Liability of true owner of card. A credit cardholder is not liable to the issuing agency for the unauthorized use of his credit card for more than $50. In order to impose liability up to that amount, the issuer of the card must show that (a) the credit card is an accepted card, (b) the issuer has given the holder adequate notice that he may be held liable in such case, (c) the issuer has furnished the holder with a self-addressed prestamped notification to be mailed by the cardholder in the event of loss or theft of the credit card, (d) the issuer has provided a method by which the user of the card can be identified as the person authorized to use it, and (e) the unauthorized use occurs before the cardholder has notified the issuer that an unauthorized use of the card has occurred or may occur as a result of loss, theft, or otherwise.

§ 17:15. Liability of the impostor.

(a) Criminal liability. When the impostor obtains accommodations or other services or goods from the hotel on the basis of the false use of the found or stolen credit card, he is

guilty of the offense of obtaining property or money by false pretenses; although there are some contrary cases where the impostor did not use or show the card until after he had received the services, accommodations, or goods.

(*b*) *Civil liability.* The impostor is liable to the person whom he has defrauded by his impersonation. As the hotel is ordinarily entitled to be paid by the issuing agency, the hotel has no cause of action because it cannot show that it has been harmed by the fraud.

When it is the agency which bears the loss, through being required to pay for the credit extended to the impostor, it can sue him for the loss — although there is the practical problem of catching him first. If as between the true owner of the card and the issuer, the former must pay, it is he who can sue the impostor.

§ 17:16. Liability of the hotel.

(*a*) *Unknown impersonation.* In the ordinary case the hotel will not be civilly or criminally liable for extending credit to the impostor where it in fact does not know and does not have reason to know of the impersonation.

(*b*) *Known impersonation or reason to know.* If the impersonation is known it is likely that the hotel employee involved will be civilly liable for the loss and perhaps the hotel as well. It is possible that the employee will be guilty of some criminal offense, although the hotel will probably not be criminally liable.

It is probable that the consequences of having reason to know of an impersonation will have the same consequences as a "knowing" case. In contrast mere suspicion or doubts should be classified with the "unknown" cases.

Chapter 18. LIENS AND EVICTION

A. The hotel lien

§ 18:1. Existence of lien.
    (a) Generally.
    (b) Nature of claim.
    (c) Care of property subject to lien.
    (d) Loss of lien.
        (1) Tender.
    (e) Recapture of property from guest.

§ 18:2. Property subject to lien.
    (a) Generally.
    (b) Exempt property.
    (c) Property of third person.
        (1) Actual ownership unknown.
            (i) Statutory provisions.
        (2) Ownership by third person known.
            (i) Statutory provisions.
    (d) Group accommodations.
    (e) Security interest of third persons.
        (1) Code states.

§ 18:3. Enforcement of lien.
    (a) Generally.
    (b) Lockout of patron.
    (c) Notice and sale.
    (d) Surplus and deficit.

B. Removal and eviction of patrons.

§ 18:4. Right of removal and eviction.
    (a) Generally.
    (b) Limitation on right of eviction.

§ 18:5. Wrongful eviction.
    (a) Generally.
    (b) Damages for wrongful eviction.

A. The hotel lien

§ 18:1. Existence of lien.

(*a*) *Generally.* The hotel has the right to hold the goods of a guest who has not paid his bill; in order to bring pressure to bear upon the guest to compel him to do so. By statute this right of lien has generally been extended to boarding and lodging house proprietors, but in the absence of statute, the right of lien is limited to the hotel and is limited to claims against guests; that is, persons whom the hotel receives as transients.

If the person has the status of a tenant, rather than a guest, the hotel does not have a hotel lien against the tenant's property but note that it may have a landlord's lien which will generally achieve the same result as a hotel lien.

(*b*) *Nature of claim.* The lien may be exercised as to all claims against the guest which are due and owing for accommodations and services furnished the guest.

(*c*) *Care of property subject to lien.* While the property is held by the hotel subject to the lien, the hotel must do no act adverse to the interests of the guest in the property. If the hotel fails to exercise that degree of care which a reasonable man would take of the property and harm is caused thereby, the hotel is liable to the guest for such negligent harm. Furthermore, if the misconduct is willful, the lien may be terminated automatically.

The property which is subject to the lien remains the property of the guest until the title thereto is transferred by its proper sale. Accordingly, if the hotel disposes of it as the hotel's own property, there is both a civil conversion and a criminal larceny or embezzlement of the property.

(*d*) *Loss of lien.* The lien is lost or terminates if (1) the hotel voluntarily surrenders the property to the guest or owner and the guest or owner is not guilty of any fraud in inducing such surrender; (2) the debt of the guest is paid in full or the hotel is offered or tendered the proper amount which is due, but refuses to accept it; (3) the parties make a binding agreement for the surrender of the lien; or (4) the hotel demands an excessive amount from the guest in payment of his debt to the hotel.

The facts: A guest drove his automobile each day and parked on the parking lot of the hotel each night. The hotel claimed that it had a lien upon the car.

Decision: The hotel did not have a lien upon the automobile because it remained in the possession and control of the guest. [Brown v. Harmon, 59 GaApp 373, 1 SE2d 33 (1939)].

The lien is not lost by the fact that other or additional security is taken for the payment of the debt owed the hotel, unless the express provision or necessary implication of the agreement as to such other security calls for the termination of the lien.

(1) Tender. In order to constitute tender within the meaning of the rule that a tender which is refused by the hotel discharges the lien of the hotel, it is necessary that the debtor offer the exact amount due in money. That is to say, a check is not a "tender" unless the hotel is willing to accept it as payment, for the reason that a check is not legal tender. There is no duty on the part of anyone to accept it, and hence the hotel does not violate any duty when it refuses to accept the check and is not to be penalized by losing its lien upon the goods.

(e) Recapture of property from guest. When the hotel has a lien it has the right to recapture the property from the guest if the latter takes the property unlawfully from the custody of the hotel, provided the hotel can do so without committing a breach of the peace. However, if the guest retaliates to a proper retaking of the property by the hotel with force of such a nature as justifies the hotel employee in inflicting bodily harm in self-defense, the employee may do so, and may use such force as would be warranted by the circumstances without regard to the existence of the lien or the hotel-guest relationship.

§ 18:2. Property subject to lien.

(a) Generally. Ordinarily all property brought by the guest onto the premises is subject to the hotel lien. In some instances, the class of property which is subject to the lien is defined by statute. In the absence of a statutory restriction, the lien extends to all clothing, except that in actual use; all baggage; and to furniture and goods brought by the guest onto the premises.

An automobile is subject to a hotel lien as in the case of any other property of the guest, although under some statutes the term "lien" is limited to "baggage," which in turn is so defined or construed as to exclude automobiles.

(*b*) *Exempt property.* Exemption statutes are strictly construed with the result that property which is exempt from execution upon a judgment is not by that fact alone exempt from the hotel lien. From this it follows that although an ordinary judgment creditor cannot reach property of the guest because it is exempt from execution, the hotel may nevertheless enforce its lien thereon.

(*c*) *Property of third person.*

(1) Actual ownership unknown. If the hotel does not know or have reason to know that the property brought to the hotel by the guest is in fact the property of a third person, the hotel may assert its lien thereon. In such case it is immaterial that the guest is merely a bailee, or an employee of the owner. It is also immaterial how the guest came into possession of the property or whether the property was lost, stolen, or obtained by fraud.

(i) Statutory provisions. A hotel lien is regulated by statutes in many states with respect to the property subject to the lien. In some instances the common-law rule above discussed is restated by the statute, as by declaring that the lien extends to all property of or under the control of the guest; although in some instances "control" is not given a literal interpretation but is held to require that the owner have entrusted the guest with the property; thereby excluding a lien on stolen goods.

By other statutes the lien is limited to property of the guest, whether or not the hotel knows of the ownership of the third person. There is some authority that if the lien, when created by statute, is not restricted to the property of the guest, the statute is unconstitutional with respect to third persons who own the property.

As a middle position, some states limit the right against the property of the third person to a lien for services rendered in connection with such property.

Statutes extending the hotel lien to boarding and lodging houses frequently create such lien only as to property of the boarder or lodger.

(2) Ownership by third person known. If the hotel knows that property in the custody or possession of the guest is in fact owned by a third person, the hotel cannot enforce its lien against such property.

As an extension of this view it is held that where accommodations have been furnished husband and wife on the faith of the husband's credit, the property of the wife is not subject to the lien therefor.

(i) Statutory provisions. In some instances, statutes have so extended the hotel lien that it is immaterial whether the hotel has knowledge of the third person's ownership. For example, where the statute states in general terms that the lien extends to property of or under the control of the guest, the lien will extend to property which the hotel knows to belong to the guest's employer, such as samples and display cases which the guest-salesman has in his possession.

When the lien does not exist if the interest of the third person is known, such knowledge may be shown by the fact that the hotel knew that the universal custom was that samples of a salesman were not individually owned by him.

(d) Group accommodations. When accommodations are obtained as a group it is generally held that the individual property of each member is not subject to a lien because of the debt for the group accommodations. Likewise, property of the wife alone cannot be held for a bill owed for accommodations furnished to the husband and wife.

(e) Security interest of third persons. Prior to the adoption of the Uniform Commercial Code it had been held that the hotel lien was superior to the title of a conditional vendor or a chattel mortgagee when the property was in the guest's possession and the hotel had no actual knowledge of the existence of the security interest of such third person. But other cases have sustained the superiority of the security interest over the hotel lien. So it has been held that although a statute extended the hotelman's lien to the owner or operator of a trailer court, such lien was not superior to a prior chattel mortgage on a house trailer where the mortgage was filed as required by statute.

(1) Code states. It would appear that the Uniform Commercial Code does not apply to the situation here considered, the prior law in such case continuing. The matter is not free from doubt for a contrary conclusion could be reached, holding the Code applicable and the security interest paramount.[1]

§ 18:3. Enforcement of lien.

(a) Generally. The lien confers upon the hotel the right to hold the property of the guest until paid, and, if not paid, to order a public sale of the property, and apply the proceeds therefrom to the discharge of the payment of the debt owed to it by the guest for accommodations, and so forth.[1a]

(*b*) *Lockout of patron.* The hotel may sometimes beat the skipping patron to the draw by locking him out of his room and thereby trapping the patron's property. This remedy does not have very great value for the reason that the regular skipper travels lightly so that he has nothing to lose.

Before using the lockout, the hotel should of course check its records to verify that there is in fact an amount due and that the hotel is not bound by any agreement to extend credit to the patron, for if the hotel seizes the patron's goods without there being any debt then due, the hotel is subject to civil liability for the conversion of the patron's property.[1b] The hotel might also be subject to criminal liability although in most states this would not be so because the hotel, acting in the honest belief that it was justified, would not have the mental state necessary to make its act criminal.

(*c*) *Notice and sale.* When the patron has left the hotel and the hotel is holding his property by virtue of a lien, the hotel does not have an immediate right to sell the property. Statutes require that the hotel wait to afford the patron the chance to pay his bill. This waiting period varies from ten days to six months under the various state statutes. Notice must then be given to the patron, by mail or posting or both, a specified number of days before the sale. The sale is a public sale.

This procedure is for the most part of little or no value to the hotel because of the fact that the experienced skipper, the guest who leaves without paying, generally does not leave sufficient property on which the lien can operate to make a sale under the lien financially worthwhile.

---

[1] The Code does not apply to "(b) to a landlord's lien; or (c) to a lien given by statute or other rule of law for services or materials except as provided in Section 9-310 on the priority of such lien ..." As a hotel lien is distinct from a landlord's lien, any exclusion of the hotel lien must be based upon clause (c). If the lien referred to by that clause may be a lien "for services" the hotel would come within its scope and thereby be excluded from the operation of Article 9 of the Code. If, however, the lien referred to in clause (c) is the same as "such liens" as are provided by § 9-310, the clause is limited to the lien of repairmen and artisans and does not extend to the hotel lien.

[1a] See Supplement p. 475.

[1b] The right to lockout will probably be limited by the due process concept noted in Supplement p. 473.

(d) Surplus and deficit. If upon the sale of the property, the proceeds of the sale exceed the amount due the hotel and the costs of making the sale, the guest or owner of the property sold is entitled to the surplus. Conversely, if the debt owed the hotel and the costs of making the sale of the particular property exceed the proceeds of the sale there is a deficit for which the guest remains liable. That is to say, the lien gives the hotel an additional remedy but does not substitute the lien in place of the debt owed by the guest.

B. Removal and eviction of patrons

§ 18:4. Right of removal and eviction.

(a) Generally. A guest may be removed or evicted from the hotel when after having been furnished accommodations he acts in such a way as would have justified the hotel in refusing to accept him initially, or when his right of occupancy or tenancy has been lawfully terminated.[2]

As a logical incident of the right of eviction, the hotel has the right to remove the property of the patron so that the rooms may be made available for another patron.

(b) Limitation on right of eviction. The hotel does not have an unlimited right to evict a guest and it may not do so when the circumstances are such that the hotel should recognize that such eviction would expose the guest to an unreasonable risk of harm. Thus a person who has been sick and annoys others by his groans or excessive demands, or a person who has acquired a contagious disease which imperils others, may not be evicted when the act of moving the person from the room may endanger his life or when it is foreseeable that the guest will be harmed by exposure.

For example, the fact that a guest makes a nuisance of himself because he is sick does not authorize the hotel to drive him out into a storm. Where it did so and the guest thereafter died from the exposure to the weather, the hotel was liable for damages for his wrongful death.

Otherwise stated, although the hotel has the right to evict, eject, or remove the guest, it must exercise care or provide substitute accommodations, as by having the guest taken to a

---

[2] See § 2:6 et seq.

Liens and Eviction

hospital, so that the guest is not exposed to any unreasonable danger in consequence of such eviction or removal.

§ 18:5. Wrongful eviction.

(*a*) *Generally.* Eviction may be wrongful because it is in violation of the rights of the patron or constitutes an improper discrimination.[3] In such case, it is immaterial whether the hotel acted carefully and with reasonable care.

In contrast, the hotel may have the right to evict but the wrongfulness of its conduct lies in the manner in which that right is exercised.[4] When the guest is evicted from the hotel, the hotel must act in a manner which is reasonable under the circumstances. Conversely, the hotel is liable to the guest if (1) it uses more force than is reasonably necessary, or (2) acts in a way which is unnecessarily humiliating or insulting to the guest.

(*b*) *Damages for wrongful eviction.* When the hotel has wrongfully evicted a guest from the hotel it is liable and must pay damages for the value of any property of the guest which is lost or disappears in the process; for any assault and battery that may occur; and for the mental distress, such as pain, suffering, and humiliation; which the hotel has caused the guest.

The hotel is also liable for the cost to the guest of bringing a subsequent lawsuit to recover his property from the hotel or from a third person.

> *The facts:* The landlord, acting in good faith, put the roomer's property out in the hall. Some of the property disappeared. The roomer sued the landlord for the loss. He defended on the ground that he had the right to evict the roomer.
>
> *Decision:* The landlord had acted in a negligent manner, as loss of the roomer's property was reasonably foreseeable. The fact that he had the right to evict the roomer and remove his property did not protect him from liability when he exercised that right in a negligent manner. [Tanko v. Collier, (CADistCol) 187 A2d 700 (1963)].

---

[3] See Chapters 2, 3.
[4] The concept of due process will act as a limitation on eviction. See Supplement p. 473.

Chapter 19. MANAGEMENT AND GOVERNMENT REGULATION

A. General principles

§ 19:1. Freedom of management.
  (a) Generally.
  (b) Trend of regulation.

§ 19:2. Hotel regulations.
  (a) Generally.
  (b) Particular applications.

§ 19:3. Power and subject of government regulation.
  (a) Power to regulate.
  (b) Subject of regulation.
  (c) Licensing.
    (1) Suspension of license.
  (d) Taxation.

§ 19:4. Classification for regulatory purposes.
  (a) Generally.
  (b) Nature of enterprise.
    (1) Discretion of legislature or administrator.
  (c) Nonclassification.
  (d) Persons bound.

§ 19:5. Regulation by legislative rule enforced by courts.
  (a) Generally.
  (b) Criminal liability.
  (c) Civil liability.

§ 19:6. Regulation by administrative rule enforced by administrator.
  (a) Generally.
  (b) Administrator defined.
  (c) Reasons for the rise of the administrator.
    (1) Future problems.
    (2) Expert knowledge.
    (3) Continuing and flexible administration.
  (d) Overloaded courts.

§ 19:7. Interpretation of statutes and regulations.
  (a) Generally.
  (b) Ordinary and logical meaning.

Management and Government Regulation

(c) Clear law.
(d) Background and effect of the law.
(e) Presumptions in aid of interpretation.
(f) Modification of the common law.

B. Administrative law

§ 19:8. The pattern of administrative regulation.

§ 19:9. The thermostat administrator.
    (a) Definition.
    (b) Particular applications.
    (c) Modifications of the pattern.

§ 19:10 The governing administrator.
    (a) Definition and nature.
    (b) Membership.

§ 19:11. — Investigation.
    (a) Generally.
    (b) Narrowing of constitutional guarantees.
        (1) Search and seizure.
        (2) Self-incrimination.

§ 19:12. — Rule making.
    (a) Generally.
    (b) Regulations as law.
        (1) Validity of delegation.
    (c) Hearings for rule making.
    (d) Finality of rule making.

§ 19:13. — Violation determination.
    (a) Generally.
    (b) Complaint and pleading stage.
    (c) The hearing stage.
    (d) Judgment.
    (e) Appeal and enforcement.

§ 19:14. The importance and finality of administrative regulation.
    (a) Generally.
    (b) Absence of voter control of administrative regulatory system.
    (c) Absence of constitutional limitations on the administrative regulatory system.
    (d) Finality of administrative determination.
        (1) Wisdom and fairness.
        (2) Discretion.
        (3) Questions of fact.

§ 19:15. Your attitude toward government regulation.
  (a) Generally.
  (b) Acceptance of government regulation.
  (c) Acceptance of the administrative system of government.
  (d) Public relations with the administrators.
  (f) Professional ethics and the long-term point of view.

A. General principles

§ 19:1. Freedom of management.

(*a*) *Generally.* A hotel is a private enterprise, privately owned, and therefore the starting point is that its business may be run in such manner as its management deems fit.

While this is true, the hotel is an enterprise within an ordered society, and accordingly finds itself subject to various regulations and restrictions to which everyone in the community is subject; such as the laws relating to fire prevention, sale of liquor to minors, and so on. In addition, the hotel, as is true of every other business enterprise, is subject to regulations aimed particularly at that business. The net result is that the freedom of the hotel is subjected to a wide range of general laws and particular hotel laws; using laws broadly to include ordinances and administrative regulations.

(*b*) *Trend of regulation.* The regulation of business has in general shown certain trends over the last century: (1) it is recognized that governments may regulate, compete with, and own any business; (2) as between state and federal governments, there has been a steady drift of regulatory power from the states to the federal government; and (3) the regulation of business is increasingly entrusted to an appointed commission which combines the function of making laws, enforcing them, and determining when they have been violated.[1]

With the application of the Federal Labor Management Relations Act, the Federal Fair Labor Standards Act, and the Federal Civil Rights Anti-Discrimination Act of 1964 to hotels, this pattern of the trends as stated above has caught up with hotels, although much of hotel life continues to be regulated by the ordinary state and local statutes and ordinances.

---

[1] See generally, Anderson, Government and Business (3d edition, South-Western Publishing Company, 1966).

§ 19:2. Hotel regulations.

(*a*) ***Generally.*** As an incident of the power to manage the hotel's building and operations, the hotel has a right to adopt regulations. As long as they are reasonable they are held valid and binding upon the parties concerned.

(*b*) ***Particular applications.*** Illustrative of the foregoing, it has been held that a hotel can properly prohibit the entrance of such persons as peddlers, and that this is not in conflict with the duty of the hotel to make its facilities available to the general public. In the interest of avoiding physical inconvenience or the making of false claims for property loss, the hotel may require that guests leave their baggage with a porter or bellboy until a room has been assigned to them. Style of dress, within reasonable limits, may be regulated as by requiring that coats be worn in the dining room. In the interest of avoiding offending others and of perhaps subjecting the hotel to criminal responsibility, it may prohibit a man visiting any woman not his wife in her room at night.

§ 19:3. Power and subject of government regulation.

(*a*) ***Power to regulate.*** Governments may regulate the business of the hotel in any of its various aspects. In most instances, the regulation will be based upon state law. As to matters which for the most part are minor in character, the hotel can be regulated by municipality or city ordinances. The federal government if it so desires may also regulate the hotel business under the present broad interpretation given to the commerce and the war power clauses.

(*b*) ***Subject of regulation.*** The regulation may take a wide variety of forms and relate to varying subject matter. For the most part, the regulation of the hotel business tends to be grouped in certain areas: (1) protection of patrons from physical harm; (2) protection of patrons from fraud; (3) limitation of the liability of hotels, as discussed in Chapter 16; (4) regulation of employment practices, as discussed in Chapter 20; (5) the prevention of discrimination, as discussed in Chapter 3; and (6) the prevention of the hotel's being used in connection with crime, as discussed in Chapter 21.

To protect patrons from physical harm, various laws relating to lighting and railings, elevators, and fire-fighting devices and equipment have been adopted. The licensing of hotels is commonly required in order to insure that they are run by persons of good moral character. Prospective patrons of hotels may be protected from fraud by prohibiting false advertising of hotel rates and by licensing "runners" and other persons soliciting business for hotels. In order to protect patrons from being short-changed with respect to accommodations and facilities, statutes may declare that certain specified minimum facilities must be provided with hotel accommodations, as by requiring all housekeeping apartments to have kitchen sinks or by requiring certain toilet facilities per specified number of rooms. As a means of protecting the community generally from crime, it is proper to require that a motel keep, and make available to the police, a registry of all guests, stating the date of their arrival, the number of rooms rented by them, and the make and license tag of the automobile in which they arrive.

(c) Licensing. Statutes commonly require persons owning or operating hotels, lodging houses, apartment houses, and so on to obtain a license to engage in such enterprises. It is proper to make the granting of the license dependent, among other things, upon the moral character of the applicant.

(1) Suspension of license. When a proceeding for the suspension of a hotel's license is begun it is generally necessary that notice be given the hotel of the hearing and of the matters with which it will be charged. While the same precision of pleading is not required as in the case of a criminal indictment, basic fairness requires that the hotel be informed of the nature of the proceedings against it and of the matters to which it must make defense.

If the notice of the suspension proceeding is too vague, the hotel must request particulars, and cannot meet the problem by merely staying away from the hearing to suspend the license. If it does, the administrative agency may proceed with the hearing in the absence of the hotel and suspend the license.

(d) Taxation. In a broad sense, taxation is a form of regulation and in some instances is imposed for the purpose of controlling or retarding the taxed activity, rather than merely raising revenue. The hotel is of course subject to general tax laws, such as those imposing taxes on real estate and taxes on income. In addition, it is proper to tax hotels with respect to characteristics found only in hotels. For example, it has been held valid to impose a tax on payments made to hotels by its transient guests.

§ 19:4. Classification for regulatory purposes.

(*a*) ***Generally.*** Statutes and administrative regulations may group together different things for the purpose of regulation as long as such grouping is reasonable.

(*b*) ***Nature of enterprise.*** For the purpose of governmental regulation, historical differences between hotels and other places providing accommodations, such as boarding and lodging houses on the one hand, and apartment houses on the other, may be ignored and all regulated by the common provision.

> *The facts:* The state industrial commission issued an order establishing minimum wages for persons employed in the "hotel industry" and defined it as including "any establishment which, as a whole of its business activities, offers lodging accommodations for hire to the public." It was claimed that this regulation was arbitrary and therefore invalid because it grouped together ordinary lodging houses with hotels.
>
> *Decision:* While lodging houses and hotels are historically distinct, the government, and a state commissioner exercising the power of the government, may classify them all together for the purpose of fixing the minimum wage to be paid by them. Such action is not arbitrary and is valid. [N. H. Lyons & Co. v. Corsi, 116 NYS2d 520, 203 Misc 160 (1952), aff'd 146 NYS2d 663, 286 AppDiv 1065, appeal denied 135 NE2d 732].

For the purpose of a rent control statute, both residential and transient or commercial hotels are to be considered subject to the statute in the absence of some clear evidence that the legislature intended to limit the protection of the statute to transient guests. Similarly, a regulation applicable to "hotels" can apply to such enterprises without regard to whether some of the guests are transient while others are permanent or residential.

(*1*) *Discretion of legislature or administrator.* Whether similar enterprises which could be treated collectively are to be so treated is a matter for the discretion of the authority making the rule, such as the legislature or the administrative officer. That is to say, the fact that a grouping or classification would be sustained as reasonable and valid does not require that the lawmaker make his rule extend to all persons who could be within such grouping. Otherwise stated, it is a matter for the discretion of the lawmaker to determine how far he wishes to go in applying the rule. For example, under some rent control statutes the distinction is made between the ordinary landlord-tenant relationship and the innkeeper-guest relationship, the rent control statute applying only to the former.

(*c*) *Nonclassification.* The fact that there are similarities between enterprises does not require that they all be classified together. Thus a separate treatment of different enterprises will be sustained as reasonable for the purpose of one type of regulation although for another type of regulation a grouping of the different enterprises would also be held proper. To illustrate, the difference between the physical construction and the use of hotels and lodging houses justifies classifying them separately and establishing different fire building code regulations for each class. Likewise a motel and a lodging house may properly be treated differently for registration and tax purposes.

(*d*) *Persons bound.* In order to prevent the evasion of a government regulation through the device of leasing the hotel building to another corporation, and so forth, the city ordinance or the statute imposing the regulation may be construed or by its express terms will apply to all persons owning, operating, leasing, and in any way managing or conducting a hotel or other regulated enterprise.

§ 19:5. Regulation by legislative rule enforced by courts.

(*a*) *Generally.* Historically, and still continuing in many instances today, regulation takes the form of a flat decree or rule laid down by legislature or the city council and imposing a penalty or liability for its breach, the enforcement being accomplished by means of ordinary court action.

(*b*) *Criminal liability.* Illustrating the above statement, the state legislature may adopt a building code requiring certain fire escapes in certain types of buildings and declare that the operation of a building without such a fire escape shall constitute a crime for which a certain penalty such as a fine or imprisonment, or both, may be imposed. In the event that a hotel, or anyone else violates such a statute, the statute is enforced by the local prosecuting attorney commencing and prosecuting a criminal proceeding in the local court against the wrongdoer. Likewise when the legislature prohibits the sale of intoxicating liquor to minors, a hotel which violates this law can be brought into the local criminal court for prosecution. In connection with the lesser offenses, the criminal prosecution is brought either before a magistrate or justice of the peace or some such similar minor judicial officer. In the case of the more serious offenses, there will ordinarily be the right to trial before a petty or small jury.

The fact that an ordinance or a statute has been ignored for a number of years does not prevent the government from enforcing it.

(*c*) *Civil liability.* In contrast with criminal liability, the legislature may impose civil liability for certain acts done by hotels or by anyone engaging in a particular kind of business. For example, a state legislature may declare that any bar or other enterprise selling intoxicating liquor shall be civilly liable in damages for the death of a patron when the bar sells liquor to him although he is visibly intoxicated and the patron on leaving the bar is killed because of or partly as the result of his being so intoxicated.

If the hotel makes an improper sale of liquor and the patron is killed because of his high state of intoxication, the suit may be brought against the hotel for the pecuniary or money loss caused the family of the patron by his death. This action is brought in the ordinary court in which automobile accident cases, sidewalk injury cases, and so forth, would be brought. In most instances there would be a trial of the matter before a judge and a civil jury.

§ 19:6. Regulation by administrative rule enforced by administrator.

(*a*) *Generally.* Instead of the lawmaker fixing the exact code or standard of conduct and the court's enforcing that code, increased use is made today of administrative rule enforced by administrative action. For example, the legislature will adopt a general law stating that there is hereby created a hotel commission which shall have authority to adopt rules and regulations with respect to certain matters, and which shall have power to enforce those rules and regulations. This means that instead of the lawmaker stating specifically just what should or should not be done, the lawmaker passes that job on to the administrator. It further means that when the rule established by the administrator is violated he has the authority to hold a hearing to determine whether there has been a violation of his rule.

(*b*) *Administrator defined.* For the purpose of this book, administrator is used in a general sense to refer to anybody performing an administrative function. The administrator, as so defined, may be merely a single official doing standardized acts or it may be a commission or board consisting of a number of members and having a wide range of discretion and authority. These aspects will be considered later.

(*c*) *Reasons for the rise of the administrator.* The great increase in the number of administrative agencies can be understood if we consider the simple case of your leaving me in charge of your hotel for the next twenty-four hours. Will you be able to give me instructions which will cover every possible situation which may arise? Can you foresee every situation which may arise? Even if you could, would you always know in advance what decision you would make when the time arose?

(*1*) *Future problems.* It is obvious that your instructions will not go very far and to a very large extent you must trust my experience and judgment, hoping that I have enough of both to do what should be done when the time arrives. Similarly, the legislature cannot foresee the problems which will arise in the hotel business, or any other business and can not tell a law-enforcing official just what should be done. Hence the legislature creates a hotel commissioner to make such rules and regulations as from time to time he shall deem necessary or proper.

(*2*) *Expert knowledge.* In the case of the lawmaker and the commissioner, there is also an additional aspect. The lawmaker does not know the ins and outs of the hotel business. Likewise he does not know the ins and outs of the transportation business, the food preparation business, the manufacturing business, and so on. It is both logical and necessary for the lawmaker to recognize his limitations and to refrain from attempting to regulate businesses with respect to which he has only a general or no real knowledge at all. Logically it is better for an industry to have the power to run it be given to an expert or a commission of experts who have the knowledge of the particular business, and, who, through devoting themselves exclusively to that business, will become increasingly expert as time goes on. Thus the demand for expert knowledge of the one regulating the business gradually pushes the subject of regulation away from the legislature and into the hands of a special commissioner or administrative agency.

(3) Continuing and flexible administration. State legislatures meet for the most part only every other year; in about one-fifth of the states every year. City councils meet more frequently but still with intervals. The result is that action taken by a legislature, in particular, and to some extent a city council, is in a sense a hit-or-miss type of control. The law or ordinance is passed today. If the law does not prove satisfactory it may be one or more years before the lawmaker can get around to adopting an amendment or otherwise changing the law. Moreover, political and economic factors may cause delay in the changing of the law.

In contrast, the administrative officer or commission has the ability, because he is concentrating on the one activity, of looking after it continuously and of changing existing regulations or adopting new ones whenever the changing circumstances indicate that that should be done.

(*d*) **Overloaded courts.** In all or in the majority of the large cities there is a staggering backlog of undisposed cases. This overload will obviously increase as the population increases. One of the solutions for the problem is to move out of the courts as many cases as possible, either by requiring arbitration or by giving an administrative agency the power to hear and determine the matter. It is therefore inevitable that as new regulatory laws are adopted they will follow the pattern of shifting away from trial by courts and into administrative agency control and enforcement.

§ 19:7. Interpretation of statutes and regulations.

(*a*) **Generally.** With the increasing number of statutes and regulations applicable to hotels, as well as to other businesses, the question of interpretation of statutes and regulations becomes increasingly important. In some instances, that statute will itself define the particular word or terms which it employs, although in other instances it is necessary to interpret what the words of the definition mean.

For the purpose of simplicity, the term "a law" will be used in this section to refer to a statute passed by Congress or a state legislature, an ordinance adopted by a city or a municipal authority, and rules and regulations adopted by an administrator.

(*b*) *Ordinary and logical meaning.* Whenever it is possible, words are to be given the meaning which they have in ordinary usage and the meaning which is logical.

If words are technical words, such as those which might be used in a building code or laws relating to sanitation, the words are to be interpreted according to their accepted and normal technical meaning.

(*c*) *Clear law.* When the meaning of a law is clear and free from ambiguity or doubt, it must be followed according to its terms. Its clear provisions may not in such case be ignored under the pretext of following the spirit of the law. This means in turn that every provision of the law must be interpreted to have effect and that a law is not to be interpreted beyond its provisions.

Illustrative of the latter, it has been held that where a liquor-licensing law established a quota system limiting the number of licenses which could be issued but expressly excluded from such limitation licenses granted to hotels, the exemption of hotels licenses was not affected by an amendment to the statute which went no further than to regulate the terms on which licenses would be granted to hotels and was silent as to any quota limitation on such licenses.

(*d*) *Background and effect of the law.* If the law itself is not clear, various factors may be considered in seeking to determine what the lawmaker intended by the law. Consideration may thus be given to the occasion of adopting and the necessity for the law; the circumstances under which the law was adopted; the evils to be remedied and the objects to be attained by it; the former law, if any, including other laws upon the same or similar subjects; the consequences of a particular interpretation; the contemporaneous legislative history; and the legislative and administrative interpretations which have already been made of the law.

(*e*) *Presumptions in aid of interpretation.* If the meaning of the law is not clear, certain presumptions are made so that in the absence of a convincing argument to the contrary the law will be interpreted according to the presumptions. Thus it is presumed that as between two interpretations one of which is reasonable and the other unreasonable, the lawmaker intended the one which was reasonable rather than the one which was unreasonable, absurd, or impossible to carry out. For example, where a state housing act required that hotel apartments have kitchen sinks, the requirement is applicable only as to such apartments in the hotel as are equipped with kitchens and does not apply to those which do not have such housekeeping facilities.

Likewise, it is presumed that it was intended that the law should be constitutional so as to be in harmony with the state constitution and the Constitution of the United States; and to favor the public interest as against private interest. Furthermore, until a law is convincingly shown to be unconstitutional, the court must regard it as constitutional and enforce it according to its terms.

(*f*) *Modification of the common law.* Most states which have a common-law background, that is, which as part of their colonial or territorial heritage possess a background of the law of England, follow the rule that laws which cut down rights which existed at common law are to be construed strictly. For example, a statute which modifies the liability of a hotel for the property of its guests is generally construed strictly on the ground that it cuts down the rights which the guest would otherwise have under the common law.

Contrary to the foregoing, a few states have adopted a statute which declares, at least with respect to laws thereafter adopted, that laws shall be construed liberally to attain their objectives and to promote justice, without regard to whether the common law is thereby modified or altered.

B. Administrative law

§ 19:8. The pattern of administrative regulation.

The pattern of administrative regulation may vary greatly from one type of administrator to another and from state to state, but two distinct patterns may be recognized. The person enforcing or applying the system may be a single individual or it may be a commission or board consisting of a number of members. For the purpose of convenience, the term "administrator" will be used in this chapter to refer to both the one-man and the multi-man type of administrator, unless it is otherwise specified that only one of these is intended.

§ 19:9. The thermostat administrator.

(*a*) *Definition.* This is not a technical title but he is the administrator who acts in the same kind of way as does a thermostat. When the specified fact exists, he acts, and further, he acts in a specified way. If the facts do not exist, he does not act.

(*b*) *Particular applications.* The thermostat administrator is illustrated by the health inspector who mechanically quarantines the building according to specified rules when a person therein has one of several specified diseases. The characteristics of this administrator is that the statute declares when he is to do what. That is, the statute says that when the named diseases are found, then he shall quarantine the building. Notice that he has no choice and does not exercise any judgment in determining what diseases require quarantining. Likewise he does not have any discretion as to what should be done when a specified disease exists. Thus he cannot determine to take the risk of not quarantining, nor to accept some less stringent type of control of the building. Note also that there is no element of trial before this administrator at which evidence may be offered to show that the disease does not exist. Instead the administrator acts on the basis of his own investigation and knowledge. Likewise there is no provision for appeal from his decision or obtaining a review by the court.

This type of administrator may also be found under some fire, safety, and sanitation laws. Here again, the statute declares when the officer does what; and he makes his conclusions on the basis of his observations and then acts on the matter in which he was "programmed" to act.

(*c*) *Modifications of the pattern.* Health and similar inspectors do not always represent the exact type of administrator described above but tend to move into the class of the administrator who will be described next. Specifically some statutes give the administrator some degree of discretion or judgment as by providing for the quarantine in case of "contagious" diseases, thus leaving it to the health officer to determine whether a disease is contagious. Similarly, the fire or sanitation code, instead of laying down specific, exact building specifications to be followed automatically may authorize the administrator to act if the conditions are "unsafe," "hazardous," "dangerous to human health;" in which case it is seen that the administrator is given some freedom of action, which the law calls "discretion" to determine whether there is conduct or a condition which comes within the scope of the statute.

§ 19:10. The governing administrator.

(*a*) *Definition and nature.* This again is not a technical name but is used to refer to the administrator, generally a commission, which has such broad powers that it is in effect the "government" within the sphere of its authority. This may be illustrated by the Interstate Commerce Commission which is a board composed of a number of members and which has (a) executive powers, in that it can investigate to determine what evils exist and what is being done, and whether a proceeding should be brought against any particular individual; (b) legislative power, in that it can make the rules and regulations which carriers and shippers must follow; and (c) judicial power, in that it can sit as though it were a court to determine cases involving violations of its rules and regulations. The governing administrator here described is thus all three branches of the government wrapped into one, within the area in which it is authorized to operate.

(*b*) *Membership.* A governing administrator is generally a board of two or more members appointed by a chief executive, such as the state governor or the United States President, with the advice and consent of the Senate. The governing administrator may also be a department head, such as the Secretary of Labor of the United States.

§ 19:11. — Investigation.

(*a*) *Generally.* The administrator of the rank here considered generally has virtually unlimited power to examine or hold investigations either to obtain information to guide it in adopting regulations or to determine whether there are any violations of its regulations. Furthermore, in order to be certain that you are complying with its regulations, the governing administrator may require you to file periodic reports.

(*b*) *Narrowing of constitutional guarantees.* When the governing administrator conducts an examination, the business examined cannot raise the usual defenses against such examination. For example, the business can be required to produce its business records so that the administrator can see if there is any violation of the administrator's regulations or of the law.

That is, the administrator can go fishing around looking for violations, contrary to the principle that a showing must first be made that there is a reasonable ground to believe there has been violation before a private citizen can be required to produce his papers.

(1) Search and seizure. If the administrator issues an order on you to testify before it or to produce your records for examination, you cannot oppose on the ground of unreasonable search and seizure since that guarantee does not apply unless the administrator makes an actual physical seizing by physically taking your records.

(2) Self-incrimination. For practical purposes, the protection against self-incrimination does not exist or can be avoided by the administrator. If you are a corporation, you cannot raise the objection of self-incrimination and the production of corporate records may be compelled even though the officer or employee producing them would also be producing evidence which would incriminate him. And whether you are a corporation or not, you can be deprived of the right to plead self-incrimination if you are given a sufficient immunity from subsequent criminal prosecution. And last but not least, the administrator may compel you to produce any records which he requires you to keep, in order to determine that you are keeping them. Hence, all that the administrator need do to have access to all of your business records is to adopt a blanket regulation specifying from A to Z what kind of records hotels must keep. The administrator then has the power to require the production of all these records to see that you are doing what he has required.

§ 19:12. — Rule making.

(*a*) *Generally.* As already stated, the governing administrator is given power to make rules. These are rules which have the force of law just as though the legislature or the Congress had adopted them. For example, a statute may authorize the governing administrator to adopt rules to control advertising of rates by hotels for the purpose of eliminating misrepresentation to the public and unfair competition.

(*b*) *Regulations as law.* At this point, you will notice that there is nothing which binds you. That is, no law or standard has yet been imposed. Acting under this authorizing statute, however, the governing administrator may draw up a set of rules to regulate or control "advertising of rates by hotels." Once adopted by the administrator, these provisions will have the force of law in that you must obey them to the same extent as though they had been adopted by the state legislature or the Congress of the United States. Whether they are called rules or regulations or anything else is immaterial. The important thing is that they are the standard by which you must guide your conduct.

(1) Validity of delegation. The attack is frequently made on administrative agencies that the granting to them of the power to make rules which have the force of law is an unconstitutional delegation to them of the authority given by constitutions to the lawmaker, and which should be exercised by the lawmaker alone. For the most part, this objection is not sustained and the "delegation" is generally held valid whether the authority to make the additional rules be granted to a governmental unit or to an administrative board or officer.

For example, a state fire safety statute may authorize each municipality to establish additional regulations and such action is not an invalid grant of legislative power. Likewise it is constitutional to create a commission to administer a statute designed to prevent false or deceptive advertising of rates by hotels. And a statute or ordinance may provide for the licensing as rooming house operators of persons of "good moral character" without defining that term and leave the matter to the administrator to apply. Such a provision is not unconstitutional as an improper delegation of legislative authority, for the reason that such provision is so well understood that no definition is necessary.

*(c) **Hearings for rule making.*** As far as your constitutional rights are concerned, the governing administrator may make its rules without any prior investigation or hearing. As a practical matter, it is likely that the administrator, whether or not required to do so by the statute creating him, will conduct some form of investigation to determine what is needed.

In some instances, the statute creating the administrator will require that a hearing be held before any rule is adopted so that persons in the affected industry may appear and testify with respect to the problems or the proposed rules of the administrator. If, however, the statute does not expressly require the administrator to hold such a hearing, it is up to the administrator to decide whether to hold any hearing, how long a hearing to hold, the scope of the hearing, and so forth.

(*d*) *Finality of rule making.* For practical purposes the adoption of a given rule or regulation by the administrator is final. The rule or regulation will not be re-examined by the courts to determine whether they agree with it or whether they would have done the same thing. Thus the rule can not be attacked on the basis of wisdom or lack of wisdom. As a matter of textbook law, it is true that the rule may be attacked on the ground that the government has no power to make the regulation in question, whether by acts of Congress, state statutes, or by administrators acting under their authority. This basis for attack has no practical meaning today since there is no limitation on the type or number of businesses which government may regulate, control, or even own.[2] In most instances, an attack on the regulation on the basis of an illegal delegation of legislative power will also fail. Occasionally, an attack upon the regulation as a denial of equal protection will succeed on the theory that the administrator made an improper discrimination, although even here the great probability is that the court will go along with and sustain the classification made by the administrator as reasonable and based on fact.

The net result is that as long as the administrator has followed the procedure prescribed by the statute which creates his office, it is most unlikely that a rule or regulation adopted by him can be challenged successfully on constitutional grounds.

§ 19:13. — Violation determination.

(*a*) *Generally.* The governing administrator can generally act like a court of law to sit and determine whether you have been guilty of violation of its rules. The procedure followed in such case tends to be like that in an ordinary law court, although for the most part there is no constitutional requirement that it be so.

(*b*) *Complaint and pleading stage.* The administrative machinery is set in motion either by someone making a complaint against the business in question or the administrator's having made an investigation and thereby discovering some-

---

[2]See generally Anderson, Government and Business (3d edition, South-Western Publishing Company, 1966).

thing that he deems to require action by him. If the proceedings have been started by a complaining individual, it is generally required that the complaint be a signed paper setting forth the particular matters of which complaint is made.

The next step is to inform the defendant business that something has been begun against it. This is done by the administrator's preparing and issuing a piece of paper, sometimes called a complaint, which is served on the defendant business. This complaint tells it of the charge or accusation made against it and specifies a time and place at which a hearing on the complaint will be held. Sometimes the defendant business is allowed to file an answer to the complaint. Otherwise the defendant business is free to raise any matter of defense it chooses when the hearing is held. The purpose of an answer by the defendant is to narrow the issues by seeing just what points are admitted by the defendant and which are not admitted. This phase of complaint and answer is similar to the pleading phase in an ordinary lawsuit.

(*c*) ***The hearing stage.*** In order to determine whether the business is guilty of a violation, the governing administrator generally holds a hearing and in most cases is constitutionally required to do so. The hearing is similar to any other trial in purpose but differs in two significant respects from an ordinary civil trial or criminal prosecution: (1) there is no right to a trial by jury and (2) the administrator is not bound by the rules of evidence. The first means that the administrator is both the judge and jury and determines whether the business has violated the rules which he has adopted. The second means that the administrator may hear and consider any matter whether or not it would be considered good evidence at a regular civil trial or criminal prosecution or excluded as hearsay or for any other reason. There is one outstanding exception to this statement, namely, the National Labor Relations Board is limited to the hearing of "evidence."

At the hearing, testimony and other evidence is offered and the witnesses of the opposing party may be examined.

(*d*) ***Judgment.*** After the hearing is completed, the administrator decides the case. Ordinarily this is not done immediately because it is necessary that the testimony of the witnesses at the hearing be typewritten or printed so that the administrator will be sure to know just what was said at the hearing.

The judgment of the administrator may take a variety of forms, depending upon the subject matter of the rule which is involved. It may be an order upon you to stop doing certain things, such as an order to stop discriminating against an employee because of his union membership; an order compelling you to do something, such as an order to change your advertising, pay a sum of money, and so on. It may on the other hand be a judgment in your favor and dismiss the complaint made against you.

> *The facts:* An employer refused to hire a job applicant because he belonged to a union. The applicant could not find a job. He brought an unfair labor charge against the employer, demanding that he be given a job and the pay that he would have received had his application been accepted instead of being rejected. The National Labor Relations Act made it an unfair labor practice for an employer to discriminate "in regard to hire or tenure of employment" because of union membership. The National Labor Relations Board was authorized to order an employer to stop any unfair labor practice "and to take such affirmative action including reinstatement of employees, with or without back pay, as will effectuate the policies of this Act." The employer claimed that a person who was never an employee could not be "reinstated" and given back "pay."
>
> *Decision:* The Act expressly made discrimination with respect to hiring an unfair labor practice. In order to give effect and to carry out the purpose of the Act it was necessary to prevent discrimination in hiring just as much as in connection with firing. It was therefore necessary to undo the wrong committed by the employer, which could only be done by ordering him to "instate" the employee. That is, give him the job from which he had been wrongfully barred, and to give him also the pay which he would have earned beginning with the date he was wrongly rejected down to the present; although from this amount must be deducted all amounts which the employee had in fact earned elsewhere during the interval or which he could have earned at employment which was reasonably available. [Phelps Dodge Co. v. N.L.R.B., 313 US 177, 85 Led 1271, 62 SCt 333 (1941)].

(*e*) **Appeal and enforcement.** After the entry of the order any party in interest who is aggrieved thereby may appeal the case to a particular court specified in the statute creating the administrator. That is, if the judgment is against you, you may appeal. If the judgment is against the complaining party or the administrator an appeal may be taken by him. The complaining party may also appeal, if, though winning, he does not win enough. For example, if you lose the hearing before the National Labor Relations Board and are required to reinstate a fired employee, the employee may appeal on the theory that he should also have been given back pay. In addition, you may appeal at the same time claiming that no order of any kind should have been made against you.

If no appeal is taken, the business against which an order or judgment has been made may voluntarily obey the judgment. If the judgment is not obeyed, it is ordinarily necessary for the complaining party or the administrator to file a petition in a regular court for an order upon the business to compel obedience. That is to say, the administrator is ordinarily not given the power to enforce its own judgments. To the contrary, to act as a check in order to balance the power of the administrator it is ordinarily provided that the administrator must ask a court to enforce the administrator's order. If the court does not believe that the administrator's order should have been entered, the court will refuse to issue an order to obey it and the business may ignore the administrator's order. This has for most purposes the same result as though an appeal had been taken and decided against the administrator. If on the other hand, the court agrees with the administrator, a court order is issued compelling obedience. If you violate this order of the court you are guilty of contempt of the court's order for which you can be punished by a fine and imprisonment.

§ 19:14. The importance and finality of administrative regulation.

(*a*) *Generally.* Apart from the fact there is more and more administrative procedure appearing in the lives of each one of us, there are certain aspects of the administrative regulatory system which are of great importance to the man in business and to the citizen. This is particularly so because in many respects the action of the administrator is final and not subject to control in any practical sense of the word.

(*b*) *Absence of voter control of administrative regulatory system.* The members of Congress and of the state legislature which make the laws are elected by the people. Administrators of the more important type can make regulations and rules which have the same force as laws but the administrator is appointed and not elected. This appointment may be made either by the executive officer alone or by him with the advice and consent of the legislative body or the upper house of such body. For example a commission may be appointed by the governor alone or by the governor with the advice and consent of a majority of the state senate.

The result is that as a voter you have no practical control over the administrator and the only way that you can make your criticism felt is to organize public opinion so strongly that the political leaders decide that something had better be done about the particular administrator. This is not the easiest thing to do for the reason that it takes a large number of outraged citizens to have significance and it is likely that the mass of the public will not understand your problems or will not care how they are handled. This means that hotelmen as a group must unite to assert their criticism in order to be effective.

(c) Absence of constitutional limitations on the administrative regulatory system. What the administrator does may have a very significant effect upon your ability to run your hotel profitably and even to stay in business. For example, rent controls might be set too low to enable you to make profit. Less direct but nonetheless real, wage controls and minimum wage laws may increase your operating costs. Fire and sanitation regulations will also increase operating costs. Is there any guarantee that these administrative regulations which "cost" you money can not go "too far?" Is there any point where the courts will say that enough has been taken from you and that you must be allowed to earn a specified return on your investment? The answer is that you have no guarantee of anything and that the fact that you may be losing money is not important. If you object that this is unfair, operates unequally, creates hardship, and so on, the United States Supreme Court will not furnish you with any aid or comfort. In sustaining a quota control plan for sugar production that Court declared the rule: "It is not for this Court to reweigh the relevant factors and ... substitute its notion of expediency and fairness for that of Congress. This is so even though the quotas thus fixed may demonstrably be disadvantageous to certain areas or persons. This Court is not a tribunal for relief from the crudities and inequities of complicated experimental economic legislation."[3]

---

[3] Secretary of Agriculture v. Central Roig Refining Company, 338 US 604, 94 Led 381, 70 SCt 403, (1950).

If you complain that the administrator's actions will reduce your earnings and will require you to increase the cost of your services to the public, the words of the Supreme Court in reply to such argument are "We are ill equipped to weigh such predictions of the economic future. Nor is it our function to act as a super-commission."[4]

(d) Finality of administrative determination. Technically you almost always have the right to appeal from the decision of an administrator if you desire to do so, but except in a rare case, you will lose the appeal. Hence, for all practical purposes you must accept as final what the administrator decides. This is so for several reasons of which the most important are the following:

(1) Wisdom and fairness. On appeal, you cannot attack the administrative action because it was unfair or unwise unless you can show that it was so unreasonable as to be arbitrary and capricious. There is no exact definition for these terms but it is clear that the administrator would be acting arbitrarily and capriciously if he would say that he was against hotels because he had had a bad room once upon a time, and therefore he would decide every case against every hotel. It is obvious, however, that in the ordinary case the administrator does not feel this way and, if he does, he will not be so foolish as to make public his prejudice.

To the contrary, in the ordinary case, all that you can really say is that you disagree with what the administrator does in the sense that you disagree with the management wisdom of his action or that his action will affect profit-making ability and so on. The fact that you are harmed economically does not, however, mean, as the law uses those words, that the administrator has acted arbitrarily or capriciously. To repeat, the court will not reverse the administrator merely because you do not like what the administrator did; nor even because the court itself does not like what he has done.

(2) Discretion. In the more complex forms of administrative control, particularly those dealing with economic and social matters, such as the hotel business, the administrator is clothed with wide discretion. This is in contrast with the

---

[4]American Trucking Associations v. United States, 344 US 298, 97 Led 337, 73 SCt 307 (1953).

simple forms of administrative control in which the administrator acts as a thermostat; for example, the health officer who is to quarantine the building when he finds that any person therein has any of the named diseases. In contrast with his mechanical performance of quarantining when there is a person sick with a named disease, is the more complex type of regulation in which the administrator is given the authority and judgment to make rules and regulations generally, or rules and regulations for the purpose of achieving a particular result, or rules and regulations in the public interest. In all of these situations the administrator may act in such way as he wishes for the attainment of the purposes specified.

The fact that you disagree with the administrator in such cases is immaterial. It is also immaterial that the court disagrees with the administrator as long as he acted in the area in which he was given the discretion to act. That is, even though the court agrees with you, it will still not reverse the administrator. This concept is seen in the statement "The Commission's conclusion here rests squarely in the area where administrative judgments are entitled to the greatest amount of weight by appellate courts. It is the product of administrative experience, appreciation of the complexities of the problem, realization of the statutory policy, and responsible treatment of the uncontested facts. It is the type of judgment which administrative agencies are best equipped to make and which justifies the use of the administrative process. ... Whether we agree or disagree with the result reached, it is an allowable judgment which we cannot disturb."[5]

(3) Questions of fact. In many, if not most cases, the correctness of the decision of the administrator depends upon what the facts are. This in turn often depends upon whether the administrator believes one witness or another. For example, assume that you fire an employee who then claims that she was fired because you discriminated against her race. You testify before the administrator that you fired her because she was a poor worker and was excessively late and absent from work. She testifies that she was a good worker and was fired only because of discrimination. The administrator is now faced with the conflicting versions of the case. If he believes you, he will decide against the discrimination claim. If he believes the em-

---

[5]Securities and Exchange Commission v. Chenery Corporation, 332 US 194, 91 Led 1995, 67 SCt 1575 (1947).

ployee, he will decide against you and in favor of the discrimination claim.

Assuming a decision against you, can you appeal his decision successfully? The answer is "No," because the court will not set aside an administrative decision as to matters of fact when there was conflicting evidence before the administrator and his conclusion is proper if any of the evidence is believed. Here again, the court will not reverse the administrative action even though the court would have decided the case differently.

In contrast, if in a case in which there was no evidence whatever of discriminatory discharge, the administrator should reach out into the air and grab the idea then there would be no evidence in support of his finding. But to return to the case as above first stated, as long as there was evidence which if believed would support his conclusion, the court will not interfere. This means that in cases of disputed facts the administrative action is as a practicable matter almost always final and no successful review can be obtained of this action.

§ 19:15. Your attitude toward government regulation.

(*a*) *Generally.* What can you do about government regulation? For practical purposes, not too much. As a citizen or as a member of a group you may at times be able to bring pressure to bear on the person appointing the administrator to tell him to tell his appointee to use more sense or even to remove the complained of administrator and appoint someone who is better qualified. But you cannot take up arms against every administrator and in many instances the administrator is doing nothing wrong in a legal sense about which you can effectively complain. Unfortunately, or perhaps fortunately, being stupid or goofing is not illegal.

(*b*) *Acceptance of government regulation.* The answer also is that you must learn to accept the facts of modern life of which the theme is government regulation of business. If you feel bad, perhaps you might be comforted that as far back as 1803 John Madison wrote that it was the natural course of events for the individual to lose liberty and the government to gain power. And after all, remember that you actually do not believe in free enterprise, that is, not free enterprise 100%. If you did, you would be in favor of abolishing every law regulating business, beginning with the Pure Food and Drug Act. Would you want to sit down at your table, or even step up to your bar, if you did not have the assurance of government protection of the purity of food and drink? What's that? You say that these things should be regulated? Well, you have just lost your membership in the Adam Smith free enterprise club, for you don't believe in free enterprise 100%. Your quarrel, you see, is really not over the regulation of free enterprise, but rather over the degree of regulation.

(c) *Acceptance of the administrative system of government.* In the future years you will find more and more of the control of business and of hotels being handled through administrators rather than the ordinary law which is enforced by a court. This system is not without its good points. The probability of your coming into contact with an administrator who understands your business, that is, as much as any outsider can understand another man's business, is far greater than of finding a judge and jury who would understand what you are doing. Although the administrative controls take up time and are annoying, a civil or criminal trial against you or the hotel would be much more so. You may feel bad about being ordered by an administrator to stop certain practices or to do certain things but you would feel worse if a civil trial imposed a dollar judgment against you or a criminal prosecution imposed a fine or imprisonment.

(d) *Public relations with the administrators.* From the short-term point of view the best thing to do is to maintain good public relations with the administrator by making him feel that you are friendly, honest, and cooperative. Administrators have only a limited amount of time or a limited budget within which to function. If you can make them feel that you are a square shooter, the average administrator will accept your word on many things, instead of requiring proof and records, and will not pursue his investigation into extreme details.

Let's draw on your experience as a hotelman. Suppose that there is a small sum of money missing from the cash register. If the employee who is the person who would be in the position to have stolen the money is one in whom you have confidence, you will probably do little more than ask him a few questions, accept his answers, and stop there. On the other hand, with some employees you would not stop with his answers but would go into the case in great detail, and would make an examination of his daily receipts, and the preceding days' receipts and so on. The point is obvious, you have your hotel to run and you are not going to play cops and robbers any more than you have to. Therefore the proper explanation of the trusted employee you accept as being the whole story and stop there. With a suspicious character you figure that this is something you better look into more deeply.

The same with the administrator. What he does and requires of you will be influenced to a very large degree by whether he thinks you are honest and complying with the law or are trying to evade it.

(f) *Professional ethics and the long-term point of view.* Let us ask ourselves why we have government regulation of business. In every case, the basic reason is that there was some evil that the lawmaker rightly or wrongly thought had to be regulated. For example, we did not have an Interstate Commerce Commission regulating rates until there was an evil of excessive railroad rates; we did not have an antitrust law until there was an evil of conspiring to charge exorbitant prices; we did not have a Pure Food and Drug Act until there was an evil of the sale of diseased and dangerous foods; and we did not have fire, sanitation, and other building codes until there was the evil of fire traps, disease, and so on.

The best thing that any business or industry can do, therefore, to avoid increased regulation by government is to adhere to such high standards that there is no "evil" within its ranks which provokes government regulation. This is not a matter of individual action, but requires the joint action of all members of the business or industry, for one bad member can create the evil which brings government regulation down upon the heads of all. Whether a business or industry can effectively police itself and require that all its members adhere to high standards is a matter for practical sense and experience to determine. In many instances it is just numerically and geographically impossible to establish industry-wide control. In many instances you just do not have the time.

After all, there is one more alternative. Have you thought of selling out and going to some native island to write your memoirs and drink martinis? But better check first because there is probably an administrator in charge of the licensing of retired hotel men who are writing memoirs, with an additional license fee for the drinking of martinis.

Chapter 20. LABOR LAW

A. General Principles

§ 20:1. Nature of labor law.
    (a) Generally.
    (b) Nature of labor law.
    (c) Scope of labor laws.

§ 20:2. The employment relationship.
    (a) Generally.
    (b) Duration of contract.
    (c) Termination by employer.
        (1) Justification for discharge of employee.
            (i) Employer as judge of services.
    (d) Termination by employee.

§ 20:3. Liability for injuries to employee.
    (a) Generally.
    (b) What law governs.
        (1) The traveling employee.
    (c) Workmen's compensation.
        (1) Coverage of accidents.
        (2) Coverage of occupational diseases.
        (3) Defenses.
        (4) Administration of compensation and amount.
    (d) Common-law liability.
        (1) Negligence of employer.
        (2) Defenses of employer.
        (3) Enforcement of common-law right.

B. Collective bargaining

§ 20:4. Applicability of federal law.
    (a) The statute.
    (b) Applicability to hotels.
        (1) Chains and related activities.
    (c) Employees covered.
        (1) Supervisory employees excluded.

§ 20:5. What is collective bargaining?
    (a) Collective bargaining defined.
    (b) Extent of duty.
        (1) Supply information.

Labor Law

        (c) Collective bargaining is negotiation.
        (d) Collective bargaining is not compulsory agreement.
           (1) Execution of a written contract.
        (e) Collective bargaining is not a truce.

§ 20:6. Collective bargaining as a mutual obligation.
        (a) Persons subject to duty.
        (b) Breach of duty as an unfair labor practice.

§ 20:7. The employees' representative and collective bargaining.
        (a) Generally.
        (b) Who may be the representative of the employees.
           (1) The representative not a union.
        (c) Election of representative.
           (1) The collective bargaining unit.
           (2) Who determines the collective bargaining unit.
           (3) The significance of the particular unit selected.
           (4) The election.
        (d) Voluntary acceptance of representative without election.

§ 20:8. The authority of the representative of the employees.
        (a) Equal representation.
           (1) Liability of hotel.
        (b) Subject matter of collective bargaining.
           (1) Grievances.
        (c) Individual contracts with individual employees.
           (1) Limitations upon freedom of hotel.

    C. Unfair labor practices of the employer

§ 20:9. Liability of hotel.
        (a) Generally.
        (b) Act of key or executive employee.
        (c) Act of supervisor.
        (d) Act of ordinary employee.
        (e) Protection from liability.
           (1) What constitutes disavowal.
           (2) Record of disavowal.

§ 20:10. Employer's right of free speech.
        (a) Generally.
           (1) Provisions of the statute.
        (b) Particular applications.
           (1) Questioning as to membership.
        (c) Relation to state law.

§ 20:11. Union domination or assistance.
        (a) Generally.

(b) Particular applications.
   (1) Limitations.

§ 20:12. Interference with employees' rights.
  (a) Generally.
  (b) The mental state.
  (c) What constitutes interference, restraint, or coercion.
    (1) Soliciting strikers to return to work.
    (2) Prohibiting use of company property for union purposes.
      (i) Discrimination as to use of property.
    (3) Distribution of union literature.
  (d) Rules directed against union activities.

§ 20:13. Discrimination in employment terms.
  (a) Generally.
  (b) Particular applications.
    (1) Union membership.
    (2) Union activity.
    (3) Mixed causes.
  (c) Union shop limitation.

§ 20:14. Discrimination for using Labor Management Relations Act.
  (a) Generally.
  (b) Particular applications.

§ 20:15. Miscellaneous acts of employer.
  (a) Generally.
  (b) Wage raises.
  (c) Lockout and shutdowns.

D. Unfair labor practices of the union

§ 20:16. Interference with employees' rights.
  (a) Generally.
  (b) Particular applications.

§ 20:17. Compelling employer to discriminate.
  (a) Generally.
  (b) Particular applications.

§ 20:18. Selection of employer's representatives.
  (a) Generally.
  (b) Particular applications.

§ 20:19. Miscellaneous acts of union.
  (a) Generally.
  (b) Strikes and hot cargo.
  (c) Payment for work not done.

Labor Law

      (d) Recognition picketing.
      (e) Excessive initiation fees.

  E.   Civil rights protection from discrimination

§ 20:20. Federal Civil Rights Act.
      (a) Prohibition of discrimination.
      (b) Applicability.
      (c) Keeping of records.
          (1) Official records.
§ 20:21. Allowable distinctions.
      (a) Generally.
      (b) Testing for qualifications.
      (c) Compensation and seniority status.
      (d) Existing employment imbalances.
          (1) Hiring of new employees.
§ 20:22. Enforcement of Civil Rights Act.
      (a) Generally.
      (b) Commission proceedings.
      (c) Court action.
      (d) Proceedings under state and local law.

A.   General Principles

§ 20:1. Nature of labor law.

(*a*) *Generally.* The hotel is subject to labor law. For the most part, this is because the hotel is an employer and the labor laws are applicable generally to "employers." Otherwise stated, labor law as it applies to hotels is for the greater part merely the general labor law applicable to all employers.

(*b*) *Nature of labor law.* This law may be a city ordinance, a state statute, or a federal statute. In some instances, the hotel, and any other employer, would be subject to all three types of law at the same time, one type governing certain problems, and so on. In addition to the applicability of the ordinary ordinance or statute, the hotel is also subject to administrative agencies acting under certain ordinances and statutes.

For the most part, the application and operation of these laws is relatively mechanical and causes no great problem. This is so because the hotel which is already in business has already met most of the problems before, and the treasurer or manager or some other officer or employee makes the periodic reports or payments required by a given statute and this pattern merely continues. In other areas of labor law, new situations and new problems may arise to confront hotel personnel.

(*c*) **Scope of labor laws.** In popular usage, there is a tendency to think of labor laws in terms of collective bargaining, unfair labor practices, and dispute settlement. While it is true that these are among the situations which present the more significant problems to the hotel management, labor laws cover a wide range of hotel-employee relationships. Other laws relate to working conditions of labor, the age and sex of employees, hours of employment and wages, time and manner of payment of wages, workmen's compensation, the right to compensated time off for voting, liability for taxes for social security and unemployment compensation, and withholding taxes from salaries, and so on.

§ 20:2. The employment relationship.

(*a*) **Generally.** While there are a number of laws affecting the freedom of action of the hotel as an employer, the basic pattern of the contract of employment remains the same as any other contract. As a starting point, the terms of the contract are the terms on which the hotel and the employee agree. For the most part, the services to be rendered by the employee are not specifically defined because it is recognized that the employee is to perform those duties that customarily go with the job in question.[1]

(*b*) **Duration of contract.** The employment contract may in the absence of statute be terminated in the same way as any other continuing performance contract, namely by the expiration of the time specified in the contract, the mutual agreement of the parties, or notice by either party to the other when no time has been specified in the contract. In the latter case, the contract of employment is terminable at "will" and it is immaterial whether the party terminating the contract has any reason or justification for so doing. Generally, either the contract or a statute will specify the amount of advance notice which must be given, if any, and also make provision for severance pay

---

[1] See generally, Anderson and Kumpf, Business Law (9th edition, South-Western Publishing Company, 1972) Chapter 19.

to the employee unless the termination is because of the latter's fault or incompetency.

(c) **Termination by employer.** The employer may terminate an employment contract, unless limited by a union contract or statute, whenever he has just cause. The existence of just cause is necessary when the contract is for a specified time, as when the hotel has hired the general manager for a five-year period, he cannot be fired within that period unless the hotel has a good cause for so doing.

Just cause for termination, although not literally required, is almost essential in some situations to avoid the complaint that the discharge of the employee was a discrimination against his union membership, or the absence of such membership;[2] or against the employee's race, color, creed, national origin, or sex[3]

(1) *Justification for discharge of employee.* The employer may properly discharge an employee when he obtained his job through fraud as to his qualifications or work experience, does not do his work, disobeys instructions, is not competent to work in a reasonably good manner, is disloyal to the hotel, or is guilty of wrongful conduct.

As in the case of any employment contract, there is an implied term that the employee shall continue both physically and mentally in such condition that he can perform the duties of his position. Consequently, when he becomes incapacitated from so doing, as in the case of addiction to narcotics, the hotel is justified in terminating his contract of employment.

When an employee contracts to devote his time exclusively to the business of the hotel he is bound thereby. While there is an implied term of every such contract that enables the employee to take care of his own needs, such as eating, sleeping, and reasonable recreation, the employee was guilty of a breach of his contract if he was repeatedly absent for several hours every evening during the busy hours of the hotel, at which time the hotel was in charge of an office boy.

Absence from the hotel is of course excused when the employee is absent because he is engaged in the hotel work, as in the case of making collections or soliciting business, as he was required to do by the terms of the contract itself.

---

[2] See § 20:13.
[3] See § 20:20.

(i) *Employer as judge of services.* When the contract declares that the employer may terminate the employment if he is not satisfied with the services of the employee, the employer is generally considered the sole judge of whether the employee is "satisfactory," as long as the employer acts in good faith.

(d) **Termination by employee.** The employee has just cause for terminating a fixed-period contract if the hotel does not pay his wages, he is required to do work which he was not hired to do, he is not permitted to perform the work for which he was hired, he is required to work under dangerous conditions, or the employee is assaulted by an officer or agent of the hotel whose action constitutes an assault by the hotel.

§ 20:3. Liability for injuries to employee.

(a) *Generally.* The law varies in the different states as to whether the hotel's liability for injuries of the employee is governed by workmen's compensation or by general common-law principles.

(b) *What law governs.* Regardless of whether it be workmen's compensation or common-law principles, it is to be noted that it is the state law which is being applied. That is to say, it is a state workmen's compensation law which applies or it is state law as to common-law principles.

The foregoing is true although with respect to certain other areas of labor law the same hotel is subject to federal statute. For example, in bargaining with employees, you may be subject to the Federal Labor Management Relations Act, although with respect to paying them for injuries sustained in the course of employment, you are governed by state law.

(1) *The traveling employee.* While it is the "state" law which applies to the extent above indicated, the question arises as to "which" state when the employee is injured while in a state other than that in which the hotel was located. For example, suppose that the employee who drives the hotel automobile in the course of his employment to the airport just across the state line is injured in the course of his employment while so driving in the other state. Or suppose that you have sent your employee to the supply city in another state and he is injured on the way. Or again, suppose that you are a chain of hotels and that supervising employees are sent from one hotel to another and one is injured in making such circuit while in another state.

Labor Law

If the workmen's compensation statute applies, the answer is generally found in the express terms of the statute, although there is a diversity of provisions as to whether when foreign services were contemplated the law of the state where the injury is sustained or the law of the state of contracting for the employment will control. If workmen's compensation does not apply and the liability is determined by general common-law principles, it will ordinarily be the law where the injury was sustained, although there is a trend which would support the conclusion that where the presence of the employee in the state in which he was injured is merely temporary, in the sense of traveling through the state, or being there for only a few days, that it is the law of the place of contracting which would govern. This statement is purposely vague, because this is one of the areas where the law is growing today, and we cannot yet be certain as to just how far it will have gone by the time you are involved in the legal proceeding over your injured employee.

(c) Workmen's compensation. If your hotel is governed by workmen's compensation, it will undoubtedly have already been doing certain acts to comply with the financing aspects of the statutes, so that ordinarily you will not have the task of determining whether the statute is applicable. That is, your hotel will be making payments of premiums to a compensation insurance carrier, or making payments to a state fund, or making payments in some way to meet the requirements of the state workmen's compensation statute or board.

(1) Coverage of accidents. If workmen's compensation is applicable to any one of your employees, he or his family is entitled to compensation at the rate specified by the statute when he is injured or killed in the course of his employment from a risk arising from his employment. Thus, your chef, assuming that workmen's compensation is applicable, is covered when in the course of preparing a meal he cuts his hand with a knife. In contrast, he is not covered if one of the other kitchen help stabs him with the knife because of a personal grudge against him having nothing to do with the performance of the chef's duties. This is for the reason that such collateral stabbing, although occurring in the course of employment, is not brought about from a risk which arises from nor is it associated with the employment. Otherwise stated, getting stabbed by another employee is not one of the risks that you would think of as going with the job of being a hotel chef.

Coverage is not limited to harm sustained on the hotel premises where it occurs while the employee's job is taking him off of the premises. Thus the driver, or other employee, you sent off the premises as part of his job is covered when injured off the premises while doing his assigned work, since the injury arose in the course of his employment out of a risk which arose from the employment.

The facts: A waitress was employed by the hotel. She was called for special duty to serve food and drink to a party held at the hotel by a fraternal organization. She began to work at 9:00 p.m. In the course of the evening while waiting on the party, the waitress became intoxicated and the hotel knew that she was in that condition when it allowed her to leave the next morning at 3:30 a.m. to drive home. She was killed in an automobile accident about 4:00 a.m. A workmen's compensation claim was made for her death. This was opposed on the ground that (1) no compensation was to be paid by the hotel for the services of the waitress after 9:00 p.m. and (2) the accident did not arise in the course of and out of her employment.

Decision: The fact that no compensation was paid by the hotel directly to the employee for the services rendered at the party did not mean that the services were not performed as part of her employment. They were performed in the conducting of the employer's business as an incident of the accommodations furnished by the employer to its guests. The services of the waitress at the party was therefore part of her work.

As the death occurred from the intoxication and the waitress had become intoxicated while working at the party, her death was the result of the intoxication and arose out of her employment.

The death also arose "in the course of the employment." That question is not to be answered by a mechanical rule as to whether the harm was sustained while at work or while in going to or coming from work. Instead the question is governed by the determination of whether the cause of the injury can properly be regarded as a hazard of the employment. Here the condition of intoxication arose through the employment and the fact that its consequence became manifest or resulted in harm after the employee had left the place of employment was immaterial. The fact that the intoxication had been the voluntary act of the employee did not bar compensation liability as the employer knew that the employee was intoxicated when she left the hotel by herself. [Henderson v. Sherwood Motor Hotel, 105 NH 443, 201 A2d 891 (1964)].

Labor Law

(2) Coverage of occupational diseases. Workmen's compensation statutes today generally provide some coverage of occupational diseases. Frequently, this coverage would not apply to the hotel employee because the statute speaks of such specific diseases as anthracosis, or injury from radioactive substances, or other named diseases which do not apply to the fact situations found in the hotel. Assuming, however, that the statute was stated in general terms of covering occupational diseases as a class without specifically naming them, certain hotel employees might sustain occupational diseases, as a kitchen worker who contracts pneumonia because constantly alternately exposed to the cold of a large walk-in refrigerator and the heat of the kitchen, or the water activities director who develops arthritis or deafness through long exposure to water.

(3) Defenses. If workmen's compensation is applicable to the hotel employee, the only defense that can be raised to bar him from such compensation is that the injury sustained was willfully self-inflicted. In most states compensation is also denied if at the time of the harm, the employee was voluntarily intoxicated.

(4) Administration of compensation and amount. Under the workmen's compensation statute, there is a board, instead of a court, which hears and determines liability for compensation. In its general features, it is an example of the administrative system of government control described in Chapter 19, with the scope of the administrator being limited for the most part to performing this court-like function.

The rate of compensaion paid is predetermined by the statute. In a very general sense it is paid in the same manner as under an accident insurance policy. Namely, according to a fixed schedule which designates so much compensation for certain specified injuries and a certain percentage of the employee's salary for a specified number of weeks for other kinds of injuries.

In general, the compensation allowed is less than would be recovered if the employee would be able to bring a lawsuit under common-law principles and win against the employer. The probability of the employee winning compensation is by far the greater, however, than his winning a lawsuit.

It is to be noted, however, that the injured employee does not have the choice of selecting whether he should go under workmen's compensation or sue under the common law. He is bound by whichever system is in force at the time he is injured.

(d) Common-law liability. When workmen's compensation is not applicable, the rights of the injured employee against an employer are ordinarily determined by general common-law principles. This means that the employee must sue the employer in a law court and show that the employer had been guilty of negligence or of committing a willful act which was the proximate cause of the harm sustained by the employee.

(1) Negligence of employer. This is the same concept as discussed in Chapter 9; namely the failure to exercise that degree of reasonable care which would be exercised by a reasonable man to avoid the occurrence of foreseeable harm. More specifically, this will embrace the employer's failure to provide the employee with a reasonably safe place to work, reasonably safe tools and appliances, and a sufficient number of reasonably competent fellow workers; and failure to warn the employee of unusual dangers peculiar to the business.[4]

(2) Defenses of employer. Under common-law rules, the employer is not liable for the injury sustained by the employee, in spite of the employer's negligence, if any one of the following three defenses can be proven: (a) the employee was harmed by an ordinary risk or danger of the employment, which he is deemed to have assumed by taking the job; (b) the harm was caused by a fellow-servant of the employee; or (c) the negligence of the employee contributed to the harm sustained by him.

(3) Enforcement of common-law right. The procedure for recovering damages under common-law principles is an ordinary lawsuit brought against the employer in a court. Basically, this is brought in the same way and with the same effect as though you sued a total stranger who has run into you with his automobile. The employee's suit, however, is the more difficult to win because of the greater range of defenses to which the employee's claim is subject, and the practical difficulty of obtaining other employees as witnesses who will testify that their mutual employer was at fault.

The amount recovered by the employee, if he recovers, is measured in the same way as in the case of the automobile col-

---

[4] See generally, Anderson and Kumpf, Business Law (9th edition, South-Western Publishing Company, 1972) Chapter 19.

lision between strangers, or any other "stranger" negligence litigation. Care should be taken by the hotel that it is adequately covered by liability insurance.

B. Collective bargaining

§ 20:4. Applicability of federal law.

(*a*) *The statute.* By the National Labor Management Relations Act of 1947, Congress has imposed upon the employer and the representative of his employees the duty of bargaining collectively and prohibited employers and unions generally from committing certain practices.[5]

In most of the larger and industrial states, similar legislation has been adopted to apply to employers whose operations are not sufficiently large or significant to bring them within the scope of the national statute. The discussion of collective bargaining which follows is based upon the Federal Act of 1947, but is also applicable to those state statutes which have followed the pattern of the federal law as above stated.

(*b*) *Applicability to hotels.* The Federal Labor Management Relations Act is applied to hotels and motels which have a sufficiently large transient trade. Any hotel or motel which caters primarily to permanent trade is excluded: specifically, the act is not applied to any hotel or motel of which 75% or more of its guests in the preceding year resided at the hotel one month or more. Any hotel or motel not excluded by this test comes within the scope of the Act if it receives an annual gross income of $500,000 or more.

(1) Chains and related activities. The fact that a hotel is below the dollar volume above specified does not exclude it from coverage by the Act if it is part of a larger operation and that operation meets the money standard. In meeting the dollar volume, income from any source is counted, so that income from a restaurant or a swimming pool is to be added to transient guest payments in determining whether the specified minimum is met.

---

[5] This Act, popularly known as the Taft-Hartley Act, amended the Wagner or National Labor Relations Act of 1935. Further limitations were imposed by the Labor-Management Reporting and Disclosure Act of 1959.

Hotel chains are within the coverage of the Act when the chain as an aggregate satisfies the total above stated, even though some of the member hotels when considered singly would not be included.

(*c*) *Employees covered.* The Federal statute covers employees of the hotel and classifies as "employees" persons not actually working at the time because of a current labor dispute, or because of any unfair labor practice. Thus an employee who has been fired because of his union membership remains an employee for the purpose of the federal statute; so that he may vote as an employee, and so on. This employee status of the separated employee is lost, however, once the employee obtains other regular or substantially equivalent employment.

(1) Supervisory employees excluded. The Federal statute excludes supervisory employees from the protection and benefits of the act. These in substance are employees who are "management," regardless of how small the area in which management judgment is exercised by them.

Specifically, the statute declares that "the term 'supervisor' means any individual having authority, in the interest of the employer, to hire, transfer, suspend, lay off, recall, promote, discharge, assign, reward, or discipline other employees, or responsibly to direct them, or to adjust their grievances, or effectively to recommend such action, if in connection with the foregoing the exercise of such authority is not a merely routine or clerical nature, but requires the use of independent judgment."

§ 20:5. What is collective bargaining?

(*a*) *Collective bargaining defined.* From the standpoint of the hotel, collective bargaining is the act of dealing with someone representing employees in making a contract for the terms of their employment; rather than dealing with each employee individually as to the terms of his employment.

(*b*) *Extent of duty.* The obligation to bargain collectively is of course to bargain collectively with the union which is the proper representative of the employees, as contrasted with another union which does not represent them.

The obligation to bargain collectively requires that the employer and the representatives of the employees meet at any place which is reasonably convenient under the circumstances. In any event, the employer cannot refuse to attend a meeting at a particular place merely on the ground that it would be inconvenient to him.

The employer does not have any right to refuse to deal with the particular persons selected by the bargaining representative unless there is such a history of past personality clashes that the presence of a given person makes it unlikely that an agreement would be reached.

(1) Supply information. To some extent bargaining collectively imposes upon the employer the duty of giving the representatives of his employees information as to his operations where such information is sought by the representatives in good faith in order for them to make intelligent demands and to appraise the validity of the employer's position.

So it has been held that the employer must furnish information as to employees' wages, the employer's financial status, job classification, length of employment, and insurance. When the employer opposes the demand for a raise on the ground that the business cannot afford it, he may be required to furnish such information relating to his financial condition as will show whether this argument is sound or not.

(c) Collective bargaining is negotiation. Under labor relation statutes it is made the duty of the hotel and the representative of its employees to bargain collectively in good faith on the terms of employment. This means that each side must meet at reasonable times and for a reasonable period of time and discuss and try to reach a common meeting ground.

Thus, the hotel violates the statutory duty to bargain collectively if it refuses to meet with the representative chosen by its employees. It is also improper for the hotel to attempt to dictate to the representative as to what man it should send to discuss the matters with the hotel. The hotel also violates this duty if it sits at the bargaining table and makes it clear that it just is not going to agree to anything.

(d) Collective bargaining is not compulsory agreement. Federal labor relations statutes and most state laws on the subject make it clear that there is no duty on the hotel to reach any agreement with the employees' representative. Conversely stated, the failure to reach a settlement is not proof that there was a lack of good faith nor evidence that their hotel had refused to bargain collectively.

The hotel is accordingly within the law when it meets with the employees' representatives, discusses the matter in a free and reasonable manner; but never gives an inch of ground and makes no concession of any kind.

It of course seems inconsistent to say that the hotel must bargain collectively but that there is not obligation to agree to anything. The explanation is a practical one. Congress and the legislatures which have followed the congressional lead did not want to destroy freedom of contract to the extent of saying the employer must agree to something with the employees' representative, because this would give the latter an unfair bargaining advantage. It would mean that the union could make any demands, secure in the knowledge that their hotel would have to give in to some extent on something or else be condemned for refusing to bargain collectively.

At the same time, the lawmaker is gambling on probabilities. Although the hotel is not compelled to agree to anything when it bargains collectively, nor is the representative of the employees, the odds are that some agreement will be reached. The law goes on the theory that if both sides can be brought to the same table and made to sit down and face each other, that a lot of hot heads will cool off and that a lot of bold statements made outside for publicity and electioneering purposes will be forgotten and the boys will get down to the real business of negotiation. Statistically analyzed, there has been a very high percentage of agreements reached through compulsory collective bargaining.

(1) Execution of a written contract. If the collective bargaining does result in a contract's being made, the employees' representative can demand that the contract be put in writing. It is therefore not lawful for the hotel to say to the representative: "Don't you trust me? Why do we have to put it in writing?" If the representative of the employees wishes to stand on their rights, the hotel must execute a written contract.

Here is where a lawyer comes in, although be very careful that he is experienced with respect to labor law and labor law contracts, or you may find that your contract does not say what you believed it to say.

(e) Collective bargaining is not a truce. The fact that the hotel and the employees' representative or representatives are bargaining collectively does not mean that all labor law warfare is called off during the period of the negotiation. Otherwise stated,

if it is lawful for the union to strike, to picket, to boycott, or for employees to slow down, be absent and so forth; all of this economic warfare activity can be continued while the collective bargaining is going on.

> *The facts:* The labor contract was about to expire and negotiations were being conducted for a new contract. In order to put pressure on the employer, the employees slowed down, were absent from work, picketed, distributed their leaflets and so on. The employer claimed that this was a violation of the obligation of the employees and their union to bargain collectively.
>
> *Decision:* The conduct of the employees was not unlawful. If the employees were permitted to use such pressure tactics upon the employer, it was likely that they would have greater strength at the collective bargaining table. That is to say, to restrict the right to use such pressure tactics would indirectly be to control the terms of the contract which would be made. There is nothing in the federal law which authorized interference with the power of either party in order to produce a bargaining equality between them and the use of pressure tactics did not show that the employees were acting in bad faith. [NLRB v. Insurance Agents' International Union, 361 US 477, 4 Led2d 454, 80 SCt 419 (1960)].

The union, however, cannot refuse to bargain until its labor warfare, such as picketing, has caused so much damage to the hotel that the latter is willing to agree to any terms.

§ 20:6. Collective bargaining as a mutual obligation.

(*a*) ***Persons subject to duty.*** Both the employer and the bargaining representative of the employees are subject to the duty to bargain collectively. They must accordingly both come to the bargaining table and do so in good faith.

(*b*) ***Breach of duty as an unfair labor practice.*** If either the hotel or the employees' representative refuses to bargain in good faith, it commits an unfair labor practice. This is not a crime for which there is a punishment; nor is it a civil wrong for which it can be sued for damages. Instead of these traditional court procedures, the innocent party makes a complaint to the National Labor Relations Board that the other party has acted improperly, and, if the Board agrees, it will order the wrongdoer to stop and to proceed to bargain collectively.[6]

---

[6] See Chapter 19 for a discussion of the administrative procedure.

§ 20:7. The employees' representative and collective bargaining.

(*a*) *Generally.* The employees select their representative at an election. The hotel is then required to recognize and deal with this representative until it loses its status as such.

(*b*) *Who may be the representative of the employees.* In most instances the representative with whom the hotel bargains is the union of which the hotel employees are members. The representative, however, may be any person or organization selected by the majority of the employees for that purpose. In such case it is immaterial that all the employees do not belong to the union which is selected as the representative. It is also immaterial that the union is a completely outside union in that none of the employees of the hotel belong to it. For example, if the hotel employees so voted, they could be represented by the teamsters' union.

(*1*) *The representative not a union.* There is no requirement that the representative of the employees be a labor union. A representative may be any type of organization, or any person that the workers select. Thus the workers can select some outstanding citizen and, if he is willing, have him represent them in bargaining with the employer.

(*c*) *Election of representative.* The federal statute provides for the election of the representatives by the employees.

(*1*) *The collective bargaining unit.* The first step in preparation for such an election is the determination of the area which is to constitute the unit for purposes of collective bargaining.

To illustrate, assume that we have a chain of ten large hotels owned by the same corporation. For the purpose of representation of the employees, we might have a number of areas. We might say (1) each hotel is a separate unit all by itself and therefore all the employees in each hotel should have their own election for their own bargaining representative; or (2) all of the hotels have basically the same problems and therefore the employees of all ten hotels should vote as a group for one representative to represent them all; or (3) the employees in the several hotels are naturally grouped into different levels or categories of skills and therefore the employees in each category should hold their own election for the election of their own representative, as by having all the maintenance workers of the ten hotels vote for their own representative, and so on. Other variations are also possible.

(2) Who determines the collective bargaining unit. As a start, a National Labor Relations Board is given discretion to select the unit for collective bargaining. It "shall decide in each case whether, in order to assure to employees the fullest freedom in exercising the rights guaranteed by [the statute], the unit appropriate for the purposes of collective bargaining shall be the employer unit, craft unit, plant unit, or subdivision thereof. ..."[7]

(3) The significance of the particular unit selected. A labor relations board can intentionally or unintentionally produce in many cases quite a power shift as between unions by its selection of given unit. For example, assume that all the maintenance workers belong to a given union. We can further assume that if the maintenance workers are allowed to go to their separate unit for collective bargaining purposes they will select that union which will then represent their views. Suppose, however, that a labor relations board should designate the employees in each hotel as a separate voting group, or all the employees of all the ten hotels as a separate voting group. Under such circumstances the maintenance workers would be in a minority and their union would ordinarily never get elected as the bargaining representative.

It is thus possible to stack the cards in advance in favor of or against a particular union by the way in which the unit is selected. In the earlier years under the federal act it was frequently charged that favoritism to certain unions had been shown in the selection of the unit. This charge is less commonly heard today.

(4) The election. The election of the bargaining representative is conducted under the supervision of the Labor Relations Board. Generally anyone may apply for the holding of an election: that is, any union, any employee, and the employer.

The election is secret, by closed paper ballot, with the selection going to the representative receiving a majority of the votes cast, even though this in fact may be a minority of the total number of employees eligible to vote. If necessary, a run-off

---

[7] § 9(b), National Labor Management Relations Act.

election may be held to determine which of the top two contenders shall be the representative.

In this election for a representative, the ballot may list "no representative" as a candidate, so that it is possible for the employees within the unit to vote that they do not want anyone to represent them and prefer to make their contracts on an individual basis. When a candidate is elected as representative, the Board certifies that result. Thereafter, it is an unfair labor practice for the employer to deal with any other representative.

(*d*) *Voluntary acceptance of representative without election.* In many cases, it is perfectly obvious in advance of any election that a given union would win the election if one were held. In such case, the hotel may voluntarily recognize the union without insisting that there be an election.

There is, however, an element of risk present. If the hotel has reached a wrong conclusion that this union would win an election, it is guilty of an unfair labor practice in refusing to recognize another union which in fact would win had there been an election. That is to say, if the hotel voluntarily recognizes Union A as the representative of its employees and bargains collectively with it, when in fact Union B would be elected if there were an election, Union B can petition the Labor Relations Board to hold an election to establish its right to be recognized as bargaining representative and compel the employer to stop recognizing Union A.

The practical solution to the matter is for the hotel to take the position with Union A, at the very beginning, "Well boys, we are certainly very happy to do business with you but a number of our employees say they want Union B. Why don't you petition the Board to order an election so that we can get the matter straightened out without any hard feelings?"

If Union A is experienced it will ordinarily not press the point because it knows that if it insists on being recognized, the employer, as well as Union B, or any employee, can petition the Board to hold an election. Union A therefore would not obtain any advantage which it could retain by being stubborn about the matter. To the contrary, it would make it look good to its members by being the one to bring about the election.

The hotel should be very tactful in handling this matter because if Union A does win the election, it will not do the hotel any good if there are already hard feelings on the part of Union A because it believed that the hotel was merely being evasive or backhanded in refusing to recognize it in the first place.

§ 20:8. The authority of the representative of the employees.

(*a*) *Equal representation.* Whoever is elected as the bargaining representative of a given unit is under the duty to represent all of the employees within that unit equally, that is, fairly and without discrimination. Even when the representative is a union, that union must speak equally for all the employees, whether they are union members or not and even though they belong to a rival union.

If the union does not speak impartially on behalf of all in the unit it is guilty of an unfair labor practice. For example, in the case where it seeks to obtain a better salary or promotion program for those employees who belong to it rather than for employees who are nonmembers. While the representative union cannot show preferences in such manner, it may of course agree to reasonable and non-discriminatory job classifications.

(1) Liability of hotel. If a hotel agrees to any contract which does not speak fairly and without discrimination for all employees in the bargaining unit, the hotel is also guilty of an unfair labor practice when such discrimination is made against employees because they are not union members, or belong to another union.

Note that discrimination because of race, color, creed, national origin, or sex, is an unfair employment practice.[8]

(*b*) *Subject matter of collective bargaining.* The parties, meaning the hotel and the bargaining representative, may put as much or as little as they choose in the bargaining contract. Under the federal statute, the contract may relate broadly to "wages, hours, and other terms and conditions of employment."

> *The facts:* The hotel had regularly paid Christmas bonuses for fourteen years. The bonus had become accepted as a regular benefit of employment and was referred to in inducing new employees to work for the hotel. The bonus was not paid for the Christmas following the year in which the union was certified as the representative of the workers. The hotel claimed that it could not afford to pay cash bonuses. The union claimed that the subject of the suspension of bonuses was a matter for collective bargaining. The hotel claimed that the bonus was a gift and therefore could be abandoned as it chose. Decide.

---

[8] See § 20:20. Age discrimination is unlawful. See Supplement p. 475.

Decision: Judgment against hotel. The bonus had such a regular pattern of payment, was based on a fixed scale, and was regarded as an inducement for new employees, that it could be regarded as a term of the contract of employment and was accordingly subject to collective bargaining. Hence it was necessary for the hotel to negotiate the matter of bonus suspension with the union. [NLRB v. Holiday Hotel Management, (CA10th) 311 F2d 380 (1962)].

(1) Grievances. The statutes requiring collective bargaining may contain some limitation upon the demands which can be made by the union. Under the federal statute the bargaining contract cannot affect the right of any individual employee or group of employees to present their grievances to the hotel at any time and to have such grievances adjusted, without the intervention of the bargaining representative, as long as the adjustment is not inconsistent with the terms of the collective bargaining agreement and providing the bargaining representative is given the opportunity to be present at the time of the adjustment so that he can see that the union contract is in fact not violated.

(c) Individual contracts with individual employees. The effect of the contract made by the hotel with the representative of the union is to establish a master blueprint on the basis of which the employer hotel may then make individual contracts with employees as he selects them. That is, the contract with the bargaining representative does not hire anyone for the hotel but merely agrees that as to any who are or become employees the terms of their employment shall be in accord with the terms of the blueprint or master plan of the union contract. In consequence, the hotel is free to employ whomever it wishes, subject to the limitations noted below, provided it does so on the terms specified in the union contract.

Moreover, if the union contract does not cover the entire area of terms of employment, the contract with the individual employee may extend to matters not so covered. Thus the contract with the individual employee may provide for hospitalization fringe benefits where nothing was said in the union contract about such matters.

(1) Limitations upon freedom of hotel. The employer, while free to employ or hire as he chooses, is still subject to statutory provisions against discrimination because of union

membership,[9] race, color, creed, national origin, or sex.[10] In addition, the union contract may to some extent limit the freedom of the hotel as by adopting a union shop provision.

C. Unfair labor practices of the employer

§ 20:9. Liability of hotel.

(*a*) *Generally.* Any employer who is subject to the National Labor Relations Board or to similar boards created under state law is restricted in his conduct with respect to his employees and to unions generally. If he engages in certain practices his acts are condemned as unfair labor practices and he can be ordered to stop by the appropriate board. In such situations the judgment of the Board may impose additional requirements upon the employer.[11]

(*b*) *Act of key or executive employee.* In most cases, particularly where there is a corporation, the hotel does not commit the wrongful act but rather it is committed by some officer of the hotel or the general manager and so on.

When the unfair labor practice is committed by the general manager or executive officer having charge of the labor and personnel problems of the hotel, his act, of course, is in the eyes of the law the act of the hotel, regardless of whether the hotel had authorized such conduct or not.

(*c*) *Act of supervisor.* When the labor practice is committed by a supervisor, who is a lesser employee who is not a policy maker nor an executive officer, it is generally held that the hotel is still liable for his unfair labor practice when the supervisor was (1) authorized to do such acts by the employer, (2) reasonably appeared to the employees to be acting officially on behalf of the employer, or (3) the employer was benefiting from the unauthorized acts without disavowing them and there was the danger that they would be repeated.

> *The facts:* Certain supervisory employees acted to assist a union which conduct constituted an unfair labor practice with respect to a rival union. The employer claimed that it was not liable for the

---

[9] See § 20:13.

[10] See § 20:20. Age discrimination is also unlawful. See Supplement p. 473.

[11] See § 19:12.

actions of these supervisors because they did not have the power to hire and fire. Was the employer liable?

Decision: Yes. The fact that the supervisors did not have the power to hire and fire did not lessen the fact that they appeared to be acting on behalf of the employer and therefore the employer was bound by their conduct. [NLRB v. Link-Belt Co. 311 US 584, 85 Led 368, 61 SCt (1941)].

In determining whether the supervisor's action appeared to be the official action of his employer, the past history of the case and of the employer's acts with respect to the union and his employees is important. The hotel should therefore do its best to avoid clashes over minor things not worth fighting about, in order to keep its slate clean for the serious cases.

(d) *Act of ordinary employee.* When the unfair labor practice is committed by an ordinary employee there is no liability therefor on the hotel when such action was in fact not authorized and the employee's acts did not reasonably appear to be official action authorized by the corporation. Thus, the hotel was not affected as long as the employee's acts were unauthorized and he appeared to others to be merely acting for himself; that is, a third person will regard him as doing a lot of talking about his own views, without his being the official or authorized mouthpiece for the hotel.

(e) *Protection from liability.* The mere fact that the hotel or the executive officers of the hotel have not done or authorized the unfair labor practice does not in itself constitute a sufficient defense. The hotel must therefore maintain a reasonably active supervision of its area of operation to determine that nothing is being said or done which if authorized by it would constitute an unfair labor practice. When appropriate, the hotel must disavow the actions of a given employee. If the hotel will actually benefit from the improper acts committed, the duty is particularly great upon the hotel to disavow, otherwise its failure to object suggests that it had authorized or had at least ratified the improper conduct.

(1) *What constitutes disavowal.* Any conduct which shows the person who would be harmed by the unauthorized conduct that the hotel did not authorize and does not ratify such conduct is sufficient. In addition to words of disavowal, the hotel must take such action as appears reasonably necessary to undo the harm that has been done and to maintain reasonable supervision to insure that there is no repetition of such conduct.

Conversely stated, the hotel cannot make a protest and then turn its back on the whole affair without checking thereafter to see that there was no renewal of the disavowed activity.

(2) Record of disavowal. Because the whole color of the transaction may be governed by whether the hotel disavowed the employee's acts and then stepped in to make such disavowal effective, it is obvious that it is important for the hotel to maintain a full record of what it had done in connection with the matter. It is recommended that the hotel maintain a file for each unfair labor practice incident. Into that file can go periodic reports with respect to the practice. Depending upon the closeness of the working relation of the hotel with its attorney, the hotel should also send to the attorney a copy of all information that it places in this unfair labor practice file.

If such records are carefully kept by the hotel for all such transactions, the records themselves may be admissible in evidence at the time of the unfair practice proceeding before the National Labor Relations Board. In any event, the hotel will have a detailed record of just what occurred and will not be required to trust to the memories of its personnel nor to their continued presence within the hotel's employment or the jurisdiction.

§ 20:10. Employer's right of free speech.

(a) *Generally.* The fact that the employer is the employer naturally tends to give weight to any expression of opinion by him. Accordingly there is the danger that such expression of opinion would be prohibited as interfering with the free action of the employees. Under the federal statute, the employer is protected in his right to speak freely, as long as he does not speak in such a way as to make it appear to the worker that it will be better for him to follow what the boss says and to stay in harmony with what he thinks, than to exercise his right to unionize and so forth.

The union is also benefited by the free speech provision.

(1) Provisions of the statute. The National Labor Management Relations Act declares that "the expression of any views, argument, opinion, or the dissemination thereof, whether in written, printed, graphic, or visual form, shall not constitute or be evidence of an unfair labor practice under any of the pro-

visions of (the federal) act, if such expression contains no threat of reprisal or force or promise of benefit."

(*b*) *Particular applications.* Statements by the employer advising or urging employees not to join the union, or stating that its leaders are Communists, have been held protected by the statute, particularly where the past history of the case did not show any strong anti-union attitude of the employer or when the union had already called a strike and was saying unkind things about the employer.

When two unions are competing for recognition, a statement by the employer that he prefers one over the other or that he prefers the one as the lesser of two evils is held not an unfair labor practice, as against the claim that it interferes with unionization efforts of the union criticized.

(1) Questioning as to membership. The free speech provision has been held not to extend to protect the employer so as to allow him to examine his employees to see if they belong to the union, as such questioning would tend to make an employee feel that he was put on the spot and would tend to discourage him from exercising his rights protected by the statute. In some cases, however, the right to ask such questions of one's employees has been sustained.

(*c*) *Relation to state law.* The fact that "free speech" is protected by the federal statute does not destroy the state law relating to slander and libel.

> *The facts:* In the course of a campaign within the union for the election of officers, one of the union factions published in the union paper statements that the plaintiffs, who were candidates for office, were seasoned criminals. The plaintiffs sued the persons who caused this publication and the union for libel. The action was brought in a state court. The defendants claimed that a state court action for libel could not be brought as the significance of speech in a labor-management setting was exclusively a matter for the National Labor Relations Board.
>
> *Decision:* The federal statute did not destroy the right under state law to sue for slander and libel, since the state has a valid interest in preserving domestic peace by the prevention of such conduct, and the carrying out of the state policy does not interfere in any way with the carrying out of the national policy under the Labor Management Relations Statute. Moreover the state action involved questions of policy and of damage with which the national law was not concerned, so that the rights of the parties would not be determined in all respects by any Board proceeding.

[Meyer v. Joint Council 53 International Brotherhood, 416 Pa 401, 206 A2d 382 (1965). The court pointed out that there was a division of authority in the state courts on the question and that some courts had held that a state action was barred because of the federal statute.]

§ 20:11. Union domination or assistance.

(*a*) *Generally.* Statutes commonly prohibit the employer from dominating a union or assisting it in any way. Under the federal statute, it is an unfair labor practice for the employer "to dominate or interfere with the formation or administration of any labor organization or contribute financial or other support to it."

The purpose of this provision is both to prevent the rise of a company union and also to prevent the employer's aiding one union either for its own sake or in opposition to a rival union.

(*b*) *Particular applications.* The practices here condemned cover a wide range of conduct which either aids or hurts a union. Violation of this provision is particularly obvious where there are two rival unions and the hotel extends privileges to one which it denies the other.

When the employer has openly been giving support and aid to one union, it is necessary that he make it clearly known within the area of employment when he withdraws his support, for in the absence of such a clear expression of his repudiation, there would be a remembering by others that the company in question was "employer-approved."

(1) Limitations. The domination-support unfair labor practice here considered does not prevent every possible conduct which could aid a union or aid one over another. For example, the mere distribution by a supervisory employee of union application blanks when two unions were competing for membership was not such "support" of the union as to be an unfair labor practice where there was no active encouraging employees to join nor pressure put upon them to do so.

Likewise the clause does not prevent the employer, by virtue of his free speech privilege from expressing his views in a fair manner which does not constitute the actual promotion of one of the unions.[12]

---

[12]See § 20:10.

§ 20:12. Interference with employees' rights.

(*a*) *Generally.* Under federal and many state statutes it is an unfair labor practice for the hotel to interfere with the rights of its employees both with respect to taking part in union activities and in refraining from doing so. The federal statute declares that it is an unfair labor practice for the hotel to interfere with, restrain, or coerce employees in the exercise of their rights to organize into unions; to form, join, or assist the labor unions; to bargain collectively through representatives of their own choosing; and to engage in various forms of labor warfare for their mutual aid and protection. The federal statute also protects from the hotel's interfering with the right of the employee to refrain from joining a union or engaging in any of the foregoing activities, with the exception of a union shop provision discussed in § 20:13.

(*b*) *The mental state.* In many instances of interference with employees' rights the employer must act with the intent to do the prohibited act, and in any case, the existence of evidence proving intent or motive is of value in determining whether conduct of the employer which interferes with the employees' rights should be regarded as a prohibited "interference." Such a mental state is not essential, however, and to the contrary, the fact that the employer acted with the best of intentions is immaterial. Thus there is nonetheless an unfair labor practice although the employer acted with the object only of keeping his employees happy and did not have any intent to do wrong.

> *The facts:* The employer voluntarily recognized a union as the bargaining representative of his employees under the mistaken belief that it represented a majority of them. Was this an unfair labor practice?
>
> *Decision:* Yes. The voluntary recognition of the wrong union interferes with the rights of the other union and of the employees represented by that union from bargaining collectively with the employer. The conduct was therefore an interference with the right of the excluded union and such employees and it was immaterial that the employer had acted in good faith. [International Ladies Garment Workers' Union v. NLRB, 366 US 763, 6 Led2d 762, 81 SCt 1603 (1961)].

(*c*) *What constitutes interference, restraint, or coercion.* To come within the condemnation of labor relations acts on the basis of interference, restraint, or coercion as to employees, it is necessary to show that there was an affirmative act done. But any form of pressure in this connection is condemned. For example, the fact that the employees lived in employer-owned housing units does not give the employer the right to discriminate in connection with the housing units as a means of carrying out his anti-union attitude.

(1) Soliciting strikers to return to work. Acts done by the hotel for the purpose of persuading strikers to return to work may or may not constitute an unfair labor practice. The actual decision in a given case depends to a large degree upon the background as indicating the actual intent of the hotel.

In general, the distinction appears to be made that there is an unfair labor practice when the request to the workers to return to work indicates that it is done with the intent or plan of (a) penalizing those workers who do not return to work, (b) bypassing the union by dealing directly with the employees instead of bargaining collectively, [13] or (c) ignoring the strike issues and seeking the return of the workers without any intent to adjust or reach an amicable settlement.

(2) Prohibiting use of company property for union purposes. A hotel can prohibit a union from soliciting for new members on the hotel premises during the working hours of the employees. If the solicitation takes place after the employees' working hours in areas open to the public, such as a parking lot, the employer cannot prevent such use of his property.

(i) Discrimination as to use of property. If the employer plays favorites by allowing one union to promote itself on company time or allows one the use of its facilities and denies such rights to others, such discrimination constitutes an unfair labor practice, even though the employer would not be guilty of such a practice if he had denied the right to all unions.

There is, however, no duty on the employer to voluntarily offer facilities to the union without being first asked for them and the failure to volunteer the use of facilities would be consistent with the employer's being cautious to avoid appearing to aid or support a union and thus commit such unfair labor practice.[14]

---

[13]As to collective bargaining, see §§ 20:4 et seq.
[14]As to the unfair labor practice of aiding a union, see § 20:11.

Where there is no adequate meeting hall in the community, except one owned by the employer, he may be required to allow the union to use the hall, at least when the union is willing to make a reasonable or customary payment for the use of the hall, and the practice had been to freely grant permission to nonunion groups to use it. If however there are other halls in the community and other ways in which the union can as a practical matter reach the employees, the fact that there is a no-solicitation rule on the premises does not cause any serious harm to the union as it can still reach the employees with its message.

(3) Distribution of union literature. The hotel can generally prevent the distribution of union literature on its premises by a general regulation prohibiting the distribution of handbills and so forth; where the regulation applies to all kinds of handbills and is applied to everyone, and not just to unions; and the regulation has been adopted sufficiently prior to the labor dispute so that it does not appear that it was adopted merely to fight the oncoming union, but to the contrary is a reasonable regulation designed to keep the premises clean.

If the regulation does not satisfy the qualifications above stated, the prohibition of the distribution of union literature is an unfair labor practice. For example, it is an unfair labor practice where the prohibition by the employer was limited in application and did not apply to handbills generally; or where because of such limited application it did not serve the purpose of maintaining the cleanliness of the property; or where by being adopted a few days after the beginning of the labor controversy it was clear that it was designed to interfere with the unionization movement.

(**d**) **Rules directed against union activities.** A hotel should avoid adopting rules that have an anti-union application the moment a labor dispute breaks out. The dispute colors the rules and leads to the conclusion that the adoption was merely to fight the union and was therefore an unfair labor practice. At the same time, the fact that anti-union rules are adopted colors other conduct and gives to other neutral conduct an anti-union tone. The net result is that the hotel is hit in two ways by the adoption of such rules.

What the hotel should do is attempt to anticipate all factual situations for which it should have rules and regulations. The broader such rules and regulations are the better. That is, a set of rules which would also be applicable to the conduct of guests, wearing apparel in different parts of the hotel, use of elevators, and persons making deliveries and repairs, and so forth, would naturally tend to appear less anti-union in character and would be more likely sustained as a reasonable regulation of hotel operations generally rather than as an anti-union measure. This conclusion is of course all the more likely to be made if the rules are adopted a very long time in advance of any labor dispute.

It is always difficult to tell someone how to run his life according to a book. There is the danger that the very act of adopting general "innocent" looking rules may stir up labor trouble in your hotel if the union people are alert enough or suspicious enough to recognize how the rules could apply to them.

§ 20:13. Discrimination in employment terms.

(*a*) ***Generally.*** Labor relations statutes prohibit any unequal treatment of employees because of their union membership or the fact that they are not members of a union. Under the federal statute, it is an unfair labor practice for an employer to make any "discrimination in regard to hire or tenure of employment of any term or condition of employment or to discourage membership in any labor organization."

(*b*) ***Particular applications.***

(1) Union membership. The non-discrimination provision bars an employer from refusing to hire or to promote, or from discharging, a person because he is or is not a union member. The prohibition is applicable to any phase of an employer-employee relationship. Thus the assignment to non-union employees of better hours than to union employees constitutes a discrimination. Promotion practices which advance one group of employees faster than another are likewise unfair labor practices when the only distinguishing feature between one employee group and the other is membership or non-membership in a union or in a particular union.

(2) Union activity. It is of course an unfair labor practice where an employee is discriminated against because he has taken an active part in union work, providing that he has done so without interfering with the performance of his assigned duties and without violating any valid rule or regulation of the hotel. Accordingly when a strike is over, the hotel must take

back its striking employees and cannot refuse to do so merely because they engaged in union activity, except in certain instances when the hotel has hired a replacement.

Likewise, it is an unfair labor practice to offer to bribe or buy off a union employee by giving him a better job if he will stop his union activities, particularly when the offer is of a supervisory position, which position by definition would take the employee out of the protection of the Federal Labor Management Relations Act.

> *The facts:* Two employees were seeking to form a union within the defendant's plant. Another employee falsely told the employer that these two employees had declared that they would use dynamite if necessary to organize the plant. When the employer heard of this false accusation, which he believed true, he fired the two employees. They filed an unfair labor practice charge against the employer and proved that the accusation was false. The employer defended on the ground that he had acted in good faith. Was he guilty of an unfair labor practice?
>
> *Decision:* Yes. The fact that he had discharged the men becaused he believed that they would harm his property does not alter the fact that he had fired men who were attempting to unionize the employees. The employer's action was accordingly an interference with unionization although he did not intend it to be such. This conclusion is reached because it would weaken the law if rumors could be circulated by rivals or personal enemies which would induce the employer to discharge particular employees without being liable for an unfair labor practice charge in the event that the accusations were shown to be false. Conversely, by holding the employer responsible, it is likely that he will not act on information supplied by others until he has made as certain as he can that it is correct. [N.L.R.B. v. Burnup and Sims, Inc., 379 US 21, 13 Led2d 1, 85 SCt 171 (1964)].

(3) Mixed causes. The employee who is fired may be a poor worker who should have been fired in any case. If he happens to be a member of a union, a question arises as to whether he was in fact fired because he was a bad employee or because he was a union member. In such case, if the trier of fact determines that the union membership was the last straw, without which the employee would not have been fired, the discharge is an unfair labor practice. If the employee would have been discharged in any case, even had he not belonged to the union, the discharge is for a proper cause and the employer is not guilty of an unfair labor practice.

(*c*) **Union shop limitation.** As a qualification of the prohibition against discrimination based on union membership, the Federal Labor Management Relations Act permits the hotel to fire non-union men if the hotel has entered into a union shop contract with the union.

Under the federal statute the hotel, with certain limitations, may lawfully agree to a provision in the union contract that although the hotel may hire non-union employees, any non-union employee must join the union in order to keep the job beyond a trial period not exceeding thirty days. Such a contract term creates a union shop, as contrasted with a closed shop under which only union members can be hired.

The union shop clause is merely lawful under the federal statute. The employer is not in any case required to enter into such an agreement and he may refuse to do so if he wishes and has the bargaining power to maintain his position.

§ 20:14. Discrimination for using Labor Management Relations Act.

(*a*) **Generally.** Labor relations statutes seek to prevent the employer from retaliating against an employee who has taken steps under the labor relations acts. For example, the federal statute makes it an unlawful labor practice for an employer "to discharge or otherwise discriminate against an employee because he has filed charges or given testimony" under the federal statute.

(*b*) **Particular applications.** This provision is to be broadly construed to prohibit any kind of discrimination which would be barred by the provision against discrimination because of union membership. The employee is protected under the federal law even though after the hearing was held by the National Labor Relations Board, at which the employee testified, the Board decided not to take jurisdiction of the matter, because the employer's volume of business did not meet the standards of the Board. The provision also prevents an employer from refusing to hire an applicant because he had filed a charge, which was then pending against his former employer.

§ 20:15. Miscellaneous acts of employer.

(*a*) **Generally.** There are a number of common acts which are not expressly declared to be unfair labor practices but which may be declared such if committed as part of a plan of discrimination against unions and so forth.

(*b*) *Wage raises.* A wage increase granted by the employer is an unfair labor practice when it is granted with the understanding that the employee in return for such raise will not join a union or will abandon the union which he has joined. It is likewise an unfair labor practice for the employer to grant a wage increase without prior discussion with the bargaining representative of the employees, particularly where negotiations for a wage increase are underway; for the reason that such conduct tends to undermine the value of the union in the minds of the workers who tend to feel that they did not need the union in order to get the raise.

(*c*) *Lockout and shutdowns.* The federal statutes do not make the mere use of a temporary lockout or a partial shutting down an unfair labor practice. If it is done for the purpose of interfering with the rights of employees to organize, and so on, it is an unfair labor practice. An employer may go out of business for any reason.

A temporary lockout may be used by the employer as part of labor warfare tactics while collective bargaining is going on. When collective bargaining takes place with a group of employers, it is proper for all of the group to shut down when the bargaining representative seeks to destroy the unity of the group by threatening a strike against one of them.

D. Unfair labor practices of the union

§ 20:16. Interference with employees' rights.

(*a*) *Generally.* In order to protect the rights of other unions and of non-union employees, it is now generally provided that a union cannot do any act of interference with workmen's rights which an employer could not do. Thus the Federal Labor Management Relations Act makes it an unfair labor practice for a union "to restrain or coerce" employees in the exercise of their right to self-organize, to form, join, or assist labor organizations, to bargain collectively through representatives of their own choosing, and to engage in other concerted activities for the purpose of collective bargaining or other mutual aid or protection. It is likewise an unfair labor practice for a union to interfere with the right of employees to refrain from any such activities, except to the extent of enforcing against them a valid union shop contract clause.

(*b*) *Particular applications.* The statute above noted prohibits a union from blacklisting an employee because he has been suspended from the union or belongs to a rival union. In general, any threat whether of personal harm or loss of his job constitutes an unfair labor practice when the object is to coerce the employee to give up his labor rights as above described.

§ 20:17. Compelling employer to discriminate.

(*a*) *Generally.* It is commonly made an unfair practice to cause or attempt to cause an employer to discriminate against an employee. Under the federal statute it is an unfair labor practice for the union to cause or attempt to cause the employer to do any act which would be an unfair discrimination because of union membership or activity as discussed in § 20:13. The federal statute also makes it an unfair labor practice to induce such discrimination by the employer against an employee who has been denied membership in the union or has been ejected from the union for some reason other than failing to pay the ordinary initiation fees or periodic dues.

(*b*) *Particular applications.* Under the above statute the union commits an unfair labor practice when it induces the employer to execute a closed shop or union shop agreement which is illegal because prohibited or because the statutory procedure required for its adoption has not been followed. The union commits an unfair labor practice when it requires that seniority questions be determined on the basis of length of union membership rather than length of employment. An unfair labor practice is likewise committed when the union causes the employer to fire the employee because he was dropped from the union membership because he had a fight with the union president.

§ 20:18. Selection of employer's representatives.

(*a*) *Generally.* It is an unfair labor practice under the federal statute for a union to restrain or coerce an employer in the selection of his representatives to act for him in collective bargaining or the adjustment of grievances.

(*b*) *Particular applications.* By virtue of this provision the union cannot refuse to bargain with an employers' association, as against the union's claim that it has the right to bargain with each employer individually. Likewise the union cannot insist that a given position be held by a union man when the employee in that position represents the employer for the purpose of adjusting grievances.

§ 20:19. Miscellaneous acts of union.

(*a*) *Generally.* In addition to the various unfair labor practices considered in the preceding sections, certain other forms of union conduct are expressly condemned by statute as unfair labor practices. In the case of the federal statute the refusal or failure of the union to bargain collectively in good faith is an unfair labor practice just the same as in the case of the employer. In addition, a number of other practices are condemned by the federal statute as unfair labor practices. These are briefly listed below with the caution that each represents an area which is so complex that an accurate definition cannot be obtained by any brief statement and that resort to a lawyer skilled in labor law becomes a necessity.

(*b*) *Strikes and hot cargo.* It is an unfair labor practice under the federal statute for a union to strike or to refuse to handle, or to induce others to strike or refuse to handle goods where the object is to coerce the employer to do certain acts specified by the statute.

(*c*) *Payment for work not done.* It is an unfair labor practice under the federal statute for a union to cause or attempt to cause an employer to pay or deliver, or to agree to pay or to deliver, any money or other thing of value, as an exaction for payment for services which are not performed or are not to be performed. This provision against feather-bedding does not prohibit the requiring of the doing of unnecessary work or the hiring of unnecessary employees to do unnecessary work.

(*d*) *Recognition picketing.* It is made an unfair labor practice to picket an employer for the purpose of compelling him to recognize the picketing union when it is not entitled to recognition.

(*e*) *Excessive initiation fees.* When a union has a valid union shop agreement with the employer, it is an unfair labor practice for it to charge an initiation fee which is excessive when viewed in the light of all relevant factors, including the practices and customs of labor organizations in the particular industry, and the wages currently paid to the employees affected.

E. Civil rights protection from discrimination

§ 20:20. Federal Civil Rights Act.

(*a*) *Prohibition of discrimination.* The hotel in its capacity as an employer may not discriminate in the hiring or firing of employees or in its relations with them, on the basis of race, color, religion, sex, or national origin. If the hotel does so, it is an unlawful employment practice under the Federal Civil Rights Act of 1964.[15]

(*b*) *Applicability.* This provision does not apply to all hotels but an exemption is made in terms of number of employees. As of July 2, 1965, the statute did not apply to a hotel unless it had at least 100 employees; in 1966 it applied if the hotel had at least 75 employees; in 1967, at least 50 employees; and in 1968 and all subsequent years, at least 25 employees. In making this calculation, only those persons are counted as employees who were on the hotel's payroll for each working day in twenty or more calendar weeks in the then current year or the preceding calendar year. Consequently, seasonal workers employed for less than twenty weeks in a year are not counted.

In addition to satisfying the above payroll test, the employer must be a person engaged in an industry affecting commerce. Further provisions of the federal statute have the effect of requiring the employer to meet the transient and dollar value test which determines whether the Federal Labor Management Relations Act will be applied by the National Labor Relations Board.[16]

---

[15] § 703. It is also made an unfair employment practice to discriminate against an employee for opposing any employment practice condemned by the Act or for testifying in respect thereto. The employer likewise commits an unlawful employment practice if he causes a help wanted ad to be run in which it is indicated that preference will be made on the basis of race, color, religion, sex or national origin.

[16] See § 20:4.

(c) **Keeping of records.** The hotel should make a written statement of the action taking by it in connection with any job applicant or employee. Care should be taken to show the basis for the action, in the event that the hotel is later charged with discrimination.

(1) Official records. Apart from the voluntary keeping of records, the Equal Employment Opportunity Commission, discussed in § 20:22, is given authority to require the keeping of records as to any of the various phases of hotel-employee transactions in which discrimination might appear, such as requiring reports as to hiring, firing, promotion, and other employment relationships.

§ 20:21. Allowable distinctions.

(a) **Generally.** The Federal Civil Rights Act does not require that every employee be treated the same as every other. Certain distinctions may be made without constituting "discrimination" provided, of course, that they are not designed or intended as discriminations.

(b) **Testing for qualifications.** The Civil Rights Act does not prohibit the testing or screening of applicants or employees for the purpose of determining whether the person is qualified to be hired, or promoted, or given a wage increase, or given special training, and so forth. The testing, however, must be carefully administered to avoid any basis for claiming that a test, although fair in its face, was used to conceal a plan or purpose to discriminate. In this connection it may be desirable for the hotel to adopt "any professionally developed ability test," as the statute expressly declares that the employer may act on the basis of such a test when fairly administered.

(c) **Compensation and seniority status.** The Civil Rights Act of 1964 has no effect upon the hotel's right of establishing compensation scales, providing for bonus pay and incentive pay, or from paying at different rates in different geographic areas. The hotel may also recognize seniority status, whether voluntarily or as part of a collective bargaining agreement with a union or other representative of its employees.

The foregoing statement is of course subject to the qualification that the plan followed by the hotel is not in fact designed to discriminate. The fact that the plan produces different results, in that one person is paid more than the other, and so forth, does not establish that there is a discrimination, for it is only discrimination when the different result is produced intentionally because of the race, and so forth, of the person who ends up in the less favorable position. Thus there is no discrimination when one employee is paid less than another solely because he is not as well qualified as the other, or because he has been employed a shorter period of time, or because his job carries with it less responsibility, and so forth. Conversely, there is discrimination when different rates of compensation are paid one employee than another because the lower paid employee is a member of a particular race, and so on.

(*d*) *Existing employment imbalances.* As of the date that the Civil Rights Act went into effect, it was possible that all of the hotel's employees belonged to the same race. Or, although members of two or more races were employed, they were not employed in the same ratio as existed in other places of employment, other hotels, or within the community in which the hotel was located. The Civil Rights Act expressly declares that the hotel is not required to readjust the "balance" of its payroll in order to include any particular percentage of each race, creed, and sex, as its employees. The hotel may therefore continue with its existing employees and no accusation of discrimination can be made on the ground that the employee ratio is unbalanced and is not in harmony with any ratio as between races, and so forth.

(1) Hiring of new employees. When the hotel hires new employees, the only obligation upon it is to refrain from discriminating as to each applicant. There is no obligation to hire with the purpose of changing the existing balance between races of employees, creed, or sex; for such selection of new employees on that basis would itself be a prohibited discrimination as to the otherwise qualified applicants who are rejected because of such a plan of favoring a given race, creed, or sex in order to change the existing employee balance.

§ 20:22. Enforcement of Civil Rights Act.

(*a*) *Generally.* The federal statute follows the commission-court plan of enforcement. A national agency, named the Equal Employment Opportunity Commission has been created.

(*b*) *Commission proceedings.* Initially the Commission inquires into whether the employer has committed an employment discrimination. This proceeding may be begun upon the complaint of the person who claims that he has been discriminated against or by any member of the Commission who believes that there has been such discrimination. The Commission then notifies the employer, makes an investigation, takes the testimony of witnesses, and determines whether or not there is "reasonable cause to believe that the charge is true." If it so determines, it does not make any ruling that there has been a violation of the law but instead seeks to "endeavor to eliminate any such alleged unlawful employment practice by informal means of conference, conciliation, or persuasion."

Provision is made for the use of state and local fair employment practice enforcement methods when the alleged misconduct occurs in a state or city which has applicable fair employment practice procedures.

(*c*) **Court action.** If the Commission has been unable to bring about a settlement of the matter within a specified time, the complaining applicant or employee is then free to bring a civil action against the employer. In this action, the court may appoint an attorney for the complaining party and free him from paying any costs or furnishing security. If the case is one of general importance, the United States Attorney General may be allowed to intervene in the action.

If the court finds that the employer has intentionally committed an unlawful employment practice prohibited by the Federal Civil Rights Act of 1964, "the court may enjoin the employer from engaging in such unlawful employment practice, and order such affirmative action as may be appropriate, which may include reinstatement or hiring of employees, with or without back pay." Any back pay allowance is reduced by the amount of pay which the complaining party had actually earned since the time of the unlawful employment practice, as well as amounts which he could have earned in that period with reasonable diligence.

(*d*) **Proceedings under state and local law.** The unlawful employment practice provisions of the Civil Rights Act of 1964 do not affect or take the place of any state statute or city ordinance on the subject. Accordingly the employer may be sued or prosecuted under a state law or city ordinance to the same extent as was possible prior to the adoption of the federal statute.

There is one exception to the general continuation of state law: a state law or local ordinance has no effect to the extent that it requires or permits the doing of any act which would be an unlawful employment practice under the federal statute.

Chapter 21. CRIMES

A. Crimes of the hotel

§ 21:1. Nature of offense.
    (a) Generally.
    (b) Special and general laws.
    (c) Nature of punishment.

§ 21:2. Illegal liquor sales.
    (a) Generally.
    (b) Intent to violate law.
    (c) Sales to intoxicated persons and drunkards.
    (d) Sales to minors.
    (e) Act of employee.

§ 21:3. Illegal use of premises.
    (a) Gambling.
    (b) Prostitution.

§ 21:4. Corruption and defrauding governments.
    (a) Generally.
    (b) Vicarious liability.
    (c) Collaboration with others.

B. Crimes of patrons and third persons

§ 21:5. Nature of offense.
    (a) Generally.
    (b) Crimes affecting the hotel.
    (c) Crimes limited to hotel situations.

§ 21:6. Defrauding hotel.
    (a) Generally.
    (b) Intent to defraud.

§ 21:7. Obtaining money or property by false pretenses.
    (a) Generally.
    (b) Elements of the offense.

§ 21:8. Bad check acts.
    (a) Generally.
    (b) Elements of the offense.
        (1) Intent.

Crimes

(2) Postdated checks.
(3) Presentment for payment.

§ 21:9. Forgery.
    (a) Definition.
    (b) Particular name.
    (c) Unauthorized signature.

C. Action of hotel against criminals

§ 21:10. Right to repel trespassers and criminals.
    (a) Generally.
    (b) Use of force.

§ 21:11. Detention for theft.
    (a) Generally.
    (b) Excessive force or unnecessary humiliation.
    (c) Detection statutes.

§ 21:12. Detention for nonpayment of bill.
    (a) Generally.
    (b) Psychological false imprisonment.
    (c) Detection statutes.

§ 21:13. Arrest without a warrant.
    (a) Generally.
    (b) Peace officer.
    (c) Private citizen.
    (d) Distinction between felony and misdemeanor.
    (e) Breach of the peace.

§ 21:14. Risk to hotel of using criminal process.
    (a) Generally.
    (b) Liability of hotel.

A. Crimes of the hotel

§ 21:1. Nature of offense.

(*a*) ***Generally.*** The hotel is subject to criminal prosecution for offenses committed by it although the nature of the punishment is affected by whether the hotel is a corporation or an individual.

(*b*) ***Special and general laws.*** The offense which may be committed by a hotel may be the violation of a statute specifically directed at hotels or statutes applicable generally. As examples of the former there are frequently license laws with which a hotel must comply and fees which a hotel must pay. Such requirements are applicable only to hotels and the failure to comply with them constitutes a crime.

The hotel is subject to various building, safety, and fire codes, which may speak specifically in terms of hotel requirements or may apply equally to all buildings of the same size and construction as the hotel. General statutes may also apply to additional activities engaged in by the hotel, such as laws regulating the sale or preparation of food or the sale of liquor.

(*c*) **Nature of punishment.** If the hotel is owned and operated by an individual, no question of the nature of the punishment arises because he as an individual is subject to fine and imprisonment as in the case of a crime committed by anyone else. When the hotel is owned by a partnership, and the partnership is recognized as a legal entity, the partnership itself is subject to fine for a crime committed by the partnership. In addition, each partner participating or conspiring to commit the crime is individually subject to fine and imprisonment. In some instances it is also held that the non-participating and non-conspiring partners are also subject to fine and imprisonment.

When the hotel is a corporation, the corporation is subject to fine, and those individuals who conspired to commit the crime or participated in the criminal acts are subject to fine and imprisonment.

§ 21:2. Illegal liquor sales.

(*a*) **Generally.** The sale of liquor is subject to various restrictions, some for the purpose of protecting the public and some for the purpose of assuring that the government will receive its taxes.

In addition to the ordinary penalties of fine and imprisonment, statutes may make the sale of liquor illegal, either generally or under certain circumstances, and declare that a building which is used for the illegal sale of liquor constitutes a nuisance which may be stopped by a padlocking of the building. Such a padlocking statute is applicable even though the defendant lives in the building.

(*b*) **Intent to violate law.** In most instances it is held that intent to do an illegal act or consciousness of wrongdoing is not essential to criminal liability for breach of a liquor law. That is

Crimes

to say, it is the fact of doing the prohibited act which imposes criminal liability, rather than the doing of such act with any particular mental state.

(c) Sales to intoxicated persons and drunkards. Statutes variously make it a crime to sell or give liquor to a person who is then intoxicated, or is a habitual or a known drunkard. These statutes parallel the "dram shop" laws which impose civil liability for the damages caused or sustained by the intoxicated person under such circumstances.

Under the criminal statutes it is generally held that a statute drafted in terms of supplying a "known" drunkard refers to the persons whose habits are so known in the community, without reference to whether they or the individual's condition were known to the vendor of the liquor. In consequence of this interpretation, the vendor of liquor is guilty of the crime although he had no intent to make an illegal sale or had any knowledge that in fact he was doing so.

(d) Sales to minors. Statutes generally make it illegal to sell, give to, or supply minors with intoxicating liquor. The fact that the vendor does not intend to violate the law or that he in good faith believes that his customer is an adult does not constitute a defense to the crime.

(e) Act of employee. Generally it is held that the employer, whether or not a hotel, is criminally responsible for a liquor law violation committed by an employee even though the employer had acted in good faith and had no reason to know that any illegal act was committed. For example, where it is illegal to sell or give liquor to a minor, the hotel will be subject to criminal penalty for violation thereof, even though the sale was made by the hotel bartender who had been instructed by the hotel that no such sale was to be made. That is, the law imposes criminal liability on the hotel or other employer even though the hotel or employer had intended that the law should be obeyed. Because of the high desirability of protecting minors, the view is taken that the employer must be subject to absolute liability for the acts of his establishment even though he was personally innocent.

> *The facts:* A statute made it a crime to sell liquor in bottles which had been refilled. The defendant operated a tavern or taproom. Without his knowledge, one of the bartenders sold several bottles which had been empty and which he had refilled with whisky. The defendant, as the employer of this employee,

was fined under the statute making such acts a crime. The defendant appealed on the ground that he could not be liable for a crime when he had had no intent to violate the law; the acts were done by another person, his employee; and further that the whisky in the refilled bottles was pure.

Decision: It is immaterial that the liquor in the refilled bottles was pure, for the statute was designed to protect from deception as well as the possibility of adulteration or harmful products. The fact that the defendant did not have any knowledge of what had been done is immaterial because the no-refill statutes, like other pure food and drug statutes, are designed to protect the public and therefore impose strict liability so that there is criminal liability if in fact there has been a refilling of the bottles, even though the employer did not know that its employee had done so. [People v. Jolley, ... CalApp2d ... , 28 CalReptr 899 (1963)].

§ 21:3. Illegal use of premises.

(*a*) *Gambling.* Statutes commonly make it a crime for a person to permit his "house" or "place" to be used for the purpose of gambling or to knowingly lease to another for gambling purposes any house, building or premises.

The hotel may find itself guilty of a violation of such a statute when it leases an apartment with the knowledge that it will be used for gambling, although there is authority that the offense of knowingly letting or leasing space for gambling purposes is not shown to be committed by the mere fact that some gambling was conducted on the premises. To the contrary, there must be "something in the nature of a liaison" between the hotel and the gambler.

A hotel is not guilty of the above offense if it exercises reasonable care that the hotel should not be used as a refuge for gambling or gamblers.

(*b*) *Prostitution.* It is also a common statutory crime to lease property with the knowledge that it will be used for prostitution. The statute may be so worded that the hotel is guilty of the offense when it provides accommodations to persons who will make such use thereof.

§ 21:4. Corruption and defrauding governments.

(*a*) *Generally.* The hotel may have criminal liability for corruption, such as giving a bribe to a fire law inspector to ignore

Crimes

violations of the law; or for defrauding a government, as by knowingly making a false return for tax purposes.

(*b*) *Vicarious liability.* When the corrupting or defrauding act is an "official" act of the governing body or persons of the hotel, no question arises as to vicarious liability for the act in question is in law the act of the hotel. A difficult question arises when it is the act of an ordinary employee, even though he is the employee to whom this area of the hotel's administration has been entrusted. For example, the employee who is responsible for the making of repairs called for by the fire laws does not make the repairs, but instead uses part of the repair money to bribe the fire inspector to ignore the violations and pockets the balance of the repair money for himself.

The question of whether vicarious liability exists in such cases, that is, whether the hotel will be held criminally liable for the crime of its employee cannot be easily answered. Two factors should be noted as tending to impose liability upon the hotel. The higher the employee stands in the job classification or ranks of the employees of the hotel, the more likely it is that the hotel will be held liable. Likewise, the more dangerous to the life and property of others, the more likely it is that the hotel will be held liable. Conversely, when the employee is a low-ranking employee or the crime is merely a matter of cheating the government without causing harm to any person, the probability increases that vicarious liability will not be imposed. The rationale which underlies the law is that when it is a matter of deciding whether an innocent employer must bear the responsibility in order to protect an innocent victim from the employee's wrong, the law will place the responsibility upon the employer who, through his power to fire and supervise, has the ability, or at least the greater ability, to prevent the commission of the wrong.

(*c*) *Collaboration with others.* If the hotel conspires with other hotels or individuals to violate any law, such as those relating to prices, civil rights, and so forth, the hotel may of course be subject to prosecution for the criminal offense done or for the crime of conspiracy.

In some instances the offense may have been committed in all innocence and for the purpose of doing a patron a favor. For example, when a hotel clerk or cashier pads the account of a patron at the latter's request, the employee is committing a crime. The hotel employee under such circumstances knows or has reason to know that the patron is going to use the padded receipt either for the purpose of obtaining greater reimbursement for expenses from his employer or for the purpose of claiming a greater tax deduction in his income tax return. The hotel employee by making or certifying the padded account is consequently doing an act which defrauds the employer or the government. The fact that the hotel employee is not willfully seeking to cheat either the government or the employer and that the hotel employee does not benefit personally by such conduct does not alter the fact that his act was a step in cheating someone of something and that he either realized that or shut his eyes to that consequence, and his act is therefore criminal in character.

B. Crimes of patrons and third persons

§ 21:5. Nature of offense.

(*a*) *Generally.* Guests, patrons, and strangers may commit a traditional crime and the fact that the crime is committed in a hotel rather than at some other place does not have any effect on criminal liability. Quite logically, the fact that the offense is committed by the guest, patron, or stranger in a hotel does not affect his responsibility for his crime.

In some cases, however, the heart of the offense may be misconduct, such as drunkenness, profanity, disorderly conduct, in a public place; in which case the fact that the conduct of the guest occurs in a hotel furnishes the element of "occurrence in a public place."

(*b*) *Crimes affecting the hotel.* In some instances, the crime committed in the hotel affects the hotel as the victim. For example, if the guest criminally sets fire to the hotel building, he commits a crime of which the hotel is the victim. Likewise if he gives the hotel a bad check, he has committed an ordinary crime although the hotel happens to be the victim.

(*c*) *Crimes limited to hotel situations.* In other instances, the offense is by definition one which can be committed only with respect to a hotel. For example, it is commonly made a crime to obtain hotel accommodations with the intent to defraud the hotel.[1]

---
[1] See § 21:6.

Statutes may also make it a crime to interfere with the business of a hotel as by soliciting or seeking to persuade persons to patronize a competitor. Thus a statute may make it a crime for a taxi driver to attempt to cause a guest to switch from the hotel which the guest specifies to another hotel which the taxi driver suggests.

§ 21:6. Defrauding hotel.

(*a*) *Generally.* Most states have some form of a statute creating a type of offense of defrauding hotels by obtaining accommodations without an intent to pay for them; although in some instances this type of misconduct has been held to come within the scope of the crime of obtaining money or property by false pretenses.

The secret removal of baggage with the intent to defraud the hotel, by depriving it of its hotel lien thereon, is commonly made a crime. Moreover, the taking by the guest of his property which is held under the hotel lien constitutes larceny since the guest is wrongfully taking the property from the possession of the hotel under the lien; even though the guest may be the owner of the property.

(*b*) *Intent to defraud.* The existence of an intent to defraud the hotel is essential to the commission of the offenses here considered. In order to aid the enforcement of the law, it may be provided by statute that certain acts shall be evidence of the fraudulent intent of the guest. Thus the statute may declare that there is prima facie evidence of the attempt to defraud when the guest uses an assumed or fictitious name, or secretly removes his baggage; or the check used to pay for accommodations has been returned for insufficient funds; or the guest came to the hotel with dummy baggage which misled the hotel; or the guest refused to pay or left the hotel without paying.

There is authority, however, that a refusal to pay is not merely evidence of fraud but is an essential element of the offense of defrauding the hotel. Thus, a statute may make it a crime to obtain hotel accommodations with the intent to defraud the hotel by obtaining accommodations without intent to pay for them, although no liability arises for such offense unless there is a demand for payment or a refusal to pay therefor.

§ 21:7. Obtaining money or property by false pretenses.

(*a*) *Generally.* Most states have by statute declared it to be a criminal offense to obtain money or property by means of false pretenses.

(*b*) *Elements of the offense.* To constitute the crime of false pretenses, it is necessary that there be (1) the intent to deceive; (2) a representation which is false, relating to a material past or present fact; (3) by which the victim is deceived and on which he relies; and (4) in consequence of which he transfers money or property to the evildoer.

The difficulty that arises here is that under some statutes the obtaining of accommodations or services, as distinguished from the obtaining of tangible property, does not constitute the offense. Such a requirement of obtaining property would of course be satisfied where the debt owed is not for accommodations, but is for food sold or other purchases made at the hotel's store, where the hotel acted upon the basis of the patron's false representation.

§ 21:8. Bad check acts.

(*a*) *Generally.* It is commonly provided by statute that a person who passes a bad check, that is, one which will not be honored at the bank because the drawer does not have sufficient funds, is guilty of a crime.

(*b*) *Elements of the offense.* The essence of the offense is the issuing by the drawer of a check not covered in his bank by sufficient funds, or any funds; although there is some uncertainty as to whether the time for testing the sufficiency of the funds is the time when the check is issued to the payee or the later time when it is presented to the bank for payment.

In some states the bad check act is not applicable unless property is obtained by means of such fraud.

> *The facts:* The defendant executed a check for $800 which was not paid by the drawee bank because of insufficient funds. The defendant was prosecuted for issuing a bad check. He raised the two defenses (1) the check was never intended to be cashed but was to be held merely as security to be used only in case the defendant defaulted on his obligation to remove certain buildings from the land of the payee, but that (2) if the transaction with the

Crimes

payee was an agreement to purchase the buildings which were to be removed, the check did not violate the Bad Check Act because the buildings had already been removed and were in the possession of the defendant at the time the check was delivered to the payee. Were these defenses valid?

Decision: While the theory of the two defenses were mutually inconsistent, the case should go to the jury to determine whether either version of the facts was true. As the Bad Check Act applies only to the giving of a check to obtain goods, it is necessary that the check be delivered as "payment" and not as a form of security which could be utilized in case of default. Likewise the statute did not apply if the check were given as payment for goods already received rather than for goods which were obtained by means of the check. [Jackson v. State, 251 Miss 529, 170 So2d 438 (1965)].

(1) Intent. It is generally necessary that the defendant have the intent of misleading by virtue of his use of the false check. To assist the prosecution in proving that such intent was entertained, it is commonly provided by the bad check statute that when there are not sufficient funds to cover the check it is presumed that it was issued with criminal intent, and that if the check is not made good within a specified period, such as ten days thereafter, the presumption of criminal intent becomes conclusive and cannot be disputed by the defendant.

(2) Postdated checks. In the absence of a statutory provision to the contrary, it is generally held that when a check is postdated there is no criminal liability arising from the fact that on the date when issued the check was not covered by sufficient funds. Other courts ignore this distinction because of the peculiar terminology of the local statute and hold that it is the fact that a bad check was issued which determines whether there is criminal liability.

The facts: A meatpacker sold meat to the defendant over a long period of time. During this time, the defendant paid for deliveries with checks that were postdated a few days. All prior checks had been paid, but the last check that was postdated had not been paid. The defendant was prosecuted for passing a worthless check and for obtaining property by false pretenses.

Decision: The defendant was not guilty. The postdated check informed the payee, by the fact that it was postdated, that there was not on deposit money to meet the check, while making the implied assurance that there would be funds present on the day it became due. The postdated check was therefore in effect a promissory note to pay on the date of the check and was thus not a "bad check" and no fraud was present. [Commonwealth v. Kellinson, 199 PaSuper 135, 184 A2d 374 (1962)].

(3) Presentment for payment. Under some statutes, the criminal liability attaches as of the date when the check is issued to the hotel or other payee. Under other statutes, there is no criminal liability until the check has been presented for payment and then dishonored by the bank on which it is drawn for insufficient funds.

§ 21:9. Forgery.

(*a*) *Definition.* In its most common form, forgery is the writing of the name of another person with the intent that others believe it to be genuine and are thereby defrauded.

(*b*) *Particular name.* When the signing is made with the intent to defraud it is immaterial what name is thus signed. For example, it is immaterial whether it is the name of a real person or of a dead or fictitious person. It is also immaterial that it is the forger's own name, when he signs with the intent of representing that it is the signature of another person having the same name.

To illustrate the preceding situation, assume two employees are each named "Henry A. Smith" and the one entitled to the smaller pay check gets the larger check intended for the other. If in such case the lower-ranking employee indorses the check intended for the other with the intent of making it appear that the other has signed, he is guilty of forgery.

(*c*) *Unauthorized signature.* When an agent exceeds his authority so that he does not have the right to sign his principal's name to a given instrument, he does not commit forgery. In such case, however, he is liable for damages to the third person who has been injured thereby, the liability of the agent being based on the warranty which the law implies when an agent acts as such: the law regarding his so acting as warranting that he is (1) authorized to act on behalf of a principal who has (2) existence and (3) capacity to contract.

C. Action of hotel against criminals

§ 21:10. Right to repel trespassers and criminals.

(*a*) ***Generally.*** The hotel, both with respect to its true hotel function and any non-hotel functions, stands in the dual position of property owner and proprietor of a public place. It accordingly has both a duty and a right to keep the premises free from third persons who seek to do harm to patrons or the property of patrons and the right to do so to protect the hotel's own property. With respect to its patrons and their property, the hotel stands in the special guardian-like position of a proprietor of a public place. With respect to protecting the hotel property, the hotel has the rights of any other land owner to protect his property.

(*b*) ***Use of force.*** The hotel may use such force as is reasonably necessary to repel trespassers and criminals.

When the circumstances indicate the necessity for quick action, the hotel is not required to warn the suspicious third person or request his withdrawal.

> *The facts:* The motel had been broken into a number of times by persons entering through the windows. Property of both guests and of the motel had been stolen. The manager of the motel received a phone call about 10:25 P. M. that two men were removing the screen of one of the motel units. The manager grabbed a shotgun and went to the area in question and in the dark saw someone apparently trying to break into the window of one of the units. He fired one shotgun shell at the intruders. The latter proved to be two boys. The manager injured one of them who although only fourteen years old was grown to man size. There was no apparent reason for the presence of the boys in the area and no explanation was given. The injured boy sued the motel for the harm caused him.
>
> *Decision:* Judgment for the motel. The person charged with the responsibility of protecting the motel and the guests of the motel may use force to do so. Under the circumstances, it had reasonably appeared to the manager that the plaintiff was attempting to make an unlawful entry into the motel unit. It was also reasonable for the manager to assume that the intruder was armed and that the intrusion could only be prevented by the use of the force which the manager applied. [Edwards v. Great Am. Ind. Co. . . . La . . . , 146 So2d 260 (1962)].

§ 21:11. Detention for theft.

(*a*) *Generally.* When the hotel or its employees have reasonable ground for believing that a patron or a third person has stolen property from the hotel or from any enterprise run by the hotel, the hotel and its employees have the privilege of detaining the suspect and preventing his escape. The case of detaining a suspect generally raises two questions: (1) whether the circumstances were such as to warrant the detention or seizure of the suspect; and (2) whether excessive force was used or unnecessary humiliation was caused in so doing. If it is established that there was no reasonable cause or if excessive force were used or unnecessary humiliation caused, the hotel is liable for a tort, such as false imprisonment,[2] or assault and battery.

(*b*) *Excessive force or unnecessary humiliation.* Although the conduct of the hotel and its employees may be otherwise privileged or lawful, either because the plaintiff was in fact guilty of the conduct with which he was accused or there was sufficiently reasonable ground for so believing, the hotel will nevertheless be liable where unnecessary force was used in the seizure or detention of the suspect or unnecessary humiliation was caused him.

Furthermore, the fact that the conduct of the hotel employees was willful does not exclude vicarious liability of the hotel, because such tortious conduct was nevertheless inspired by the purpose of doing their jobs.

> *The facts:* The plaintiff left the defendant's store and went to the drugstore next door. Two of the managers of the store, wearing the green jackets of the store's employees, burst into the drugstore and seized the plaintiff. They twisted his arms behind his back, causing him pain, and loudly and repeatedly stated that they wanted the meat which he had taken from the store which he was concealing underneath his coat. The plaintiff opened his coat and showed that he was not carrying anything underneath it. He sued the store for assault and battery by its employees.
>
> *Decision:* Judgment for plaintiff. While the acts of the two managers constituted a willful tort, namely assault and battery, it was committed by them in the course of their employment, for the purpose of furthering their employer's business and therefore the store was vicariously liable for their conduct. [Greenfield v. Colonial Stores, 110 GaApp 572, 139 SE2d 403 (1964)].

---

[2] As to the elements of false imprisonment generally, see § 8:4.

(c) *Detention statutes.* In some states statutes give police officers, merchants, and their employees, the right to detain a person who is reasonably suspected of shoplifting and to interrogate such person in a reasonable manner and for a reasonable time, providing further that if these elements of reasonableness are satisfied, no civil liability arises for false imprisonment, assault, battery, false arrest, slander, or similar offenses. Such statutes, however, are generally merely declaratory of the law: that is to say, the courts would reach the same conclusion even without such a statute.

The facts: The plaintiff and her granddaughter were shopping in the store of the defendant. Shortly after they left, someone seized their shopping bag and in a loud and threatening manner stated that they had a white dress in the shopping bag and demanded to see the contents. This person was requested to show his credentials but he declared that he did not have to do so and continued in such a loud manner that the grandmother, in fear for their safety, let him see the contents of the bag, which did not include any white dress or anything for which they had not paid. It was later learned by the plaintiff that the stranger was an employee of the defendant's store, although they had at first thought that he was a criminal assailant. As the result of the above transaction, the plaintiff and her granddaughter were detained two minutes or more. The plaintiff sued the defendant for false imprisonment. The latter defended on the ground that it was protected by a statute such as that described in the preceding text.

Decision: Judgment for plaintiff. The statute giving a merchant the right to detain and examine in a reasonable manner at a reasonable time, merely re-enacts the rule of law which was recognized even without any statute. The employee of the defendant had not acted in a reasonable manner as he had failed to identify himself or at least refused to do so when requested by the granddaughter. Such identification is particularly essential when the stopping of the plaintiff occurs in public as otherwise the plaintiff would not be able to determine whether the person was an authorized employee or a criminal assailant.

The fact that the transaction lasted only two or more minutes did not make the conduct of the defendant's employee any the less a false imprisonment of the plaintiff.

The conduct was likewise a false imprisonment although there was no detention by actual force; it being sufficient that the plaintiff had submitted to a request for inspection because of fear of being harmed if the plaintiff did not comply with the request. [Lukas v. J. C. Penny Co. 233 Or 345, 378 P2d 717 (1963)].

§ 21:12. Detention for nonpayment of bill.

(a) *Generally.* A person who has not paid for what he owes, whether for accommodations or other purposes, may be detained by the hotel for a reasonable time to investigate the facts of the case, but the offense of false imprisonment is committed if he is detained for an unreasonable length of time or in an unreasonable manner on the basis of the belief that he has not paid. After the patron has made payment of the full amount claimed, he has of course the right to leave and any detention thereafter becomes a false imprisonment.

(b) *Psychological false imprisonment.* Contrary to the general rule that a detention by force or fear is essential, it has been held that there is a false imprisoning of a patron when he has been publicly accused of lying, with the result that, although he is free to leave, he feels that he must stay until his innocence is established lest by leaving he give bystanders the impression that he is guilty.

(c) *Detention statutes.* Some statutes protect the hotel from liability for an honest mistake in arresting or causing the arrest or detention of a patron for nonpayment with intent to defraud. Such statutes specifically declare that there shall be no liability when the hotel has acted to arrest or to detain the patron in an honest belief that the patron was guilty of the intent to defraud or had defrauded the hotel.

§ 21:13. Arrest without a warrant.

(a) *Generally.* An arrest may be made without a warrant by both a private citizen, such as an ordinary hotel employee; and by a police or peace officer. The validity of the arrest made without a warrant is affected by the identity or status of the person making the arrest, as to whether he is an officer or a citizen; the nature of the offense, as to whether it is a felony or a misdemeanor; where the offense was committed with relation to the arresting person or officer, as in or out of his presence; and whether in fact any offense was committed or the person making the arrest merely believed that it had been.

(b) *Peace officer.* A peace officer may arrest without a warrant when (1) the person arrested has committed in the presence of such officer a misdemeanor involving a breach of the peace, or (2) the person arrested has committed a felony in or out of the presence of the officer, or has attempted to commit a felony in his presence, or the officer reasonably believes that such person has committed a felony, although in fact none was committed by anyone. In some jurisdictions, statutes have widened this power of arrest by removing the qualification that the misdemeanor must be one which involves a breach of the peace while in other jurisdictions the power to arrest has been narrowed to those instances in which arrest is necessary to prevent escape.

> *The facts:* The manager of a store saw a man with a bulge under his coat run out through the rear entrance of the store and drive away in a waiting automobile. The same thing occurred ten minutes later. Some items were missing from the clothing racks in the area where the man had been. The manager phoned the police, giving them the description of the man and the automobile. A police car arrested the fleeing man on the charge of larceny. He objected on the ground that he had been arrested without a warrant.
>
> *Decision:* What constitutes probable cause which justifies arresting without a warrant cannot be determined by any fixed formula, but must be resolved from the facts of each case. The conduct of the man, the bulge underneath his coat, and the fact that items were missing from the store constituted reasonable ground for believing that the man had committed a felony and therefore could be arrested without a warrant. [Peltas v. United States (CA Dist Col) 203 A2d 170 (1964)].

(c) **Private citizen.** A private citizen, that is, an ordinary person or hotel employee who has not been sworn as a police or peace officer to protect or maintain the peace, can arrest without a warrant when (1) the person arrested has committed in the presence of such person a misdemeanor involving a breach of the peace, or (2) the person arrested has attempted to commit or has committed a felony in the presence of the private citizen, or a felony has in fact been committed by someone and the private citizen reasonably believes that such person is the one who committed it.

(d) **Distinction between felony and misdemeanor.** As the power to arrest without a warrant is defined in part in terms of felonies and misdemeanors, it is essential to distinguish between the two. By the modern law, if the only punishment authorized for a given crime is the payment of a fine, the offense is a misdemeanor. If on the other hand it may also be punished by imprisonment in the state penitentiary or by execution of the defendant it is classified as a felony.

Under this system of classification, it is the nature of the punishment which could be imposed by the court rather than the actual punishment which is imposed in a given case which determines the character of the offense.

In some jurisdictions the distinction between felonies and misdemeanors has been abolished.

(*e*) **Breach of the peace.** In those jurisdictions in which the power to arrest without a warrant for a misdemeanor is limited to those which involve a breach of the peace, it is necessary to define the phrase "breach of the peace." "In general terms, a breach of the peace is a violation of public order, a disturbance of public tranquility, by an act or conduct inciting to violence or tending to provoke or excite others to break the peace, or, as sometimes said, it includes any violation of any law enacted to preserve peace and good order. By 'peace,' as used in the law in this connection, is meant the tranquility enjoyed by the citizens of a municipality or community where good order reigns among its members."[3]

§ 21:14. Risk to hotel of using criminal process.

(*a*) **Generally.** The hotel faces the danger of civil and criminal liability as in the case of any other person when it improperly causes the initiation of criminal proceedings against a patron or any third person; including liability for the initial detention, the arrest, and subsequent trial.

(*b*) **Liability of hotel.** If the hotel acts without justification in causing the prosecution of the patron or other person, it may be guilty under the circumstances of the particular case of the civil offenses of false arrest, or false imprisonment, or malicious prosecution. This ordinarily does not present too much of a risk although it may cause police officers to delay, to doublecheck the facts, which delay may be just what the skipping patron or the thief needs to make his exit from the county or the state.

The situation in which the greatest potential for liability arises is that which is found when the hotel causes the arrest of a

---

[3] 2 Wharton's Crim Law & Proc (Anderson Edition, Lawyers Co-operative Publishing Co, 1957) § 802, pp. 655-6.

patron. If there is any possibility that the patron is innocent of wrong, the hotel should be very careful to see that he is treated with a minimum of restraint necessary and that he be allowed every chance to phone to persons who could establish his innocence or could bring money to pay his debt. If the hotel acts in a vengeful or excessive manner there is the danger that it will be held not to have acted in good faith and its conduct may not only subject it to liability for damages for the harm done but may also subject it to liability for exemplary or punitive damages.

> *The facts:* The hotel made an agreement to extend credit to the guest. Ignoring this, the hotel falsely claimed that the guest was defrauding it and caused his criminal prosecution. The guest was acquitted and then sued the hotel.
>
> *Decision:* Judgment for guest. The action of the hotel in repudiating the credit agreement and asserting that the amount due under the credit agreement had been fraudulently incurred was unjustified and consequently made the hotel liable for malicious prosecution of the guest. [Saner v. Bowker, 69 Mont 463, 223 P 1056 (1924)].

Chapter 22. THE ANATOMY OF A LAWSUIT

§ 22:1. The problem.
    (a) Generally.
    (b) The typical lawsuit.

§ 22:2. The pre-pleading stage.
    (a) Time for commencement of the action.
    (b) Form of action.
    (c) The court.
        (1) Exceptions.
    (d) The parties.
    (e) Commencement of action.
    (f) Service of process.
        (1) Necessity of prompt action on being served.

§ 22:3. The pleading stage.
    (a) Generally.
        (1) Systems of pleading.
    (b) The plaintiff's complaint.
        (1) Necessity of prompt action on receiving the complaint.
        (2) Relief from default judgment.
    (c) Defendant's alternatives.
        (1) Defendant's answer.
        (2) Counterclaim or cross complaint.
        (3) New matter.
    (d) Plaintiff's alternatives.
        (1) Plaintiff's reply.
    (e) Classification and determination of issues.

§ 22:4. Pre-trial procedure.
    (a) Generally.
    (b) Motions to end case without a trial.
        (1) Motion for judgment on the pleadings.
        (2) Motion for summary judgment.
    (c) Pre-trial conference.
        (1) Forced settlements.

The Anatomy of a Lawsuit 413

        (d) Discovery.
            (1) Common-law procedure.
            (2) Modern procedure.
        (e) Depositions.

§ 22:5.   The trial.
        (a) Generally.
        (b) The trier of fact.
            (1) Equity cases.
            (2) Administrative proceedings.
        (c) The basis for decision.
            (1) The basis for testifying.
            (2) Inferences and presumptions.
        (d) Conduct of the trial.
        (e) Charge to the jury and verdict.
            (1) Generally.
            (2) The determination of the truth.
            (3) Function of the judge and jury.

§ 22:6.   Taking the case from the jury.
        (a) Generally.
        (b) Voluntary nonsuit.
        (c) Compulsory nonsuit.
        (d) Directed verdict.

§ 22:7.   Attacks upon the verdict.
        (a) Generally.
        (b) New trial.
            (1) Test of mistake by jury.
        (c) Judgment N.O.V.

§ 22:8.   Damages.
        (a) Generally.
        (b) Compensatory damages.
            (1) Compensatory damages for personal harm.
        (c) Punitive or exemplary damages.

§ 22:9.   Judgment and costs.
        (a) Generally.
        (b) What are costs.

§ 22:10.   Appeals.
        (a) Generally.
        (b) Action of appellate court.

§ 22:11. Execution.
    (a) Generally.
    (b) Garnishment.
        (1) Availability of procedure.
        (2) Defenses of garnishee.

§ 22:1. The problem.

(*a*) *Generally.* The object of a legal system is to ascertain the facts of a controversy and to apply the law thereto. This should be a very simple matter except that it is sometimes very difficult to tell what did happen and the exact rule of law to fit the case may not have been declared. This perhaps is an over-gloomy statement of the situation for there are many cases in which the risk of being unable to prove the facts is relatively slight and in which the law is relatively or definitely certain. Nevertheless, even at its best you will see from the following steps of a lawsuit that the best course is to avoid litigation by running your hotel in such a way that you minimize the possibility of being sued.

(*b*) *The typical lawsuit.* In the following sections a lawsuit will be analyzed step by step. Actually the procedure in one state may differ in many details, but the general plan will follow that set forth. Moreover, the following analysis will take the lawsuit from its beginning and run it through to its greatest length. In actual practice, many suits will not go that far.

For the purpose of simplicity, the procedure will be discussed in terms of pre-pleading stage, the pleading stage, the trial stage, post-trial proceedings, appeals, judgment and costs, and execution.

§ 22:2. Pre-pleading stage.

(*a*) *Time for commencement of the action.* The kinds of action which will generally be brought against a hotel are subject to time limitations called statutes of limitations. This means that, if the action is not brought within a specified time, no action can ever be brought and the claim is barred. For example, in many states, an action to recover damages for personal injuries must be brought within two years after the injury is sustained. In the case of an action for product liability under the Uniform Commercial Code, the plaintiff has four years in which to bring the action.

(*b*) **Form of action.** The action which will ordinarily be brought against the hotel will be called a civil action or a civil action for damages. In some states still retaining the old common-law names, this will be called an action of trespass. This is the form of action which is brought when the plaintiff is injured by the condition of the hotel's premises or the operation of the hotel's automobile.

The hotel is of course legally capable of committing other civil wrongs and may therefore be sued in the form of action appropriate to such other types of claims. For example, if the hotel builds onto the neighboring land, the neighboring landowner may obtain an injunction in equity to prevent such construction, or in certain cases could sue in ejectment to cause the ouster of the hotel from such part of the plaintiff's land as had been encroached upon. Again, in many states, the names of these other actions have been changed from these common-law names and the action will either be called a civil action or a provisional remedy.

(*c*) **The court.** As is the case of any lawsuit, the plaintiff cannot bring his case wherever he chooses. To the contrary, he must bring it in a court which by statute or constitution has been given the power to hear the particular type of case involved. For example, the plaintiff claiming for damages for harm done because of the condition of the hotel's premises cannot bring suit against the hotel in a court which is only authorized to hear divorce actions.

Furthermore, the hotel may only be sued in a particular county or district. Specifically, the hotel can only be sued in the county or district in which the hotel is located because as a general principle of law, a defendant can only be served in the county or district where he can be found. As the hotel will most likely exist only within a given county or district where its hotel building is located, it can only be reached or served there. This rule is of course for the convenience of the hotel for its does not have to go traveling away from home in order to defend the claim asserted against it.

(1) Exceptions. As an exception to the rule above stated, it is generally provided that suit may be brought in the county or in the foreign state in which the harm is sustained where the claim is one for damages arising from the operation of a motor vehicle. Thus, if the hotel business is run in County A but the hotel automobile is being driven on hotel business in County B,

a suit may commonly be brought in County B when the hotel automobile is involved in a collision in County B which harms the plaintiff. Likewise, if the hotel automobile is driven out of the state, non-resident motorist statutes will ordinarily be applicable. Under such statutes, the use of an automobile in another state automatically appoints the secretary of state or some other official of that state as agent to receive service of process directed against the operator or driver of the vehicle.

If the hotel is a corporation, and particularly if it is a corporation formed under the laws of another state, it is likely that the plaintiff will be permitted to serve a particular local government official who is designated as the statutory agent of the corporation for the purpose of being served with process.

(d) *The parties.* The action against the hotel may be brought against the hotel alone. In many cases, the plaintiff will be allowed to join both the hotel and some employee involved. For example, a plaintiff harmed by the negligence of the hotel employee while the latter is acting within the course of his employment may in most states sue both the employee and the employing hotel in one action.

In some cases, the plaintiff may join the hotel and an independent contractor. Thus the plaintiff who is injured because of the maintenance contractor's failure to maintain the hotel elevators in good condition, may join both such contractor and the hotel, the latter not being released from liability because of the employment of an independent contractor. In product liability cases, the plaintiff in many states will be permitted to join the hotel which served or sold him the harmful product and the dealers or manufacturer who had supplied such goods or product to the hotel.

(e) *Commencement of action.* There are a variety of ways in which the action may be commenced. In the old common-law courts, an action was commenced by filing an order with the keeper of the court records to issue a writ to the sheriff. This writ of summons ordered the sheriff to inform the defendant to appear before the court on a particular date. This method of commencing an action is still followed in some states.

By way of contrast, an action in a court of equity was begun when the plaintiff filed with the court a complaint in which he set forth the facts about which he complained. That is, the action was itself started by the beginning of the pleading stage by the filing of the first pleading, namely, the plaintiff's complaint. No writ was issued, and a copy of the complaint was itself served on the defendant. In many states, and in the federal courts, the procedural reforms of the last several decades have extended this practice to all legal actions. They are accordingly commenced today by the filing of the plaintiff's complaint.

Some states still preserve the former distinction between law and equity and their distinct methods of commencement while others give the plaintiff the option of commencing the action by either method. This latter plan has the advantage of enabling the plaintiff to start the action quickly without taking the time to prepare his complaint where quick action is needed because (1) the statute of limitations period is about to expire or (2) the defendant is about to leave the jurisdiction and if service is not made within 24 hours or so it may be impossible to ever effect service.

(*f*) *Service of process.* The defendant must be served with some paper for the purpose of making him subject to the jurisdiction of the court and to notify him that the action has been begun. This paper may take a variety of forms. It may be a writ, a notice, or a summons, or, the complaint itself.

Ordinarily, there is no problem in serving the hotel because of its fixed location where its building is located. As a minimum, the plaintiff will ordinarily be able to have service made upon the hotel by making service at the hotel building upon the owner, proprietor, corporate executive officer, or an agent or employee in charge of the hotel.

(1) Necessity of prompt action on being served. As soon as the hotel is served it should communicate at once with its attorney and with its insurance company. The attorney will want to investigate before the facts have changed; witnesses have moved away; and, if possible, to talk to witnesses before they have been discovered and talked to by the plaintiff's attorney. It is therefore to the advantage of both you and your attorney for you to notify him at once.

By the terms of your insurance policy it is generally necessary that you give your insurer prompt or immediate notice in order that it also can make an early investigation of the facts. When notice to the insurer is required, it is likewise generally provided that the failure to give notice as required shall bar any right of the hotel against the insurer. In the absence of a contrary statute or some special circumstance, such a forfeiture provision is given effect and means that it is just the same as though you did not have any insurance policy.

§ 22:3. The pleading stage.

(a) Generally. After the action has been commenced, the next stage of the proceedings is to get before the court a statement of the facts as viewed by each party so that it can be seen to what extent the parties really disagree over the facts.

(1) Systems of pleading. Apart from variations as to the names of pleadings, the time for filing them, and so on, there are two basic systems of pleading in the United States. The older or common-law system requires that a party be very specific and set forth all facts material to his case. The modern system, frequently described as the federal or notice-giving system, only requires the setting forth of such facts as give notice to the other party of the substance of the claim being asserted. For example, the plaintiff's complaint by the latter system might be nothing more than the statement that the plaintiff fell on a certain day in the lobby of the defendant's hotel because of the hotel's fault. In contrast, the common-law system of fact pleading would require a pleading of just where the fall took place, what caused the fall, and in what respects the defendant was negligent or at fault, and so on.

(b) The plaintiff's complaint. The first pleading filed in the action is the complaint of the plaintiff. In some states this may have already been filed as a means of commencing the action. If the action was not commenced in this manner, the plaintiff must file the complaint.

After the complaint is filed, a copy is served on or sent to the defendant. The defendant must make some reply thereto, ordinarily within 15 or 20 days. If he does not, the plaintiff ordinarily wins the case by default and a judgment is entered in his favor against the defendant.

(1) Necessity of prompt action on receiving the complaint. Here is a danger spot in litigation. Namely, that you will let the 15 or 20 days for replying to the complaint slip by without doing anything about it. Remember, your attorney needs time to examine the facts before he will know just what type of paper or pleading he should file in reply to the plaintiff's complaint. You should therefore give him all the possible time you can by

notifying him of the fact that you have been served with the complaint and forwarding it to him.

Your liability insurance policy will in most cases require that a copy of the complaint be forwarded to it promptly, immediately, or forthwith. Again, the failure to comply with the policy provision in this respect will ordinarily forfeit your rights under the insurance policy with respect to the neglected claim, although under special circumstances it may be held that the forfeiture provision is not effective.

(2) Relief from default judgment. If through carelessness or for any other reason, the defendant hotel fails to file anything in reply to the complaint and the plaintiff obtains a default judgment against it, is there anything that the hotel can do about it? In many states, the hotel, if it has a good excuse for the neglect and can show in addition that it probably has a good defense to the action if it were given the chance to formally prove such fact, it will be allowed to proceed to do so. In many states this is called petitioning to open the judgment for the purpose of making a defense.

While this remedy may frequently be invoked, it is not always certain that it will be allowed, so that the hotel should not take it for granted that if its employees fail to act promptly in informing the hotel that service has been made of the complaint, that the hotel can thereafter be rescued by obtaining the opening of a judgment in this manner.

(c) Defendant's alternatives. After the complaint is filed, the defendant must take some step in court. Although he is directed to file an answer, the defendant has the right to say "Let's wait until later about my answer. There's something about your case or your claim that we should first discuss."

Specifically, the defendant before answering the plaintiff's complaint may point out errors relating to the case thus far. This the defendant does by filing what are sometimes called preliminary objections. For example, the defendant may claim that he was never served; or that the action has been brought in the wrong county, or in the wrong court, or that there is something wrong about the plaintiff's complaint. What happens at this point may end the case, depending upon the nature of the objection made. If the objection is upheld or sustained, the case may be ended, as when the objection is that the action is brought in the wrong court, and it is held that is true; or the plaintiff may be granted leave to correct his mistake, as when his complaint does not conform to the statutes or rules of court and he is then given leave to correct his mistakes by filing a new or amended complaint.

One of the objections which the defendant may raise is that the plaintiff's complaint, even if believed, does not set forth a claim or cause of action which the law recognizes and that the plaintiff is therefore not entitled to recover. This objection is often called a motion to dismiss or a demurrer. If this objection is sustained, the action of the court has the effect of saying that the plaintiff has nothing about which to complain and the case is over, in favor of the defendant, subject of course to the right of the plaintiff to file an amended complaint to state his case better, if he can, or to take an appeal or otherwise challenge the action of the court.

(1) Defendant's answer. If the defendant loses on his various preliminary objections or motions above described, he must then file an answer, which either admits or denies the facts averred by the plaintiff. Under the common-law system of pleading, the defendant must ordinarily deny the plaintiff's claim fact by fact, and, wherever possible must aver just what did happen as opposed to what the plaintiff claims. Under the notice system of pleading, it is generally sufficient that the defendant merely state that certain matters are denied, or he may even make a blanket denial of the entire plaintiff's claim as by saying that: "All facts averred by the plaintiff are denied."

For example, if the plaintiff averred that on a given date he fell in a given part of the hotel building because of the negligence of the hotel consisting of its failure to take certain specified precautions and that in consequence the plaintiff suffered specified harm, the hotel might want to deny part or even all of these facts. To illustrate, if the claim is a false claim in that the plaintiff never was even hurt on the premises of the hotel, the hotel will deny the entire claim. On the other hand, the hotel may not dispute the fact that the plaintiff was harmed nor that the hotel's negligence was the cause thereof, but the hotel disputes that the plaintiff has suffered the damages claimed by him. For example, the plaintiff has claimed damages for permanent disability whereas the hotel claims that there was not more than a few days of disability. Similarly, the hotel might admit all parts of the plaintiff's claim but dispute the amount which the plaintiff said he spent for doctor bills. In these two situations, the hotel could admit the facts relating to the occurrence, the fact of plaintiff's being harmed, and of the defendant's being negligent, but attack the damages claimed by denying that the plaintiff was injured or sustained damages to the extent claimed. Or the hotel may wish to admit that the facts occurred as claimed and that the plaintiff sustained the damages alleged, but wish to deny some or all of the facts on which the liability of the hotel is based. To illustrate, the hotel may wish to deny that part of the plaintiff's complaint which states that the automobile which ran over the plaintiff was being driven by an employee of the hotel while acting in the course of his employment. In the ordinary case, if the employee is outside the scope of his employment there is no liability for the harm caused by him. The fact of his being in the course of his employment is therefore a pivotal fact in the determination of the lawsuit.

(2) Counterclaim or cross complaint. It may be that the hotel has some claim against the plaintiff. For example, if the plaintiff sued because of harm done by the hotel-driven automobile, the hotel may take the position that its automobile was properly driven and that it was the plaintiff's fault which caused the collision and that the plaintiff should pay the hotel for the damage which had been sustained by the hotel car.

This making of claims back against the plaintiff is called, depending upon the local procedure, either a counterclaim or a cross suit.

(3) New matter. The position which the hotel takes may be that it admits all the facts as claimed by the plaintiff but because of some additional fact not set forth by the plaintiff, the latter had no right to sue the hotel. For example, the hotel may wish to claim that although the plaintiff had the right to recover as far as would appear from his complaint, there is the additional fact that the hotel had already paid the plaintiff a cash settlement in return for which the plaintiff gave the hotel a release. That is, according to the hotel, the plaintiff gave up the claim against the hotel in return for the money received from the hotel.

Whenever there is some additional element which the hotel claims constitutes a bar to the plaintiff's claim, the hotel is allowed to put that additional matter in its answer. Frequently this additional information is called "new matter."

The pleading of new matter is not limited to cases in which the hotel admits the claim of the plaintiff as far as it goes and then raises the new matter as a defense. The hotel can also take the alternative positions that the plaintiff's claim is not valid but that even if it were valid it would be barred. By way of illustration, the hotel can take the position that the plaintiff who allegedly fell because of the condition of the premises can not recover because the hotel was not negligent, but that even if the hotel was negligent the plaintiff was barred by his contributory negligence.

(d) *Plaintiff's alternatives.* After the defendant files his answer, the plaintiff may generally file preliminary objections to the answer. Similar to the pattern of possible objections which the defendant could raise, the plaintiff may, in certain instances, take the position that a counterclaim cannot be asserted in the court in which the case is pending, that the answer is defective in form, or that the counterclaim is not legally sufficient as a claim or the new matter is not legally sufficient as a defense. These various objections are disposed of by the court and the case moves on.

(1) *Plaintiff's reply.* In most instances, the pleadings will have come to an end by this time. The case may be such, however, that the plaintiff is allowed one more pleading. For example, if the defendant under new matter has raised the defense of a release given by the plaintiff, the plaintiff may wish to admit the release but then claim that the release is void because obtained from the plaintiff by fraud or when the plaintiff was in such a mental or physical state that the plaintiff had no capacity or ability to agree to anything.

If the plaintiff is permitted to file a reply, it is generally provided that the defendant may make preliminary objections thereto, or file a motion to dismiss or a demurrer. Beyond this point, it is generally provided that pleadings may not go.

(e) *Classification and determination of issues.* Generally, all of the pleadings in an action will raise only a few or perhaps one question of law, or one question of fact, or both questions of law and questions of fact. To illustrate, the whole case may turn on the question of fact whether the defendant gave the plaintiff notice of the condition of the premises. The nature of the case may be such that if it is true that the hotel gave such notice it was not negligent and the hotel is then not liable to the plaintiff. Conversely, if the notice was not given, the hotel was negligent and was accordingly liable to the plaintiff.

By way of contrast, it may be admitted that the notice was given but the plaintiff takes the position that more than notice was required. It is then a question of law of whether the hotel was legally required to do more than give notice or whether it had gone as far as it was required to do when it gave the notice. Here the question is one of law. If the question is decided in favor of the defendant hotel, judgment will be entered in its favor; if decided in favor of the plaintiff, he will recover against the hotel.

If the only questions involved are questions of law, the court will decide the case on the pleadings alone since there is no need for a trial to determine the facts. Conversely, if questions of fact are involved, then there must be a trial to determine what the facts really are. If there are both questions of law and fact there must be a trial, and if the trial is before a jury, there will be a division of labor: the judge deciding the questions of law and the jury deciding the questions of fact, as will be described in § 22:5.

§ 22:4. Pre-trial procedure.

(*a*) *Generally.* In a strict sense, everything that has occurred up to this point is pre-trial procedure for the reason that the trial has not yet been held. There are, however, a number of procedural steps which may take place before trial which are often classified as pre-trial proceedings because they are modern innovations added on to the common-law or statutory form of procedure. The classification is arbitrary because some of the steps may be regarded as an extension of the pleading system and in many states are so classified, while other steps may be pursued while the parties are pleading and in some instances even before the pleading has begun.

(*b*) *Motions to end case without a trial.* We have already considered as a part of the pleading stage the objection, motion to dismiss, or demurrer which is used by one party to show that the pleading of the other party does not state a cause of action or a defense which is valid. In many states there are two or more types of motions which can be made for the purpose of putting an end to the case without getting into a trial.

(1) Motion for judgment on the pleadings. After the pleadings are closed, many states permit either party to move for a

judgment on the pleadings. When this motion is made, the court examines the entire case up to that point as shown by the pleadings and then enters judgment according to the merits of the case as shown by the record.

(2) Motion for summary judgment. In some states, a party is allowed to bring into court sworn statements or affidavits which show that a claim or defense is false or a sham. This procedure can not be used when there is a substantial dispute of fact concerning the matters to be proved by the use of such affidavits.

(c) **Pre-Trial conference.** In many states a pre-trial conference may be called by the court on its own initiative or upon the application of any party to the action. This conference was originally intended to be only a round table discussion by judge of the court and the attorneys in the case with the object of eliminating matters which were not in dispute, agreeing on just what issues were to be determined at the trial, and cleaning up in advance procedural matters relating to the trial.

The pre-trial conference is not intended as a procedure to compel the parties to settle their case. It not infrequently results, however, that when the attorneys discuss the matter with the court, they recognize that the differences between the conflicting points of view are not so great as originally believed or that one side has less merit than at first appeared; in consequence of which, the attorneys are able to come together and meet on a common ground and settle the case. With the increasingly staggering overload of court dockets, the pressure to settle cases becomes increasingly greater.

(1) Forced settlements. The pre-trial proceeding presents a danger area for the hotel or any other person in a defending position. It may well be that in a given case it is better for the hotel, and its insurer, to make a payment to the plaintiff and bring an end to the case, for the litigation if prolonged may be more costly to the hotel than the payment which it or its insurer makes to the plaintiff.

There is at the same time the danger that the plaintiff will make a false claim and then pressure will be brought to bear on the hotel's attorney to compromise the claim rather than defend against it. This opens the door to fraud in that persons will make exaggerated and false claims trusting that there will be just enough semblance of validity to their claims that the pre-

The Anatomy of a Lawsuit

trial conference judge will seek to persuade the hotel to give the plaintiff something.

(**d**) *Discovery.* In the federal courts and in many state courts following the federal rules, parties to litigation have an almost free right to obtain discovery from the other parties and from third persons. The exact significance of this is more readily apparent if we first consider the common-law practice.

(1) Common-law procedure. Prior to the modern reform, any party could before the trial, or before bringing an action, ask anyone any questions he chose; but whether the other person would answer was a matter which was up to him. That is, you could investigate a claim but you could not compel any answer nor compel the production of any information if the person questioned was hostile to you and did not wish to cooperate with you.

There was accordingly a race by parties to a lawsuit to reach the witnesses first; each party hoping that if he would examine a given witness first he could thereby induce that witness to refuse to answer the investigator for the other party. The result of this technique was extreme secrecy without either party knowing for certain just what witnesses would be called by the adverse party nor what those witnesses would say when the trial actually took place. Those who criticized this system pointed out that it was a game of surprise in which no one knew what the trial would bring. Those who favored this system said that that was good because you would not be able to manufacture false testimony to overcome my truthful witnesses.

There was indeed an advantage in the old system of shaking a lying witness apart by producing evidence which showed that he was lying, without his having any opportunity other than the spur of the moment to think up some way out of his perjurious dilemma. Unfortunately, sometimes the one who was shaken by the surprise was the attorney whose client consciously or unconsciously had deceived him; and it was not until the moment of truth arrived at the trial that the attorney could see the entire picture and recognize that his client or his client's witnesses were not in fact telling the truth.

(2) Modern procedure. Under the modern procedure a wide range of examination may be conducted before trial by both parties not only of third persons but also of each other. The theory here is that everyone learns just what everyone else

knows and the trial then becomes a matter of presenting the known facts in an orderly way rather than a battle of wits and of witnesses.

Under this modern procedure, one party can seek virtually as much information before the trial as he would be permitted to ask at the trial, and in certain respects his scope of pre-trial examination is even wider than at the trial.

In terms of procedural forms, in many courts a party can (1) send a questionnaire to the other party asking him any questions about the facts of the case; (2) send a request to the other party to admit formal matters, such as the execution of a document; (3) require the adverse party and witnesses to appear before an examiner and answer under oath what they know about the case and state the names of other witnesses; (4) obtain a court order to allow the examining, inspecting, and photographing of books, records, buildings, and machines; and (5) obtain a court order to make a physical or mental examination of a party when his condition has a bearing on the case.

This system eliminates the evils of surprise but it also eliminates the beneficial aspect of surprise since the perjurer is now forewarned of the evidence which would otherwise trip him and it becomes just a matter of little more perjury for him to conjure up a rational excuse or explanation for the conflict within his testimony or between his testimony and the other evidence.

More important, the discovery procedure easily lends itself to being used as a means of harassing a party and of subjecting him to unnecessary and needless inconvenience and expense. In many instances, the criticism is heard that the net effect of the discovery procedure is to try the case twice, once by the discovery procedures and once by trial. When the adverse party is a corporation with scattered officers and employees it becomes particularly annoying if discovery is repeatedly had of different officers and employees or the examination is obtained of its many records. The acuteness of the problem arises where the defendant is a multi-state operation such as a chain hotel and the witnesses and employees who have been involved in the transaction giving rise to the lawsuit have thereafter been assigned to different jobs in different branches. As the witnesses are spread to the four points of the compass, the discovery procedure obviously spreads out over a larger geographic area.

The evils here depicted are not without remedy. It is generally provided that a court may be petitioned to enter a protective order against any excessive or abusive use of discovery, as well as for other grounds. But the very necessity of seeking a protective order in resisting proceedings is itself a burdensome thing. Moreover, the general inclination of the courts is to refuse to restrict the discovery proceeding. The net result is that the modern lawsuit brings with it the added threat of harassment by discovery procedures.

(*e*) ***Depositions.*** Ordinarily a witness testifies in court at the time of the trial. In some instances it may be necessary or desirable to take his testimony out of the court before the time of the trial. This is the situation when he is aged or infirm and may die or be too ill to testify by the time of the trial. It is likewise true if he is about to leave the state or country so that he will not be available or within the reach of a subpoena at the time of the trial. In such cases, a party in interest, after giving proper notice to the adverse party and to the prospective missing witness, may require such witness to appear before someone authorized to administer oaths, and to answer questions and to submit to cross-examination; all this testimony being recorded stenographically and then filed with the court as the testimony of the missing witness if, when the trial arrives, he is in fact then missing.

§ 22:5. The trial.

(*a*) ***Generally.*** The trial is the phase of litigation in which a trier of fact determines the facts of the case; the principles of law applicable to such facts are applied; and a conclusion as to liability or guilt is reached. As earlier described in this chapter, it is possible that the parties may never reach a trial, as where the case is disposed of prior to trial for some reason, as when certain preliminary objections are sustained, and so on.

(b) ***The trier of fact.*** In most cases which are brought against a hotel the facts are determined by a jury, unless all parties to the action agree that the case be heard without a jury. This is based upon the principle that if the legal controversy is one which should have been tried by a jury at common law, either party to the action has a constitutional right to demand a trial with a jury. But if the parties agree to waive such jury, the case may be heard by the judge alone, or in some instances referred to a master or referee specially appointed by the court for such purpose.

(1) Equity cases. When the hotel is a party to an equity proceeding there is no right to trial by jury. This merely follows from the historical accident that in equity there is no constitutional right to a jury trial. Thus if an action is brought in equity to enjoin the hotel from doing certain acts, neither the plaintiff nor the hotel would be entitled to a jury trial.

The equity judge, if he desires, may submit questions to a jury in the same way that you might retain a body of experts to give you a report on a particular matter. That is the verdict of the jury is only advisory and the equity judge who appointed the jury is not bound by their decision; whereas in the case of an action at law the determination by the jury is binding in the absence of basic error.

(2) Administrative proceedings. When new causes of action are created by statute and enforced by administrative boards or agencies,[1] there is no constitutional right of trial by jury, the theory being that where the right was unknown to the common law, the right to trial by jury did not exist and accordingly the guarantee of the trial by jury does not extend to these hitherto unknown areas. For example, the discharge of an employee because of union membership never gave rise to any cause of action at common law; and being a new form of action it may, as is the case, be entrusted to an administrative agency to determine whether there is a breach of the duty imposed by that law.[2]

(c) The basis for decision. The trier of fact, whether it is a jury, the judge, or an administrative body, can only decide questions of fact on the basis of the evidence presented before it. The evidence usually consists of the questions put to the witnesses in the court or trial and their answers to the questions. This is called the testimony. The evidence may also include real evidence, consisting of tangible things, such as the piece of the broken chair and so on involved in the accident, and other things to be seen, which are offered in evidence on the theory that seeing is better than hearing. In some cases the trier of fact may be taken to view the premises: that is, go look at the actual place where the harm occurred although here it is

---

[1] See Chapter 19.
[2] See Chapter 20.

necessary that there be an explanation on the record as to whether the place is exactly the same as it was when the harm occurred, and, if not, in what respect it has changed.

(1) The basis for testifying. The witness who testifies in court or before an administrative agency is usually a person who had some direct contact with the facts in the case, such as a person who saw the events occur or who heard one of the parties say something. In certain cases, where the ordinary layman cannot appreciate or evaluate the significance of the facts, it is also proper to allow persons to testify on the basis of their expert knowledge in the particular field, stating their opinion as an answer to a hypothetical or theoretical question put to them at the hearing or trial, or as a statement of the conclusion reached by them as the result of observation of the facts in the case or the making of tests and experiments.

(2) Inferences and presumptions. As a general rule, each important fact of the case must be established by proof. Conversely, that which is not proven does not exist. In some instances, however, the law permits the trier of fact to conclude that if one fact is proven, another closely related fact may be deemed proven, without direct proof of its existence. For example, when the condition of the premises causes harm to the hotel's invitee, and he sues the hotel, he must prove as a fact that the hotel was negligent. Under certain circumstances, however, the rule of res ipsa loquitur applies which, as discussed in § 9:14, means that once the peculiar way in which the plaintiff was harmed is proven, the trier of fact may without further proof infer that the hotel was negligent. Thus the falling of the ceiling on the guest of the hotel during the night allows the jury to infer that the hotel was negligent, as described in § 11:22.

Similarly, in many states, the fact that an employee is driving an automobile which bears the hotel's name may give rise to a presumption that he was at the time driving within the course of his employment. This is not a final determination or proof of the fact, for the presumption does not prevent the hotel from showing that such was not the case, that is, from rebutting the presumption.

There are definite limitations as to how far inferences and presumptions can go in taking the place of actual proof, and the law will not just "assume" that a fact exists or does not exist because you want it to do so.

The facts: The defendant was a finance company. Its collector of delinquent bills rented a room in the plaintiff motel. He used this room as his office, doing his work of collecting delinquent accounts and reporting to the defendant by phone. Shortly after midnight, the collector-employee threw a burning mattress out of his room. The fire spread and damaged the motel. The motel then sued the employer finance company. The employer defended on the ground that the employee was not acting in the course of his employment. The motel claimed that since the employee was in the motel with all his working papers received from his employer, and did his work from his room, that it was to be presumed that he was acting in the course of his employment.

Decision: Judgment for the defendant. The rebuttable presumption that an employee driving the employer's automobile is acting within the course of his employment does not extend to other transactions. Hence the fact that the employee had possession of his employer's papers did not create a presumption that the employee was acting within the course of his employment at the time the mattress caught on fire. As the motel failed to offer any proof that the employee was acting within the course of his employment, the defendant-employer could not be held vicariously liable. [Gumm v. National Homes Acceptance Corp. (CA7th), 339 F2d 993 (1965)].

(*d*) **Conduct of the trial.** Ordinarily a case is one of several listed or assigned for trial on a specified day or during a specified trial period. When the case is called, the attorneys seat themselves at tables before the judge and the jury is selected and sworn. The attorneys then usually make opening addresses to the jury. Details vary in different states, but the usual pattern is that each attorney states to the jury what he intends to prove at the trial. After this step, the presentation of the evidence begins.

The plaintiff's attorney calls his first witness and questions him. This is the direct examination of the witness since it is made by the attorney calling the witness. After the direct examination, the opposing attorney questions the same witness in the effort to disprove his testimony. This is cross-examination. The opposing attorney may also call other witnesses to discredit or impeach the credibility of the witness.

After the cross-examination, the plaintiff's attorney may ask the same witness more questions in the effort to overcome the effect of the cross-examination. This is redirect examination. It may be followed by further examination by the defendant's attorney, called recross-examination.

After the examination of the plaintiff's first witness has been concluded, the plaintiff's second witness is then examined in the same way as the first. This is repeated for each of the plaintiff's witnesses. Then the plaintiff rests his case, and the defendant's witnesses are examined. The pattern of examination is the same as above stated, except the defendant's attorney conducts the direct and redirect examination, while the plaintiff's attorney now conducts the cross- and recross-examination.

When all witnesses have been examined and all the evidence has been presented, each attorney makes another address to the jury, a summation, in which he sums up what he has proved and argues to the jury that it decide for his client.[3]

(e) *Charge to the jury and verdict.*

(1) Generally. After the final address of the attorneys, the judge charges the jury. By this, he summarizes the evidence and explains the law which applies. He then tells the jury to retire and consider the case in the light of his charge and to return a verdict. The judge leaves the jury free to determine the facts but they must apply to such facts as they find the law stated by the judge. The jury deliberates in secret in the jury room.[4]

(2) The determination of the truth. The validity of the jury system, and of any system of trial is based upon the premise that the jury or other trier of facts is able to determine the true facts. In many fields of the law, the sciences have greatly aided the trier of fact in determining what is the truth, as in the case of finger prints, ballistics, blood tests, and so forth. Unfortunately, in the ordinary type of lawsuit brought against the hotel there is very little that is scientific and the trier of fact must fall back on which witnesses the trier believes. Even this may not be difficult in some cases for the skill of the attorneys may have made it clear to the trier of fact, ordinarily the jury, where the truth of the matter lies.

There is nevertheless a great area in which the jury's decision is nothing more than a guess or a hunch or is merely an averag-

---

[3]Anderson and Kumpf, Business Law (9th edition, South-Western Publishing Co. 1972) Chapter B.
[4]Op. cit., chapter B.

ing out of the different opinions of the jury, as by adding together what each juror would give the plaintiff, if anything, and then dividing by twelve. What is the difficulty?

Let's reduce the problem to the simplest terms. Have you ever taken care of two small children? Assume they are playing in the next room. Suddenly cries of combat rend the air and you go into the next room to find the two locked in battle. When you reprimand them and ask who started it, you are greeted with the unanimous reply: "He did." Can you tell in fact who began the fight? If you think you can, are you not really being guided by a prejudice against one of the children on the basis that he had started so many prior fights that he must have also started this one?

The jury is in much the same position. For example, they were not present when the plaintiff fell in the hallway of the defendant hotel and neither was anyone else. Now some time, even years, later, the jury will attempt to reconstruct what happened and why. No hotel employee was present and actually knows what happened; not even the plaintiff who fell actually knows what happened. The plaintiff does not know exactly what happened for all the plaintiff knows is that he tripped and fell on an object. But does the plaintiff realize what the plaintiff was doing the moment before he fell, so that he can give a truthful picture of the scene? It seems clear that what he knows of the scene is what he himself reconstructed in his mind immediately after falling. If he had had a clear picture of the scene before he fell, obviously he would have seen the object over which he fell and presumably would not have fallen. Now, having fallen and knowing very well that the offending object is there, he attempts to determine whether he could have seen the object before he fell.

The problem of determining what happened becomes the more complex when we have neutral or impartial witnesses. For example, suppose that you are walking down the street and hear what you interpret as an automobile collision. Hearing the sound, you look toward its source and then see something. You do not see what happened because what happened occurred before you heard any sound. What you see is what existed x seconds or parts of a second after the event occurred. The less acute your hearing; the poorer your eyesight; the more you were concentrating on other matters; and so on, the longer will be the x-second interval of time between the actual event and your "perception" thereof and the more difference will there be between what actually did occur and what you saw. That is why two equally honest witnesses can testify in flat contradiction to each other as to the color of a traffic light: one took just enough time longer than the other to "see" the light, and by that time it had changed.

On top of this is the matter of image memory and word equivalents. Remember now that we have our jury trial a long time, even years, after the event occurs. Do you have a clear image of some significant event which occurred three years ago? You probably think you do. You may even say most emphatically "I'll never forget the expression on his face, ..." but actually if you were shown a perfect photograph of the event you would be surprised to find that there were so many details which you have forgotten or so many things that you have "remembered" that were not so.

This takes place because our minds are not perfect filing cabinets. When we store away that past image, parts of it drop out, like a jigsaw puzzle that is tilted and parts of other images pour over into the particular image in question.

Then on top of all this, can you accurately describe the image which you do have in your mind? Try for example, to describe the degree of lighting in the hallway in which the guest fell. Was it brightly lit, well lit, semi-lit, dimly lit, partly dark, or dark? Can you pick just the right word to describe the degree of lighting, even when you have the hallway in front of you today; let alone remembering what it was several years ago? Obviously neither you nor I by our eyes alone can measure nor by our words describe scientifically and accurately the exact degree of lighting.

Yet notice how all innocently a witness can change the whole complexion of a trial. This witness describes the hallway as dark, whereas someone else might say that the lighting was dim. Add also the problem of eyesight variation that might make the hallway seem dark to one and merely dim to another. Note also that these variations in eyesight can exist although there is not a condition so serious as to be a "defect" which an attorney could show on cross-examination to discredit the witness.

If the whole problem is not yet sufficiently confused, consider where the witness was before he saw the hallway. One witness may have been asleep in a darkened room and, on getting up, was going down the hallway. His eyes are still accustomed to the dark room and he does not notice that the hallway is particularly dark. Another witness has just finished shaving with an electric razor in front of a bright fluorescent light and is rushing out of his room and down the hall so that he will not be late for an appointment. The sudden contrast between the fluorescent lights and the hall will undoubtedly make the hall seem very dark to this witness.

And finally, we have the great problem of communication. If I say the hall was dimly-lit will each of the twelve good men and true on the jury know just how lit the hallway was or will we have twelve different mental pictures in their respective minds as to what "dimly-lit" means? Now observe how vital this is to the determination of the facts and the trial of our case. In one form of words or another the judge is going to tell the jury at the end of the trial: "Now jury, you will return a verdict in favor of the plaintiff if you find that the hotel was negligent in that it did not adequately light the hall in such a way as to avoid the harm which a reasonable man would foresee." Thus uncertainty progresses by geometric bounds, for now we have

$$\begin{bmatrix} \text{uncertainty as to how well lit the} \\ \text{hall really was} \end{bmatrix}$$

times

$$\begin{bmatrix} \text{uncertainty as to what a reasonable} \\ \text{man would do} \end{bmatrix}$$

as the evaluation which the jury must make in reaching its verdict. Even more uncertainties are generally introduced for the questions of whether the hotel had made reasonable inspections or had reason to know of the condition of the hallway and whether the plaintiff had acted like a reasonable person or was guilty of contributory negligence are also thrown into this kettle of jury deliberation.

Somehow, in spite of all these difficulties, the trier of facts decides what happened, or in substance what it thinks happened and your liability is determined on this basis.

In the foregoing, the problem has been discussed in terms of the trial by jury. The basic difficulties of determining today what happened yesterday remains even though there is a trial without a jury, as by a judge or an administrative board. The only difference between the jury and the non-jury methods is that the complexities tend to be reduced as we move from twelve persons on the jury down to a smaller board and down to a single judge. Likewise, those who oppose a jury will take the position that the trial by judge or trial by administrative board will tend to be the more logical, because of experience and training, and less subject to illogical or arbitrary influences.

(3) Function of the judge and jury. The general rule is that the judge determines the law and the jury determines the facts. This tends to oversimplify the role played by the jury because it gives the impression that the judge and jury have equal importance in determining the outcome of the case. Actually, in the great run of cases there is no question about the rule or rules of law to be applied. The big question in the case is what were the facts. In consequence, unless there is a new principle of law to be developed or an old principle of law to be reversed, your big question mark as you go into the court is what will the jury find as the facts?

Approaching the same conclusion from another direction, it has been repeatedly noted that the courts say that where it is debatable whether the hotel was negligent or whether the plaintiff was contributorily negligent, the case must go to the jury. This means that in every case where there is a conflict of testimony, the case must go to the jury to make the choice between the possible alternative conclusions.

It is to be emphasized that this does not mean that when the evidence is fifty-fifty or an even toss either way that then the jury is called into action. Instead of being limited to the narrow, evenly-balanced case, the jury is required to determine every case when reasonable men believing one group of witnesses would reach one decision and other reasonable men believing another group of witnesses would reach a different decision. Otherwise stated, only in the very clear cases where there can be no doubt between reasonable men as to the conclusion to be made can the court decide negligence or contributory negligence. The very fact that there is a lawsuit is a pretty fair indication that the two parties have different ideas about what happened and will present conflicting testimony on which the issues are debatable and which therefore takes the case to the jury.

From the practical point of view this means that in the great majority of cases which might be brought against the hotel, the case will go to the jury with the freedom to find the facts as the hotel claims they were or as the plaintiff contends they were; and with the freedom to make judgments that certain conduct shall be deemed negligent or not negligent.

The facts: The hotel had employed the bellboy, aged 17, for some six months during which time no complaints had been made as to his conduct and there was no reason to suspect that he would commit any improper act. Upon taking ice to the room of a guest, he was offered some liquor and took a few gulps from a bottle at about 10:00 P.M. At about 3:00 A.M. the next morning, a guest for whom he handled baggage gave him another drink. At about 4:00 A.M., the guest who originally offered him a drink invited him into the room when he brought up more ice. He stayed in the room for about an hour and had three or four drinks. He then went to the hotel desk and looked through the register for the room number of any girl who was alone. He then took a passkey from the hotel desk, apparently going by the switchboard operator and the desk man in order to do so. At about 5:00 A.M., he went with the key he selected to the room of the plaintiff, entered her room and committed rape. He then left and when later found admitted all the facts as above stated.

The plaintiff sued the bellboy and the hotel, claiming that the hotel was liable on the theory that it had been negligent. A verdict for $25,000 was returned against both defendants. The hotel appealed on the ground that there was no proof that it had been negligent.

Decision: Judgment for plaintiff. The jury's verdict against the hotel established that the hotel was negligent and therefore liable. As the jury was the trier of fact, its conclusion that the hotel was negligent could not be set aside unless it was against the manifest weight of the evidence and was clearly erroneous. "There was evidence presented at the trial that [the bellboy] had been drinking while on duty and that he was absent from his post for two periods of about one hour each. There was evidence that in order to get the passkey to the rooms, [the bellboy] had to pass near a switchboard operator and a night attendant who could have determined that he had been drinking while on duty. We do not say that the evidence on these points is conclusive, but the evidence was such that a jury might reasonably come to the conclusion that the hotel staff could have and should have known of [the bellboy's] absence from his post when he was upstairs drinking and they should have seen [the bellboy] go in and take the passkey, and a jury could reasonably find negligence in that they should have guarded this key more carefully and did not. Whether we agree with the jury's conclusion or not, we have no basis for substituting our opinion of the evidence for the one it gave. The verdict is clearly not against the manifest weight of the evidence. . . . We must indulge in every reasonable presumption to uphold a verdict." [Danile v. Oak Park Arms Hotel, 55 IllApp2d, 203 NE2d 706 (1965)].

Notice that in the above case the court goes on the basis that the jury's verdict stands not because the court believes that the jury was correct, but that even if the jury was wrong, it was not so far wrong as to be obviously wrong. Otherwise stated, as long as the matter is within a debatable area where there are two sides to the matter, the jury may take either side and the court will not reverse it merely because the court would have reached a different conclusion. Moreover, even when the jury is wrong, the court will not interfere unless the jury is so clearly wrong that there can be no question about it.

Consider also the significance of the case in terms of the degree of supervision which the hotel must maintain over its bellboy in order to avoid the possibility that it may be held negligent and liable for his misconduct outside of the scope of his employment. Then multiply this by the number of employees on the premises and the extent of precautions becomes substantial. Notice also that the decision virtually imposes absolute supervisory liability upon the hotel as discussed in § 5:4. That is to say, in effect, the result of the case is the same as saying that whenever an employee of the hotel causes harm while on the hotel premises, the hotel is liable to the injured guest for that harm although the employee was not in the course of his employment at the time and regardless of the absence of any fault on the part of the hotel.

§ 22:6. Taking the case from the jury.

(*a*) *Generally.* At several points in the pleading stage it is possible to bring before the court a question of law in the effort to have the case ended then and there by the decision of the court on the question of law. Similarly, during and after the trial it is possible to take certain steps for the purpose of taking the case away from the jury and thereby bringing it to an end.

(*b*) *Voluntary nonsuit.* The plaintiff may be unhappy with the progress of the trial. He may stop the trial in most jurisdictions by taking a voluntary nonsuit and then begin another suit at a later date.[5]

(*c*) *Compulsory nonsuit.* After the plaintiff has presented his case the defendant may request the court to enter a non-

---
[5]Op. cit., chapter B.

suit of the plaintiff on the theory that the plaintiff's evidence, even if believed, does not entitle him to recover.[6]

(*d*) *Directed verdict.* At the end of the trial, either party may request the court to direct the jury to return a verdict in his favor. If the plaintiff could not recover even though all his evidence were believed, the court should direct the jury to return a verdict for the defendant. Similarly, the plaintiff is entitled to a verdict when, the defendant's evidence, even if believed, does not establish a defense.[7]

§ 22:7. Attacks upon the verdict.

(*a*) *Generally.* After the verdict has been returned by the jury it is still possible to attack their action either on the ground that they have acted improperly or that they should never have been allowed to act at all.

(*b*) *New trial.* After the verdict has been returned, any party dissatisfied therewith may move for a new trial. If it is clear that the jury has made a mistake or if newly-discovered, material evidence that could not have been discovered sooner is available, the court orders a new trial before a new jury.[8]

> *The facts:* The manager of a store signed the complaint on which was issued a warrant for the arrest of employees who worked in a store which was unlawfully open on Sundays. The warrant was void because it did not identify the person to be arrested. The employee who was arrested under the warrant was detained for approximately two hours by the arresting officer and the justice of the peace and was then released on the ground that the warrant was void. She sued the manager for false arrest. The jury returned a verdict in her favor for $2,000. The manager claimed a new trial on the ground that such damages were excessive.
>
> *Decision:* The amount of damages awarded by the jury was excessive. There was no evidence of any loss of wages, loss of future earning power or ability to be employed, or actual physical harm. All that the plaintiff could show was the inconvenience, embarrassment, and humiliation of being detained by the law for approximately two hours. This did not entitle her to damages of $2,000. Moreover there was no element of malicious conduct on the part of the defendant which would justify greater

---

[6]Op. cit., chapter B.
[7]Op. cit., chapter B.
[8]Op. cit., chapter B.

than compensatory damages. While the amount of damages is ordinarily within the province of the jury to determine, the court may set aside a verdict as excessive if the amount of the verdict is so large that it indicates that the jury was influenced by passion, partiality, prejudice or corruption, or entertained a mistaken view of the case. This exception is here applicable and the verdict must be set aside and a new trial ordered because of the excessiveness of the verdict. [Winters v. Campbell,] ... WVa ..., 137 SE2d 188 (1964)].

(1) Test of mistake by jury. The mere fact that you disagree with the jury or even that the judge disagrees with the jury does not mean that there is a "mistake" because of which the law will set aside the jury's verdict. If the jury's verdict could have been reached by reasonable men believing one set of the witnesses, the jury has not made a mistake. You will notice that this is the same test which was already applied in determining whether the case should be decided by the jury. If it is debatable on the facts, the case goes to the jury: if they decide either way in the debatable case, no one can say that the decision is wrong.

Now we can see the full significance of the jury's function for not only does it decide the heart of all the vital disputes but in the great bulk of cases the circumstances will be such that the jury's decision will be final.

Notice the element of hazard this introduces in litigation. But do not think that you can escape completely from this risk for when a case is tried without a jury, by a judge or by an administrator, the basic elements of uncertainty remain unchanged although there is some simplification in the sense that there is only one judge or a smaller number of administrators than there are jurors.

(c) **Judgment N.O.V.** If the verdict returned by the jury is clearly wrong as a matter of law, the court may set aside the verdict and enter a judgment contrary to the verdict. This in some states is called a judgment non obstante veredicto, or as it is abbreviated, a judgment n.o.v.

§ 22:8. Damages.

(a) **Generally.** Most lawsuits to which the hotel will be a party are actions in which the plaintiff seeks to recover money damages from the defendant. Other forms of relief may be

obtained by legal proceedings, such as an order or injunction to require the defendant to perform some act or to prevent him from performing a specified act.

When damages are sought questions arise as to how the damages are to be measured and whether punitive or exemplary damages may be imposed in addition to compensatory damages.

(b) *Compensatory damages.* The object of a lawsuit is to require the defendant to pay the plaintiff such amount of money as compensates or makes up for the harm caused by the defendant. This is not as simple a matter as it sounds for it is often a difficult matter to determine the value of what the plaintiff has lost. If he has lost or been deprived of property it is necessary to determine the value of the property at the time of the loss: not the cost of the property to the plaintiff, nor the cost of purchasing a replacement, but instead the second-hand value of the property at the time of the loss.

That is to say, if the hotel is responsible for the theft or disappearance of the guest's overcoat, the plaintiff is entitled to compensatory damages equal to the second-hand value of the coat at the time of the loss but not what the guest had paid for the coat nor what it would cost him today to buy the same coat.

(1) *Compensatory damages for personal harm.* The hotel may be liable under certain circumstances for damages caused the guest when the latter is physically injured by the act of the hotel's employee or of another guest or third person. This injury may also include mental harm as when the hotel guest has experienced pain and suffering in consequence of the physical injury, or has been put in fear or humiliated. In such cases, the question of valuation, in order to determine what damages will compensate, is made increasingly difficult because there is no mercantile standard or market value for determining the "price" of pain, suffering, or mental distress.

(c) *Punitive or exemplary damages.* In addition to the compensatory damages, which seek to compensate for the harm, the guest may in some cases recover additional damages which are imposed to punish or make an example of the hotel for the outrageous way in which it has acted. That is, if the conduct of the hotel shows personal malice or a willful disregard of the rights of the guest, such additional damages are properly allowed.

For example, if the hotel breaks into the room of a female guest in the night, and without cause evicts her from the hotel, and in the presence of others falsely declares that she is a prostitute, the guest is entitled to recover not merely compensatory damages for her mental distress but the hotel will ordinarily also be required to pay damages which are punitive or exemplary because of the outrageous character of its conduct.

§ 22:9. Judgment and costs.

(a) *Generally.* If a new trial is not granted or a judgment n.o.v. is not entered the court enters a judgment on the verdict. Generally whoever is the winning party is awarded costs. In equity actions and in some statutory proceedings, the court has discretion to allocate costs, as by awarding them to the winner, to dividing them between the parties, or having each party bear his own.[9]

(b) *What are costs.* Costs ordinarily consist of the fees charged for filing papers with the court, for having the sheriff make service or other officers take official action, the statutory fees paid to the witnesses, the jury fee, if any, and the cost of printing the record, when required on appeal. Costs do not include compensation for the time spent by the party in preparing his case or in being at the trial, the expense of going to his attorney's office or to the court, the time lost from work because of the case, or the fee paid to his attorney. In some statutory actions the recovery of a small attorney's fee is authorized. Thus, a mechanic's lien statute may authorize the recovery of an attorney's fee of 10 per cent of the amount recovered, or a 'reasonable attorney's fee.' "Costs" thus represent only a small part of the total expenses actually sustained in litigation.[10]

§ 22:10. Appeals.

(a) *Generally.* A party aggrieved by a judgment may appeal, either because he did not win or did not win enough.

The appellate court does not hear evidence. It only examines the printed or typewritten record of the proceedings before the lower court, to see if there was an error of law so bad as to require a reversal or modification. The parties' attorneys file

---

[9]Op. cit., chapter B.
[10]Op. cit., chapter B.

arguments or briefs and generally make an argument orally before the appellate court.[11]

(*b*) *Action of appellate court.* If the appellate court does not agree with the law as applied in the case, it generally sets aside or modifies the action of the lower court and enters such judgment as it decides the lower court should have entered. It may also set aside the judgment of the lower court and send the case back to hold a new trial or to enter a new judgment in accordance with the opinion of the appellate court.[12]

§ 22:11. Execution.

(*a*) *Generally.* If a losing defendant does not comply with the final judgment in the suit, the plaintiff may execute on the judgment.

If the judgment is for the payment of money, the plaintiff may direct the sheriff or other judicial officer to sell as much of the property of the defendant as is necessary to pay the plaintiff's judgment, and costs. In most states the defendant is allowed an exemption of several hundred dollars and certain items of property, as personal clothing and tools of his trade.[13]

(*b*) *Garnishment.* In most states a plaintiff may direct execution on a debt owed by a third person to his defendant or upon property of the defendant in the possession of a third person. Thus the plaintiff suing the hotel may garnish the hotel's bank account, the account being technically a debt owed by the bank to the hotel. In some states, or under some liability insurance policies which do not permit a direct action by the injured claimant against the insurer, the procedure for the claimant to follow is to obtain a judgment against the hotel and then garnish the obligation of the insurance company to the hotel.

This procedure is commonly called attachment and the third person is called a garnishee. The third person may raise any defense which the original debtor could raise if he were being sued.

(1) Availability of procedure. When garnishment is allowed prior to judgment, it is generally restricted to cases in

---
[11]Op. cit., chapter B.
[12]Op. cit., chapter B.
[13]Op. cit., chapter B.

which the original debtor is guilty of fraud or of concealing himself, or is not a resident of the state. When employed after judgment obtained by the original creditor against the original debtor, the fact that the judgment has been obtained in itself entitles the original creditor to garnish without proof of fraud or any other particular circumstances.

In some states, the procedure of garnishment does not exist as a distinct procedure but is made part of a judgment execution procedure.[14]

(2) Defenses of garnishee. In post-judgment garnishment, the garnishee may raise defenses which he has against the original debtor.[15]

---

[14]Op. cit., chapter B.
[15]Op. cit., chapter B.

Chapter 23. HOW TO BE A GOOD CLIENT

§ 23:1. How you can help.
  (a) Generally.
  (b) Scope of this chapter.

§ 23:2. Regulations to protect from litigation.
  (a) Generally.
  (b) Avoidance of litigation.
  (c) Establishing the basis for decision.

§ 23:3. Inspection witnesses.
  (a) Generally.
  (b) Selecting the best witness.
    (1) Insurance adjuster and outsiders as witnesses.
    (2) High-ranking hotel employee.
    (3) Non-litigation object of inspection.
  (c) Inspection of premises.
  (d) Inspection of property damage.
  (e) Inspection of injury of claimant.
    (1) Limitations.
  (f) Entry into rooms without permission.
    (1) Entry to prevent crime.
    (2) Entry because of sickness or condition of patron.
  (g) Eviction and removal.
    (1) Removal of property.

§ 23:4. Reports.
  (a) Generally.
  (b) Utility of reports and records.
    (1) A written memory.
    (2) Missing witness.
  (c) Danger of report making.
    (1) Wrong basis for defense.
    (2) Impeaching and contradiction of witnesses.
  (d) Supervision of report making.
    (1) Integrity.
    (2) Communication.
  (e) Time of making report.
  (f) What a good report should contain.
  (g) Areas for reporting.
    (1) Employment.

            (2) Routine examination of premises.
            (3) Liability claim inspection.
            (4) Entry into rooms.
            (5) Eviction.
§ 23:5.   Names, addresses, and telephone numbers.
            (a) Generally.
            (b) Change of address.
            (c) Telephone numbers.
§ 23:6.   Preservation of condition and things.
            (a) Generally.
            (b) The premises in question.
            (c) The movable property in question.
            (d) Photographs.
§ 23:7.   Notice and forwarding papers.
            (a) Notice to your attorney.
            (b) Notice to your insurer.
            (c) Form of notice.
            (d) Identity of person receiving telephone notice.
§ 23:8.   Unemotional evaluation of claims.
            (a) Generally.
            (b) Reasons for distorted claims.
                (1) False claims.
                (2) False cause of harm.
                (3) False extent of harm.
            (c) The hotel's open mind.
§ 23:9.   Free speech may be expensive.
            (a) Generally.
            (b) Unnecessary provocation.
            (c) Discrimination charges.
§ 23:10. Do not expect an easy answer all the time.
            (a) Generally.
            (b) Society's desire for flexibility.
            (c) The jury question as the answer.

§ 23:1. How you can help.

(*a*) *Generally.* I suppose we all agree that a person should go see his doctor before he is so sick that it becomes difficult if not impossible for the doctor to make him well. I suppose we also agree that the person should make a mental or written note of his significant symptoms so that he can give his doctor a more accurate basis on which to diagnose the case. There should likewise be hardly any dispute that after having seen the doctor, the sick person should follow his instructions.

The general aspects of the matter are much the same when instead of patient and doctor we have client and attorney, and to make the matter have even a more direct message, when we have a hotel and its attorney. Otherwise stated, there is much that the hotel can do to increase or decrease the amount of litigation in which it will be involved. Likewise, there is much that the hotel can do to make the case against it more difficult to defend.

(*b*) *Scope of this chapter.* It is the purpose of this chapter to gather together some of the practical aspects of being a client or a potential client which should reduce the amount of litigation which you have and also assist your attorney in defending you better when you are sued. As in the case of all general rules of human conduct, the suggestions made herein are generalities and are hence subject to exceptions and qualifications. Nevertheless, they should prove helpful as a point of beginning, to be contracted or expanded in the light of what is practical for your particular hotel, and by what your personal experience and your attorney suggest.

§ 23:2. Regulations to protect from litigation.

(*a*) *Generally.* The hotel has the power to adopt reasonable and proper rules to govern its operations. Assuming that the rules are reasonable and proper notice has been given of them, they are binding upon all patrons, even with respect to guests whom the hotel is required to receive without discrimination.

(*b*) *Avoidance of litigation.* The existence of a regulation on a particular subject may have the psychological effect of persuading persons not to sue the hotel. People are in general law-abiding and rule-obeying. If there is a regulation in existence, of which the patron of the hotel is given due notice, the average patron is likely to feel that he must obey it and is bound by the regulation. While he might try to cut corners or cheat on the regulation when nobody is watching, he does not feel that he can ignore the regulation to the extent of suing the hotel as though the regulation never existed. Hence if the hotel stands on its regulations, the patron will probably feel that he is getting all that he is entitled to and that he has no legal rights against the hotel.

(*c*) ***Establishing the basis for decision.*** In most areas of free enterprise, the parties may by their agreement fix their relative rights and duties. When this is so, the parties may either make an express agreement; or the one party may adopt regulations, which then become binding on the other party when the latter has knowledge or notice of such regulation and does business with the first party, — his assent to doing business having the effect of agreeing to abide by the terms on which the other party through his regulations has announced that he will do business. Hence in many instances, the principle which the court will apply in determining the rights of the parties may be regulations adopted by one of them and assented to or acquiesced in by the other. This is equally true with lawsuits against hotels.

Hence the rights of the hotel with respect to many of the difficult and uncertain matters within your state may be solved, to the extent that the foregoing is true, by the simple device of adopting rules on the subject in question.

§ 23:3. Inspection witnesses.

(*a*) ***Generally.*** Many situations can arise in which a lawsuit will depend upon the word of your employee or officer against the word of the claimant or plaintiff. There may not have been any witnesses, or if there were; at the later date when you need them, such witnesses cannot be located.

It is thus a sound precaution for your employee or officer to handle trouble situations in pairs or as a team. Thus it becomes the word of two employees against the one claimant. Now of course, the law does not weigh the testimony of witnesses by bulk and say that two witnesses weigh greater than one witness and therefore the hotel employees are telling the truth. Nevertheless, there is the greater chance that with your two employees present you will be the better able to find out just what did happen because you have the statements of two people on which to base your conclusions. Moreover, there is an undoubted human factor operating that the jury will tend to believe the side with the greater number of witnesses, in spite of the fact that the judge tells them that they should not do so. This is particularly likely to be true when the extra witness is a physician who has his professional integrity as well as his personal integrity to uphold, as considered later in this section.

(*b*) **Selecting the best witness.** When the hotel selects a person to be an additional observer, it is obviously desirable to select the highest ranking employee on the premises at that time who is the best qualified to speak in the area involved, assuming that the matter is one which could give rise to serious litigation. For example, if the question is observing the physical injury of the guest, it is clear that the house physician or any physician should be selected when possible, whereas if an inspection of the physical condition of the premises is involved, a high employee in the maintenance or repair department would ordinarily be the better choice.

No simple rule can be laid down in advance because of the wide variation between the size and nature of the hotel operations as between different hotels, and the differences between the duties and backgrounds of different employees in different hotels, although each may have the same job classification or official title. The thing to remember is that a jury (a) is going to be more impressed by the testimony of a witness with particular training in the field involved than an ordinary witness and that (b) the higher the rank of the employee within the hotel the more they are likely to believe his testimony. Like all generalities, it must be recognized that this is not always so, but since all we can do at this point is to make the best guess possible as a guide for the future it is preferable to think in terms of the above suggestions.

(1) Insurance adjuster and outsiders as witnesses. In many instances you will not have anyone in your employment who is particularly qualified to speak as an expert with respect to the matter involved. In such case, the answer is to call in the outsider, such as a neighboring physician, who is qualified to make the examination of the matter which is called for. When the matter comes within the scope of your insurance coverage, the problem may often be solved by notifying the insurer immediately and having the insurer send an adjuster. Even when you are not covered with respect to the claim by insurance, it may still be advantageous to call in at your own expense a professional claim adjuster.

The calling in of an outsider also has the advantage of creating a neutral or impartial witness. There is always the danger that the jury will not be convinced or will doubt witnesses who are your own employees, because the jury may feel that your own employees will testify in your favor merely to save their jobs. This suspicion of bias is generally eliminated or at least reduced when outsiders testify on your behalf.

There is the danger, however, of delay when outsiders are called in. It may be that the conditions to be observed cannot be preserved in their exact present condition for a sufficiently long time to enable an outsider to come to the hotel and observe. If the circumstances appear to warrant it, a desirable combination would be to have both your employee make his observation "at once" and then have an outsider make his observation as soon as possible. Your employee should make a re-examination at the time when the outsider conducts his, in order to tell the outsider whether there has been any change of the condition being examined, and if so, its extent and nature.

(2) High-ranking hotel employee. Whenever possible, the hotel should have as one of its witnesses a high-ranking employee. He will ordinarily be more intelligent and more perceptive, and will create a greater impression of integrity upon the jury. There is of course the danger the jury may feel that, however honest he may be, the high-ranking employee is not the man who has actual daily contact with the subject matter and therefore does not really know what this particular matter is about. It is for this reason that where the matter is outside of the daily experience of the high-ranking employee, the hotel should also make use of such an employee as does have daily contact or dealing with the matter in question.

There is another psychological advantage in having a high-ranking employee as a witness. The case may be a borderline case in which the patron is not going to sue the hotel if the patron feels that the hotel has been reasonable about the matter. If you send a lower classification employee to the patron, the patron may feel slighted that you have sent just the "office boy." Moreover, there is the very real hazard that the lower classification employee does not have the experience and the understanding to handle the situation as adroitly as the higher-ranking employee, and in many cases does not have any real interest in so doing. Hence the sending of the lower ranking employee may get everything off on the wrong foot and in itself tip the scales and make the patron feel so hurt or insulted that the patron brings suit.

This feeling of hurt and insult on the part of the patron will be the greater as the act of the hotel invades the patron's privacy. You can readily see how the patron may be humiliated by the fact that it is a minor employee entering the patron's rooms instead of a high-ranking employee. This feeling of the patron is probably influenced by the belief, whether warranted or not, that the high-ranking employee is not going to talk about the incident, whereas within a few hours everyone in the hotel will have heard the story from the ordinary employee. If the incident is one which has any potential for embarrassment this feeling that the guest is now branded within the hotel increases the humiliation and anger of the patron and again may be just what is needed to make the patron bring suit against the hotel.

(3) Non-litigation object of inspection. Because this chapter is directed to the problem of being a better client, inspection has been here discussed only in terms of preparing for a lawsuit. It is of course to the advantage of the hotel to have a "good" inspection made of any matter in order for the management of the hotel to know just what is going on and in order to determine whether any corrective measures should be taken; either with respect to the past conduct of employees or to prevent future repetitions of the difficulty.

(c) **Inspection of premises.** If any claim is made that injury has been sustained because of the condition of the premises, immediate investigation should be made of both the injured person and the part of the premises in question. With respect to the premises, the highest employee of the department which has charge of the area involved should make the inspection when reasonably possible. If this employee does not have actual daily contact with the area involved, the inspection should be made jointly with the employee who does.

The strategy underlying this suggestion is to have either one or two employees who will be able to testify that from personal experience he knew the area, such as the stairway on which the patron fell; that he had seen this area every day or other reasonably short period of time; that it was or was not in the same condition in which it was when he had seen it the last time before the injury; the condition in which it was at the time of the injury; and if either of these witnesses is called to speak as an expert witness, whether such practice as was followed by the hotel was a proper practice in the industry, and so on.

(d) **Inspection of property damage.** When the claim is made that property of the patron has been damaged, the hotel should have someone examine the damage who has familiarity with property of the same kind, if such is possible. For ex-

ample, if damage is done to fabrics or clothing, it is probable that a woman employee of the hotel will be a better witness than the ordinary male employee who would not know what the materials were and could not very well describe what he saw. Of course, even the woman employee may not be a fit witness where the property is so valuable or unusual as to require an expert opinion.

In contrast, if the guest's automobile is damaged, the hotel's auto mechanic should be the witness. If the hotel does not have such a person of sufficient experience, an outside mechanic or an insurance adjuster should be called. In many cases, the amounts involved will not be so great and you will be content to leave the matter up to the insurance adjusters; although this should not be done unless the conditions to be inspected are of such a nature that the delay in bringing in the adjuster will not cause any change and the premises will be in exactly the same condition when the adjuster sees them as when you could examine them today.

(e) *Inspection of injury of claimant.* Here the inspection witness should of course be a physician whenever possible. If not, the next best thing is to take the employee with the longest experience from among such of the higher-ranking employees who is on the premises at the time. Sometimes you may have little or no choice because at the particular time there is no one on the premises with any particular experience. In such case, a physician from the neighborhood or a nearby hospital should be sought. If no better witness is available, a traffic policeman or a state trooper may be a good witness although his experience is limited to a particular kind of injury.

In any case, where outsiders are called in, do not rely on them alone, but have your own employee or employees observe the claimant's condition as soon as possible and also at the time when the outsider arrives in order to inform the latter what changes have taken place.

(1) Limitations. It must be remembered that these statements are very general suggestions and that in the given case they may have no practical value because the injury of the claimant is internal and therefore not observable to the untrained witness, or observation may require a personal examination of the claimant which would not be proper or allowable in the absence of consent by the claimant or except by a physician. Nevertheless, there may be something to observe in any

case, and every bit of information helps defend the case against you.

(f) Entry into rooms without permission. Whenever the hotel makes an entry into the rooms of a guest or tenant or enters the room of any patron while the patron, or members of his family, or his guests, are present therein, the entry should be made or accompanied by a high-ranking employee, together with either a physician or a police officer depending upon the reason for making the entry.

(1) Entry to prevent crime. If the entry is made because the hotel believes that a crime is being committed against its patron or is being committed by the patron, the employee entering the hotel room should be accompanied by a police officer, whether a house detective or other employee sworn as a peace officer, or a regular member of the local police force, or a state trooper, or county peace officer.

This is desirable not only because it provides the additional witness but also because it confirms the hotel's statement of why it made the entry. The ordinary jury is going to feel that if the hotel made the entry for any improper reason it would not have brought a cop along. Since it did bring an officer, it obviously believed that something was going on which required a police officer. Since in certain situations the hotel has no right to enter the guest's room except when a crime is being committed, or some other privilege-creating circumstance exists, it is obviously important to make the jury believe that the entry was made in good faith, in a reasonable manner, and for a purpose recognized as proper.

(2) Entry because of sickness or condition of patron. If the hotel enters the patron's rooms because it believes that there is an emergency which requires medical care or the taking of the patron to a hospital, the employee making the entry should of course be accompanied by a person with medical knowledge, such as a physician, when the circumstances so permit. If the entry is made without a physician, the action of the hotel may be viewed with suspicion unless it is clear that there was no opportunity to secure a physician first.

For example, the hotel may learn that the smell of gas is seeping out under the door of a housekeeping apartment. Under such circumstances the delay to find a physician could very well prove fatal and consequently the hotel is justified in entering the patron's rooms without the presence of a physician. While the absence of a physician presents a hazard to the hotel, the cases in which this situation would arise are generally so clearly loaded with danger to the patron that the medical observer is not essential at the time of entry. For example, if other employees testify that the entire area smelled of gas, the jury is hardly likely to find that the hotel was not acting properly when it entered the rooms from whence the smell of gas came. Moreover, there is generally corroborating evidence in these emergency cases because undoubtedly the hotel has summoned the local hospital, or police patrol car, or fire house, or gas company, and so forth. The jury will necessarily be impressed by the fact that such outsiders were called for a gas emergency condition and will accept such fact as clinching the point as to why the hotel entered the patron's room.

(g) *Eviction and removal.* In the case of evicting the patron from the premises, it is always desirable that the ordinary employee be accompanied by a high-ranking employee, and where eviction is predicated upon criminal conduct, by the house detective or other police officer.

This is of course desirable when eviction is only proper if cause be shown. But the presence of such witnesses is also desirable in any case, because although the hotel in the given situation has the right to terminate the patron's occupancy, the right to do so is always qualified by the requirement that the hotel act in a manner which is reasonable, and even when it is necessary to use force to effect the eviction, it is still necessary for the hotel to use only such force as is reasonably necessary. Hence it is important that the hotel have good witnesses to testify both to the cause for the eviction and the manner in which it was conducted.

(1) Removal of property. If the patron is evicted or removed to a hospital, the hotel must take care of the property of the patron. If the removal is only for a temporary purpose and is not intended to terminate the hotel-patron relationship, as when the patron is taken to the hospital, the property of the patron will frequently not be removed. Here the testimony of a high-ranking employee that nothing was removed is of course of great value if a claim is later made by the patron that certain articles are missing.

If the eviction or removal of the patron results in a termination of the relationship to the hotel, there is ordinarily a removal of the patron's property and belongings from the rooms. In this case, an inventory of the goods should be made, and should be supervised by a high-ranking employee.

§ 23:4. Reports.

(a) *Generally.* At various stages or phases of hotel operations, examinations or investigations will be made, either as a matter of routine, or because some unusual event has occurred. For example, there will be the regular, periodic examination of the condition of the premises, the more or less irregular and intermittent examination of applicants for jobs, and the very irregular inspections made in connection with someone being hurt on the premises.

Whatever the nature of the occasion or its frequency, the hotel should make a written report which it should preserve in its files, and depending upon the nature of the matter involved should send a copy to its attorney and to its insurer.

(b) *Utility of reports and records.* The making of a record or a report means just so much more paper work, just so much more filing, and so on. Nevertheless this added labor is well worth the effort and is indeed essential when litigation or controversy arises thereafter.

(1) A written memory. If a report is not made the hotel will be trusting to the mere memory of man to recall at a later date just what had happened. The risk involved here is apparent for few persons, if any, have a perfect, photographic memory that will retain all details accurately and indefinitely.

It is of course true that many times some occurrence will stamp itself in your memory because of its dramatic or terrifying nature so that it is likely that you will remember much of the transaction for a long time. But details will be forgotten and your half-recollection may be very misleading. Moreover many controversies arise out of transactions which at the time appeared routine so that there was no reason for you to remember what happened. For example, you rejected an applicant because the applicant just did not seem right for the job and it is not until some time later that the claim is made that you were guilty of improper discrimination in refusing to employ that applicant. Can you remember now just why you had rejected the applicant? Can you remember in a way which will convince the law that you acted on the basis of a sound judgment and not a

How to be a Good Client

prejudice? Or by way of further illustration, a person bites on a piece of glass while eating at your restaurant. No harm is apparently done and you have forgotten all about the matter until some time later when you find a large damage claim being asserted against you for harm and mental distress sustained by the patron. Do you know today what happened back then?

The making of the report substitutes a permanent writing for a fleeting memory. Moreover, it eliminates the task of trying to guess what is an important transaction which should be remembered. If you keep a report on every transaction, there is no question of selecting those which will give rise to litigation, because regardless of what transaction does give rise to litigation, you have your report.

The report can serve a double function as an aid to memory. When your attorney is preparing the case for you, the report will enable him to check the memory of your witnesses and the witnesses will be able to check against the report as to just what happened. Likewise at the trial itself, if your witness has forgotten what happened, he will be permitted in most cases to look at the report, in order to refresh his memory.

(2) Missing witness. In many instances, by the time the lawsuit against you comes to trial the transient persons who were your witnesses have long since gone, and even employees may no longer be with you. It is possible that you might not have any witnesses to produce at the trial. Your attorney already will have safeguarded against this as far as he was able to do so by the taking of the testimony of witnesses by deposition as soon as he learned that there was a transaction which might give rise to a claim against you.

You can strengthen your position at the trial by maintaining regular reports. For if you have a regular system of making reports, the very fact that the reports were made in a regular systematic way vouches for the accuracy of any one report. Hence in many states, such reports will be admissible in evidence as business records, even though the person who prepared the report is not available and even though it cannot be determined who such person actually was.

(c) Danger of report making. Great care must be exercised in making a report, because you can harm your position greatly by a report which does not accurately set forth the facts as they actually existed.

(1) Wrong basis for defense. The written report tends to be the basis around which the hotel's case will be built. When you discuss the matter with your attorney or he discusses the matter with your witnesses, it is easy to understand that in case of any misunderstanding or ambiguity in the statements of witnesses, reference will be made to the report to get the facts straight. If the facts in the report are actually not "straight," it is apparent that the entire case of the hotel may be built on a wrong premise and the hotel in effect walks into a trap which has been created by itself. If the hotel did not prepare for the facts as they actually existed but instead prepared for the facts that is assumed to exist on the basis of the erroneous report, it may find itself unable to meet the actual facts, shown by the plaintiff, upon such short notice.

This danger may be lessened or avoided by the taking of depositions of the plaintiff and his witnesses in advance of the trial, since any conflict between the plaintiff's version of the facts and the report would at once become apparent.

(2) Impeaching and contradiction of witnesses. Under one theory or another, the adverse party can require the production of routine inspection reports. If at the trial the witness for the hotel who prepared the report says anything which is inconsistent with the statements in his report, the plaintiff may use the report to contradict the witness on the theory that he cannot be telling the truth today because the report made for the hotel shortly after the occurrence said something else. This can at least cast doubt on the merits of the hotel's case, unless the discrepancy can be reasonably explained; and may in fact cause so much doubt that the jury concludes that the witness for the hotel is not telling the truth, and consequently may decide the case against the hotel.

In the situation above considered, the report was used to show that the witness who made the report was not telling the truth at the trial and was therefore a person who was a liar who should not be believed at the trial. In contrast with this use of the report, which is confined to the person who made it, the report once admitted in evidence can contradict the testimony of any witness or witnesses by providing a different version of the facts which the jury may choose to believe in preference to the version narrated by such other witness or witnesses at the trial.

(*d*) **Supervision of report making.** In view of the importance of reports, they should be made correctly or not made at all. To make them correct, a comparatively high-ranking employee of the hotel should examine carefully each report filed and if necessary, discuss with the employee just what he meant to say in order to verify that the report as submitted does state what the employee intended. This of course means just that much more office work for someone in the hotel system when they should be busy running the hotel. But again the answer is that there are so many potential frauds facing the hotel that defensive measures must be taken in all directions.

(*1*) *Integrity.* The hotel employee in charge of reviewing reports must be particularly careful to detect any conscious or unconscious whitewashing of the situation in order to make it appear that the person making the report was not at fault. Thus, the reviewing employee must check carefully to see that the reporting employee is really telling the truth and the whole truth. This is not an easy task for the reporting employee may be subconsciously distorting the facts to show that he is not at fault, without realizing that he is doing so. It is human nature for us to seek the loop-hole and to reach the conclusion that really we were not at fault. For example, there is a natural reluctance on the part of the maintenance employee to admit that he improperly left a scum of soap on the marble floor. If he admits it, there will be a tendency to reduce the size of the spot so that it would not constitute a menace to navigation and the report will make it appear that the patron was guilty of contributory negligence for not walking around it. And this employee who is thoroughly familiar with the area and the lighting will probably not see why the patron, who was a stranger in the place, did not perceive that the floor was wet, and inevitably his reporting is colored by the fact that he thinks the whole matter was the plaintiff's fault.

The employee reviewing the reports must get to the truth as it will appear to jurors who are also strangers to the premises, and he must take great care in eliminating personal opinions of the reporting employee or the distortions which he makes; again, even in the best of good faith.

The reviewing employee has an unpleasant task in this respect because he must at the same time be careful to avoid making the employee feel that he thinks the latter is a liar. The hotel must continue in business and the reporting employee and the reviewing employee must still work together. The latter's effort to get to the truth must therefore not destroy such harmony as existed between these two employees prior to the reviewing of the report.

In most instances this difficult situation can be handled by the reviewing employee by saying to the reporting employee: "That is a good report which you have made, but we should go into a few of the details a little more fully. Now you have seen trials in the movies and on television, and you know how the opposing attorney does his best to batter and tear down the witnesses. Let's just go all through this report and see if an opposing attorney could tear it down in any way. Remember I believe you because I know you. But a jury never saw you before and will not know you. Therefore we must be sure that what you say cannot be twisted to mean something else and that the jury will also believe you." After this type of introduction the reporting employee will ordinarily feel that he and the reviewing employee are fighting on the same team and will not develop any antagonism when the reviewing employee turns the report inside out to find its errors and flaws.

(2) Communication. Having established in his mind what the facts of the case really are, the next problem of the reviewing employee is to determine that the report as filed actually says what happened. This is merely a matter of words, of the proper vocabulary, of communication. But here both the reporting employee and the reviewing employee may unconsciously fail to say in words exactly what they have in their minds. The fact that they are thoroughly familiar with their own hotel may tend to lead them into this trap. The reviewing employee must therefore read slowly and think carefully to see that the words and events check with each other.

(e) Time of making report. A report should be made at the time the reported events occur or as soon thereafter as possible. If too much time intervenes, the making of the report may fail of its purpose because the persons making the report have already forgotten or have begun to forget some of the details. Moreover, if not made at the same time or very close after the time of the transaction the report may not be admissible as evidence at the trial nor used by a witness to refresh his memory as to the past.

In many cases, it is obvious that events will occur so fast that there is not time for making reports until everything is all over.

In other cases, notes may be made as the events take place on the basis of which the report itself is thereafter made.

(*f*) **What a good report should contain.** The standard is easy to state: a good report should set forth every important fact in the case and every important fact relating to proving the case and locating witnesses. The application of this standard to a given case may cause some difficulty. As the starting point, it is necessarily recognized that a report cannot set forth every word that was said and everything that was seen. Necessarily the report is a boiling down or condensation of all this. It also requires the weeding out of some matters which will not be important. This opens the way to error as discussed in subsection (d) above. It is highly desirable that you discuss these matters with your attorney in advance of any trouble so that you have a pattern of questions or report forms ready when the trouble comes.

With respect to the physical form of the report, the hotel should devise such forms of report as best suits its needs. A few mechanical details should be observed: the report should be dated, in order to show that its execution was at the same time or contemporaneous with the events in question. The report should also be initialed or signed by any party taking part in the making of the report and should indicate the capacity in which a person acted. Somewhere on the report should appear the typed or printed names of all persons signing the report and their addresses and phone numbers. This is for the convenience of the hotel in identifying the signer and in making contact with him.

(*g*) **Areas for reporting.** It is desirable to discuss with your attorney what areas should be covered by reports in your hotel, for what may be beneficial, or even essential, to one type of hotel operation might be merely an unnecessary burden to another. For example, if the hotel has only a small employee staff, the reports suggested below may not be worth the keeping. Whereas, if the hotel has a substantially large or a large employee staff, such reporting systems are highly desirable.

(1) Employment. Reports should be carefully kept as to employees and applicants for employment with respect to such matters as show that the decision of the hotel was based upon the merits of the given case rather than upon prejudice against

union membership, or the absence of such membership, or prejudice against race, color, creed, sex, or national origin.[1]

As the hotel may be liable to a third person harmed by its employees, either on the theory of vicarious or supervisory liability,[2] it is important that the report on the hiring or job assignments show that the hotel acted with the prudence of a reasonable man in employing the given employee. Furthermore, with respect to the supervisory liability of a hotel, there should be reports to show a continuing supervision of employees after they had been hired initially.

(2) Routine examination of premises. As the hotel is under the duty to make its premises, furniture, fixtures, and so on, reasonably safe, or to warn patrons of danger, the hotel must necessarily make periodic inspection of its premises.

In order to make sure that all things are checked each time and to make sure that there is an adequate check, a check list of the entire hotel should be made, showing just what is to be inspected, and if necessary how the inspection is to be done. Separate check lists may be made for items on different time schedules. For example, the lobby floor must be inspected daily whereas the hotel sign on the roof, depending upon its construction, probably needs only to be inspected every six months.

The making of such check lists greatly simplifies the making of inspection reports because the inspecting employee can merely check off on the list each item as he covers it. Such lists also save the hotel some training worries in that a new employee can be easily informed of what checking must be done by handing him the check list report form.

The foregoing suggestions must of course be read in the light of your experience, the nature of the operations of your hotel, and the advice of your attorney. There is no necessity for you to spend all day making reports and the extent of your inspections and their nature will obviously vary with the nature of the hotel plant, its size, and the nature of your operations, and even the time of the year and weather conditions. The important thing is that you maintain such inspection of your premises as satisfies your legal obligation to make reasonable inspection to keep the

---

[1] See Chapter 20.
[2] See Chapters 5, 6.

premises in a reasonably safe condition for your patrons. All that is here suggested is that you make such reporting as shows that you have done just this and what it is that you have done.

(3) Liability claim inspection. Apart from the regular inspection that the hotel will make of its premises, are the inspections and reports which should be made when some claim is asserted against it because of harm caused by a condition of the premises, food or drink sold in the hotel restaurant, the operation of the hotel automobile, and so on.

Here the report should set forth all the facts which contributed to the occurrence of the harm, as well as these can be determined; the investigation or inspection should be conducted by the persons as suggested in § 23:2; and evidence should be preserved and photographs taken as described in § 23:6.

(4) Entry into rooms. Whenever an entry is made into the rooms of a patron without the patron's permission, a report should be made of that fact; the report being made by the person suggested in § 23:2, and setting forth the material facts which show that the entry was proper and not an unlawful invasion of privacy.

If the entry was made into the patron's rooms because of the belief that a crime was committed therein, the report should be initialled or signed in some way by the hotel detective or any police officer who was actually present. If the entry was made because of the condition of the patron and a physician was present, he should furnish a signed statement as to the condition of the patron which statement should be attached to the report.

(5) Eviction. Whenever a patron is evicted, a report should be made of the circumstances and justification for such action. The object is to enable the hotel to be able to defend against false claims that the eviction was discrimination because of race, color, creed, sex, or national origin; or that it was in violation of the obligation of the hotel with respect to this particular patron.[3]

This should be done even when the hotel has the right to terminate the relationship at will; because it could still be claimed that such termination at will was inspired by a purpose to discriminate against the patron.

---

[3] See Chapter 3.

§ 23:5. Names, addresses, and telephone numbers.

(a) *Generally.* At various times it is important to know the names, addresses, and phone numbers of persons who were directly involved in transactions that have since gone into litigation. This becomes an acute problem where the persons in question were transients or licensees only temporarily in the hotel building. Even in the case of employees who are more or less permanent, there are often such delays in litigation that you cannot be sure that they will still be available at the future date when you need them.

Consequently, it is advisable whenever the name of any person is obtained to also print or type his name so that there is no question as to the spelling of the name thereafter; to obtain his address, and any proposed forwarding address; and to obtain any phone number which he may have.

(b) *Change of address.* Persons who are potential witnesses on your behalf might move away or employees leave or go to another city. In order to protect yourself, keep a record of the addresses of your witnesses as up-to-date as possible. In many instances, the witnesses will not be difficult to locate because they have merely moved to another place in the same city and by the time you need them the new telephone book is available showing their new addresses. In many cases, however, you can imagine that the witness has departed and since you do not know to what city he has gone it is impossible to look for him if you do not have the necessary information already.

To some extent, your attorney will have guarded against this difficulty, assuming that you have given him timely notice, by taking the testimony of the potential witnesses before they have gone away. But even if this has been done, you should still assist your attorney by keeping a record of new addresses and phone numbers of the potential witnesses, whenever such information comes into your possession.

(c) *Telephone numbers.* Whenever possible, make a note of the telephone number of any potential witness and of any change of number which comes to the attention of the hotel. In some instances it will be easier to contact a witness by a phone than it will be seeking to find the new address to which he has moved. Often the phone number, or the changed phone number that the telephone operator will give, provides the hotel with the means of finding out the whereabouts of the witness.

§ 23:6. Preservation of condition and things.

(*a*) ***Generally.*** Independently of whether there were witnesses who saw what happened, it is a great advantage to your attorney and your insurer, and to the various experts that they may bring, to see the premises and the things involved in exactly the same condition as that in which they were at the time the harm was sustained by the plaintiff.

When harm is caused someone, the hotel should therefore not only give prompt notice to its attorney and its insurer, but should do its best to freeze things as they are until after such other persons have examined the place. The preservation of conditions and things relate generally to (1) keeping the premises exactly as they were when the plaintiff was injured; (2) keeping and separately preserving the harm-causing substance or thing; and (3) photographing the area or premises, particularly where it is clear that a change will take place and that such changes cannot be stopped or where the area is such that it cannot be described adequately by words and of course cannot be brought into the court room physically.

(*b*) ***The premises in question.*** When the patron or other claimant sustains injury because of the condition of the premises, the part involved should be roped off and left exactly as it is until your attorney and your insurance company have examined the area, made photographs and tests, and so on.

There are of course various factors which would make it impossible or highly undesirable to follow this rule. For example, some conditions will naturally change by themselves. If the patron has fallen on snow or ice on the sidewalk or on a wet spot on a tile or marble floor, it is obvious that the melting of the snow or ice, or the natural drying of the spot on the floor is going to "destroy" the evidence. In such case all that the hotel can do is to observe the condition and set forth that information in the report considered under § 23:4, and if the condition would be revealed by a photograph, to take photographs of the area.

The plan of roping off and keeping the premises unchanged also becomes impossible where either the patrons and the public must use the area or it would be highly inconvenient for them to use an alternate route. It may be that the hotel will have no choice other than to make repairs as soon as possible and not seek to preserve the premises in their original condition. In such case, it may be desirable to have the head repairman make a signed statement as to the conditions which he found.

(c) *The movable property in question.* When the patron sustains injury because of personal or movable property, the hotel will probably be in a position where it can put the property in storage awaiting further examination by its attorney and the insurer. For example, if a chair breaks, the hotel can hold the chair in storage awaiting the turn of events.

In the case of a patron in the restaurant being made ill apparently from food eaten in the restaurant, the hotel should seek to isolate the particular food which caused the harm, assuming that it is identified while the balance of the food in question is still in the restaurant kitchen. If it came from a can or jar, the hotel should try to locate and isolate the can or jar. If the foodstuff in question is perishable, the hotel should communicate with its attorney at once so that arrangements can be made to send the foodstuff out for chemical analysis.

(d) *Photographs.* If there is any reason to believe that the hotel will not be able to keep everything just as it was at the time the patron was harmed, and if the hotel is not able to contact its attorney, the hotel should phone a photographer to come and take photographs of the area or thing. It is best if the hotel's attorney makes arrangements for this because much depends upon the manner of taking the photograph. Much depends upon the height of the camera, the angle of the shot, and so on, and the impression that the photograph gives can greatly affect the hotel's case. Accordingly, the hotel attorney should check with the photographer or hire the photographer in order to make certain that the photographs will be taken properly. Nevertheless, if the hotel cannot reach its attorney, it should hire a photographer who has had actual experience in photography for the preservation of evidence, if possible. After the photographs are made they should each be signed or initialled and dated and the subject matter identified in order to avoid any uncertainty as to the identity of the photographs when they are used in preparing the case or if they are offered in evidence at the trial.

§ 23:7. Notice and forwarding papers.

(a) *Notice to your attorney.* Give your attorney notice of every event which may give rise to any claim against you. You should not attempt to judge whether it is a good claim or a bad claim. Nor should you try to prophesy whether a claim will grow out of an incident which has occurred. In many cases, the prompt notice to your attorney becomes doubly important because it may be that the only witnesses that you have in your favor are transient guests who may be leaving the city and the state within a very short time. If you delay before notifying your attorney, or never notify him at all, it becomes difficult, and sometimes impossible, for him to locate these witnesses even for the purpose of taking their depositions to use at the trial.

The requirement of giving notice to your attorney is not based on any legal obligation in the sense that you are breaking a contract or law if you fail to notify him. It is merely a matter of common sense that since you are retaining the attorney you should do your best to help him bring about the result which you desire.

When any papers are received, such as letters and notices sent to the hotel, or legal process and pleadings served on you or sent to the hotel in connection with a lawsuit, the hotel should promptly forward such papers to the attorney.

(*b*) *Notice to your insurer.* Under your liability policy, notice together with the subsequent furnishing of proofs of loss, is generally mandatory in the sense that the hotel cannot recover on its policy if notice of loss is not given to the insurer within a time specified and proofs of loss are not furnished to the insurer thereafter within the period of time likewise specified by the policy. It is a question for the hotel to determine, whether such notice and proof should be attended to by its attorney or should be taken care of by the hotel.

The typical liability policy will also require the insured hotel to forward all process and papers served upon it, and to cooperate in the defense of any action. The hotel must perform according to these terms and if it fails to do so, its insurer is not bound by the terms of the hotel's policy.

(*c*) *Form of notice.* In addition to the hotel's attorney and insurer, the hotel may be required to give notice to other persons such as the supplier from whom it has purchased goods, food, and so on, notifying that there has been a breach of warranty; to tenants in the hotel, who are being notified that the lease is being terminated by the hotel; and to other persons with whom the hotel has business dealings. In order to preserve a permanent record of the notice given, as well as that of satisfying statutory or policy requirements in others, the hotel should always give a written notice which expressly states just what the notice is about and why it is being given. In some instances, it will be necessary to proceed more quickly than by mail. In such case a telephone notice is proper, but in order to provide a record of having given the notice, and to satisfy any requirements which may make a writing necessary, the hotel should promptly send a confirming letter, stating that it is confirming the notice which has been given over the telephone, and then repeat just what had been stated.

(d) *Identity of person receiving telephone notice.* Whenever notice is given to a person by telephone, the hotel should ask for that person's name and title. This information should then be placed in the report or file on the matter so that at a later date if the giving of notice is disputed the hotel can pinpoint the person receiving the notice by telephone. In addition, the hotel will have sent a confirming letter, and will be able to produce the carbon copy to support the testimony of the giving of oral notice by phone.

§ 23:8. Unemotional evaluation of claims.

(a) *Generally.* It is only human nature for a defendant to be prejudiced in his attitude against a person making a claim against him, and against the claim so made. Thus it is a natural reaction to believe that a given claim is false because the thing alleged just could not happen in your first-class hotel. The difficulty is that such things often can and do happen, for the simple reason that the frailties of man and the mathematical probabilities are almost always in favor of the breakdown of the most elaborate set of precautions at some time or other.

A blind and stubborn attitude that "it can't happen here" can lead into needless and expensive litigation which could have been avoided by a recognition that it could happen and did happen, that someone was tired, that someone forgot, that someone goofed; and the harm was done. It is therefore of prime importance that the hotel act unemotionally and scientifically in seeking to learn the truth when inquiring of its employees with respect to the incident and in dealing with its attorney.

(b) *Reasons for distorted claims.* Out of a given number of claims made against you as a hotel a substantial number will be distorted in some respect.

(1) False claims. Sometimes the distortion is intentional and the claim is fraudulent either in whole or in part. For example, the plaintiff seeing an "accident background" in your hotel makes a false claim of having sustained harm. To illustrate, the patron upon becoming aware that there is some slippery substance on the marble or tile flooring, and seeing no one around, sits carefully down on the ground and then sets up loud cries of anguish and pain. When your employees or other patrons come upon the poor, unfortunate patron, a sad tale of woe and fault on the part of the hotel is related. Of course all of this is false and if the patron continues his false story in court, his statements constitute perjury. But the great difficulty is how can you tell when the claim of harm sustained without witnesses is perjurious or true? Even with witnesses how can you be sure that the witnesses are telling the truth when their testimony supports the patron, or whether they were merely fellow conspirators who have joined forces with the patron to make the perjured statements in court on behalf of the claimant patron?

(2) False cause of harm. More frequently the distorted claim is one in which it is true that the patron sustained harm but there is distortion as to the manner in which the harm was sustained or the extent to which the patron has been harmed. For example, it may be true that the plaintiff fell in your hotel but the patron may not realize why he fell. To illustrate, the patron fell on the dimly-lit stairs when he did not see the first step because he was carrying so many bundles in his arms that he could not see where he was stepping down. Under these circumstances, the fact that the hall was dimly-lit had nothing to do with the harm for it was the bundles which obstructed his view and they would have done so regardless of how bright the hallway was lighted. The chances are great, however, that after the patron has fallen, the patron will not realize just how much the bundles in his arms obscured the stairs. If the patron, seated on the ground with his bundles strewn about him surveys the scene of his disaster, he is likely to ignore the fact that he had bundles or that they obstructed his view and will perceive only that the stairs were dimly-lit and blame his misfortune upon that fact.

Or again, the plaintiff may realize just what was the cause of harm but falsely testifies that it was the hotel's fault in not lighting the area properly.

(3) False extent of harm. In other cases, it is true that the patron sustains harm on the hotel premises for a condition or cause for which the hotel is liable. Nevertheless distortion enters into the picture because the patron has made an exaggerated claim of the extent of damages that he has sustained. Consider, for example, the low-cost, nearly wornout suit, that the plaintiff was wearing when he slipped and fell on a grease spot on the hotel floor. Not infrequently it thereby is transformed into a brand new, highly expensive, imported suit; and the grease, instead of having come right out with a few cents worth of cleaner, was to the contrary as enduring and permanent as the Rock of Gibralter and utterly ruined the plaintiff's clothing. Similarly it is claimed that slight bruises or sprains actually sustained by the patron have caused great pain and suffering, requiring large outlays of cash and the incurring of future liability for medical, hospital, and nursing care, and of course, have caused permanent disabilities. In many of these cases, the plaintiff is making a perjured statement as to the consequences of his "truthful" injury: the distortion entering the picture in terms of the consequences of the harm to the patron.

In many cases, the claim of the patron as to the harm sustained is distorted although not intentionally or consciously so. For example, the injury actually sustained by the patron on your premises may make the patron become aware of some prior or latent condition, but, and with all honesty, the patron now blames the whole matter on the hotel.

Distortion almost invariably enters into the area of stating a money value for non-money losses. For example, the patron, because of the fault of the hotel has sustained pain and suffering, or sustained a temporary disability or a permanent disability. For such loss the plaintiff is entitled to claim money damages from the hotel. But how much money? What is the money value of one day's pain and suffering? It is clear that there is no precise nor even a reasonably accurate method or technique of determining the loss in such situation. Consequently the plaintiff claims whatever he thinks the pain and suffering are worth. Here is where the distortion enters into the picture, for even when the patron is acting in all honesty it is obvious that he will have an exaggerated idea of what his pain and suffering are worth.

To illustrate, the patron who has been hospitalized for one month may say that he would not go through that again for a million dollars. Does that mean that the pain and suffering were worth a million dollars? You and I as members of a jury might well conclude that this patron in his entire life will not earn a million dollars and therefore it is a little difficult for us to believe that one month of his life, even when attended by pain and suffering, could have a value of a million dollars.

Also you and I might very well say that we would not take a million dollars in return for our health, our eyesight, or our ability to walk, and so on. Yet if we are to be jurors it is doubtful whether we would feel that a million dollars or more should be paid to the patron just because his health has been impaired, although permanently; or he has lost his sight; or he has been made a permanent invalid as the result of the harm sustained in your hotel.

Furthermore practically every injured person suffers in varying degrees fron his friendly mis-advisors. For example, the patron's friends, in order to make him feel better, or because they want to sound important and know-it-all, may assure the patron that he should not worry because the hotel is a big, rich hotel, and carries large insurance, and the patron will have no trouble in collecting a nice, fat sum, say a million dollars. Not infrequently, either or both the friendly advisors and the injured patron are misled by something they had read in the paper or a magazine about someone who had a similar injury and who received a million dollars damages for his claim. In many instances, the recollection of what was recovered in the other proceeding is wrong to begin with or the prior account was merely the entry of the verdict for the huge amount, and the newspaper never published what the claimant in the other action actually received after the verdict was set aside or reduced, or if it did, our injured patron and his friends missed that edition. Or even if the verdict was not changed, there were significant factors differentiating the other case from the patron's case, such as difference between the earning power of the other plaintiff and of the present injured patron, or of the inclusion of punitive damages in the former proceeding.

*(c) **The hotel's open mind.*** In view of the fact that the patron's claim may be totally true, totally false, or true in part and false in part, it is obvious that the hotel must keep an open mind in investigating the facts and in conferring with its attorney. The hotel, as is true of every other litigant, should not automatically make a compensating distortion by jumping to the conclusion that the plaintiff is a willful liar and that there is no basis what-

soever for his claim. An open mind which is free from automatic prejudice will enable the hotel to think more clearly about the case, make it easier to find the truth, easier to know when to defend against the claim, and to know when and in what amount to compromise the claim.

§ 23:9. Free speech may be expensive.

(*a*) *Generally.* The experienced hotelman knows how to handle patrons. Pride in his profession and in rendering the most courteous service will generally restrain him from speaking his mind, however much the guest or patron deserves such comments.

There is danger, however, that the less experienced will not carry over this same attitude of speaking softly into other areas of hotel life where the hotel is not dealing with the public but with individual claimants, labor unions, suppliers of goods, and so on.

(*b*) *Unnecessary provocation.* Not infrequently, the failure to be silent or to speak gently has merely caused a slight irritation or hurt on the part of the claimant to be magnified by him many fold until his "getting even" with the hotel or "showing them" becomes such a goal or obsession with the claimant that it is no longer possible to reason with him or to work out a compromise acceptable to both parties.

(*c*) *Discrimination charges.* Statements of the hotel with respect to labor unions and its employees in general may be very dangerous as constituting evidence of an attitude of hostility to a particular group or union. If the hotel is charged with an unfair labor practice,[4] or an unlawful employment practice,[5] its past conduct and attitudes become important in making the decision whether a hotel's present act was inspired by a purpose to discriminate against a worker or workers because of their union membership or lack of such membership; or because of their race, color, creed, sex, or national origin. If there is a prior history of outspoken hostility to various groups, there is a greater probability that one such group or individual will seize upon the hotel's current action and claim that it was dis-

---

[4] This is a violation of labor management relations statutes, as described in Chapter 20.

[5] This is a violation of civil rights anti-discrimination statutes as described in Chapter 20.

crimination-inspired. Likewise, with a background of hostility, the agency or commission having charge of such matters is more likely to conclude that the act in question was discrimination-inspired. To the contrary, if no witness can testify to any discriminatory statements ever made by the hotel, there is a good chance that it will be held that the hotel did not commit any improper practice. In short, the hotel with a clean slate is much more likely to win against a claim of discrimination than one which has repeatedly spoken or acted in a discriminatory manner.

§ 23:10. Do not expect an easy answer all the time.

(a) *Generally.* By now you have seen that the law is not a fixed, rigid set of rules. At first thought it would be much simpler to run your hotel, or to live your life, if you had, or if your attorney could give you a set of exact rules that you could always follow.

(b) *Society's desire for flexibility.* Society, however, does not wish to be bound by fixed and rigid rules, but wants its law to be able to change and grow with the times. This is not done just for the sake of annoying you; but flexibility is emphasized so that we can change and move toward justice, which is the ultimate goal of our legal system.

Because of this flexibility of the law and its potential for growth, your attorney will in many cases not be able to give you the exact answer to your question "will I be liable?" The law may not yet have been decided in your state and, even if decided once, there may be other factors which tell or suggest to the intelligent lawyer that the court might change the law or that a different result might be obtained with a different jury.

(c) *The jury question as the unknown answer.* In many instances, the law does not lay down any exact rule but refers the matter to the jury to determine the facts, to apply the competing rules of law, and then to return a verdict in harmony with their conclusions. As you have already seen, the statement that a question is a question for the jury means that the jury can decide the case either way on the facts, and that no judge or higher court will reverse or set aside the jury for what it has done.

In terms of guidance for you, it means that no guide can be given to you. All that your attorney can say is that if there is a dispute as to any significant or substantial question of fact, you cannot tell in advance of the trial whether the law requires a judgment for you or against you. All that you know is that there is no answer until the jury has returned its verdict, and that once it has done so, that verdict is, under the circumstances described, final and cannot be upset. This means that your attorney can merely answer you "It depends."

Your attorney, however, can guide you; and with your experience, you can recognize that there are certain steps which you can take either before or after a given situation has arisen; namely those which you would expect of a reasonable man. Having taken such precautions or done such subsequent acts in good faith and in a reasonable manner, you will not be liable for the harm sustained by the plaintiff, assuming of course that the jury believes what you have done and how you have done it. The best protection you can have is a carefully selected staff, a good attorney, and a good insurance company.

And good luck!

1974 SUPPLEMENT

Instructions: The numbers of sections, pages, and notes used in this Supplement are the same as in the preceding pages of the book.

§ 2:5, p 22

If a hotel sends someone to take care of or examine a guest, it is liable for the harm sustained by the guest if such person is not a qualified physician or a nurse and the guest sustains harm because improper treatment is recommended. Stahlin v Hilton Hotels Corp. (CA7 Ill) 484 F2d 580 (1973) (hotel sent an employee who was not licensed as a nurse and who failed to recognize the actual serious condition of the guest).

§ 3:6, p 39, n 3.

Some courts are giving a very broad interpretation to what constitutes "state action" for the purpose of the Fourteenth Amendment, going to the extreme of finding such action when there is merely a general law which permits individuals to act or when there is a law providing for the licensing of private individuals. Management should therefore lean over in favor of following any federal standards so that it would not be material whether the action of the hotel should be deemed "state action."

§ 7:2, p 87, n 1.

The Maya case was reversed on its facts in Dillon v Legg, see § 9:3. This reversal merely means that California is now placing the stopping point for liability at a different place. It does not alter the underlying philosophical concept that wherever the line is drawn, it is in the last analysis determined by "socio-economic and moral factors" and not by logic or mathematics.

§ 11:3, p 164, n 1a.

In some states, the distinction between licensees and invitees has been abolished and the hotel will owe a duty of exercising reasonable care under the circumstances without regard to whether the injured person was a licensee or an invitee. See Supplement to 11:6.

§ 11:6, p 168, n 1a.

(c) Negligence rule. Under the common law, the liability of the hotel to a person coming on the premises, was stated in terms of whether such person was a trespasser, a licensee, or an invitee. This approach to the problem is being abandoned by some states in varying degrees. Several courts have gone to the extreme of ignoring whether the person harmed on the premises is a trespasser, a licensee, or an invitee; holding that in all cases, the occupier of the premises must exercise reasonable care, that is, the care which a reasonable man would exercise to prevent the occurrence of foreseeable harm. The occupier, namely the hotel, by this view, has the duty to take reasonable steps to prevent such harm without regard to whether the potential victim is a guest or a trespasser. One court has carried this rule to the extent of holding the occupier of a parking lot is liable where the occupier knows that people customarily cut across the lot to patronize a neighboring coffee shop and one such pedestrian is injured by falling down the edge of the parking lot where a retaining wall had fallen away, on the theory that the occupier knew or should have known that pedestrians would cross the lot during the night and a reasonably prudent man would foresee that in the dark the condition of the lot made harm to such persons probable or foreseeable.

Some courts have taken an intermediate position and treat trespassers as before but abolish the distinction between licensees and invitees, so that the occupier owes the same duty of care to all lawful visitors, and whether one is a licensee or an invitee is merely a circumstance to be considered by the jury in applying the ordinary rule of negligence.

In some states the distinction between licensees and invitees has been retained in name but destroyed in fact by requiring a licensor to warn the licensee of dangers of which the licensor knew or in the exercise of reasonable care should have known.

§ 12:2, p 200, n 1a.

The strong trend of the modern cases is to imply a warranty of habitability when premises are leased for residential purposes. This reverses the common law under which no warranty arose unless expressly stated.

§ 14:2, p 220, n 1.

The concept of strict tort liability is a relative newcomer to the law of product liability, being scarcely more than a decade old. If a product is sold or supplied to another, there is liability for harm which results if the product was defective and the defect caused harm, even though the defendant was not negligent and without regard to whether the injured person had direct dealings with the defendant. Some states impose the additional requirement that the defect be of so serious a character that the product is unreasonably dangerous to the user. Strict tort liability is imposed without regard to whether the transaction is a sale, a lease, or a goodwill give-away.

§ 14:2, p 222, n 1a.

The damages recoverable under the strict tort liability concept differ from state to state. Some states permit only recovery for personal injuries. Other expand this to include property loss and some include economic or commercial loss. In such latter states, there is little difference between the several theories of product liability insofar as damages recovered are concerned.

§ 18:3, p 325, n 1a.

In some states, it is held that when a hotel asserts its lien or locks out a patron, the action of the hotel constitutes "state action" within the meaning of the Fourteenth Amendment to the federal constitution. In consequence of this conclusion, it is held that the hotel cannot act without giving the patron a notice and having a hearing by an impartial arbiter to determine if the patron in fact owes the hotel. Although this view has been expressly recognized by only a few lower court cases, it is relatively certain that it will be the law of tomorrow when viewed in the broader perspective of consumer protection. That is, the same concept applied in these hotel cases has been applied to conclude that a finance company cannot repossess an automobile without a notice and hearing, that a gas or electric company cannot discontinue service for nonpayment without a notice and hearing, and that a landlord cannot distrain or seize goods of the tenant for rent without a notice and hearing. Viewed as an aggregate, the pattern for the future is clear and unmistakable.

§ 20:8, p 373, n 8.

By federal statute, job discrimination on the basis of age is prohibited as to employees between 40 and 65 years of age. Act of December 15, 1967, P.L. 90-202, 81 Stat 608, 29 USC § 621.

INDEX

Absolute liability, see Supervisory liability
Accidents
    Workmen's compensation 361
Accommodation parties, see Checks
Accommodations and discrimination
    Civil Rights protection...................... 38
        Federal Civil Rights Act................ 39
        Non-hotel services 40
    Nature of 34
    Price of................................... 34
    Refusal of
        Improper................................ 37
        Proper 35
    Right to enter hotel 32
Act of God................................... 250
Addresses, see Good client
Administrative regulation, see Government regulation
Administrator, see Government regulation
Age
    Accommodations
        Improper refusal 37
Allergy
    Sold products liability
        Drugs, cosmetics, and preparations 230
        Food and drink 227
        Merchandise and sporting goods 231
Amusements
    Discrimination 40
    Supervisory liability......................... 62
Anatomy of lawsuit
    Appeals 441
    Costs 441
    Damages 439
    Execution 442
    Judgment 441
    Jury 437
    Pleading stage............................. 418
    Pre-pleading stage.......................... 414
    Pre-trial procedure 423
    Trial..................................... 427
    Verdict................................... 438
Apartment house 17

INDEX

Appeals, see Anatomy of lawsuit
Appliances, see Premises liability
    Electrical and gas appliances and fixtures
Arrest
    False, see False arrest
    No warrant, see Crimes
Assault, see Intentional torts
Assignee 242
Assumed name, see Checks
Assumption of risk 145
Athletic events, see Amusements
Automobile
    Guest's property protected 255
    Hotel, see Hotel automobile

Bad check, see Crimes
Baggage 283
    Guest's property protected 254
Bailee, see Supplied products liability
Bailor, see Supplied products liability
Bank, see Checks
Banquet accomodations
    Premises liability
        Floors 175
Bathtubs 192
Battery, see Intentional torts
Boarders 16
    Right of occupancy or possession 24
Boarding house 17
    Guest's property 271
Breach of contract, see Liability-imposing conduct
Breach of statute 143
Burden of proof, see Definitions and relationships
    Guest's property, see Guest's property
    Premises liability, see Premises liability
Business tenants, see Supervisory liability

Care
    Degrees of, see Negligence
    Reasonable, see Reasonable care
Causal relationship
    Intervening force 88

INDEX

Necessity of 84
Proximate cause 86
Checks
    Accommodation parties...................... 292
    Acquisition by hotel 292
    Assumed name 316
    Dead patron's check 317
    Definitions 290
    Execution by hotel employee 306
    Forgery 309
    Lack of authority 309
    Liability of drawee bank 304
    Liability of hotel's bank.................... 308
    Liability of parties
        Check negotiated by patron 299
        To hotel 299
    Liability on warranties...................... 302
    Negotiation by hotel 297
Children
    Contributory negligence..................... 140
        Claim of child 144
    Hotel automobile liability 215
    Premises liability, see Premises liability
Civil Rights, see Accommodations and discrimination
Claims
    Death, see Death claims
    Evaluation of, see Good client
    False 467
    Inspection reports 461
Cleaning 111
Client, see Good client
Clothing 283
Clubs, see Private clubs
Code
    State adopting Uniform Commercial Code 473
Collective bargaining, see Labor law
Compensatory damages 440
Concessionaire
    Supervisory liability, see Supervisory liability
    Vicarious liability, see Vicarious liability
Concessions
    Discrimination 41

INDEX

Conduct. see Liability-imposing conduct
Construction, see Premises liability
Contagion, see Premises liability
Contract, see Breach of contract
Contractors, see Independent contractors
Contributory negligence
    Assumption of risk 147
    Determination of............................ 147
    Effect of 141
        Nature of defendant's conduct 143
    Guest's property
        Loss by fire 275
    Imputed 143
    Plaintiff 138
    Premises liability
        Falling objects........................... 194
        Floors 176
    Furniture 190
    Guardrails, ramps, and stairs 185
    Lighting 185
    Plumbing fixtures 193
    Walking areas and walks 179
Corruption, see Crimes
Cosmetics, see Sold products liability
Costs, see Anatomy of lawsuit
Counterclaim 421
Credit cards 318
    Liability
        Hotel 319
        Impostor................................ 318
Crimes
    Arrest without warrant 408
    Bad check acts 402
    Corruption and defrauding governments 398
    Criminals and trespassers.................... 405
    Defrauding hotel........................... 401
    Entry to prevent 452
    False pretenses 402
    Forgery 404
    Liquor 396
    Nature of hotel offense...................... 395
    Nature of patron offense 400

INDEX

Nonpayment of bill 408
Premises
    Illegal use 398
  Prevention 111
  Theft 406
  Use of criminal process 410
Criminals, see Crimes

Damages
  Battery. 97
  Compensatory, see Compensatory damages
  Exemplary, see Exemplary damages
  False arrest. 102
  Guest's property, see Guest's property
  Intentional torts
    Property directed 105
  Lawsuit, see Anatomy of lawsuit
  Punitive, see Punitive damages
  Vicarious liability 74
Dangers. 160
Dead patron, see Checks
Death Claims
  Effect of death. 115
  Survival action 117
  Surviving action 117
  Wrongful death action 116
Defamation
  Proof of 106
  Privileged statements. 107
  Reputation injury 105
Defect, see Premises liability
  Condition or defect
Definitions and relationships 15
  Assault. 97
  Battery. 96
  Burden of proof 29
  Checks, see Checks
  Guest-hotel relationship
    Creation of 20
    Termination of 25
  Guests and patrons
    Duties of. 21

INDEX

Hotel-tenant relationship
    Termination of 28
Medical care
    Emergency 22
Delivery, see Guest's property
Departure, see Guest's property
Depositions 427
Design, see Premises liability
    Construction or design
Detention
    False imprisonment 98
    Nonpayment of bill, see Crimes
    Theft, see Crimes
Direct liability
    Independent contractors 80
    Vicarious liability compared 72
Discovery 425
Discrimination
    Accommodations, see Accommodations and discrimination
    Labor law, see Labor law
Disease
    Accommodations
        Proper refusal of 36
    Occupational
        Workmen's compensation 363
    Premises liability, see Premises liability
        Contagion and disease
Doors, see Premises liability
Drink, see Sold products liability
    Food and drink
Driver
    Care, see Hotel automobile
        Liability
            Motorist's duty of care
    Fit driver 210
    Unfit driver 82
Drugs, see Sold products liability
Drunkards, see Intoxicated persons

Electrical appliances and fixtures, see Premises liability
Elevators, see Premises liability
Elevator shaft 188

INDEX

Emergency
   Action, see Negligence
   Medical care, see Definitions and relationships
Emergency vehicles.............................. 213
Employees
   Acts of, see Supervisory liability
   Checks, see Checks
      Execution by hotel employee
   Guest's property................................ 265
   Vicarious liability, see Vicarious liability
Employees' rights, see Labor law
Employment
   Relationship, see Labor law
   Reports.. 459
   Scope of
      Vicarious liability........................... 75
Entertainment, see Amusements
Entry
   Reports.. 461
   Rooms, see Violation of privacy
   Without permission
      Sickness..................................... 452
      To prevent crime............................ 452
Equity cases..................................... 428
Eviction
   Hotel-guest relationship
      Termination................................. 427
   Inspection witnesses........................... 453
   Reports.. 461
   Right to....................................... 326
   Right to enter................................. 32
   Wrongful eviction.............................. 327
Execution, see Anatomy of lawsuit
Exemplary damages............................... 440
Expert
   Express warranties............................. 225
Express warranties, see Sold products liability

Falling objects, see Premises liability
False arrest, see Intentional torts
   Supervisory liability........................... 64
False imprisonment, see Intentional torts

INDEX

False pretenses, see Crimes
Federal Civil Rights Act, see Labor law
    Hotels under, see Accommodations and discrimination
        Civil rights protection
Felony.. 409
Fire
    Guest's property, see Guest's property
        Loss by fire
    Premises liability, see Premises liability
Firemen... 163
Fixtures, see Premises liability
Floors, see Premises liability
Food, see Sold products liability
Foreseeability, see Negligence
Forgery, see Crimes
    Checks, see Checks
Fraud
    Checks, see Checks
    Drugs, cosmetics, and preparations............... 230
    Vicarious liability 80
    Labor law, see Labor law
Furniture, see Premises liability

Gambling.. 398
Garnishee 443
Garnishment 442
Gas appliances, see Premises liability
    Electrical and gas appliances and fixtures
Gasoline station 40
Good client
    Addresses.. 462
    Answers... 471
    Claims... 466
    Condition and things
        Preservation of 463
    Forwarding papers 464
    Free speech..................................... 470
    How you can help 445
    Inspection witnesses 447
    Litigation
        Regulations to protect from 446
    Names... 462

INDEX

Notice 464
Reports 454
Telephone numbers 462
Good will................................... 3
Government regulation
   Administrative regulation 335
      Importance and finality of............ 347
      Pattern 339
   Administrator
      Governing............................. 341
      Thermostat 340
   Attitude toward 351
   Classification 333
   Freedom of management 330
   Hotel regulations....................... 331
   Interpretation
      Statutes and regulations 337
   Legislative rule 334
   Power and subject of 331
Grievances................................ 374
Guardrails, see Premises liability
Guest..................................... 16
   Duties of, see Definitions and relationships
   Objecting, see Objecting guest
   Unconscious, see Unconscious guest
Guest-hotel relationship, see Definitions and relationships
Guest's property
   Boarding house......................... 271
   Burden of proof 275
   Damages 286
   Delivery or deposit 284
   Departure of guest...................... 260
   Liability
      Contract modification 276
      Limitation by regulation.............. 276
      Strict................................ 248
         Exceptions to 250
   Loss by fire............................ 274
   Persons causing loss.................... 272
   Property of person not a guest 266
      Patron of non-hotel enterprise 268
   Property retained by guest 263

INDEX

Room 264
Statutory regulation 278
    Extent of liability 280
    Property to which applicable 282
Transportation of 265
What property protected 254
When entrusting begins 258

Halls, see Premises liability
    Doors and halls
Handrails 183
Harm
    Apprehension of, see Supervisory liability
    Rescue 91
Highway, see Hotel automobile
Hotel 15
Hotel automobile
    Liability
        Duty to persons on highway 214
        Expectable conduct of others 216
        Motorist's duty of care 209
        Nature of vehicle 212
        Use of vehicle 212
    Vicarious liability, see Vicarious liability
Hotel regulations, see Government regulation
Hotel-tenant relationship, see Definitions and relationships

Imaginary man 122
Impersonation 319
Impostor
    Checks 312
    Credit cards 318
Imprisonment, see Intentional torts
    False imprisonment
Independent contractors
    Guest's property 265
    Leased premises liability
        Negligent repair 208
    Premises liability
        Maintenance 187
    Vicarious liability, see Vicarious liability
Injuries, see Labor law

INDEX

Liability
    Injuries to employee
Insects 197
Inspection
    Liability claim 461
    Premises liability 193
    Witnesses, see Good client
        Inspection witnesses
Insurance, see Liability insurance
Insurance adjuster 448
Intentional torts
    Assault 97
    Battery 96
    Contributory negligence 143
    Defamation, see Defamation
    False arrest 98
    False imprisonment 98
    Malicious prosecution 98
    Mental distress 103
    Principles 96
    Privacy, see Violation of privacy
    Property directed 105
Intoxicated persons 397
Intoxication 254
Introduction
    Absolutes and arbitraries 5
    Justice 10
    Law 11
    Understanding the law 5
    Why bother 3
Investigation, see Violation of privacy
Invitees, see Premises liability

Jewelry 283
Judgment, see Anatomy of lawsuit
Jury, see Anatomy of lawsuit
Justice, see Introduction

Key
    Guest's property 249
    Supervisory liability 253

Labels 223

INDEX

Labor law
  Allowable distinctions 390
  Collective bargaining
    Applicability of federal law 365
    Employees' representative 370
      Authority of 373
    Mutual obligation 369
    What is 366
  Discrimination
    Employer compelled to 387
    Employment terms 383
    Labor Management Relations Act 385
  Employees' rights 380
  Employer 385
  Employer's representative 387
  Employment relationship 358
  Federal Civil Rights Act 389
    Enforcement of 391
  Free speech 377
  Liability 375
    Injuries to employee 360
  Nature of 357
  Union
    Acts of 388
    Assistance or domination 379
Labor Management Relations Act, see Labor law
Landlord liability, see Leased premises liability
Landlord-tenant relationship 18
Lawsuit, see Anatomy of lawsuit
Lease
  Premises liability 172
  Termination of 28
Leased premises liability 198
  Landlord agreement to repair 207
  Landlord liability
    For retained land 205
    To tenant 200
    To third persons 202
Liability
  Absolute, see Absolute liability
  Checks, see Checks
  Claims 461

INDEX

Credit cards, see Credit cards
Direct, see Direct liability
Guest's property, see Guest's property
Labor law, see Labor law
Liability-imposing conduct, see Liability-imposing conduct
Sold products, see Sold products liability
Statutory, see Statutory liability
Supervisory, see Supervisory liability
Vicarious, see Vicarious liability
Liability-imposing conduct
   Breach of contract................................ 47
   Fields of.. 43
   For tort.. 44
Liability insurance
   Sold products liability............................ 233
   Tort liability.................................... 45
Libel.. 106
Licensees, see Premises liability
Licensing.. 332
Liens
   Enforcement of.................................. 324
   Existence of.................................... 321
   Property subject to.............................. 322
Lighting, see Premises liability
Liquor, see Crimes
Litigation, see Good client
Lockout.. 386
Locks.. 27
Lodgers.. 16

Maintenance
   Entry into rooms................................ 111
   Premises liability
      Guardrails, ramps, and stairs................ 184
      Lighting.................................... 187
Medical care
   Causal relationship.............................. 91
   Patron, see Definitions and relationships
Mental distress, see Intentional torts
Merchandise, see Sold products liability
Mice.. 197

INDEX

Minors	397
Money	
Statutory regulation	283
What property protected	255
Motel	16
Names, see Good client	
Negligence	
Care	124
Elements of	120
Emergency action	127
Foreseeability	125
Omission to act	127
Proof of	133
Sold products liability	
Drugs, cosmetics, and preparations	230
Food and drink	227
Test of	122
Vicarious liability	76
Non-guests	
Emergency medical care	24
Supervisory liability	57
Nonpayment of bill, see Crimes	
Notice, see Good client	
Guest's property	279
Objecting guest	23
Opinions	225
Parol evidence rule	307
Patron	
Crimes	400
Duties, see Definitions and relationships	
Medical care, see Definitions and relationships	
Peace officer	408
Photographs	464
Picketing	388
Plumbing fixtures, see Premises liability	
Policemen	163
Premises	
Illegal use, see Crimes	
Premises liability	
Burden of proof	171

INDEX

Children	169
Condition or defect	172
Construction or design	173
Contagion and disease	196
Doors and halls	180
Electrical and gas appliances and fixtures	191
Elevators	187
Falling objects	193
Fire	195
Floors	174
Furniture	189
Guardrails, ramps, and stairs	183
Invitees	157
Licensees	164
Lighting	185
Nature of	156
Plumbing fixtures	191
Rodents and vermin	197
Scope of invitation or license	165
Guest's visitor	167
Screens and windows	188
Stranger	169
Trespassers	168
Walking areas and walks	177
Preparations, see Sold products liability	
Price, see Accomodations and discrimination	
Privacy, see Violation of privacy	
Private clubs	41
Products	
Sold, see Sold products liability	
Supplied, see Supplied products liability	
Property	
Guest, see Guest's property	
Intentional torts, see Intentional torts	
Joint	144
Liens, see Liens	
Removal of	27
Prostitution	298
Protection	
Entry into rooms	109
Persons on street	64
Third persons, see Supervisory liability	

INDEX

Proximate cause, see Causal relationship
Public authority 250
Public enemy 250
Public relations................................ 3
Punitive damages 440

Racial discrimination 38
Ramps, see Premises liability
    Guardrails, ramps, and stairs
Rates... 35
Rats 197
Reasonable care, see Supervisory liability
Reasonable man, see Negligence
    Test of
Receipt 285
Registration 20
Relationships, see Definitions and relationships
    Causal, see Causal relationship
Removal, see Eviction
Renovations.................................... 160
Rent 28
    Nonpayment, see Crimes
Repairs
    Guest's property 257
    Leased premises, see Leased premises liability
    Premises liability........................ 160
    Time for................................. 194
Reports, see Good client
Reputation, see Defamation
Rescue... 91
Restaurant
    Discrimination 40
    Guest's property 269
Revolving doors 181
Rodents, see Premises liability
Rooms
    Entry, see Violation of privacy
    Guest's property, see Guest's property

Salesmen
    Accommodations 37
    Guest's property 284

INDEX

What property protected	258
Search and seizure	342
Screens, see Premises liability	
Sickness	452
Signature	
Checks	
Execution by hotel employee	306
Forged	310
Signs	223
Slander	106
Sold products liability	
Avoidance or restriction of liability	232
Cosmetics, drugs, and preparations	229
Express warranties	222
Food and drink	226
Merchandise and sporting goods	231
Other warranties	225
Theories of liability	220
Who may sue	234
Solicitors	33
Sporting goods, see Sold products liability	
Stairs, see Premises liability	
Guardrails, ramps, and stairs	
Statute, see Breach of statute	
Statutory liability	
Guest's property, see Guest's property	
Hotel automobile	82
Sold products liability	231
Stranger, see Premises liability	
Strikes	388
Supervisory liability	
Absolute liability	54
Business tenants	69
Concessionaire	67
Vicarious liability distinguished	83
Employee	66
Willful act	79
Harm	58
Nature of	51
Persons on street	64
Reasonable care	53
Third persons	60

INDEX

Vicarious liability compared 52
Warning 58
Supplement to text 1974 473
Supplied products liability
    Bailee 240
    Bailor 241
    Third persons 242
Surveillance, see Violation of privacy
Survival action, see Death claims
Surviving action, see Death claims

Taxation 332
Telephone numbers, see Good client
Tenants 16
    Business, see Business tenants
Theft, see Crimes
Third persons
    Acts of, see Supervisory liability
    Crimes 400
    Supplied products liability, see Supplied products liability
Torts, see Intentional torts
Transportation 265
Trespassers
    Premises liability, see Premises liability
    Right to repel, see Crimes
        Criminals and trespassers
Trial, see Anatomy of lawsuit

Unconscious guest 22
Union, see Labor law
Union shop 385

Valuables 253
Verdict, see Anatomy of lawsuit
Vermin, see Premises liability
    Rodents and vermin
Vicarious liability
    Concessionaire 82
    Corruption and defrauding governments 399
    Employees 74
    Hotel automobile 81

INDEX

Independent contractors 80
   Nature of 72
   Scope of 73
   Supervisory liability compared, see Supervisory
      liability
Violation of privacy 108
   Entry into rooms 109
   Investigation 114
   Public privilege 113
   Surveillance 109
Vision 212
Visitor
   Contributory negligence 140
   Right to enter 33

Walking areas, see Premises liability
Warning
   Hotel automobile liability 212
   Premises liability 160
   Sufficient, see Supervisory liability
Warrant, see Crimes
Warranties
   Checks, see Checks
   Express, see Express warranties
   Sold products liability, see Sold products liability
Watches 283
Weather conditions
   Floors 175
   Walking areas and walks 178
Who may sue, see Sold products liability
Windows, see Premises liability
   Screens and windows
Witnesses, see Good client
   Inspection witnesses
Workmen's compensation 361